A HAVEN AND A HELL

A Haven and a Hell

THE GHETTO IN BLACK AMERICA

Lance Freeman

Columbia University Press
New York

Columbia University Press
Publishers Since 1893
New York   Chichester, West Sussex
cup.columbia.edu
Copyright © 2019 Columbia University Press

Library of Congress Cataloging-in-Publication Data
Names: Freeman, Lance, author.
Title: A haven and a hell : the ghetto in black America / Lance Freeman.
Description: New York : Columbia University Press, [2019] | Includes bibliographical
references and index.
Identifiers: LCCN 2018027639 (print) | LCCN 2018042390 (ebook) |
ISBN 9780231545570 (electronic) | ISBN 9780231184601 (cloth : alk. paper)
Subjects: LCSH: African American neighborhoods—Social conditions. |
African American neighborhoods—Economic conditions. | Discrimination in
housing—United States—History. | United States—Race relations—History.
Classification: LCC E185.86 (ebook) | LCC E185.86 .F765 2019 (print) |
DDC 363.5/90973—dc23
LC record available at https://lccn.loc.gov/2018027639

⊗

Columbia University Press books are printed on permanent and durable acid-free paper.
Printed in the United States of America

Cover design: Noah Arlow

CONTENTS

CONTENTS

ACKNOWLEDGMENTS

I thank Hyun Hye (Cathy) Bae for her tremendous assistance in completing this book. Brianna Peppers also was of great help in sourcing archival materials. My colleagues Derek Hyra and Rachael Woldoff offered encouragement and thoughtful feedback on my ideas for the book. My editor, Eric Schwartz, provided invaluable guidance in shepherding the book to completion.

Finally, I thank my mother, Eleanor Freeman, who I wish had lived to see the completion of this project.

INTRODUCTION

His was a true rags-to-riches-to-rags story. After working as a barber and Pullman Porter in sundry western cities, he arrived in Chicago in the late 1890s with only a few dollars. He went on to build a real estate and financial empire that inspired awe and pride among members of his race. By the third decade of the twentieth century, he could boast of a bank bearing his name, a bank reputable enough to become one of the few on the South Side of Chicago to belong to the association of elite Chicago banks—the Chicago Clearing House Association.[1] He owned so much of the property on State Street between Forty-Seventh and Forty-Eighth Streets that the street took on his name and was called the "Binga Block."[2]

Jesse Binga's rise paralleled the rise of Chicago's black ghetto in the early twentieth century. Indeed, in many ways Binga rose to fame and fortune *because* of the rise of the ghetto. He made his fortune buying white-owned properties and opening these properties up to space-starved Negroes. His bank and insurance company provided financial services to a clientele shunned by white-owned banks. He also married into money, wedding the sister of John "Mushmouth" Johnson, who made his fortune providing another service to the captive Negro audience—illegal gambling or "numbers." In short, the ghetto created a captive market that an enterprising Jesse Binga capitalized on to make his fortune.

Binga was no mere bystander to the rise of the ghetto. Aside from making his fortune off the ghetto, he acted to shape the ghetto, both the institutions within it, such as his bank, and its physical boundaries. To be sure, white racism and a refusal to have Negroes as neighbors gave rise to a color line that hemmed Negroes inside the ghetto. But Binga was an active participant in determining where the color line and boundaries of the ghetto would be drawn. In acquiring white-owned properties, he was carving out space for blacks in what was formerly hostile white territory. The acquisition of properties by "race men" such as Jesse Binga meant additional housing opportunities for the race. The expectation was that once property fell into a race man's hands, it would be made available to black families. Indeed, Binga was often depicted as a champion of the race's interests as he acquired property in formerly all-white neighborhoods, displaced the current occupants, and opened these same properties to Negroes.[3] In 1909, a local black newspaper reported that although "whites now occupy the building, they will be put out May 1st to make room for colored people."[4] To be sure, it was unlikely that Binga was motivated purely by race pride; he most likely knew he could charge blacks more rent than whites due to blacks' constrained housing choices.[5] But his actions allowed members of his race to access "good houses and flats,"[6] thus expanding housing options for a people desperate for space.[7] And for this, along with his considerable philanthropy, he was considered a true "race man," someone who advanced the interests of his race, and was held in the same regard as such early-twentieth-century luminaries as W. E. B. Du Bois, Booker T. Washington, and the entertainers Bert Williams and Jack Johnson.[8]

The ghetto was instrumental in Jesse Binga's rise, and it would play a key role in his downfall as well. The proximate cause of Binga's collapse, which culminated in the demise of his bank and his imprisonment for fraud, was the Great Depression. Personal shortcomings and a proclivity for mixing the bank's finances with his own played their role as well.[9] But the business model of the Binga State Bank, dependent as it was on the ghetto's fortunes, was inherently risky. In an era before federal deposit insurance and diversified financial conglomerates, a bank was only as strong as its debtors. The Binga State Bank provided much needed credit to the burgeoning black ghetto, but its solvency was at the mercy of the ghetto's economic fortunes. When times were good, Binga and his bank prospered. But the ghetto was financially vulnerable. Its inhabitants were poorly paid in insecure jobs. The housing stock was among the oldest and most dilapidated and was shunned by the majority of the population. White financiers refused to accept housing stock in the ghetto as collateral.[10] When the Depression hit, many ghetto residents lost their jobs and could not make their mortgage payments. It comes as no surprise that the Binga State Bank collapsed in short order. Jesse Binga's fortune plummeted along with that of his bank. He could not even make bail when indicted for embezzlement, and he died virtually penniless.[11]

A HAVEN AND A HELL

Jesse Binga's story illustrates the twofold nature of the relationship between the ghetto and black America. Although much has been spoken and written about the ills of the ghetto, this perspective tells only one side of the story. Thanks to the work of numerous historians, we know the modern ghetto was the result of blacks migrating en masse to urban centers in the early twentieth century and creating new types of urban spaces heretofore unseen on the American landscape. The term *ghetto*, initially used to define a space where Jews in sixteenth-century Italy were confined, seemed an apt moniker for these spaces inhabited by blacks. Like the Jews in the ghettos of Venice, blacks were confined to specific spaces. Moreover, these spaces were marginalized, stigmatized, and typically undesirable. Ghetto residents in both medieval Venice and urban America were stigmatized for residing in these spaces. Moreover, whatever their compunctions about residing in the ghetto, its inhabitants, then and now, had little choice about residing there. The ghetto, whether in its sixteenth century incarnation or its modern one, was not the result of Jews or blacks voluntarily congregating together.

Unlike the ghetto of Venice, however, black ghettos grew in size and salience so that at various times they have been viewed as America's most pressing problem. Given the ghetto's salience in America's urban life, it is not surprising that scholars have produced a voluminous scholarship on it. We know that white racism manifested through private actors was largely responsible for spawning the ghettos in the early twentieth century. Historians have also shown how federal and local governments became senior partners in reinforcing and expanding the walls of the ghettos starting during the Great Depression and extending several decades thereafter.

We know that ghettoization made it difficult for blacks to participate in the American Dream of upward mobility and stability through homeownership as they were either denied access to homeownership or relegated to owning property in declining neighborhoods where ownership proved a dicey proposition. We also know that the confinement of blacks to the ghetto has made the celebrated *Brown v. Board of Education* victory in 1954 a hollow one across dozens of northern cities as black children still attend segregated schools more than half a century later.

Furthermore, the relegation of blacks to the inferior ghetto and white flight in combination precipitated an "urban crisis" in which many of American cities faced bankruptcy as they struggled to support a poor and declining population on a steadily dwindling tax base. Social scientists have also shown that living in the ghetto has stunted the life chances of millions of blacks. The toll of inferior schools, higher crime, lack of jobs, and social isolation has only marginalized ghetto residents even further.

Thus, the ghetto's role as a hell for black Americans is clear. The ghetto has served as an instrument of subjugation for blacks. Like slavery and Jim Crow, it has been an institution that stifles dreams and serves the interests of others.

But the ghetto has also been more than that. As Jesse Binga's experience illustrates, the ghetto has been a haven, too, a place where many have improved their lot. Although Binga's rise and fall were dizzying, for many blacks the ghetto has provided incremental but extremely important steps toward a better life and fuller inclusion in American society.

This book chronicles the role of the ghetto as an institution in influencing black American life. The spatial and temporal focus of the book is expansive, which means some specific factors are glossed over or excluded altogether. Perhaps most importantly, this book focuses on ghettos outside of the eleven states that were part of the Confederate States of America during the Civil War. Although ghettos did and do exist in the South, the race relations and economic context were different enough during vast stretches of the period studied to warrant the exclusion of this region here. Nevertheless, even outside the South there were significant differences between ghettos in various parts of the country—say, Harlem in New York and Watts in Los Angeles. There are a number of excellent histories of specific ghettos, which I draw on. A close reading of these histories, however, reveals that these communities as institutions in black life share a number of similarities that allow for a cogent general narrative about ghettos outside the southern United States.

The book proceeds chronologically, and for each period covered, the context and meaning of the ghetto is similar enough to categorize the period as an era. Of course, history does not unfold evenly across time or space. Some events typical of a particular era will of course occur in other periods as well. The categorization of eras should thus not be treated too literally in the reading of this book.

Chapter 1 defines the concept of the ghetto as used in this book and covers the period 1880 to the Great Migration starting in the 1910s. Beginning with the period covered in this chapter and continuing until the era of fair housing, I rely primarily on demographic criteria to demarcate the ghetto. I consider historical, demographic, and social criteria to demarcate the ghetto after the onset of fair housing in the late 1960s. The chapter considers the origins of the ghetto and what this space meant to black America as a whole prior to the Great Migration.

Chapter 2 discusses how blacks' actions served as the critical catalyst for the creation of the ghetto in the first place. The Great Migration from the South to the North was a voluntary act in which blacks took a bold and oftentimes dangerous step to improve their lot. To be sure, whites' reactions to the black migration are what turned what would likely have been ethnic enclaves that would fade away over time into durable ghettos instead. But blacks did not meekly march into the ghetto but in many ways sought to use the ghetto as a mechanism for becoming acquainted with modernity, building racial pride, and advancing the race. The discrimination encountered by blacks in northern cities meant the ghetto was hardly a promised land of milk and honey. Yet it was in the ghetto that the American Negro encountered modernity. Blacks proved their humanity by surviving and thriving in the city. There were many, including some black leaders, who were doubtful that the race could survive in the city, although this belief seems preposterous now. But blacks did not die out; they survived to such an extent that terms such as *urban* and *inner city* have become synonymous with the term *black* in many contexts. The book places blacks' incipient urbanization within the context of that time. At a time when the overwhelming majority of blacks in America and indeed the world were rural and many were skeptical of the races' ability to survive the rigors of city life, blacks' surviving and thriving in the cities were of great symbolic value to the race.

The ghetto in fact provided more than proof that blacks were modern and capable of surviving in the city. It was in the ghetto that black art and culture were taken to new levels through the New Negro movement. It was the ghetto that enabled blacks to regain some of the political power lost after Reconstruction. Black ward bosses, councilmen, aldermen, and congressmen became part of the political landscape and wielded political power. The ghetto also provided a means for upward mobility. Simply by moving from the economically backward South to the North, blacks were able to partake of a much more productive economy and make economic gains for themselves. Although they continued to be overrepresented on the margins of the economy, many and eventually most of them were eventually able to escape poverty in this era. Moreover, the ghetto produced a captive clientele with a modicum of disposable income that allowed some black entrepreneurs to thrive and become wealthy. Chapter 2 makes the argument that the ghetto was thus instrumental in changing blacks' status in early-twentieth-century America.

Chapter 3 describes hellish conditions brought on by the Great Depression and how the dreams of a black metropolis were thus cut short. Yet during this time the race's complex stance toward ghettoization began to crystallize in reactions to the federal government's foray into the housing market. It was at this time that the federal government put its stamp of approval on and reinforced the walls of the ghetto. The book goes beyond merely describing the ways in which the federal government institutionalized the ghetto—a story told elsewhere in the literature. Rather, it considers how blacks reacted to the federal intrusion into solidifying the ghetto. For blacks in northern ghettos, this federal intrusion posed a dilemma—on the one hand, it was a chance to wield newfound political power and sway the federal government to earmark federal resources for the race for the first time since Reconstruction, but on the other hand it was also another instance of state-sanctioned segregation. In recasting this story, the book elucidates the role blacks played in shaping public policy toward the ghetto—a heretofore overlooked aspect of the ghetto's history.

While activists complained bitterly about the federal government's fostering of segregation through redlining and the refusal to lend to blacks who tried to move into white neighborhoods, many applauded and even demanded slum clearance and segregated public housing in the ghetto. The book explores this complex reaction toward ghettoization and shows that acceptance of some forms of ghettoization was not necessarily a foregone conclusion. The desire to maintain the ghetto as a haven along with the demand for the opportunity to live where one wanted emerged concretely at this time.

Chapter 4 recalls the mid-twentieth-century transformation of the ghetto's role in black life. Although the ghetto was instrumental in helping change blacks' status during the first wave of the Great Migration, the role of the ghetto itself changed as the status of blacks changed. As blacks slowly broke into the wider American society, the role of the ghetto as a haven and springboard for upward mobility slowly began to recede. While whites were beginning to be accept blacks in other domains of public life (e.g. employment, professional sports), white resistance to residential integration proved more formidable. And so the ghetto persisted and even grew after de jure segregation was outlawed. Even during a time, especially the 1950s and 1960s, when blacks were achieving many "firsts" (e.g., the first black cabinet secretary, the first black Supreme Court justice, and so on) and civil rights were being expanded, ghettoization was intensifying, and the ghetto was physically expanding as millions of black migrants continued to stream north in search of a better life. This chapter describes the ghetto's evolution in the postwar era to play different roles in the life of black Americans. For the millions of blacks escaping the Jim Crow South, the northern ghetto was still a promised land—a place for aspirations. This was the time of the largest migration of blacks from the South to the ghettos of the North, dwarfing the migration that had occurred up to that time. For these migrants, the ghetto continued to provide a modicum of social mobility. Some translated this hard-earned mobility into property ownership within the ghetto. Others sought the American Dream of a home in suburbia to go with their newfound mobility.

It was also in the mid-twentieth-century that the federal government, acting in conjunction with local governments, affected the physical fabric of the ghetto through urban renewal—a larger version of the slum-clearance programs that had begun during the 1930s. As was the case in the 1930s, blacks' reactions to urban renewal offer a prism through which to view and understand the variegated ways blacks perceived the ghetto, both as a haven to be protected and as a hell to be dismantled, its occupants dispersed, or to be rebuilt from the ground up.

Thus, by midcentury the ghetto's role in black life was multifaceted. For those escaping a serflike existence in the South and those who had achieved some mobility within the ghetto, it was still a haven. For others, the overcrowded and rundown housing typically found in the ghetto made it a hell that they wished to escape. For an increasing number of blacks, who could achieve neither the black American Dream in the ghetto nor the American Dream outside it, anger and resentment would grow and fuel the widespread urban unrest of the 1960s.

The turbulent 1960s is the subject of chapter 5. Chronicled here are the depopulation, the collapsing housing market, and the frustrations of ghetto residents that sparked waves of violent unrest. This chapter also describes how the frustration that fueled the 1960s urban unrest also served to fuel a second wave of black nationalism, with the ghetto becoming one of several proposed homelands for a separate black nation. Although various locales were proposed as an independent homeland, the ghetto was the place where the nationalist dream came closest to fruition. The separatist sentiment of the 1960s never sparked a mass movement among blacks, but it did help spawn many cultural and community institutions, some of which remain active and influential today. This chapter thus illustrates how the ghetto was perhaps the most visible space of black anger during the 1960s while at the same time becoming a space for autonomous black empowerment.

Chapter 6 describes the evolution of the ghetto in the post–civil rights era. As the social acceptance of blacks throughout America slowly translated into acceptance of their residence outside the ghetto, the walls of the ghetto not only expanded but became more porous. In the post–civil rights era, the ghetto was not the home of most blacks in the North. Although full integration is a long way off still, a majority of blacks outside the South do not reside in majority-black neighborhoods. The ghetto in many ways thus became depopulated and forlorn. The irony is that although *forlorn* is an apt adjective for the economic and social conditions that created the late-twentieth-century ghetto, more ink has been spilled about this particular type of neighborhood than about perhaps any other. It is this so-called underclass ghetto that has captured the attention of social scientists and spawned the voluminous literature mentioned earlier.

The ghetto of this era was in many ways qualitatively worse than the ghetto of earlier years. Crime, joblessness, family dissolution, and mass incarceration rolled over it with devastating consequences. Chapter 6 demonstrates how this devastation, combined with the rise of newer black meccas in the Sunbelt and prosperous black suburbs in the North, rendered the ghetto's role as a haven nearly obsolete. Despite the devastation wrought by joblessness, rising crime, and mass incarceration, the persistence and successes of the community-development movement in this same period are illustrative of how many residents continued to view the ghetto as a place to fight for and protect.

Chapter 7 takes stock of the three major forces shaping the twenty-first-century ghetto—mass incarceration, the subprime crisis, and gentrification. Mass incarceration grew in part from political reactions to rising crime from the 1960s through the 1980s. The chapter shows that although mass incarceration may have contributed to falling crime rates at the end of the twentieth century, this policy exacted a heavy toll in the ghetto on both criminals and the innocent alike. The subprime lending crisis wreaked havoc in middle-class black neighborhoods typically not thought of as ghettos in the pejorative sense. But the crisis illustrated that despite a facade of distinctiveness and stability, the middle-class enclaves were not immune to some of the same forces that had disadvantaged the ghetto earlier in the twentieth century.

Gentrification, which often evokes strong emotions over the changing character of ghetto neighborhoods, also demonstrates how the ghetto remained a haven for many. This perception is apparent both in the often visceral reactions to gentrification among those fearing the loss of the ghetto's character and in the actions of black gentrifiers, many of whom could choose to live elsewhere but for a variety of reasons see the ghetto as a haven and wish to make their home there. Chapter 7 thus shows how in the early twenty-first century the ghetto has continued to be a hell, buffeted by mass incarceration and the subprime crisis, even while its role as a haven has persisted.

The conclusion summarizes the key findings of the book, distilling the patterns that explain how the ghetto has variously been a haven and a hell for blacks, sometimes occupying these two roles simultaneously. Over the course of its history spanning more than a century, the American ghetto has served as a haven for blacks when white supremacy denied blacks opportunity to live fully. At times, as in the case of the Jim Crow South, white supremacy threatened the very survival of blacks. At other times, white supremacy stifled blacks' opportunity to express themselves politically. And there were times when a much more benign form of white supremacy simply served to remind blacks that they still remained on the margins of American society. During these times, the ghetto provided a space for blacks to thrive culturally, economically, and politically and simply to feel at home.

Although white supremacy may have given blacks the impetus to seek a haven in the ghetto, it also often manifested in ways that would make life there a hell. Moreover, the recession of white supremacy could ironically also wreak havoc in the ghetto as the most able and upwardly mobile blacks no longer sought refuge there.

The conclusion uses this distillation of findings to explore how planners and policy makers might respond to a ghetto that has been both cherished and loathed. The policies aim to address the circumstances that have too often made the ghetto a hell, while recognizing that even in the second decade of the twenty-first century it remains of haven for some blacks.

A NOTE ON TERMINOLOGY

The terms *African American*, *colored*, *black*, and *Negro* are used interchangeably throughout the book. *Colored* and *Negro*, however, are used only when their use was in vogue during the time period being discussed.

"The South" refers to the eleven states that were part of the Confederacy. "The North" is often used as a shorthand way to describe the entire region outside the former Confederacy, including the West Coast and Mountain states.

Chapter One

THE EMBRYONIC GHETTO

A young black man arriving in New York City at the age of nineteen, Joe Hamilton was enamored with the bright lights and hustle and bustle of the city. He admired the confident swagger and dapper clothes of the young men in his neighborhood. He admired their style and the way they strolled the streets seemingly always on their way to someplace exciting and important. His goal was to remake himself from a green country boy to a sophisticated city gent. Although job options were limited and the pay was too little to help support his mother and sister, it was enough for drink and an occasional night on the town. Soon he was able to adopt the style and swagger of those he previously admired, becoming a regular at the local watering hole, where the regulars included gamblers, pickpockets, murderers, and women of ill repute. Able to access only the most meager of jobs, he instead acquired status among those on the margins of the underworld. He soon succumbed to the bottle, barely able to keep a job or a roof over his head. His girlfriend tired of his drunkenness, putting him out and inspiring such a fit of rage in him that he murdered her. Before long, he was incarcerated, following the path of his father, whose imprisonment had left his family without a home and brought them to the city in the first place. Joe's quick descent from a green awestruck newcomer to an alcoholic denizen of the underworld and eventually an inmate in prison was one that his contemporaries had seen many times before. Although they were sad about his fate, they did not dwell on his tragic life, for he was "only one more who had got into the whirlpool, enjoyed the sensation for a moment, and then swept dizzily down."[1]

For those familiar with life in the American ghetto, this story seems all too common. A young man with limited options for achieving status or success via conventional means turns to the street to gain a modicum of respect as well as to mind-altering substances to numb the pain of a stunted existence. Before long, his life on the edge runs afoul of the law, and he becomes enmeshed in the carceral state, as his father was before him. The inner city is a dead end, a place of sorrow and stunted ambition.

This story, however, taken from Paul Dunbar's novel *The Sport of the Gods*,[2] takes place at the turn of the twentieth century, before the birth of the ghetto, as dated by contemporary social scientists, and the ensuing social problems that would become its hallmark. The social problems chronicled in *The Sport of the Gods* appear to be a case of art imitating life and not just the fanciful details of a story tailored to appeal to the masses' prurient interests. Writing at the same time as the publication of Dunbar's novel, W. E. B. Du Bois, a pioneer of urban sociology, described the neighborhoods of recent Negro migrants as hotbeds of "dirt and vice," "New York's most dangerous slum[s]." Indeed, Du Bois pinpointed crime as the "most sinister index of social degradation and struggle," which he further laid at the doorstep of "bad homes, poor health, restricted opportunities for work and general social oppression."[3] Indeed, in cities across the North, blacks found themselves in the least-desirable environs. An Indianapolis newspaper editor complained that blacks were "compelled to live in alleys, or broken down barracks, while at the mercy of rental agents and have as next door neighbors frequently, the most vicious classes."[4]

High rates of crime and social dislocation were common among blacks in the urban North. Social statistics first became available in the last decades of the nineteenth century and were used by policy makers and social reformers. Although these statistics were often put to the dubious use of justifying pseudoscientific race theories, they also documented the precarious position of late-nineteenth-century blacks in urban America.

Using his pioneering methods of social investigation, Du Bois found that Philadelphia blacks were incarcerated at anywhere from 20 percent to 138 percent the rate of whites from 1879 to 1895, which he felt was indicative of the crime problem among members of the race, even after accounting for the unreliability of arrest statistics and prejudice against Negroes. The pressures of stunted opportunity were also evident in family life among Philadelphia Negros in the late nineteenth century. Du Bois observed high rates of cohabitation among Negroes, which he attributed to "the difficulty of earning income enough to afford to marry."[5] Moreover, the death rate was some 20 percent higher among Philadelphia blacks in the 1890s.[6]

Novels such as *The Sport of the Gods* and the observations of early social scientists such as Du Bois tell a similar tale about life for late-nineteenth-century urban blacks in the North—for them, life was harsh. Indeed, these conditions were *hellish*. Did they, however bad, constitute a ghetto? Although few would argue otherwise about life for black Americans in the urban North before the Great Migration, which commenced in 1916, many instead date the rise of the ghetto to the first or second decade of the twentieth century and the Great Migration.

American ghettos, those large sections of many American cities that are home to tens of thousands of blacks and few others, are a twentieth-century result of the Great Migration and the forces that shaped blacks' incorporation into modern American cities. But significant numbers of blacks lived in the urban North prior to the Great Migration, which commenced during World War I. As discussed later, blacks residing in the late-nineteenth-century urban North experienced the forces of ghettoization that would bedevil later generations of blacks, but at this point they did not form the critical mass that would allow these spaces to function as true havens for the race. We thus begin our chronicle of the ghetto by examining the experiences of urban blacks in late-nineteenth-century America.

WHAT IS THE GHETTO?

The term *ghetto* originated in sixteenth-century Venice to describe a section of that city where Jews were forced to live, a section that happened to house a copper foundry, or *geto*. Soon thereafter, Jewish sections of other European cities came to be referred to as *getos*. The term persisted for several centuries, reaching its most notorious use during the Holocaust of the 1930s and 1940s, when the Nazis imprisoned Jews in ghettos as part of their "final solution." In the United States, the term *ghetto* became synonymous with the large agglomerations of blacks in American cities in the wake of World War II, as evidenced by the publication of *The Negro Ghetto* by

Robert Weaver in 1948, the first book using the term in its title in reference to black America.

The moniker seemed to fit the black belts that were prevalent across much of urban America. Like Jews in Nazi Europe, blacks were stigmatized outcasts. Like Jews, who were forced to wear yellow stars of David, blacks could not hide their identity. Jewish ghettos were overcrowded, crammed with many more people than the spaces were built to house. Likewise, Harlem and the South Side of Chicago were packed with black families living doubled up and even tripled up. Jews did not choose to live in the ghetto; they were confined there by walls and the barrels of guns. Blacks, too, were confined to the black belts through the use of restrictive covenants, terror, and discrimination. Finally, using the term *ghetto* to describe black belts in America might have been a way to prick the conscience of white Americans, who spent the better of part of a decade railing against the evils of the Nazis' racist creed while ignoring racism at home. In the 1930s and 1940s, it was not uncommon for the black press to compare the racism in the United States with Nazi master-race practices. When congressmen threatened to filibuster a fair-employment act, the *Chicago Defender* likened the "august buildings" that house the Senate and House of Representatives to the "Nazi Reichstag."[7] And so the moniker *ghetto* stuck.

More recently, social scientists have debated the definition of the term *ghetto*. Two prevailing definitions are what sociologist Mario Small calls the strong and the weak conceptions of the ghetto.[8] The *strong conception* focuses on the political and social forces that create the ghetto. Subscribers to this view see the ghetto as a distinctive, identifiable place "that is perpetuated by the dominant society and is a form of involuntary segregation."[9] Peter Marcuse's description of the ghetto as a "spatially concentrated area used to separate and to limit a particular involuntarily defined population group (usually by race) held to be, and treated as, inferior by the dominant society" is an exemplar of this approach.[10]

The weak conception, explained by Douglas Massey and Nancy Denton in *American Apartheid*, focuses on demography and conceptualizes ghettos as places that meet a certain demographic threshold. Arguing that the black ghetto is a unique institution, Massey and Denton contrast the ghetto to ethnic enclaves inhabited by many immigrant groups during the late nineteenth and early twentieth century. They point out that whereas the ghetto was overwhelmingly black, immigrant enclaves were heterogeneous places consisting of many groups. They indicate, however, that most immigrants and ethnics did not live in the enclaves. Finally, according to Massey and Denton, such enclaves were fleeting. The "Little Italys" and "Polestowns" of late-nineteenth- and early-twentieth-century America were transitory phenomena that would be relegated to the dustbin of history once immigrants and their offspring assimilated into America. Thus, Massey and Denton argue, the transitory nature of European immigrant enclaves stands in stark relief to the enduring presence of the ghetto.[11]

Prior to the passage of fair-housing laws in the 1960s and 1970s, these different definitions were distinctions without difference. Virtually all blacks in northern metropolitan areas lived in predominantly all-black neighborhoods, and a variety of actions by white individuals and the state conspired to keep them in these neighborhoods. Moreover, these spaces were stigmatized in the minds of white America. In the last decades of the twentieth century and the first decades of the twenty-first, however, these distinctions matter. As we shall see, increasing numbers of blacks live in integrated neighborhoods. Some have moved to formerly all-white neighborhoods, while some ghetto neighborhoods have experienced gentrification or an influx of immigrants from Asia or Latin America or both. Moreover, large numbers of blacks have chosen to live in upscale, predominantly black neighborhoods. All of these patterns are inconsistent with ghettoization as described earlier.

The topic of this book is the black ghettos in the urban American North. For the periods prior to the fair-housing era that began in the late 1960s, virtually all predominantly black neighborhoods were ghettos. Even the most privileged blacks could escape segregated neighborhoods only with great effort. For analytical purposes, it thus makes sense to consider all black neighborhoods in the periods under discussion. As described in more detail in chapter 6, this broad definition is less applicable after the passage of fair-housing laws. For this later period, neighborhoods with a history as ghettos (e.g., Harlem, Chicago's South Side) and relatively poor black neighborhoods are still considered ghettos.

WHEN DID THE GHETTOS ARISE?

With the definitions of the ghetto in hand, we can return to the late-nineteenth-century urban North, when blacks formed a miniscule portion of the urban milieu. The conditions where they lived were deplorable, but were they living in a ghetto in this period?

In most northern cities, the black population as a proportion of the total population was in the low single digits. Ghettos as they exist today, where tens of thousands of blacks and virtually only blacks reside, did not exist in the late nineteenth century. The small numbers of blacks and the concomitant absence of large-scale ghettos have led some historians to infer that the ghetto is a twentieth-century creation resulting from the Great Migration and that blacks' residential patterns in the late nineteenth century did not bear the hallmark of discrimination or stigma that we associate with the ghetto. The first wave of in-depth historical studies that appeared in the 1960s and 1970s clearly demarcate the ghettoization of the twentieth century from the black urban experience of the late nineteenth century. Describing the experience of blacks in Chicago after the Civil War, the historian Allan Spear writes, "[Blacks] continued to face discrimination in housing, employment, and[,] even in the face of civil rights law, public accommodations. *But they were not confined to a ghetto.* Most Negroes, although concentrated in certain sections of the city, lived in mixed neighborhoods."[12] David Katzman's history of Detroit in the late nineteenth century, *Before the Ghetto*, reaches a similar conclusion. Katzman, examining census manuscripts from the 1880s, shows that although blacks were concentrated on the east side, there were few if any all-black blocks, and most blocks with blacks also had substantial numbers of whites.[13] Historical accounts of the black experience in Cleveland and Philadelphia also stress the lack of a black ghetto in these respective cities prior to the twentieth century. Consider the historian Kenneth Kusmer's assertion that "the fact that most blacks lived within fairly well defined areas of the city at this time, however, does not mean that a black ghetto existed in Cleveland."[14] Likewise, the historian Roger Lane writes, "Philadelphia as late as 1900 had the largest black population of any city north of the Mason-Dixon line, as the census counted 62,613 Afro-American residents. . . . But even Philadelphia could not support a 'ghetto,' as its black housing was not always segregated by household, court, or alley, certainly not by street or block."[15]

A second group of scholars sees pre–Great Migration race relations and consequently the residential patterns that reflected these relations as being more fluid. Mid-twentieth-century housing reformer Charles Abrams argues:

As long as the Negro had been a small and docile minority in the North, the feeling that Negroes always destroy social status and market values never gained widespread acceptance. In Washington, D.C., Baltimore, and Philadelphia, Negroes lived in small clusters near the better white dwellings, and, before 1915, they lived in almost every section in Chicago and a third of the city's Negroes living in areas that were less than 10 per cent Negro occupied. The Negro's presence in cities rarely caused a white exodus; it would in fact have disturbed the equanimity of the whites in those days if their maids and butlers moved too far from the town houses.[16]

Describing nineteenth-century New York, historian Marcy Sacks writes, "Until the early twentieth century blacks lived within integrated Manhattan neighborhoods."[17]

In what is perhaps the seminal work on the black ghetto, *The Negro Ghetto*, published in 1948, the public intellectual and later secretary of the U.S. Department of Housing and Urban Development (HUD) Robert Weaver described the North prior to the Great Migration as a place where residential segregation patterns were starkly different than those following the onset of migration from the South beginning in the 1910s. In the second chapter of his book, "Concentrated but Not Always Separated," Weaver played down the importance of discrimination in determining the housing experiences of blacks during this era. He wrote, "Such concentration of colored residents as existed was due chiefly to the voluntary actions of Negroes (largely inspired, of course, by their need for each other's society in a community which rejected them in many phases of its life) and to their restriction, because of income, to low-rent housing."[18] Such a description is clearly inconsistent with conceptions of the ghetto offered earlier and is more akin to an ethnic enclave. Weaver also noted that although these blacks' housing was generally poor in quality and sometimes substandard, "it was not unlike the sort of housing which American cities in the North offered to all poor groups."[19] Weaver did note that blacks often paid more for comparable housing, which is suggestive of discrimination. Moreover, he pointed out that blacks who claimed that prior to the Great Migration things were rosy were perhaps being nostalgic.

But in considering Weaver's overall description of the urban patterns of pre–Great Migration blacks, we cannot overlook his ideological inclinations. Operating in the tradition of Du Bois and influenced by the then recently released book *An American Dilemma: The Negro Problem and*

Modern Democracy by Gunnar Myrdal,[20] *The Negro Ghetto* is a work suffused with the notion that social science could combat the primary cause of race antagonism—ignorance. With it, Weaver aimed to dispel the falsehoods that motivated housing segregation in the first place. Faulty arguments such as the claim that Negroes lowered property values were clearly in Weaver's sights when he wrote *The Negro Ghetto*. Consistent with this attack on ignorance, Weaver also aimed to put the ghetto in proper historical context and to show that blacks and whites did at one time live together:

Few Americans realize that widespread enforced residential segregation on the basis of color is relatively new in the North and that complete spatial separation of the races is not characteristic of urban living in the South. Were they to reflect upon these facts, many would be less certain that the Negro ghetto will and must persist. At the same time such knowledge would be helpful and perhaps encouraging to the small minority of municipal officials, city planners and housers who realize the impediments to sound city planning and urban redevelopment which result from involuntary and enforced residential segregation.[21]

In this seminal work on the ghetto, Weaver clearly considered the ghetto a recent creation resulting from irrational fears and misunderstandings. Moreover, the alternative—blacks and whites living in the same neighborhoods—was a reality of the not too distant past.

Fast-forward half a century, and many social scientists make an argument similar to Weaver's that spatial patterns between blacks and whites reflected the relatively fluid social relations between the races. Drawing on the work of several urban historians, Massey and Denton assemble data showing that segregation at the ward level was relatively low between blacks and whites as late as 1910. Moreover, blacks in the urban North lived in wards that were overwhelmingly (at least 90 percent) white prior to the Great Migration.[22] Massey and Denton describe a nineteenth-century city that was not conducive to segregation of any type, including that experienced by blacks. The lack of specialized land uses and almost nonexistent transportation systems that could move great numbers of people over significant distances precluded much in the way of spatial separation of differing groups. Moreover, Massey and Denton paint a picture of relatively fluid race relations, specifically in the North, where discrimination did not play an important role in determining housing patterns for blacks and where blacks and whites shared residential spaces. Blacks lived in bad housing, to be sure, but this was due to their low-income status rather than to their race per se. Massey and Denton go as far as to write, "To the extent the disadvantaged residential conditions of blacks in the nineteenth century can be attributed to prejudice and discrimination, it is to prejudice and *discrimination in employment rather than in housing.*"[23]

The economists David Cutler, Ed Glaser, and Jacob Vigdor date the rise of the ghetto to 1890 at the earliest, reasoning that the rise of the ghetto coincided with the mass migration of blacks to urban centers. They assemble the most systematic evidence of black segregation in the 1890–1910 period, showing, based on ward-level data, that blacks were not that segregated. The levels of segregation as measured by the dissimilarity index (showing how evenly spread blacks were throughout a given city) were modest (average of 0.47 based on ward-level data), and levels of isolation as measured by the isolation index (showing the average percentage of blacks in the typical black person's neighborhood) were lower still.[24] Taken together, the historical descriptions and quantitative evidence assembled would seem to settle with a high degree of certainty the question of whether ghettos existed prior to the Great Migration.

Although the evidence clearly marks a difference in ghettoization coinciding with the Great Migration, we should be careful not to overstate the distinction between pre–Great Migration black "enclaves" and the ghettos that arose thereafter. The term *ghetto* was used more often later because the conditions in which black Americans lived resonated with the conditions of the Jewish ghettos.

There certainly appears to have been widespread housing discrimination against blacks in the late nineteenth century that limited their housing options. Notwithstanding Weaver's and Massey and Denton's claims about the unimportance of housing discrimination, consider a sample of testimonies from various black newspapers in the nineteenth century.

Being one of those persons who have been obliged to do house-hunting through the columns of our paper, the *Gazette*, I wish to offer up my feeble voice in protest of the injustice of being refused the privilege of renting a good house simply because the color of my skin is a shade darker than my fellow man. Day after day this repulse is given me in plain and very poor English "I don't rent to your kind of people."[25]

How can we working women who have to do that way, clothe ourselves comfortably or save a cent to take care of us when we are sick? And if we lose a place we haven't sufficient funds laid up to buy food. The color line is drawn on us at the dry goods store, the grocery, the market, by the landlord and real estate men, from whom we have to purchase and rent, and out in service of all of these charge the colored man or woman 20 or 35 percent more than they do the white purchaser or tenant.[26]

Nowhere in the northwest portion of the city [Washington, DC] can a colored person obtain a house when an agent or owner has a possible chance of renting to a white person. What is true in Washington, D.C. is true in every northern and eastern city. Respectable colored people cannot not only rent but cannot buy properties in respectable localities.[27]

There are blocks upon blocks, street after street, right here in Indianapolis, miles of thoroughfare "for rent," "lease" "sale" that are just as completely barred against the entrée of a "colored family," no matter how respectable or able financially, as is the Harem of the Sultan of Turkey against the inquisitive gaze of the tourist within his gates. The same condition exists in Chicago, Cincinnati, Detroit, Cleveland, Columbus, Buffalo, Brooklyn, New York, Boston, Philadelphia and the thousand and one small cities and towns that intervene and lie beyond.[28]

The unjust discrimination indulged in Northern cities by rental agents and real estate owners, against respectable colored people is most humiliating and trying. There is very little difference in meanness, if any, between the spirit that causes it and that which made the Jim Crow car in the South possible.[29]

There seems to be a mutual understanding among capitalists and real estate dealers who have been conspicuous in contributing to this development of our city, that [the] colored man, no matter how respectable, how intelligent, how thrifty, is not to enjoy in common with other citizens the right to live in as good a style as his means will allow him. If a house becomes vacant, if it has modern improvements, if it be in a decent neighborhood, the word is invariably given that no colored tenant shall occupy it.[30]

The first two quotes give firsthand testimony of the experience of housing discrimination. Elite Negroes' recollections of the late nineteenth century also attest to the problem of housing discrimination. The first black family to move into the idyllic all-white LeDroit Park subdivision outside Washington, DC, in 1893, were greeted with a bullet through their window. The second black family, that of Robert Terrell, a well-known attorney and the first black justice of the peace in Washington, DC, and his wife, Mary Church Terrell, suffragette and founding member of the National Association for the Advancement of Colored People (NAACP), were rebuffed on account of their race when attempting to purchase a home in that same neighborhood. Only the intervention of a white friend, who bought the house for them and immediately resold it to them, allowed them to acquire the house. Such accounts are the closest we have to actual evidence of housing discrimination in the pre–Great Migration era.[31] But there is also an abundance of secondhand evidence, as the four quotes indicate. From editors of black-owned newspapers in the North, these statements suggest that housing discrimination was widespread and not an isolated or occasional occurrence. They describe the near impossibility for blacks to obtain housing in wide swaths of the urban North.

Consider also the opinions of urban experts in this period. The white journalist and social reformer Ray Stannard Baker, writing in 1908 about early-twentieth-century Boston, wrote, "A strong race prejudice exists against renting flats and houses in many white neighborhoods to colored people."[32] Jacob Riis, one of the earliest investigative journalists, wrote extensively about the lives of the poor and in his writings included a fair amount about the travails of the black poor as well. Riis described extensive discrimination faced by blacks. "Where he [the landlord] permits them to live, they go; where he shuts the door, stay out. By his grace they exist at all in certain localities; his ukase banishes them from others. . . . Until recent times—the years since a change was wrought can be counted on the fingers of one hand—[they were] practically restricted in the choice of a home to a narrow section of the West Side [of New York City]."[33]

W. E. B. Du Bois also described the housing market as unfriendly toward blacks. About late-nineteenth-century Philadelphia, Du Bois wrote, "The undeniable fact that most Philadelphia white people prefer not to live near Negroes limits the Negro very seriously in his choice of a home and especially the choice of a cheap home. . . . The sentiment [unwillingness to live near Negroes]) has greatly lessened in intensity during the last two decades, but it is still strong."[34] This perspective was undoubtedly influenced by the firsthand accounts he obtained as part of his survey of blacks in Philadelphia. Among the accounts Du Bois recorded in his manuscript were:

A— paid $13 a month where the preceding white family paid $10.

B— paid $16; "hear that former white family paid $12."

G—, the Negro inhabitants of the whole street[,] pay $12 to $14 and the whites $9 and $10.

The houses are all alike.[35]

Riis and Du Bois, writing about New York and Philadelphia, respectively, approximately a decade apart, drew the similar conclusion that what we called housing discrimination was pervasive in these cities and that it had observable impacts on blacks. Tellingly, both Riis and Du Bois thought the housing market was *improving* for blacks, which contradicts the notion that housing discrimination started with the onset of the Great Migration or immediately preceding it. Of course, Riis and Du Bois's perception of the changing intensity of discrimination may be wrong. But that they would have such a perception suggests pervasive housing discrimination had been occurring for quite some time before they published their books and that this discrimination was not a new phenomenon.

On the eve of the Great Migration, the author of a survey of housing conditions in Springfield, Massachusetts, wrote, "In the districts where the colored people are in the majority bad housing features are among the most serious in the city. This is usual in cities that have Negro districts." The author went on to construct a story attributing bad housing conditions to "the Negro suffer[ing] under severe handicaps. He is usually segregated if not by law then by custom."[36]

In addition to testimonials and contemporary opinions, we can also consider indirect evidence consistent with widespread discrimination. This indirect evidence takes several forms, one of earliest being the actions of progressive reformers. As early as 1856, progressives noted how housing discrimination restricted the housing options of blacks in ways that were deleterious. Indeed, one of the first model tenements in New York City was built for blacks because their housing conditions were so poor. Describing this model tenement, one of the proponents of such housing wrote, "The number of families in the building is 87 . . . all of whom are colored. The reason for selecting this class of tenants is that they are usually forced into the worst kind of dwellings, and are deprived of most social privileges and consequently were specially deserving commiseration."[37] Progressives, although certainly more enlightened than most whites about race matters, certainly did not see blacks as equals to whites. Moreover, as this quotation suggests ("forced into"), blacks often could not access better housing. That blacks would be the beneficiaries of one of the first model tenements, despite their pariah-like status, speaks to both the horrific conditions they must have endured and the significant obstacles they faced in securing housing.

The evidence on how urban housing markets operated in this period is also suggestive of widespread housing discrimination against blacks. In marketing their housing, realtors often took the step of indicating which offerings were available for blacks. The historian Christopher Robert Reed quotes an ad for a flat "for colored people only" in the *Chicago Tribune*.[38] *New York Age*, a black newspaper, ran an ad in 1890 describing "Flats for Respectable Colored Families Only." Another *New York Age* ad in 1889 listed "First Class Apartments for Colored People." Indeed, in late-nineteenth-century black newspapers one can literally find hundreds of ads for apartments designated as "For Colored." Figures 1.1 to 1.4 exhibit only a few. The implication of these types of advertisements is that other housing or at least a significant portion of it was off-limits to blacks.

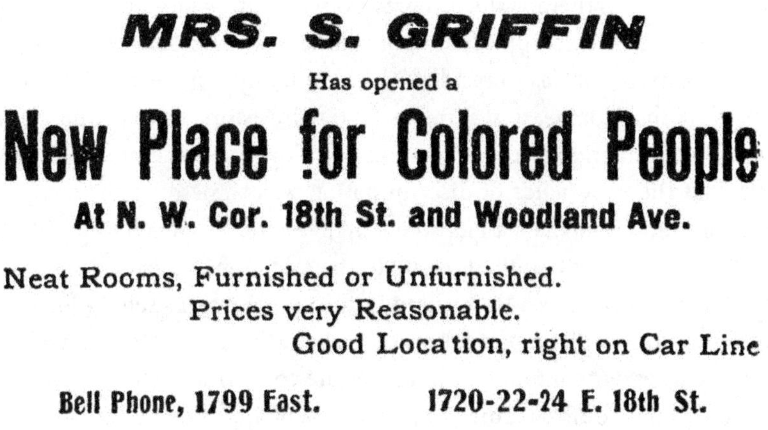

MRS. S. GRIFFIN

Has opened a

New Place for Colored People

At N. W. Cor. 18th St. and Woodland Ave.

Neat Rooms, Furnished or Unfurnished.
Prices very Reasonable.
Good Location, right on Car Line

Bell Phone, 1799 East.   1720-22-24 E. 18th St.

FIGURE 1.1 Ad in *Kansas City Rising Sun*, November 2, 1907.

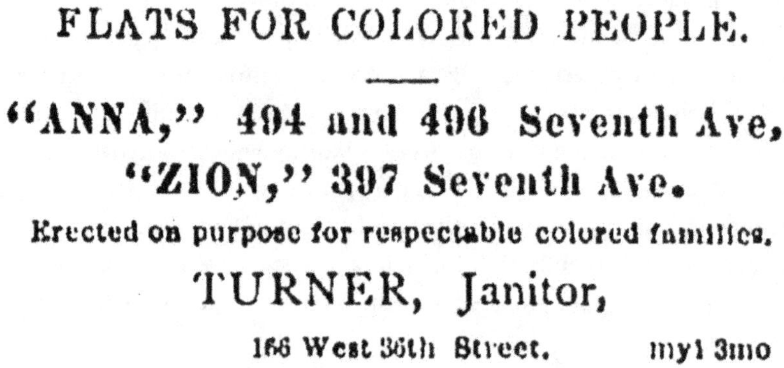

FLATS FOR COLORED PEOPLE.

**"ANNA," 494 and 496 Seventh Ave,,
"ZION," 397 Seventh Ave.**

Erected on purpose for respectable colored families.

TURNER, Janitor,

166 West 36th Street.   my1 3mo

FIGURE 1.2 Ad in *New York Freeman*, October 9, 1886.

FOR RENT—ROOMS—No. 221 Court street, suitable
for colored families; rent low.   au 18-2t*

FIGURE 1.3 Ad in the *Cincinnati Daily Gazette*, August 18, 1877.

Some black entrepreneurs, seeking to capitalize on the discrimination experienced by blacks, aimed to create housing that they could market directly to blacks. In 1887, a group of black entrepreneurs started a development company in Middlesex County, Massachusetts, with the stated aim to "purchase and build suitable places in desirable locations in Cambridge to rent for homes thereby shielding us from an outrageous and foolish discrimination that exists on account of color and is a hindrance to our procuring desirable places to reside."[39] The company ran ads in black newspapers in the Northeast seeking potential investors. Perhaps its claims about discrimination were just a marketing ploy. It seems more likely, however, that the experience of discrimination was something the company thought would resonate with its potential investors. In a world where blacks' housing choices were limited owing to their economic means, such an ad would make little sense. Each share in the company was selling for $25, a not inconsequential amount for most blacks at that time. Moreover, blacks with the wherewithal to invest in real estate companies, who, Massey and Denton claim, could "acquire a residence befitting their status,"[40] would probably have looked askance at such ads if housing discrimination were indeed a rare occurrence.

A final piece of indirect evidence is suggested by economic theory. Cutler, Glaeser, and Vigdor argue that housing markets where blacks paid higher prices for equivalent housing than whites was consistent with widespread collusion among whites to restrict the housing options of blacks.[41] This makes intuitive sense. Whites' refusal to lease or sell property to blacks in effect restricted the supply of housing available to blacks. The restriction of supply is a cause of rising prices, as taught in Econ 101.

Contemporary observers frequently noted that blacks paid higher prices than whites for housing of the same quality. Du Bois noted regarding the testimonies of several respondents in his study of black Philadelphia, "Here is a people compelled to live in a less pleasant quarters than most people, and pay for them somewhat higher rents."[42] This was also the observation of a British study of living standards in twenty-eight U.S. cities in the first decade of the twentieth century.[43] Social reformer Mary Ovington also wrote about New York City around the same time, "The shelter afforded is poorer than that given the white resident whose dwelling touches the black, the rents are a little higher."[44] Jacob Riis documented the premiums paid by blacks, quoting a real estate firm: "We find the former [blacks] cleaner than the latter [lower grades of foreign white people], and they do not destroy the property so much. *We also get higher prices.*" Riis also listed a rental schedule that illustrated the higher rents this realtor charged to blacks.[45] Even Robert Weaver, who painted a relatively rosy picture of pre–Great Migration housing patterns among blacks, acknowledged in 1948 that blacks often paid more for equivalent housing, as noted earlier in this chapter. Curiously, Weaver failed to make the connection between the higher prices blacks paid for housing prior to the Great Migration and the widespread discrimination that was probably responsible for this trend.

The preceding discussion provides substantial evidence that blacks faced pervasive housing discrimination in the nineteenth and early twentieth centuries in urban areas outside the South. One can, of course, find some evidence to suggest housing discrimination was not problematic. For example, a newspaper editor in Pittsburgh wrote, "It is not difficult to rent a house, except in some few localities, and any unprejudiced person who walked around this city would be surprised to find so many prominent streets upon which our people own property and rent."[46] But such a view seems to have been in the minority, as indicated by both the testimonials and the indirect evidence summarized here.

Discrimination alone, however, is not the only hallmark of the ghetto. Stigma is another of its attributes. That blacks lived in areas that were physically poor seems beyond dispute. Numerous scholars have described the fetid living conditions experienced by urban blacks prior to the Great Migration.[47] The poor physical condition of areas where blacks lived and the fact that these spaces were black contributed to their stigmatization.

Social scientists have documented the stigmatization of black spaces in current times.[48] But negative perceptions of black spaces by whites apparently date back to at least the middle part of the nineteenth century. In 1903, a description of why Gotham Court, one of the first model tenements in New York City, became a slum noted: "In the first place it was decided that the house should be occupied solely by colored persons. This meant, as it always does in this city, that the house could never be occupied by respectable white people afterward, there being the strongest possible feeling on this part of tenants in this respect, so that when the class of respectable negroes moved away from that neighborhood it became absolutely hopeless to secure for the building tenants of the right kind."[49]

Jacob Riis also described how black residential spaces were stigmatized. In addition to pointing out how blacks were typically charged more for the same units, he summarized landlords' rationale: "white people will not live in the same house with colored tenants, or even in a house recently occupied by negroes."[50]

Historian Roger Lane writes that the "red-light district was partially located in the area with the densest black settlement. One reason was political, in that while the police and magistrates were not usually capable of eliminating vice, they could at least set bounds to it. And 'little Africa' was ideally suited in all respects. . . . The legitimate black elite was not strong or independent enough to protest effectively, to keep it out of their neighborhoods." Lane also writes, "residential segregation forced more closeness in the respectable middle class than it wanted."[51] Writing about Cleveland in the first decade of the twentieth century, historian Kenneth Kusmer describes how vice districts developed in close proximity to the city's budding black residential sections.[52] The historian Allan Spear makes similar observations about pre–Great Migration black Chicago and infers that the association of black districts with vice was no mere coincidence.[53] Law enforcement made a conscious decision to tolerate vice in certain neighborhoods—those already viewed with disdain, including black areas.

The association of black areas with red-light districts appears to have been pervasive, much like housing discrimination in general. Describing black neighborhoods in the first decade of the twentieth century, the civil rights advocate Richard R. Wright wrote, "In more than one large city the distinctively Negro neighborhood is the same as, or next to, that district which seems, by the consent of the civil authorities, to be given up to vice."[54] True, Wright was writing in 1908, when some black ghettos had already begun to coalesce. But Riis was writing nearly two decades before then, and Lane's account of black Philadelphia was of the 1860–1900 period.

The evidence presented thus far in this chapter shows that political and social forces, in the form of widespread housing discrimination, relegated blacks to second-class housing. We must therefore ask whether those who date the birth of the ghetto to the first decades of the twentieth century or the Great Migration that accompanied World War I are wide of the mark in their assessments of when the black ghetto began. In addition to anecdotes, a number of scholars have presented segregation indices for cities in the late nineteenth century and at the turn of the twentieth.[55] These data show moderate levels of segregation based on the dissimilarity index and the isolation index. Certainly by the standards of the twentieth century, the segregation levels presented by these authors are relatively moderate. The moderate levels of segregation indicated by the dissimilarity index mean blacks were relatively evenly spread throughout given cities. The moderate levels of segregation indicated by the isolation index mean that, on average, blacks lived in areas where other groups had a significant presence.

The segregation analyses, however, are based on ward-level data. Census tracts have served as the basis of the vast majority of segregation analyses conducted since the middle of the twentieth century. Tracts are geographic entities developed by the U.S. Census Bureau for the purpose of disseminating data on areas that approximate what people think of as neighborhoods. Tracts typically have around 4,000 persons. In contrast, wards are geographic entities developed for political purposes. Wards are also typically much larger than tracts. Cutler, Glaeser, and Vigdor note that wards in Philadelphia in 1910 had 33,000 persons on average.[56] Moreover, because ward boundaries are local political jurisdictions, their sizes vary dramatically across local jurisdictions. For these reasons, segregation indices based on ward-level data should be interpreted cautiously.

Unfortunately for those studying segregation patterns prior to the Great Migration, census tracts were not adopted until 1910 and even then only in a handful of cities. Census data from 1880 until 1950, however, do contain information on each respondent's "enumeration district." An enumeration district, as the name implies, is a unit of geography created for the purpose of enumerating rather than disseminating census data. Enumeration districts represent the geographic area where each enumerator (the person who went door to door collecting census data) was responsible for collecting information. The size and shape of the district were designed to be compact enough so that the enumerator could cover the area in a few weeks, and the boundaries had to be contained within the larger geographic entities for which tabulated data were provided.[57] I have shown elsewhere how class segregation among blacks varied prior to the 1960s and that enumeration districts can be a valid proxy for neighborhoods.[58] Table 1.1 shows comparative statistics for wards and enumeration districts in 1900.

Enumeration districts are much smaller than wards and perhaps more importantly are more uniform in size. The standard deviation, which measures the extent to which the distribution clusters around the mean, is much smaller for enumeration districts than for wards. With an average size of 1,522, enumeration districts are smaller than tracts, which have been frequently used in analyses of twentieth-century segregation. But the size of enumeration districts is closer to census block groups, a geographic entity some argue is preferable for measuring segregation.[59] For assessing the types of neighborhoods blacks were living in prior to the Great Migration, enumeration districts may indeed be superior to wards.

TABLE 1.1
Comparison of Wards and Enumeration Districts in 1900

	Average Size	Median Size	Largest Size	Smallest Size	Standard Deviation
Ward	9,325	5,360	152,343	116	12,549
Enumeration District	1,522	1,454	8,469	37	717

Source: Author's tabulation of Integrated Public Use Microdata samples (Ruggles et al. 2010).

The Integrated Public Use Microdata samples produced by the University of Minnesota identifies each census respondent's unique enumeration district.[60] Recently, full count versions of census data have been produced for select years. For the period prior to the commencement of the Great Migration (1920) the 1880 census data are available, which allow us to calculate segregation indices for northern cities in 1880 to get a sense of quantitative levels of ghettoization at that time.

Table 1.2 illustrates segregation indices for northern cities with the largest black populations in 1880. Compared to the "chocolate cites" of the late twentieth century, the black population in northern cities was typically small. Only three cities had a black population greater than 25,000. The dissimilarity indices for these cities are listed in the third column. Values higher than 0.6 are considered high, from 0.3 to 0.6 moderate, and lower than 0.3 low. A noticeable pattern emerges. Cities in states bordering slave states or in former slave states (Delaware, Kentucky, Maryland, Missouri) tend to have dissimilarity scores in the low or moderate range. In contrast, most of the northernmost cities—such as Boston, Brooklyn, Chicago, Indianapolis, New York City, and Philadelphia—have dissimilarity scores in the high range. For readers unfamiliar with historical studies of residential segregation, this pattern might seem counterintuitive. Residential

TABLE 1.2
Residential Segregation in 1880 (Ranked by Size of Black Population)

	City Population	Black Population (% of Total Population)	Dissimilarity Index	Isolation Index
Washington, DC	147,200	37.8	.33	.44
Baltimore	332,300	16.1	.42	.29
Philadelphia	847,100	3.7	.61	.21
Louisville, KY	123,700	16.9	.38	.26
New York (Manhattan)	1,206,200	1.6	.64	.11
St. Louis	350,500	5.4	.46	.15
Kansas City	55,700	14.6	.19	.17
Cincinnati	255,100	3.2	.54	.11
Brooklyn	566,600	1.4	.58	.06
Lexington, KY	16,600	45.6	.29	.54
Indianapolis, IN	75,000	8.7	.40	.17
Chicago	503,100	1.3	.69	.15
Boston	362,800	1.6	.65	.15
Wilmington, DE	42,400	12.8	.21	.15
Pittsburgh	156,300	2.6	.53	.10

Source: Author's calculations of Integrated Public Use Microdata samples (Ruggles et al. 2010).

segregation was lower in states that had chattel slavery and that would later implement Jim Crow. The lower segregation indices in the urban South reflected the physical proximity between slaves and their masters even in urban areas. After the Civil War, blacks often lived on side streets and in back alleys that were close to their places of work as domestic servants for whites.[61] Northern cities, however, were already exhibiting high levels of segregation even at this early date.

In assessing the ghettoization of blacks in the late nineteenth century, we should be concerned about more than the extent to which blacks were evenly distributed among blacks. What was the racial composition of the neighborhoods that blacks lived in? Did blacks live completely isolated from whites in all black enclaves? The fifth column in table 1.2 presents isolation indices, which tell us the average percentage of blacks in the typical black person's neighborhood. In none of the cities save one, Lexington, Kentucky, in 1880 did blacks on average live in neighborhoods that were majority black. In a number of cities, the neighborhoods where the typical black lived was overwhelmingly nonblack. This evidence is more consistent with the notion that ghettoization did not start until the onset of the Great Migration some decades later.

But we cannot focus on only one piece of evidence, the isolation index, and conclude that ghettoization was not a relevant phenomenon in the late nineteenth century. True, the isolation indices in the cities listed in table 1.2 are generally low. But the isolation index is influenced by the size of the black population in the respective cities.[62] As can be seen in table 1.2, blacks constituted a very small percentage of these cities' populations, in many instances in the low single digits. That the isolation indices were as high as they were given the paltry number of blacks in these cities in 1880 belies the notion that the forces of ghettoization were inert at this early date.

A recent study by John Logan and his colleagues is consistent with the quantitative analyses presented earlier. They also based their study of segregation on enumeration districts and in analyzing data for 1880 concluded, "Black separation from whites in northern cities was much greater and appeared much earlier than has previously been documented."[63]

A final point to consider when weighing the evidence on late-nineteenth-century ghettoization is the context of the times. Ghettoization is about using physical space to separate, stigmatize, and subjugate a group of people. The ghettoized are pariahs condemned to second-class status at best. Although the North did fight against the Confederacy in part to halt the spread of slavery, the racial climate in northern cities throughout the nineteenth century can hardly be described as anything but hostile. The many histories of black life in nineteenth-century urban America are replete with tales of disenfranchisement in the political sphere, segregation in public schools, employment discrimination, and just plain racial hostility. As Gilbert Osofsky indicates in the title of the first chapter of his history of Harlem, life for blacks in the New York of the 1890s was "no crystal stair." Employment discrimination was rampant.[64] Lane describes in detail how Philadelphia's blacks were excluded from the burgeoning industrial sector.[65] The historian Christopher Reed describes a similar scenario in nineteenth-century Chicago, where blacks were for the most part limited to a few personal-service occupations.[66]

Indeed, one need only look at the struggle for blacks' civil rights in the late-nineteenth-century North to take the temperature of the racial climate there. In most northern states, blacks lacked the right to vote in 1865. Even with the passage of the Fifteenth Amendment, which assured the vote for all male citizens, northern blacks found many of their civil rights circumscribed. In several northern states, schools remained de jure segregated well into the 1880s.[67]

Given these experiences in employment, education, and politics, it would be surprising if the racial animus that so limited blacks' opportunities in these spheres did not extend to housing as well. If blacks' humanity was viewed with suspicion, their right to suffrage granted only grudgingly, and their access to public spaces often defined by the policy of "separate but equal,"[68] how likely would it be that they could freely settle anywhere they wished, limited only by the size of their purse?

More likely, blacks' options were limited through the experience of ghettoization during the late nineteenth century. Their numbers were small enough, however, that this ghettoization did not result in ghettos on a scale that we would recognize today. This interpretation is consistent with the quantitative evidence in tables 1.1 and 1.2. Yet the *process* of ghettoization was under way by the final decades of the nineteenth century, so the birth of the ghetto should rightly be dated to the late nineteenth century.

A HELL OR A HAVEN?

Without bread all is misery.

—WILLIAM COBBETT, BRITISH JOURNALIST (1763-1835)

For southern blacks after the Civil War, their first concern was survival. Once the nation reneged on General William Tecumseh Sherman's promise of "forty acres and a mule," they found themselves with few options to secure their daily bread. With no money or land and skills only suitable to their previous work as slaves—primarily agrarian work—most blacks found themselves working for their former masters in a state of semiserfdom. The withdrawal of federal troops and the South's revoking of blacks' civil rights after Reconstruction left the mass of blacks there economically beholden to whites, without civil rights and at the mercy of terrorist groups such as the Ku Klux Klan. For a small number of blacks who became ensnared in convict leasing in the South, life may have been even worse than it was during slavery. Slave owners had some incentive at least to make sure the slaves were healthy so they could work productively or fetch a fair price. Prisoners in many convict-leasing programs could not even count on that.[69] Without this "health insurance," the landscape for the mass of black Americans after Reconstruction was indeed a bleak one.

Given the abysmal conditions in the South, one might have expected the North to play the role of promised land earlier than it did. To be sure, racial subjugation was less harsh and pervasive in the North than in the South in the period after Reconstruction. While the civil rights accorded by emancipation to blacks in the South were slowly being taken away after Reconstruction, they were slowly expanding in the North. As in the South, northern states voted for the Thirteenth, Fourteenth, and Fifteenth Amendments, but several northern states went further. Prodded by activist groups such as the National Equal Rights League, eighteen state legislatures passed civil rights laws during the 1880s. Blacks were less successful in eradicating school segregation, but most northern states had de jure if not always de facto integrated schools by the end of the nineteenth century.[70] The racial climate in the North was often violently hostile; Lane describes how urban blacks in the North often felt the need to be armed because of the racial antagonism they experienced.[71] But this antagonism paled in comparison to the state-sanctioned terror that ruled the South.

But for at least four reasons the incipient ghettos of the late nineteenth century did not play the role of a haven in which the race's interests could be advanced. First, the small numbers of blacks in the budding ghettos limited the extent to which blacks could create their own institutions. True, de facto segregation in social life meant that blacks in the North had to create their own institutions. Black churches both long standing and fleeting arose to serve the faithful. Numerous other civic and fraternal organizations arose. Some, such as the National Equal Rights League, were able to achieve a little success regarding blacks' civil rights, as noted earlier.[72] Black businesses catering to blacks rather than to whites also began to arise at this time across Northern cities. A number of black newspapers arose in the period between Reconstruction and the commencement of the Great Migration. But, as the historian David Katzman surmises, the black population was too small to support enterprises that were anything but meager. The small black population in conjunction with the limited resources of the black community meant most black institutions remained small and fleeting in this period.[73]

Second, the small size of the black population in the North limited black political power. In the age of the political machine, blacks could wield power to the extent they could stay united as a voting bloc. Loyalty to the political machine would be rewarded with political appointments, as when Robert Pelham Jr. was appointed clerk in Detroit's revenue collector's office or when Edwin Horne, the songstress Lena Horne's grandfather, was appointed assistant inspector of the Combustible Division of the Fire Department in Brooklyn, New York, in 1899—an impressive feat for a Negro at that time—as reward for joining the Negro affiliate of the Tammany Hall Machine.[74] More commonly, Negroes were appointed to less-glamorous, menial positions, such as street sweeper or janitor, as patronage rewards. A letter to the editor of the *Indianapolis Freeman* describing the opportunities for blacks in Los Angeles in 1889 stated, "At the last city election Afro-Americans turned the balance of power, giving them two policemen, one Clerk in Assessor's office and all the janitor work in the public buildings."[75]

Occasionally a black could be nominated for and win elective office. Loyal black Republican operatives were sometimes nominated for local offices. Partisan loyalties were strong enough in many instances for whites to vote for blacks nominated by their party. David Augustus Straker of Detroit is such an example, elected to the position of Wayne County

(Detroit) Circuit Court commissioner. John Patterson Green was elected to the Ohio House of Representatives.[76]

Blacks who obtained patronage positions were obviously beholden to whites who wielded political power, but the few black elected officials in the late-nineteenth-century urban North were also beholden to whites. For example, the majority of John Patterson Green' s district was white. Because of the small size of the black population in the North, black politicians had to rely on white politicians to be nominated. Blacks could wield little independent political power.

The third reason the incipient ghettos in the North did not serve as a haven is that the small size of the black population and the relative weakness of black institutional life left the race with a leadership class more concerned with burnishing their own status than with advancing the interests of the black masses. The small black elite prior to the Great Migration generally owed their status more to whites than to other blacks. Indeed, a disproportionate share of the "colored aristocracy" owed their very existence to whites: they were the descendants or offspring of interracial liaisons between masters and slaves in the antebellum era. As the offspring of high-status whites, they often enjoyed the benefits of education and social connections with whites and sometimes inherited substantial property even when they were still legally slaves. After emancipation, these advantages gave them a head start over other blacks in term of socioeconomic mobility, and as result they were a major component of the elite class in the late nineteenth and early twentieth century.

The small size and relative poverty of the black population in the urban North meant the most prosperous black businessmen and entrepreneurs made their living by servicing whites. They were often in personal-service occupations such as barbering or catering, where the subservient nature of the business made it acceptable for blacks to hold such skilled and remunerative positions. A number of blacks became relatively wealthy (at least compared to other blacks) in the urban North in these occupations and often operated their own businesses. Moreover, their servicing of elite whites gave them an up-close and personal view of the ways and mores of the upper crust—behaviors they would emulate to distinguish themselves from the black masses. A contemporary news article portrayed this "colored aristocracy" as making their living as "caterers or head waiters at top metropolitan hotels" and described most of the men of the "colored 150" as stewards of clubs or in charge of private yachts, "with their positions giv-ing them opportunities to learn the ways of cultured white men."[77] Describ-ing nineteenth-century black Detroit, Katzman writes, "Most of the black upper class in nineteenth-century Detroit were in either professional, white collar, or entrepreneurial occupations. The Physicians [*sic*], dentists, and attorneys had mostly white practices, and the managers and clerks worked for white business or were in government service."[78]

It is perhaps not surprising, given their economic and sometimes bio-logical proximity to whites, that many-nineteenth century Negro elites saw themselves as distinct from the mass of darker blacks. Indeed, Katzman goes so far as to describe the Negro elite as belonging to a distinct caste "between the white caste and the general black caste," noting that in Detroit members of this elite black class intermarried with one another and refused to accept upwardly mobile blacks into their social circles.[79] This view of the black elite as a distinctive class, however, was seldom shared by whites, espe-cially toward the turn of the twentieth century, when the color line hard-ened and allowed exceptions for none with any trace of African ancestry.

The elite blacks' circumstance as a well-educated group with sophisti-cated cultural tastes and manners and their perception of themselves as the natural leaders of their race, yet their denigration by the wider white soci-ety, occasioned in them a contradictory and almost schizophrenic stance toward the black masses. On the one hand, they often subscribed to a sense of noblesse oblige, holding charity balls to benefit poor blacks or helping sponsor settlement agencies to relieve the poor and to help recent migrants adapt to city life.[80] They also practiced the politics of respectability, hoping their genteel manners and sense of refinement would simultaneously prove to the world what the race was capable of if given the chance and demon-strate to their social inferiors the proper way of behaving in public.

On the other hand, elite blacks, many of whom were anxious about their status in a society that denigrated all persons of color, had distant social relations with the black masses and went to great extremes to distinguish themselves from their more plebeian brothers. Du Bois described their aloofness thus: "They are not the leaders or the ideal-makers of their own group in thought, work, or morals. They teach the masses to a small extent, mingle with them but little, do not largely hire their labor."[81] They attended different churches, participated in different social clubs, intermarried only with each other, and objected vociferously when whites failed to note the distinctions between them and "lesser" blacks. Complaining that whites lumped the "vicious element of the race" together with the "more respectable element," one black newsman editorialized that "white men ought to sufficiently master that old spirit of caste-prejudice as will enable them to recognize virtue, though it be in ebony."[82] The rejection of a colored businessman by a professional association despite his not being a "burly Negro or one from the class of rowdy Negroes but a representative of decent, sober enterprising members of the race" was an outrage to another black editor.[83] The contradictions of this class are captured in a description highlighting both their frivolity and their noblesse oblige: "The eyes of the more fortunate have been turned toward the needy, and united efforts are being made to relieve their wants. There was a grand rally in this direction last evening in the character of a charity ball, which was attended by the wealth, beauty and distinction of the city. This evening the elite colored society lent to the lord by giving a pound party for the relief of the poor suffering in their midst."[84] Although the cause was certainly worthy, the attention given to appearances raises the question of whether the primary purpose of the event was to marshal resources for the poor or to demonstrate one's social status.

Finally, the elite blacks' efforts to secure housing in neighborhoods commensurate with what they perceived to be their status inevitably meant attempting to move away from the mass of poorer blacks, who were confined to the worst districts. As noted earlier, however, class was no shield against pervasive housing discrimination. Nonetheless, some elite blacks were able to pierce the color line in housing.

Kusmer describes early-twentieth-century Cleveland's elite blacks as living in "predominantly white neighborhoods scattered throughout the East Side (where the Negro masses lived) and occasionally on the West Side." Charles W. Chestnutt and his family, among the richest of Cleveland's Negroes, lived in an integrated upper-middle-class neighborhood.[85] Mary Church Terrell, part of the "Black 400" elite social set in Washington, DC, was able to move into the overwhelmingly white LeDroit Park section of the nation's capital, albeit after an arduous search in which she bumped repeatedly into an almost impenetrable color line. And in 1898 Lena Horne's grandparents, Cora and Edwin Horne, part of the so-called Negro Talented Tenth because of their education and middle-class income, were able to purchase a home in what was then Stuyvesant Heights, an integrated neighborhood in Brooklyn.[86] This area would later become Bedford-Stuyvesant, one of the largest black ghettos of the twentieth century.

The extent to which these instances were isolated or characteristic of the Negro elite class is unclear. Membership in this class was not based solely on income or occupation. As Du Bois argued in *The Philadelphia Negro*, the acquisition of wealth did not automatically confer elite status.[87] Du Bois himself defined this group according to moral considerations and questions of expenditure, reflecting his personal judgment. Skin color and comportment—attributes not measured in census data—were often just as important in determining who was part of the pre–Great Migration Negro elite.[88] Thus, it is nearly impossible to calculate segregation indices that would tell us of the degree of residential intermingling between this Negro elite and the Negro masses in this earlier era. There is also evidence to suggest that although there was some spatial distance between the Negro elite and the Negro masses, it was not that large. Describing the homes of the "Negro 400" of Chicago, the historian Christopher Reed lists addresses such as 383 East Forty-Fourth Street and 3531 Federal Street. But both of these addresses would become firmly ensconced within Chicago's black belt in the early twentieth century, suggesting that in the late nineteenth century they were not too far from where the Negro masses lived. Likewise, Du Bois described Philadelphia's Seventh Ward as having the "worst negro slums in the city" but being situated only blocks away from the "best negro residence sections of the city page."[89]

Whatever their successes in distancing themselves spatially, the Negro social elite's strenuous attempt to distinguish themselves from the black masses did not go unnoticed. Rather, these efforts to maintain social distinctions helped breed a mutual contempt. In 1880, an article entitled "Wealthy Colored People in New York" described the colored elites and the black masses as being separated by a "wide gulf" and their relations as being characterized by sworn enmity.[90] Black news editors regularly criticized and mocked the elites, reflecting the editors' and their audience's often scornful feelings for this group: "We condemn now as we did then any effort by the colored people of this city to establish any such society. Any efforts of any Negroes who desire to imitate 'de whi' folks and set themselves up as being 'blue vein' holier and better than thou Negroes should and we believe will meet the eternal condemnation of all the colored people of Wichita."[91]

Another family of "means and consequent influence" was criticized for refusing to take part in "colored enterprises and organizations" and for doing little to advance the interests of the race in Cleveland. The article mocked Mr. Seales, noting that "not more than one tenth of the colored Cleveland population would know him or his family if they stood face to face with him in the public square."[92] An early-twentieth-century observer summed up the situation across the North: "In the South the most intelligent and best educated Negroes are, generally speaking, the leaders of their race, but in Northern cities some of the ablest Negroes will have nothing to do with the masses of their own people or racial movements; they hold themselves aloof. . . . Their associations and their business are largely with white people."[93]

Clearly the elite held themselves aloof and apart from their disadvantaged brethren. This aloofness bred a mutual hostility that, as Du Bois noted, precluded this group from being viewed as leaders of the race. Thus, the ideology of many putative race leaders at this time, which sought to draw sharp social distinctions between different classes of blacks, left the ghetto without a cadre of leaders unabashedly committed to ghetto residents' interests. The Negro elite of the pre–Great Migration era focused on distinguishing themselves from the black masses rather than on serving as "race men." They often lived outside the incipient ghettos and did not identify with the blacks who made their homes there.

A more race-oriented Negro elite was beginning to emerge in northern cities around the turn of the century, however. In time, this new elite, who owed their success to the masses of the race, would eclipse the old mixed-race elite. But it would take the critical mass of Negroes created by the Great Migration to complete this coup.

The fourth and final reason the incipient ghettos of the pre–Great Migration did not serve as a haven was the lack of economic opportunity for blacks in the North at this time. Carter G. Woodson, writing in 1918, described the occupation options for "educated Negroes" in the pre–World War I North as "waiters, porters, butlers, and chauffeurs."[94] Although the North's economy was growing rapidly owing to exponential growth in manufacturing and concomitant services, blacks, with few exceptions, were excluded from the Industrial Revolution and the concomitant clerical, industrial, and professional occupations.

When considering jobs such as office boy, clerk, doctor, and lawyer, Du Bois wrote in his chronicle of black life in Philadelphia's Seventh Ward in the 1890s, "All these careers are at the very outset closed to the Negro on account of his color." He reported the case of a black woman who upon graduation from high school sought work as a stenographer and a white pharmacist who bragged, "I wouldn't have a darky to clean out my store, much less stand behind the counter."[95]

According to Forrester B. Washington, as late as the eve of the Great Migration in Detroit, "The idea of using Negroes in considerable numbers in any of the industrial plants of the city would have been looked upon as so iconoclastic that the factory owner or superintendent who attempted it would have been considered irrational from a business point-of-view. The Negro was thought to be irredeemably slothful and inefficient and incapable of enduring the intensive work of northern industry. Above all it was thought that black and white labor could not be mixed."[96]

Indeed, in *Half a Man* Mary Ovington cites the census of 1900 to show that only 9 percent of black men were employed in manufacturing or mechanical pursuits, whereas nearly 40 percent of white men were.[97]

As a consequence, neither the North nor the ghettos forming there in the aftermath of Reconstruction were seen as any type of promised land. When blacks thought about leaving the South en masse, they typically focused on places where blacks could do the type of agrarian work they were doing already, but this time for themselves. Oklahoma and the Southwest, for example, were often seen as possible sites where blacks could acquire land and achieve independence from whites. Further evidence of spaces that were viewed as offering respite from oppression in the South can be gleaned from the National Baptist Convention of 1889. At this convention, a resolution was passed saying that "this convention believes that the truest interests of our people are in acceptance of the Horace Greeley doctrine of 'Young man go West' where we may obtain lands and grow up with the country, and we ask the President to appropriate $100,000,000 to aid the colored people to leave the South."[98] Likewise, in Cobb County, Georgia, "Negroes held a meeting in favor of colonization in some Northwestern states."[99] In another instance, it was argued that "the American Negro is an excellent farmer . . . but he finds it hard to get control of the land and he pays much too dearly for all that he makes on the crop lease rent system.

The new talk of organized colored migration to the Northwest is interesting and pertinent.... [The Negro] would thrive financially, he would not find the climate unbearably cold for him, he would enjoy good schools and other advantages of civilization not available in Mississippi."[100]

GHETTOIZED WITHOUT A GHETTO

Prior to the Great Migration, blacks in urban centers in the North *were* ghettoized. They were relegated to stigmatized spaces that only a fortunate few could escape. Yet their small numbers precluded the development of a true ghetto—an all-encompassing Negro space that was a world unto itself. Negro spaces were much smaller then, sometimes only a building or a few blocks. Thus, although trapped in marginalized and stigmatized spaces, the Negroes of this era were not as spatially isolated as they would become decades later. Even if blacks' spaces were stigmatized in a physical sense, they were typically not that far away from whites' spaces.

But we should be careful not to confuse a lack of spatial isolation with fluid race relations. Even in the urban North, blacks were relegated to second-class citizenship. In many instances, civil rights were granted only grudgingly, and de facto segregation in schools was not uncommon. Perhaps most importantly, blacks were virtually excluded from one of humankind's epochal transitions—the Industrial Revolution. As a result, Negroes struggled to survive and were for the most part confined to the most menial livelihoods. The evidence forces us to conclude that the lack of large-scale ghetto comparable to what we know today merely reflected the demographic reality—too small a Negro population more than the fluidity of race relations.

The absence of a large modern-style ghetto in the United States prior to the Great Migration was not the only result of the relatively small size and economic marginalization of the Negro population in northern cities. An absence of institutions with the power to inspire the race and effect change on the national level was another result.

All this would soon change. In the summer of 1914, a Serbian nationalist fired shots in Sarajevo that would reverberate around the world. Among the reverberations was the rise of the modern American ghetto.

Chapter Two

THE AGE OF THE BLACK ENCLAVE

In 1890, Jesse Binga, whom we met in the introduction, arrived in Chicago with a mere ten dollars to his name. He would become one of the richest black men in America. Beginning with the acquisition of run-down properties in the nascent black belt on Chicago's South Side, he used sweat equity to transform these properties into buildings that earned a handsome return. Combining business acumen with the luck of marrying the heiress to the John "Mushmouth" Johnson "policy" fortune,[1] Binga was able to open the first black-owned bank in Chicago. With the advent of the Great Migration in the 1910s, Binga found a clientele happy to patronize his bank so as to avoid discriminatory white banks. At its apex, Binga State Bank was described by a contemporary observer as "one of the leading banks owned and operated by Negroes anywhere."[2] In 1917, Binga moved to 5922 South Park Avenue (now South King Drive) in an upscale neighborhood on the South Side. In making this move, he was doing what almost any successful businessman might—relocating to a neighborhood commensurate with his wealth and prestige.

Jesse Binga's race, however, meant that despite his wealth, prestige, and reputation as one of Chicago's leading citizens, there would be no welcome mat for the Bingas on South Park Avenue. Indeed, the Bingas' home was bombed repeatedly to intimidate them into moving out and to send a signal to any other "uppity Negroes" who might share such lofty aspirations.

Binga refused to be intimidated and stood fast in the face of repeated terrorist attacks. For Binga, moving would mean giving in to racists and setting a bad example for the race.[3]

Although white terrorists could not evict Binga, whites could and did move from the neighborhood. By 1930, Binga's home would be firmly ensconced within the black belt as white flight transformed the neighborhood into the southern edge of the ever-growing black belt.[4] A century later the neighborhood remains overwhelmingly black.[5]

Around the time Binga was moving away from Chicago's black belt into an all-white neighborhood, another notable black leader, the noted scholar and agitator W. E. B. Du Bois, was moving from a predominantly white neighborhood in Brooklyn to what was rapidly becoming *the* black belt of New York City—Harlem.[6] Du Bois's motives for moving from Brooklyn to Harlem are unknown. An original member of the NAACP, Du Bois championed an integrationist ideology. For him to accept segregation was to accept inferiority. But his position on segregation was evolving. Du Bois increasingly saw the benefits of segregation for black solidarity and self-improvement.[7] Perhaps he wanted to be closer to what was rapidly becoming the most famous Negro city in the world.

Was Du Bois's move from a predominantly white neighborhood in Brooklyn to Harlem part of this evolution? We can only speculate, but it would have been consistent with such an evolution.

The experiences of these two black titans of the early twentieth century illustrate the changing role of the ghetto in the life of black America. Rather than being a marginal space that blacks were relegated to, as the black belts of the nineteenth century were, the ghetto in the early years of the Great Migration was a space where the race advanced, sometimes spectacularly, as in the case of Jesse Binga. It was also a space that attracted some elite blacks, such as W. E. B. Du Bois. Yet we are also reminded that it was a space that few blacks in northern cities could escape for long, as Jesse Binga's experience also attests.

Like Binga, numerous blacks encountered all manner of roadblocks when attempting to move out of the ghetto. Moreover, blacks' confinement to the ghetto would create manifold problems and a durable legacy of inequality. Yet the increased ghettoization of blacks in the early twentieth century also coincided with the Golden Age of the Ghetto. The ghetto was a haven for the race. It was a place for economic mobility, political enfranchisement, and cultural expression. The claim here is not that the intensified ghettoization of blacks at the start twentieth century was some idyllic period when blacks of all classes rubbed shoulders in smoky salons listening to jazz or debating the latest "Negro poetry." But relative to the ghettoization prior to that time or after it, early-twentieth-century ghettoization produced more benefits to black America than ghettoization did at any other time. Indeed, we could go as far as to call the Great Migration ghettoization the era of the black enclave. To the extent that enclaves are defined by their voluntary nature and where "members of a particular population group . . . congregate as a means of enhancing their economic, social, political and/or cultural well development,"[8] ghettos that came into being with the onset of the Great Migration were enclaves in some important ways.

THE MIGRATION

As noted in the previous chapter, there were only a small number of blacks in the North in the late nineteenth and early twentieth century. Their numbers remained small because a lack of economic opportunities outside the South meant that life in the North, even with greater civil liberties, would be harsh. World War I would change all of that. First, the war had a tremendous impact on the U.S. economy. What the belligerents thought would be a quick war over in a few months turned into an epic total war of attrition. Their resources stretched to the limit by 1916, the Allied powers turned to the United States to bankroll and supply their war machine. Buoyed by increased demand from the European countries at war, the American economy boomed.

Second, the war dampened immigration from Europe as many would-be immigrants were conscripted to fight or work to support their homelands' war efforts. The war, too, made Americans more skeptical of immigration, and this attitude culminated in the restrictive Immigration Act of 1917. Immigration from Europe, which had supplied a significant component of labor for the rapidly industrializing United States, slowed to a trickle.

Finally, as the United States edged closer to joining the fray and eventually did in 1917, the U.S. military needed manpower to fight the war. The increased need for labor at the same time that immigration was being shut off from Europe made employers increasingly open to hiring black workers.

Indeed, the need became so great that labor agents would travel south to recruit workers. Thus, World War I created labor shortages that pulled black migrants northward.

Conditions in the South, always poor from a political or social perspective, also worsened economically as the boll weevil pest decimated much of the cotton crop. This devastation made it harder for already hard-pressed black agricultural workers to make ends meet and provided the push behind their moving out of the South.

The result was the commencement of the Great Migration, which would see millions of blacks move out of the South over a period of nearly fifty-four years from 1916 to 1970. The impact of the migration in the early years was dramatic. Cleveland's population of black southerners grew from 2,703 in 1910 to 21,527 in 1920 and 49,440 in 1930. Detroit saw the number of black southerners explode from 1,608 in 1910 to 33,309 in 1920 and 80,376 in 1930. Chicago's southern-born black population, which stood at 22,973 in 1910, nearly tripled to 61,200 in 1920, and then that number more than doubled to 146,520 in 1930. Philadelphia's southern-born black population doubled between 1910 and 1920 from 35,692 to 68,781 and then nearly doubled again to 219,655 in 1930. New York City saw its number of black southerners increase from 34,711 in 1910 to 60,680 in 1920 and 137,109 in 1930. It also saw a big spike in black immigrants from abroad, their numbers increasing from 11,022 in 1910 to 31,049 in 1920 and 51,762 in 1930. Outside of the South, the number of southern-born blacks increased from 531,853 to 866,236 between 1910 and 1920 and increased further to 1,519,325 by 1930. Thus, in the span of twenty years the southern-born black population outside the South nearly tripled, increasing by almost a million.[9]

Table 2.1 shows the residential segregation patterns for the northern metropolitan areas with the largest black populations. Recall that the dissimilarity index tells us how evenly spread blacks are throughout a metropolitan area. In this case, it tells us the extent to which blacks and whites lived in the same enumeration districts. By 1920, blacks were already highly segregated from whites, with an average dissimilarity score of 0.65—higher than the threshold of 0.6, which is generally considered a high level of segregation.

The isolation index in the fourth column tells us the average proportion of black residents in a black person's enumeration district. Although blacks were unevenly spread throughout metropolitan areas, they were not as yet

TABLE 2.1
Residential Segregation in Cities with Large Negro Populations, 1920

City	Black Population	Dissimilarity Index	Isolation Index
New York City	225,999	.72	.38
Philadelphia	180,480	.69	.37
Chicago	120,545	.81	.34
Baltimore	117,953	.67	.50
Washington, DC	103,693	.56	.51
St. Louis	88,906	.77	.54
Pittsburgh	60,130	.59	.20
Kansas City	48,807	.68	.46
Louisville, KY	48,182	.56	.41
Detroit	43,824	.71	.30
Cincinnati	38,072	.71	.41
Cleveland	35,655	.77	.36
Indianapolis	35,216	.68	.50
Boston	29,720	.72	.26
Average for metro areas with at least 5,000 blacks in 1920		.65	.29

Source: Integrated Public Use Microdata full-count samples (Ruggles et al. 2010).

isolated in all-black neighborhoods. Indeed, in only a few metropolitan areas did blacks live in neighborhoods that were majority black on average.

But the processes of ghettoization described in the previous chapter were intensifying in the 1920s as more and more blacks poured into the urban North. This was the time when ghettos began to take on their modern form, reaching populations of tens or even hundreds of thousands. The ensuing ghettoization planted the seeds for the extreme isolation blacks experienced the rest of the twentieth century. Although these black belts were rarely called ghettos in the early twentieth century, the near imperviousness of these spaces to blacks wishing to move out of them and the disadvantage and stigmatization visited upon them made the term *ghetto* an apt moniker that ably captured the social significance of these spaces.

But the rise of the modern ghetto also means that it could serve as a haven of sorts. Black agency should not be overlooked in this era. Moreover, the role of the ghetto as a haven where the interests of the race were advanced is also part of the story. The context and conditions of the Great Migration were what made the early-twentieth-century ghetto a haven despite the virulent racism blacks would encounter in the North. The start of World War I and the cessation of immigration from Europe ramped up demand for

American-made goods among the belligerents, creating desperate labor shortages in the North. Although blacks had largely been excluded from the industrialization sector prior to the war, they now had a chance at least to gain a toehold there. The war provided the opportunity for large numbers of blacks to support themselves and perhaps just as importantly to participate in manufacturing—the most rapidly modernizing sector of the economy. Opportunity knocked, and blacks answered the door, turning a sliver of economic opportunity into a gateway for their full incorporation into modern America. The economic opportunity afforded by the Great War, the experience of fighting in the war, and the new assertiveness, independence, and pride among those who migrated created what might aptly called the age of the black enclave. It was a time when blacks voluntarily came together to enhance their economic, social, political, and cultural well-being.

OF THEIR OWN VOLITION?

The strongest evidence of the ghetto as a haven is given in the actions of blacks such as W. E. B. Du Bois, whom we encountered at the beginning of this chapter. Blacks were voluntarily moving en masse into the ghetto. But was the migration that precipitated the development of the ghetto as voluntary as Du Bois's move to Harlem appears to have been? Several factors suggest it was. True, the average Negro migrant did not have the options of a man like Du Bois. With a PhD from Harvard, the editor of the leading black periodical of the time, and one of the founders of the premier civil rights organizations of the twentieth century, the NAACP, Du Bois was better positioned to overcome the strictures of race than perhaps any black person in America. Nevertheless, for the migrants who participated in the migration, moving North, regardless of whether this meant moving into the ghetto, offered the opportunity to "secure steady employment," to "be among the better side of our Race," and to "receive very good wages and where I can educate my 3 little girls and demand respect and intelegence [sic]."[10]

Moreover, not only was the migration voluntary, but blacks had to hurdle considerable obstacles to migrate, walking miles to take the train north and even risking arrest for merely citing poems about migrating north.[11]

Nor was the migration merely a pell-mell race, with blacks eager to escape anywhere. As the historian James Grossman writes, "Many black southern-ers were uncertain about the North. Despite the 'sudden revelation of a new world' pictured by labor agents and rumors, the wisdom of an equally sudden decision to leave was questionable. Many people were not prepared to abandon home and community until they could learn more about what the North might offer them. Where would they go? What would they do? Until they could secure answers, many cautious black southerners chose to stay home."[12]

To answer these questions, migrants often wrote to black newspapers in the North or even visited the North to see it for themselves.[13]

Moreover, in migrating north the migrants went against the stated wis-dom of many race leaders. Most prominent among these leaders, of course, were Booker T. Washington and his acolytes, who counseled blacks to stay not only on the farm but in the South as well. There was Washington's well-known counsel in his "Atlanta Compromise" speech urging blacks to "cast down your buckets where you are." And in an article entitled "The Negro in the North: Are His Advantages as Great as in the South?" Washington gave a detailed argument for the advantages of staying in the South.[14] Wash-ington died before the Great Migration picked up full steam in 1916, but with the increased opportunities in the North Washington might have over time looked more favorably on migration. But his acolytes continued to beat the drum of staying put. Consider a patronizing diatribe published in the late Washington's organ *The Southern Workman.* The author essentially blamed blacks' plight in the South on their shiftlessness and concluded: "Women be industrious, be economical. Teach your children to work. Teach them to be saving of their time and money: send them to school. Teach them to be law-abiding. Make your home and family the best on earth. If all unite in doing these things there will be no hard times for the white or the black, but we will have prosperity here in our Southland."[15]

But it was not only Booker T. Washington's acolytes who advised against moving North. The militant abolitionist Frederick Douglass advised against migration during the 1880s.[16] Moreover, as late as 1915 the editorial page of the militant *Chicago Defender* advised against migrating.[17] The reasons for counseling blacks to stay put were pragmatic. The great demand for black labor in the North in 1916 was due in large part to the world war. What would happen once the war ended? Would the migrants face the same obstacles to employment in the North that they long had—hostile unions and unfriendly employers? Black leaders recognized the indispensability of black labor to the South and thought the option of migrating could provide blacks with the leverage to demand greater rights.[18] Moreover, there was a long tradition among accommodationists and militants alike of looking to independence through land ownership and yeoman agriculture. Blacks had been brought to this continent to work in agriculture, continued to work in agriculture upon emancipation, and could be expected to work in agriculture for the foreseeable future. As one writer stated in 1918, "The rapid acquisition of [land] has long been pointed to as the best evidence of the ability of the blacks to rise in the economic world."[19] By farming and owning their own land, blacks would achieve what was viewed as the best way forward for black Americans.

Despite all of these obstacles and the counsel of race leaders, blacks still migrated to the northern cities. Clearly, the migration of blacks to the North was voluntary.

Of course, the voluntary movement to the North does not necessarily imply a voluntary move into ghettos upon arrival there. Blacks might have eagerly migrated north, only to be shocked and disappointed at being confined by various means to all-black neighborhoods. In this way, the ghettoization was involuntary in spite of the voluntary nature of the migration from the South. This interpretation, although possible, seems implausible. As previously mentioned, migrants did not jump up and move en masse to the North. Many migrants carefully weighed their options, wrote letters of inquiry, and even took it upon themselves to visit their intended destinations first.[20] The pros and cons of migrating as well as the conditions the migrants would likely face were the topics of much discussion. In addition, earlier migrants to the North related to their brethren the conditions the would-be migrants would likely face.[21]

The notion that blacks were migrating unwittingly into the ghetto thus seems implausible. It might be the case that blacks had full knowledge that they would be relegated to the ghetto but migrated north anyway because doing so was better than remaining in the South. How *did* blacks feel about being relegated to the ghetto?

For the mass of migrants who would form the bulk of the ghettos coming into existence, their relegation to the then nascent ghettos appears not to have been a primary concern. To be sure, blacks wanted to live in decent housing and neighborhoods. Perhaps most importantly, they wanted the choice to live where they desired and could afford. Both black migrants and other blacks shared this sentiment. The black intelligentsia and others protested vociferously against racial zoning laws that proscribed where someone could live based on his race. These laws were seen as degrading to the race and an attack on the vital rights of blacks as American citizens.[22] When the NAACP won the *Buchanan v. Warley* (25 U.S. 60) case in 1917, with the Supreme Court ruling such laws unconstitutional because they violated property rights, blacks celebrated the win as a "great victory" for the race.[23] Booker T. Washington's admonition "to quit thinking of the parts of cities that can't be lived in, but begin to beautify the parts that can" seemed to be a decidedly minority opinion.[24]

To be sure, blacks wanted decent housing and the right to choose where to live. If the neighborhood was decent, its racial composition was probably a secondary concern at most, for a number of reasons.

First, as we have already seen, blacks had long been discriminated against and confined to often deplorable quarters in northern cities. Discrimination perhaps intensified with the growing black population, but this was a change of degree, not of kind. Because migrants were somewhat aware of conditions in the North, they likely would have expected to be consigned to black neighborhoods.

Second, the end state of the process of ghettoization was unknown. Blacks had previously faced discrimination and were confined to certain sections of northern cities, but these areas never had the concentration or number of blacks that would come to represent the twentieth-century ghetto. The conditions and circumstances of the twentieth-century ghetto were as yet unknown. Indeed, the migration to the cities and the formation of ghettos represented a grand experiment. Blacks had always been a rural people, residing in the South under clearly drawn lines of inferiority. Living in the urban North, where conditions were freer, as part of the industrial proletariat was something altogether new. For the mass of blacks to have clearly defined positions on this unknown would have been unlikely.

Third, the evidence left by the migrants themselves suggests little in the way of concern with being confined to the ghetto. Many migrants wrote to ask of information about moving to the North. Migrants asked for job references and attested to their own credibility. Nary was a word said about living in integrated neighborhoods. Not surprisingly, migrants were most concerned about their ability to make a living after moving. For example, in the dozens of letters collected by Emmett J. Scott, Booker T. Washington's consigliere and special adviser of black affairs to the U.S. secretary of war, information about possible employment reigned paramount.[25] After all, without the ability to support one's self, all other concerns become moot. So we should not be surprised that relative to the migrants' concerns about their livelihoods, residential integration was a minor concern.

This is not to say that migrants were concerned *only* about jobs. They did consider issues aside from making a living—the education of their children being a prime example. The education blacks received in the South was notoriously bad. Thus, migration offered an opportunity to improve the education of their offspring, as suggested by these examples from letters collected by Scott:

Please gave me some infamation about coming north. . . . i want to get where i can put my children in school.

I would like to get a place where I could proply educate them.

I am planning to leave this place on about May 11th for Chicago and wants ask you assistence in getting a job. I has been here all my life but would be glad to go wher I can educate my children where they can be of service to themselves, and this will never be here.

What class of work do you get men? I am writing you to know that I may obtain an employment through you. I want a good paying job that I may be able to educate my children.

I am a Negro mechanic, having served the paint trade since 1896, 30 years of age, married, no booster, a graduate of N. Y. trade school, first honor, class of 1906, wish to change location for better educational advantages for my children consequently will be glad to have you endeavor to place me. Hoping to hear from you at earliest convenience. Willing to accept position in any good north western city, with white or colored firm.[26]

Beyond education, migrants were anxious to escape the land of white supremacy. They wanted to be treated like men, to be free from mob violence, and to have a chance not to be cheated. They wanted a better job, freedom to patronize stores of their choosing, and an escape from the noose. The North offered all of that. For the migrants, being able to send their children to decent schools, not having to address white folks as "sir" or "ma'am," and not having to ride in separate train cars were important.

The absence of inquiries about the racial composition of potential neighborhoods is therefore all the more conspicuous. Migrants were focused laserlike on using migration to the North as a way of bettering their condition. Having a job that paid better than what they were used to was instrumental to achieving that end. Migrants were also keenly aware of the liberties available to blacks in the North that were not available in the South. Thus, the lack of integrated housing does not appear to have negated the allure of the North.

The context in which ghetto formation was taking place also cannot be overlooked. For blacks coming from the South, whites, even northern ones, represented potential trouble. In the South, an act or language misinterpreted could mean humiliation or even death. Many migrants expressed hesitancy to sit next to or talk to whites because they feared how their actions might be misconstrued: "I can ride in the electric street and steam cars anywhere I get a seat. I don't care to mix with white what I mean I am not crazy about being with white folks, but if I have to pay the same fare I have learn to want the same accommodation."[27] In due time, migrants of course came to understand racial protocols in the North. The risks of humiliation or violence were orders of magnitude lower in their new environs, but interracial contact was nonetheless often freighted with anxiety and hostility. In contrast, the ghetto, whatever its shortcomings, offered a respite from the white world, a place where blacks did not have to worry about racial violence. As Mahalia Jackson sang, the ghetto was a place where the black person "could lay down his burden of being a colored person in the white man's world and lead his own life."[28]

THE GHETTO AS BEACON

The connotation of the term *ghetto* as a denigrated place that a people are involuntarily relegated to does not fully capture the experiences or symbolism of the early-twentieth-century black belts. For many blacks, the nascent ghettos were "black metropolises" pregnant with possibilities because, relatively speaking, movement into the ghetto was a step up for most of the newcomers. Moreover, the movement into the ghetto coincided with the "New Negro" identity that was taking hold in black America. The New Negro looked with pride at things black and saw the ghetto as an opportunity to build up the race.

As described earlier, for most migrants the nascent ghettos' conditions were, however bad, better than what they left behind. And in at least one instance, the case of the most famous and populous black ghetto—Harlem— conditions were indeed good. Originally built as an upscale suburb to Lower and Midtown Manhattan, Harlem came to be known as the most famous black neighborhood in the world in large part due to one black realtor's enterprising efforts. The original developers of Harlem overshot and built far more housing than was demanded. Facing the prospect of ruin, some landlords rented to blacks. Philip A. Payton Jr. accelerated and amplified this process by offering to lease even more units in Harlem to blacks. Payton also capitalized his business in part by appealing to race pride. Encouraging black investors, he said, "Buy, if you want to be numbered among those of the race who are doing something toward trying to solve the so-called race problem."[29]

Relegated to the slums of the Tenderloin and San Juan Hill, many blacks jumped at the chance to live in modern buildings in a neighborhood of broad boulevards. After initial resistance by whites to the black influx, white flight ensued, and what began as a few buildings being marketed to blacks became an entire neighborhood.

Blacks no doubt moved to Harlem for a number of reasons, but chief among them was the fact that the housing there was better than what was available to them elsewhere. Harlem soon overtook San Juan Hill as the primary black neighborhood in New York City. Its physical size and dimensions came to presage those of the modern twentieth-century ghettos— much larger and more exclusively black than the preceding center of black New York, San Juan Hill, which stretched only a few blocks.

Harlem came to be a physical symbol of the "New Negro" movement. "New Negro" was a moniker used to describe the attitudes and actions of blacks in the second decade of the twentieth century, and the New Negro can perhaps best be defined by contrast to the "Old Negro." Whereas the Old Negro was willing to adapt to the constraints imposed by white supremacy, the New Negro sought to smash those constraints. The Old Negro moved but only within the South and remained in agriculture. The New Negro forsook the South and began to acquire a toehold in industry. Whereas the Old Negro asked for fair treatment and pointed out the folly of being poorly treated, the New Negro militantly demanded just treatment. Whereas the Old Negro would argue that "the negro is treated better in America than elsewhere,"[30] the New Negro was not afraid to list the litany of offenses that America was guilty of—including disenfranchisement, lynching, and the denial of education—and to demand that these injustices be rectified.[31]

Also fundamental to the shifting attitude among blacks was an increase in race pride. This race pride meant blacks were no longer ashamed to be black or descended from Africans. The most well-known manifestation of this increased race pride was the United Negro Improvement Association, which promised blacks glory if they returned to Africa. But there are other lesser-known examples, such as the Moorish Science Temple, which preached self-determination and pride of noble ancestry.

The increased pride induced an alternative reaction to the reality of segregation. Few if any blacks favored legal segregation, but their reactions to the omnipresence of segregation varied. There was the Tuskegee approach, which essentially counseled blacks to keep their heads down and make the best of their situation so that with time they would earn the respect of whites and the concomitant privileges of citizenship. Conversely, the Niagara position, as personified by W. E. B. Du Bois and the NAACP, argued for immediately demanding the rights that were due blacks as citizens. The New Negro expressed a race pride that fused these two approaches. Blacks would work to build their own institutions, but that would be because they wanted to and were proud to be with and uplift other blacks, less so to impress whites regarding blacks' worthiness. Moreover, blacks would cede no ground in their demands for civil rights.

This thinking may have permeated reflections on being ghettoized. One black Chicagoan neatly summed up the distinction between being segregated and coming together for race pride:

Segregation presupposes a force from without which seeks to compel those of the same race or nationality or religious belief to remain among themselves, separated from those of another groups supposedly superior. Grouping together either for purposes of living or religious worship or for other purposes, with the idea of developing a group or race consciousness and this to develop "pride of race" presupposes a force from within—that is a conscious desire of the people themselves to develop the latent powers within their own group through intensive application.[32]

The distinction blacks made between segregation and separation probably animated thoughts about the budding black ghettos for most migrants. Segregation meant state or mob sanction and the denial of rights and access to institutions. Separation, however, was voluntary. Reverend Ernest Lyon, a well-respected former ambassador to Liberia, gave a speech, described as "well-received" in the black press, underscoring this point. "Segregation has given us the great church organizations of color, and all other institutions which wield power among us. It has given us our own lawyers, physicians, college presidents, journalists, banking institutions, and foreign diplomatic representatives. Without it we would not have a representative in the City Council of Baltimore today."[33] This separation-not-segregation sentiment is also reflected in the prevailing views about intermarriage. Most blacks felt antimiscegenation laws were unjust and believed that whom one chooses to marry should be a private matter. In practice in their own lives, however, many blacks frowned on interracial unions and spoke disparagingly of those who decided to marry outside of the race. Frederick Douglass's second marriage to a white woman drew much scorn from some blacks.[34]

Increased race pride may have thus contributed to an increase in ethnocentrism among blacks and subsequently less desire for living in integrated neighborhoods. Indeed, the "black metropolises" that were springing up in northern cities inspired a great deal of race pride. Whereas the majority of blacks in the South were not only poor but subjugated and forced to be subservient to whites, the increased variety of roles available to blacks in the urban North was something to trumpet. Consider the case of a southern church service in which congregants debated the wisdom of migrating North: "One man in the audience, who had been to Detroit, could constrain himself no longer and stood up to inform the audience that there were also colored street car conductors and motormen and that he had seen them with his own eyes."[35]

The construction of the Eighth Regiment Armory specifically for black soldiers in the black belt of Chicago in 1915 also illustrates the prideful opportunities manifested in the ghetto. Building segregated quarters for a segregated army in the heart of a budding black ghetto is in many ways the epitome of segregation and white supremacy, yet the armory and the soldiers in it inspired a great deal of pride among blacks. For a people who supposedly were cowardly and lacking the discipline to be soldiers, the armory was a concrete testament to black soldiers' manhood. According to one newspaper, there was "much rejoicing" among blacks in response to the armory, and the militant *Chicago Defender* described the laying of the cornerstone as an "epochal" event for the race that would announce "to rising generations of Afro-Americans that they are citizens with every right of any other citizen."[36] The armory was thus acclaimed despite literally being an edifice built specifically to segregate blacks.

Moreover, residential segregation gave blacks the leverage to demand political patronage, which white politicians sometimes obliged. Chicago was perhaps the epitome of this relationship, with one observer noting that the political machine in Chicago "secured the allegiance of the Negro electorate by granting to it a fair share of the patronage which was distributed in the event of victory."[37] For example, blacks demanded that Governor Alfred E. Smith appoint a black judge in Harlem and agitated for the staffing of local hospitals by blacks.[38]

Migrating to the ghetto meant not only higher pay and freedom from Jim Crow but also the possibility of assuming roles that were heretofore reserved exclusively to whites. Of course, blacks could have been appointed as conductors or motormen or could have been soldiers without being ghettoized. But the existence of the black belt provided the space for these opportunities to manifest without interference from whites. Would whites have welcomed black motormen and conductors in their neighborhood or an armory for an all-black regiment? Most likely, they would have resented blacks taking good jobs and would hardly have been receptive to armed black men stationed in their midst.

Even the prospect of masses of blacks living as modern city-dwellers was enough to instill some pride. A contemporary white observer marveled that a race that could have a city like Harlem, with "magnificent Negro churches, luxurious Negro apartment houses" and all the other makings of a modern metropolis, could indeed achieve anything.[39]

Again, context is important. This was a time when most whites' opinions of blacks ranged from the ignorant belief that blacks had barely evolved from lesser primates to the more "enlightened" view that blacks were a backward race that needed time to become "civilized." The types of whites holding these opinions ranged from hooded Klansmen to progressive teachers, one of whom said, "Colored children are restive and incapable of abstract thought; they must constantly be fed with novel interests and given things to do with their hands."[40]

The idea that such a primitive race could thrive in the city was viewed with incredulity; as one historian in this period noted, "Students of Social Problems are now wondering whether the Negro can be adjusted in the North."[41] The anthropologist Franz Boas found it necessary to devote an entire article against "the belief that the Negro is unfit for more modern civilization."[42] Even progressives sympathetic to the plight of blacks would nevertheless write, "The masses of colored people are not yet fitted to survive and prosper in the great northern cities,"[43] and "The 'race tradition' of the Negro . . . [is] essentially agricultural. He is not adapted by either his African or his American experience, to urban conditions, and, consequently, when he goes to the city he becomes a serious problem."[44] No less a figure than the former director of the U.S. Census Bureau, W. G. Wilcox, reportedly believed that migration to the cities would result in the extinction of the black race.[45]

The black migration to the urban North galvanized whites to employ various tactics—including racial zoning, neighborhood "preservation" groups, restrictive covenants, and terror—to ensure that the growing black population was funneled into the many burgeoning black belts. Blacks essentially had three choices: to stay in the South, to migrate to the North and simply endure ghettoization, or to use ghettoization as an opportunity to build the black metropolis. In creating the black metropolis, the race would create conditions that advanced the interests of the race. Moreover, in doing so, they transformed the stigmatized minighettos of the late nineteenth century into havens for the race that would serve as embarkation points for inclusion in modern American life.

THE BLACK METROPOLIS

Concentration in the ghetto fused with increased race pride to create conditions conducive to the idea of a black metropolis. Blacks would come together to create a parallel city without interference from whites. Working together, blacks would achieve culturally, economically, and politically what had heretofore seemed impossible for them.

The Cultural Impact of Ghettoization

The idea of a black metropolis perhaps reached its apogee in the realm of culture. This was the time of the Harlem or Negro Renaissance. This was an artistic movement with decidedly political ends—to use the arts to demonstrate the undeniable humanity of blacks. If a race could produce fine literature, poetry, music, and the like, who could deny their inherent humanity? And if they were indeed human, why were they denied full equality?

There was truly a flowering of Negro arts in this period, with writers such as Claude McKay and Langston Hughes, poets such as Countee Cullen and Clarissa Scott Delany, and musicians such as Louis Armstrong having a profound and permanent impact on American and, indeed, Western culture. The extent to which this artistic and literary flowering succeeded in reducing racism is debatable. Certainly the world became increasingly aware of blacks' creative and artistic capabilities to an extent heretofore unknown.

But was the confinement of the mass of blacks to urban ghettos necessary for such a flowering to occur?

Certainly, migration to the city was necessary. Only in a city was there the clustering of artists, audiences, writers, publicists, and patrons necessary for a renaissance to occur. Moreover, New York City as a center for the arts and literature made a natural home for Negro arts and literature as well. The infrastructure of galleries, patrons, publicists, publishers, and the like was already in place in New York.

To be more specific, we could ask if being confined to a few square miles on the island of Manhattan somehow fostered the Harlem Renaissance. Had blacks been scattered about New York, albeit in the poorest neighborhoods, it seems unlikely that Harlem or any other place would have attained the stature of the "Negro capital" of the world. The ghettoization of virtually all blacks in Harlem—rich and poor, educated and illiterate, laborer and artist, southern and Caribbean—included black artists and writers from across the globe. This concentration of blacks perhaps created a new black culture that was more than the sum of its disparate parts.

Beyond the cultural milieu that was fostered by the intermingling of the black diaspora in Harlem, the spatial concentration of blacks there probably nurtured the renaissance in at least three ways. First, the Harlem Renaissance was not just a spontaneous flowering of Negro creativity but an artistic movement spurred on and nurtured by a handful of black elites, so the genesis of this movement benefitted from a clustering of creative talents in the circumscribed area of Harlem.[46] Patrons, intellectuals, and artists could and did easily rub shoulders in living rooms, nightclubs, and the like. Once the movement was under way, would-be artists and writers were drawn to Harlem as a place to express their creative talents. Edward Waldron describes Langston Hughes's summary of the interaction of segregation with the allure of Harlem for black creative types: "Harlem was like a great magnet for the Negro intellectual, pulling him from everywhere. Or perhaps the magnet was New York, he had to live in Harlem for rooms were hardly to be found elsewhere unless one could pass for white, or Mexican or Eurasian and perhaps live in the Village. . . . Only a few of the New Negroes lived in the Village, Harlem being their real stamping ground."[47]

The artists, musicians, and writers in Harlem benefited from proximity to one another. It's no surprise that biographers and historians alike have described the migration of many a budding artist and writer to the beacon that was Harlem.[48]

Second, the concentration of blacks in Harlem created a physical space for the Renaissance to unfold. Besides the living rooms of Renaissance stalwarts such as James Weldon Johnson and Walter F. White, the 135th Street YMCA and the New York Public library (now the Schomburg Center) across the street hosted poetry readings and literary events that provided budding artists the opportunity to hone their craft, gain exposure, and meet other creative types. Had blacks been scattered about the city, would the YMCA have tailored its programming to blacks? Given that the YMCA was a segregated institution, perhaps yes. But there would have been less reason for this YMCA to be located in Harlem in the first place other than that there was a spatial concentration of blacks there. Likewise, the public library as a public institution in a state without legal segregation would have been unlikely to turn its focus to black literature.

Finally, Harlem itself provided the raw material for much of the creative outpouring. Harlem was an undeniably black space, but more than that it was an *attractive black space*. Upon reaching Harlem for the first time, Cab Calloway and his band "drove around, awestruck by the whole scene. It was beautiful. Just beautiful."[49] Harlem attracted what both anecdotal reports and some empirical evidence suggest was the most elite concentration of blacks in the world at that time.[50] And, as pointed out earlier, Harlem had originally been built for an upscale clientele and was still relatively physically attractive in the early part of the twentieth century. For a downtrodden people used to being confined to "alleys, broken-down ramshackle tenements, on the fringe of where white people live," Harlem's broad boulevards, new tenements, and spacious brownstones must have seemed like a Negro utopia worth writing about.

The cultural flowering that was the Harlem Renaissance was therefore due at least in part to the spatial concentration of blacks in Harlem. Ghettoization fused together disparate parts of the black diaspora, resulting in a richer, more cosmopolitan culture. The concentration of perhaps a few hundred thousand blacks on the northern tip of Manhattan created conditions ripe for serendipitous encounters between artists, writers, patrons, and the like. Moreover, it allowed space for the renaissance to occur.

A smaller, less-celebrated flowering of Negro arts and letters also occurred later on the South Side of Chicago in the 1930s and 1940s. Here the black belt provided much of the raw material for this flowering, which produced well-known works such as *Native Son* (1940) by Richard Wright. A space for Negroes to congregate and collaborate was another by-product of the burgeoning ghetto, with groups such as the South Side Writers meeting in the heart of the black belt at the Lincoln Center.[51]

Of course, most of the nascent ghettos in the North were not home to an artistic movement that approached the size and significance of what was happening in New York or even Chicago in later years. The spatial concentration of blacks in Harlem was a necessary but insufficient condition by itself for the renaissance to occur.

Nevertheless, the Harlem Renaissance had an impact that extended far beyond the blacks in Harlem. Although the vast majority of blacks living in the ghettos of the North were not in Harlem, they and their descendants would feel the influence that Harlem had on both black culture and the larger American culture. Citing the Harlem Renaissance as one of the positive outcomes of ghettoization is therefore not a stretch.

Politics

The idea of a black metropolis had implications in the political world as well. As the population in black belts swelled from the in-migration of southerners, black political power swelled as well, albeit not always commensurate with the demographic growth that undergirded this increase in political power. Blacks were not disenfranchised in the North as they were in the South. Voting as a bloc, blacks could in many places swing an election. Contemporary observers anticipated how more black people would translate into more black political power: "The Southern Negroes will give us political power in this city. They will not be bought. Their very segregation will mean power, and the time is not far distant when we will have Negroes in the legislature, state senate and U.S. Congress because of the vote of southern Colored Migrants [sic]."[52] An editorial in the *Philadelphia Tribune* celebrated the migration because it would provide the opportunity to elect colored congressmen in Illinois, New Jersey, New York, Ohio, and Pennsylvania who could take on the "rotten democracies" in the South and defend the race against the "Bourbon South."[53] In short order, this wish came to pass, as the sociologist Charles S. Johnson noted: "Negro law makers are multiplying out of a situation [ghettoization] [into] which they have been forced in defiance of law."[54]

Blacks could and did make demands in return for their votes. Sometimes this meant civil service jobs for black workers. In Chicago, the burgeoning black belt translated into votes that the local machine cultivated through support for black-belt politicians and patronage appointments in city hall. Indeed, patronage appointments of blacks were visible enough during the first administration (1915–1923) of Mayor William "Big Bill" Thompson that Chicago City Hall came to be called "Uncle Tom's cabin."[55] In other instances, patronage of blacks meant services and amenities in black neighborhoods. Harlem Hospital is a case in point. Blacks agitated for and were eventually successful in getting the hospital to include blacks on the staff. Such a change was in many ways symbolic. And opening up Harlem Hospital to black medical workers also provided opportunities for black medical professionals, however small their numbers may have been. These opportunities helped prove that blacks were human and could succeed in highly skilled positions, such as doctor or nurse.

The increase in political power in this Great Migration period represents only a change in magnitude rather than in kind. As noted in the previous chapter, even prior to the Great Migration blacks were able to leverage their numbers into patronage appointments. The increase in voting power thus meant more patronage.

But the increasing size of the black belts also eventually translated into a change in the *kind* of political power blacks wielded as well. First, blacks acquired positions as aldermen or councilmen. In Chicago, Oscar DePriest was the first black alderman and later became the first black elected to the U.S. Congress in the twentieth century.[56] In Cleveland, Thomas W. Fleming became the first black to be elected to the city council. Philadelphia sent two blacks to the state legislature, Samuel B. Hart and William H. Fuller, as a consequence of the ghettoization of blacks. Moreover, whereas the few black elected officials prior to the Great Migration were often nominated due to back-room machinations by white political machine bosses, the black politicos in this new era owed their positions to the black masses. In the nineteenth century, a loyal black political machine member might have been rewarded with nomination for an elective office. But the office in question would not have represented a particular Negro community because the Negro community was too small to have its own elected officials. Ultimately, the political boss, not the black masses, was responsible for that black politician being in office. As an editorial in the *Chicago Defender* explained the new situation, "Unless we are diligent in fighting our own cause, we cannot expect to leave the job to somebody else. We believe that these successes and victories are but the first steps to real power and a voice in affairs at Washington, a voice unfettered by jobs held at the mercy or whim of some white political leader, but held because the man in office has a mandate from the voters of his race and of his home district to be there."[57]

The black politician's power was of course limited because he was often usually the lone black person in a legislative body. We should not overstate the significance of the few lone black politicians elected to municipal government as a result of ghetto formation.

But we should also not understate the symbolic importance of these black politicians, either. In the aftermath of black politicians being driven from office in the South, these few black elected officials in the North represented the only real and living evidence of black enfranchisement. As elected officials, they were referred to as "honorable," whether whites liked it or not; they had real power, however circumscribed; and they stood as beacons of hope for what blacks could accomplish. Thus, the political power that blacks acquired by means of their numbers cannot be evaluated solely according to the limited material gains traded for those numbers. For black Americans, their politicians were also an exhibition of their agency and ability to help shape their world.

This is one of the ways that the nascent ghettos of the early twentieth century proved to be a haven. They were a space where black political power, however limited, could coalesce to speak for the race.

The Ghetto Economy

If ghettoization achieved the greatest notoriety in the cultural realm— through the Harlem Renaissance, for instance—the aspirations of the ghetto were the greatest and the most widespread with respect to the notion of a self-sufficient black economy. Blacks rich and poor, accommodationist and nationalist, viewed segregated ghettos as places where blacks would create a parallel economy that shielded blacks from the racism of whites, provided opportunity for blacks, and created black wealth.

Prior to the Great Migration, black leaders argued that economic self-sufficiency offered the race a way forward. First, as Booker T. Washington claimed, if blacks could be successful businessmen "producing what the world wants, whether it is a product of hand, heart or head, the world would not long stop to inquire what is the color of the skin of the producer."[58] Thus, successful black businessmen would skirt racism and show the folly of race prejudice.

Second, black businesses would advance the economic fortunes of the race. At an Atlanta University conference on Negro business in 1899, one speaker argued that rather than relying on whites for jobs and being restricted to menial positions, blacks could create their own businesses and staff them with other blacks as they saw fit. Labor problems could be solved. "Employment for colored men and women, colored boys and girls must be supplied by colored people."[59] Another participant suggested that

the solution of the much-talked-of Negro Problem is for us to enter into business. Let us keep our money among ourselves. Let us spend our money with each other.

Every Negro who successfully carries on a business of his own, helps the race as well as himself, for no Negro can rise without reflecting honor upon other Negroes. By Negroes sticking together and spending whatever they have to spend with their own race soon they would be able to unite and open large, up to date, dry goods, millinery, hardware and all other establishments as run by their white brothers, thereby giving employment to hundreds who otherwise have nothing to do.[60]

Finally, black people would serve as the natural clientele for black businesses, thus ensuring their success. Booker T. Washington and W. E. B. Du Bois had their differences, but on this point they concurred. Du Bois wrote in 1899, "It is density of negro [sic] population in the main that gives the Negro business-man his best chance."[61] And Washington elaborated on this point a few years later:

But where the great masses of the Negro population are, there are the best opportunities for Negro business men. Experience has shown, I believe, even in the North that the largest opportunities for the Negro in business are in providing for those needs of other members of his race, which the white business man, either through neglect, or lack of knowledge, has failed, or been unable to provide. The Negro knows the members of his own race, he knows the Negro people of his neighborhood, in their church, and in their family life, and is able to discriminate in his dealings with them. This superiority in the matter of credits is in itself a business advantage which competition cannot easily deprive the Negro [of].[62]

Although Washington was explaining why it would be advantageous for black businessmen to locate in the South, his logic was perhaps even more compelling in the case of the northern ghettos. True, blacks did create successful business enclaves in the South, as Atlanta and Durham, North Carolina, attest. But black business success in the South, like all types of success for blacks there, was tenuous because of the South's virulent racism. If blacks were too successful, whites would find a reason to put these "uppity Negroes" in their place. A case in point is the destruction of the black commercial district in Atlanta in 1906 after the alleged rapes of several white women by black men. Rumors swirled and mobs of whites rampaged through the black section, killing dozens and destroying many black businesses.[63]

In the nascent ghettos of the North, conditions were ripe for Negro business to achieve the success suggested by Du Bois and Washington. With the onset of the Great Migration, black ghettos in some northern cities reached sizes that surpassed the entire populations of all but the largest southern cities. Moreover, this population explosion was taking place in compact, circumscribed spaces. In addition, if whites in the South lacked the knowledge to provide for the needs and wants of the Negro, this was even more true in the North, where blacks were relative newcomers and many of the whites were recent immigrants themselves, with no experience in or knowledge about catering to a black clientele. Finally, despite being frozen out of the best jobs, northern blacks were still economically better off than their brethren left behind in the South. Blacks' incomes were also higher in the urban North than in the South, which translated into more disposable income and in turn into a stable and more reliable customer base.

Indeed, Du Bois and Washington were prescient in their assessment of the role of demography in creating opportunity for black business. Just as Washington predicted, a number of enterprising blacks stepped into the void left by the absence of white enterprises to serve the ghetto. Anecdotal reports abound of black entrepreneurs setting up shop, particularly in the largest black ghettos in cities such as New York and Chicago. Contemporary observers described Harlem variously as a place where blacks owned "their own grocery stores, and meat markets, their own savings and loans associations"; where "two colored banks are to be put into operation";[64] and where "Negroes have gone into business, the real estate business, the insurance business, the amusement business, and a dozen other kinds of business, large and small."[65]

The Windy City was described as a place where blacks were "conducting an increasing number of business enterprises" and where a "conspicuous development of business enterprises" was occurring.[66] More generally, the ghettos of the North were described as places where "small Negro enterprises were increasing rapidly."[67] It was in those businesses—in particular, banking, insurance, real estate, and personal grooming—where familiarity and intimacy with black culture were an advantage and where black businesses had their most visible successes.

Such was the folk wisdom on members of the race solving their economic problems through cooperation. The evidence suggests that although the "black economy" came nowhere near close to solving the economic problems of the race, tangible advances were made.

In banking, the former slave Richard R. Wright established the first black bank in the North, Philadelphia's Citizens and Southern Bank and Trust Company. Chicago was home to two black-owned banks, the Binga State Bank, which we encountered previously, and the Douglas Bank, the largest black-owned bank in the country during the 1920s. Indeed, a disproportionate share of the largest black-owned banks were located in the ghettos of the North.[68] Insurance was another industry where blacks could achieve notable success. Shunned by white insurance companies, the budding black metropolises would provide fertile ground for black-owned insurance companies. As in the case of black-owned banks, a disproportionate share of the largest black-owned insurance companies were also located outside the South.[69]

In the realm of personal grooming, Anthony Overton made his fortune in Chicago, becoming one of the wealthiest blacks in America and erecting the imposing multipurpose Overton Building, which remains a landmark to this day. In Indianapolis, Madame C. J. Walker became one of America's first female self-made millionaires on the success of her hair-care products specifically marketed to blacks. The thing that united all of these businesses was that they relied on other blacks for clientele.

A parallel fourth estate also evolved to serve as the voice of the oppressed and to act as an "uplift agency." The black press was where blacks could learn about the latest accomplishments of the race as well as keep abreast of all manner of slights, indignities, and terrorism that the race endured. Although the mass of black America remained in the South, it was in the ghettos of the North that the true organs of the race emerged. The *Chicago Defender*, the *New York Amsterdam News*, and the *Pittsburgh Courier* were among the most famous black newspapers, and all were based in the North. Black papers based in the South knew that reporting the truth, especially as it related to race relations, could at best bring a rebuke from white terrorists or at worst lead to murder.[70]

There were black newspapers in the urban North in the later nineteenth century (some of which were referenced in the previous chapter). It is also true that the black press could serve a black clientele without blacks being confined to the ghetto. There still would have been "Negro firsts" to report and atrocities perpetuated against the race to chronicle. But, like most news outlets, the black press relied on advertising to survive, and, of course, it was businesses serving the ghetto clientele that were most attracted to advertising in the black press. Moreover, the expanding size of the ghetto provided a much larger and attractive audience for potential advertisers. In this way, the ghetto made the black press a viable business possibility in many cities.

Beyond these anecdotes, the census data, too, suggest that in the ghettos of the North opportunity for black enterprise arose. In the South, de jure segregation created a captive market for black entrepreneurs. In the North, however, de facto segregation in the form of ghettoization allowed black entrepreneurs in northern cities to actually surpass their southern counterparts. Consider figure 2.1, which shows the average amount of retail sales by black establishments in states with the largest black population inside and outside the South, adjusted for the size of the black population in 1929. Retail sales in the seven southern states with the largest black populations typically lagged well behind sales in the seven northern states with the largest black populations.

We may also consider whether the degree of segregation in northern cities affected black enterprise. Although ghettoization was nearly universal, the resultant degree of spatial isolation varied a great deal from city to city. For example, in 1930 the level of isolation measured using enumeration

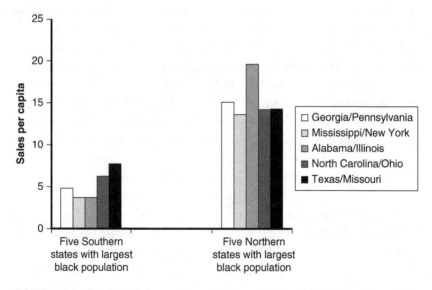

FIGURE 2.1 Per capita sales in black-owned stores, 1935. *Source*: Based on data in U.S. Census Bureau 1935.

districts ranged from a high of 0.92 in Chicago to a low of 0.05 in Stamford, Connecticut. Recall that the isolation index measures the average percentage of blacks in a black person's neighborhood (here defined by enumeration districts) in each city. Using the larger measure of neighborhood with which to calculate black spatial isolation, Robert L. Boyd also found that "when segregated Black communities arose in northern cities, the participation of Blacks in retailing was promoted by Black spatial isolation."[71] Boyd's conclusions were based on a comparison of the rate of retail self-employment across the twelve nonsouthern cities with the largest black populations.

A complementary question to whether blacks decided to go into retail is how successful they were when they did. In 1930, the U.S. Census Bureau conducted a census of retail business for cities with at least 50,000 blacks. Figure 2.2 plots the level of racial isolation in that city against the degree of per capita retail sales. Per capita retail sales are the aggregate amount of retail sales by black-owned retailers divided by the black population. Although the sample is small, the relationship is clearly positive. The more racial isolation, the greater the per capita retail sales among black retailers.

All of this evidence is consistent with the notion that ghettoization did foster the development of a protected "Negro market" and aid the growth of black enterprise.[72] The spatial concentration of tens of thousands of blacks

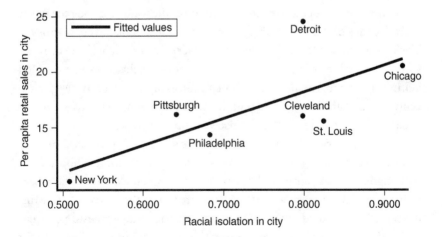

FIGURE 2.2 Per capita retail sales by racial isolation, 1930. *Sources*: Compiled from data in U.S. Census Bureau 1935 and Ruggles et al. 2010.

in some cities, the New Negro ideology that promoted black independence and self-reliance, and the relative improvement in blacks' economic fortunes due to migration to the cities combined to enhance opportunities for black enterprise. By no means did black enterprise approach the size and diversity necessary to be a self-sufficient black economy that many dreamed of, but there were at least three tangible benefits to the growth of black enterprise nonetheless.

First, at least a few blacks gained significant wealth, and many more were able to make a living for themselves and their families through black enterprise. Anthony Overton, Jesse Binga, and Madame C. J. Walker are but a few of the blacks who prospered because of the ghetto. Second, the success of black businesses was taken as a reflection of the abilities of the entire race and not just of the individual entrepreneur. Being able to successfully start and manage a business enterprise was further evidence of the race's humanity. As Charles S. Johnson eulogized in 1930, the Binga Bank, "a Negro Bank[,] is more than an institution for financial savings and transactions—it is a symbol of the Negroes' aspirations to enter the commercial life of the nation and it is a mark of his faith in the ability and competence of his own."[73] Negro entrepreneurs advanced the race when they were successful. Third, these black-owned business provided goods and services that were wanted in the black community. To the extent that ghettoization made the provision of these goods and services possible, this was a benefit to the black public at large.

Finally, when we consider how ghetto formation affected the race in the early decades of the twentieth century, we can also look at the fortunes of blacks who resided there vis-à-vis other blacks. In the twenty-first century, when we think of the ghetto, we think of a place that houses those left behind, the unfortunate ones who cannot escape. The early-twentieth-century black ghetto was different: it was a place of aspirations—a haven where blacks strived to better themselves and their race.

Figure 2.3 suggests those aspirations were successful. It is based on 1920 U.S. census data using enumeration districts as proxies for neighborhoods. Although the 1920 census did not collect data on educational attainment or income, it did record occupation. Researchers at the University of Minnesota have translated the respondent's occupation into a measure of occupational prestige and a score representing the median earnings for that

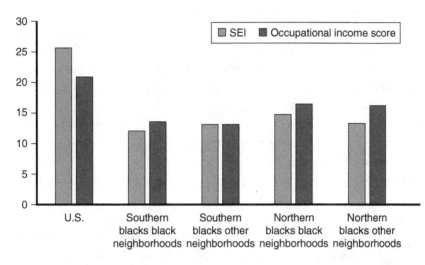

FIGURE 2.3 Socioeconomic status in Negro enumeration districts, 1920. *Source*: Author's tabulation of Integrated Public Use Microdata (Ruggles et al. 2010).

occupation.[74] These two indicators thus give one a sense of the socioeconomic status of an individual, based on his or her occupation.

As measured by these two indicators, blacks in predominantly black neighborhoods in the North had the highest socioeconomic status among blacks in the country, even slightly higher than northern blacks living outside the ghetto. To be sure, blacks, wherever they lived, were confined to lower-status occupations than whites; figure 2.3 makes this clear. But the ghetto of the early Great Migration was not a place for those left behind; rather, it lured the most upwardly mobile blacks with heretofore unknown opportunities.

A GHETTO AND AN ENCLAVE

The Great Migration transformed black America and the nation's "race problem" more broadly from a sectional obsession to a nationwide issue. It also marked the birth of the modern ghetto—that is, large city-size sections of cities that were almost exclusively black. Although blacks voluntarily moved into these incipient ghettos, they in many ways had no choice, given that the only other option was remaining in the degrading Jim Crow South.

Blacks gained a toehold in the manufacturing sector of the North, but it was just that, a toehold. Theirs were the dirtiest, most dangerous, and lowest-paying jobs. The color line forced Negroes to pack themselves like sardines into overcrowded, dilapidated ghettos with housing that most whites shunned. Almost uniformly they experienced more discrimination than recent white immigrants. The walling of blacks into ghettos would create a legacy of urban problems that would endure for at least a century. Many of the urban ghettos that were born in the first decades of the twentieth century remain black ghettos nearly one hundred years later. Many contemporary observers and numerous historians have told the travails of these ghettos.[75]

But it would be a mistake to view the incipient ghettoization solely through the prism of future and enduring urban problems. Ghettoization also coincided with the arrival of the "New Negro." The New Negro had a sense of racial pride and self-reliance that was at the time ambivalent about integration and was perhaps more focused on surviving and upward mobility. Moreover, the degradation of blacks in the larger culture, where they were perceived as a barely human "primitive" race, generated in many blacks a desire to demonstrate their true humanity, whether in the arts, in business, or in politics. Ghettoization entailed many costs that have been discussed elsewhere and are taken up in subsequent chapters. But the ghetto also provided blacks with the platform to demonstrate their humanity and in ways that created benefits to the race that also endure to this day. This other aspect of ghettoization was not lost on the migrants themselves. As two migrant sisters commented later, "Harlem was as close to Heaven as we were going to find on this earth."[76]

Chapter Three

THE FEDERALLY SANCTIONED GHETTO

With much fanfare in August 1937, the New York City Housing Authority opened the Harlem River Houses for Negroes. The new federally funded housing development had modern conveniences and was viewed as a modest step toward addressing the discontent that had boiled over in rioting in Harlem two years earlier.[1] Harlem was not unique in being the site of federal housing largesse. Thousands of public-housing units were set aside for blacks in other cities across the country.[2] Outhwaite Homes in Cleveland, for example, opened for blacks in 1935.

Eight decades later, even with the integration of Major League baseball, the desegregation of the armed forces, the decision in *Brown v. Board of Education*, the civil rights movement, and the election of the first black president, both the Harlem River Houses and Outhwaite Homes remain devoid of whites. Harlem River Houses has diversified a bit, now being 24 percent Hispanic, but whites are absent. Outhwaite Homes remains 99 percent black.[3] Such was the durable racial imprint left by the federal government's foray into the ghetto.

The impetus for federal involvement in the ghetto and other aspects of the economy was, of course, the Great Depression. For blacks, the economic devastation wrought by the Great Depression obliterated distinctions between the ghetto as a place for aspirations and opportunity and elsewhere. Mere survival was the paramount concern in the ghetto, as it was elsewhere across the nation and indeed in large swathes of the industrialized world. During the Great Depression, the ghetto was no longer a haven in the sense that it was no longer a place to flock in order to advance economically. But neither was it a hell in the sense that conditions were especially bad in the ghetto compared to other places. Times were extremely hard everywhere.

Nevertheless, the Depression era would prove pivotal in the role the ghetto would play as a haven or a hell in the future. Federal involvement in the housing market meant the federal government had to take a stand regarding the budding black belts in the North. With the adoption of policies that reinforced the ghetto, what I call the "federally sanctioned ghetto" came into being. The federally sanctioned ghetto is a ghetto where the federal government's enormous influence and resources came to bear, solidifying patterns that have persisted in many cities to this day. For this reason, understanding how the federal government came to sanction the ghetto lays the groundwork for our understanding of how the ghetto would come to perpetuate inequality in the decades to come.

Blacks' reactions to the federal government's sanctioning of the ghetto is also revelatory for understanding how blacks themselves saw the ghetto during the Great Depression. Understood literally, a ghetto is a place of confinement, marginalization, and stigmatization—a place to be escaped at the first opportunity. But, as we shall see, blacks' reactions to the federally sanctioned ghetto suggest they did not necessarily see it that way. Rather, they came to see the ghetto as a spatial manifestation of the race itself and therefore to consider any resources that could be obtained for the ghetto as reason for pride.

An examination of the federal government's foray into the ghetto thus provides us with important insights into the ghetto's role as a haven and a hell. It helps us to understand one of the mechanisms through which the ghetto would become a hell, federal policy, and yet at the same time supports the argument that the ghetto was indeed viewed by its inhabitants as a haven. This chapter begins by briefly describing the conditions that would galvanize the federal government to act.

The chapter then turns attention to two major initiatives with long-lasting implications for the ghetto, mortgage lending and public housing. It examines how the federal government put in place mortgage-lending practices that would undermine the ghetto. We shall see that although public housing initially seemed to enhance the ghetto's role as a haven, it was in fact planting the seeds for future inequality. The Great Depression would thus prove pivotal in the role of the ghetto as either a haven or a hell.

THE GHETTO IN THE GREAT DEPRESSION

Economic historians consider the Great Depression, which began in October 1929, to be the worst economic downturn in the history of the modern world. Millions lost their jobs as the economy contracted. The stock market crashed, banks failed by the hundreds, and it would be more than a decade before the economy completely recovered.

For an already economically marginalized group such as Negroes, the Great Depression was a catastrophe. The progress that the race was making through migration to the northern ghetto came to halt. The era of the New Negro, in which blacks would use the arts to prove their basic humanity, was over. Instead, mere survival became the central concern.

In Detroit, joblessness reached a staggering 60 and 75 percent among black males and females, respectively. In Cleveland, well more than half of black males and females were unemployed. Harlem, the "black capital of the world," did not escape the plague of unemployment, with some 60 percent of its population without work.[4] The last-hired blacks became the first fired. Most blacks had relatively low incomes even in good times and thus had little in the way of savings to cushion the blow of prolonged unemployment. Nor was misfortune limited to the Negro masses. As previously noted, Jesse Binga saw his bank fail in 1930. The black real estate magnate, John Nail, likewise saw his fortunes fade. And W. E. B. Du Bois lost his home in the chaos of the Great Depression. Cabarets and night clubs that catered to whites and mixed crowds were closed.[5] The Great Depression thus put an end to the dream of a self-sufficient black metropolis and the artistic/cultural movement known as the Harlem Renaissance.

Not surprisingly, the belief in the northern ghettos as "promised lands" took a back seat to the need to survive. People struggled to acquire enough food to eat. In Oklahoma City, black and white workers banded together for a hunger march that culminated with marchers raiding a grocery store to feed their families.[6] Recent migrants to Baltimore became so desperate that they turned to the police for food and in some instances to jail cells for shelter rather than going hungry and enduring the elements.[7] Others, such as Harlem resident Emil Heike, took their own lives to end the misery

that jobless desperation had wrought.[8] To avoid being swamped with indi-
gent migrants, the City of Detroit limited its relief program to those who
had been in the city at least a year.[9]

The elite art of the Harlem Renaissance, which had sought to prove
blacks' humanity by demonstrating the cultural and intellectual heights
that the race could achieve and that often portrayed the incipient black ghettos as a "promised land" for blacks, faded away. In its stead came a social
realism that chronicled the struggles of everyday blacks in the ghetto with
documentary-like precision. The literature penned in this tradition drew
on the authors' own experiences; these authors covered the black belts as
journalists, investigating Works Progress Administration projects and even
their own deprivation in living in the black belt through the Great Depression. Their stories thus provide a window into life in the black belts in the
depths of the Great Depression.[10]

The view they provided was a bleak one indeed. Material hardship was
ever present. The black belts featured in the writings of authors such as
Chester Himes and Richard Wright featured blacks who could not afford
to pay for heat, did not know how they would pay the rent, and resorted to
armed robbery to put money in their pockets.[11] The black belts were gray
places where, as Richard Wright put it, "whites were looming overhead like
a great natural force."[12] The forces that created and maintained the black
belts were neither benign nor reflective of the agency and will of black folks.
They were the same forces that kept blacks in the worst jobs and living a
second-class existence. It was whites who decided where blacks could live,
what they could be or do, and where they could go, leading Bigger Thomas
in Wright's novel *Native Son* to wonder, "Why [do] they make us live in one
corner of the city? Why don't they let us fly planes and run ships?" To Bigger, blacks were "*prescribed*" to live in a corner of the city "tumbling down
with rot."[13] In the fiction of social realists, the burgeoning ghettos of the
North were depicted as anything but a promised land.

With jobs scarce, the North no longer beckoned to black southerners the
way it had in previous decades. Indeed, the historian James N. Gregory
writes that many southern migrants returned to the South, where their relatives at least had access to food and shelter in the form of a home they
owned, a garden, and a few farm animals.[14] As figure 3.1 shows, the number of black southerners in the North, after increasing rapidly from 1910
to 1930, almost leveled off in the 1930s, the decade of the Great Depression.

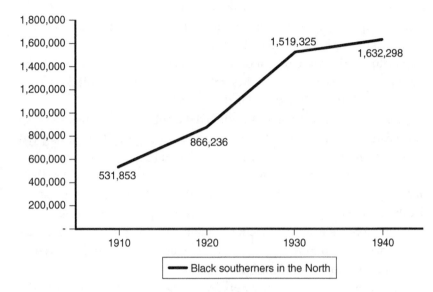

FIGURE 3.1 Number of black southerners in the North, 1910–1940. *Source:* Author's tabulation of Integrated Public Use Microdata (Ruggles et al. 2010).

THE FEDERAL FORAY

In response to the economic calamity of the Great Depression, the federal government became deeply involved in the American economy and never looked back. A host of programs, initiatives, and regulations were passed to jumpstart the economy and help struggling Americans as part of a "new deal." The housing market would prove to be an important focus of the New Deal.

Until the Great Depression, housing policy had been a local matter, and the federal government had taken a laissez-faire approach. It had with few exceptions built little in the way of publicly financed housing up to this point.[15] The financing of housing was the exclusive domain of the private market, with states providing only regulatory oversight. Building codes and zoning regulations were also state and local matters. The federal government did pass the Standard State Zoning Enabling Act in 1926, which served as a template for states to pass legislation that would enable municipalities to enact zoning. But it allowed the federal government solely an advisory role.

The only significant action on ghettoization by the federal government was the Supreme Court's ruling in *Buchanan v. Warley* (245 U.S. 60 [1917]) that racial zoning was unconstitutional. This victory, however, proved to be pyrrhic as the construction of the ghetto continued apace through the use of restrictive covenants, whites' refusal to rent or sell to blacks, terror, and, when all else failed, white flight.[16]

The Great Depression, however, altered the political landscape, allowing the federal government to intervene in housing a big way. The housing and real estate industries were particularly hard hit during the economic downturn. In response to millions of Americans not being able to pay their mortgages and losing their homes to foreclosure, the widespread failure of banks due in part to borrowers not being able to repay their mortgages, millions more being evicted or facing eviction, and the legions of construction workers becoming unemployed, the federal government moved to resuscitate the moribund housing market.

After a few ineffectual attempts by the Hoover administration, the remaking of the housing market began in earnest under President Franklin D. Roosevelt. The government's thrust into the housing market was multifaceted but, broadly speaking, distilled two approaches: easing access to credit so that more Americans could purchase (or keep) their homes and the development of government-owned affordable housing. Both of these efforts would have important implications for the ghetto, and, indeed, their effects reverberate to this day.

On the homeownership side of the ledger, the most significant move was the establishment of the Home Owners Loan Corporation (HOLC). The HOLC allowed homeowners at risk or in default to refinance their mortgages at lower interest rates, thus saving millions of Americans' homes from foreclosure. Also noteworthy were the HOLC's impacts on the practice of mortgage financing: it introduced and standardized the self-amortizing thirty-year mortgage, which allowed for lower monthly payments spread over the life of the mortgage and was widely adopted by home financiers.

So far so good: these practices benefitted millions of Americans by helping them avoid foreclosure and henceforth making homeownership more feasible. Blacks, too, stood to benefit from the HOLC, and black newspapers took it upon themselves to advise their readership on "how to get help under Home Owners Loan" and to explain the particulars of the HOLC for those contemplating whether to seek such aid.[17]

In order to refinance the millions of mortgages at risk of foreclosure, the properties under threat had to be appraised. Because the HOLC was refinancing properties across the country, standardized methods of appraisal nationwide had to be developed. The HOLC successfully developed methods that took account of a property's age, construction, neighboring sales trends, and the racial composition of the area. Black neighborhoods or those at risk of a black influx were almost invariably assigned the lowest grade and deemed the highest risk. Even black middle-class neighborhoods consisting of relatively new construction were given the lowest grade.[18] Despite literally redlining black neighborhoods—that is, denying them certain services because of their racial composition—the available evidence suggests the HOLC did refinance loans in black and other red-coded neighborhoods, albeit at higher interest rates.[19] Although the HOLC refinanced mortgages in areas it deemed risky, its underwriting standards influenced practices in the private market.[20] As part of the nascent federal banking system, the policies and practices adopted by the HOLC filtered into professional real estate organizations and other parts of the federal banking bureaucracy, including the Federal Housing Administration (FHA). Although there is debate on the extent to which the HOLC influenced private lenders and the FHA, it can be asserted that its coding/grading scheme undoubtedly cast a shadow on many black neighborhoods as places too risky to lend to.[21]

Perhaps more profound for the ghetto were the FHA's actions. The FHA's key innovation was the provision of mortgage insurance for qualifying properties. Such properties had to meet certain construction standards as well as to be located in areas that, among other criteria, were deemed "economically stable" and unduly burdened by "adverse influences." In practice, the latter two criteria were almost synonymous with white neighborhoods because mixed and black neighborhoods were seen as economically unstable and blacks themselves were viewed as an "adverse influence." Lest there be any confusion over the meaning of the term *adverse influences*, the *FHA Underwriting Manual* specifically stated, "If a neighborhood is to retain stability, it is necessary that properties shall continue to be occupied by the same social and racial standards."[22]

Like the HOLC, the FHA needed to develop a systematic method for appraising properties. Indeed, the lack of standardized appraisal methods and inattention to neighborhood dynamics were considered prime causes of the mortgage crisis in the first place.[23] The FHA-sponsored study *The Structure and Growth of Residential Neighborhoods in American Cities* (1939) encapsulates the FHA's discriminatory stance toward blacks.[24] Homer Hoyt, an economist with the FHA, and his research team analyzed reams of data collected for real property surveys by the federal government during the 1930s with the purpose of providing mortgage lenders with an analytic framework for assessing a property's risk. They aimed to illustrate how a city could be analyzed with the intent of assessing the level of risk associated with various neighborhoods. Not surprisingly, the racial composition of a neighborhood was identified as a consistent predictor of the least-desirable neighborhoods. The higher the proportion of nonwhites, the less desirable the neighborhood.

This conclusion is not particularly noteworthy. As Hoyt himself acknowledged, "This is principally reflective of the economic conditions of the nonwhite population." Moreover, Hoyt noted, "There are many slum areas tenanted by whites which are in as poor or worse condition than areas tenanted by nonwhites. The same cities may also contain areas occupied by colored races where acceptable housing conditions prevail." More insidious, however, was Hoyt's assessment of racial integration and transition: "In wholly white areas, the gradual filtration of other than white races tends to slowly change the character of neighborhoods. *The presence of even one nonwhite person in a block otherwise populated by whites may initiate a period of transition.*" And "the presence of nonwhite persons influences rent directly only in those blocks partially occupied by nonwhite persons. In some cities, rents in wholly white blocks adjacent to wholly or partially nonwhite blocks may be affected. It is in the twilight zone where members of different races live together that racial mixtures tend to have a depressing effect upon land values—and therefore, upon rents."[25]

Hoyt's assertions about the dangers of mixed neighborhoods appear to be based on prevailing opinions and stereotypes rather than on any systematic analysis. No evidence is provided in Holt's voluminous study to support the conclusion that "racial mixtures" had a depressing effect. *The Structure and Growth of Residential Neighborhoods in American Cities* painstakingly correlated the proportion of nonwhites on a block with rents, structural deficiencies, and other neighborhood traits. But, as mentioned earlier, Hoyt attributed blacks' location in less-desirable areas to their lower economic status. Nowhere in this document with its forty-one illustrations and twenty-five tables was evidence provided showing that the introduction of nonwhites to a neighborhood depressed property values. Indeed, the only evidence on the matter contradicted the notion that racial mixtures depress property values:

What are the actual qualitative differences in the housing of different racial groups in American cities? Data on rents in the dwelling units in the 64-city sample reveal that the average rent of dwelling units in blocks occupied exclusively by the white race was $23.08, in blocks occupied by a mixture of white and other races was $14.90 and in blocks occupied exclusively by nonwhite persons was $9.34. The gradation of rent reveals qualitative differences of housing between white and nonwhite races. The differences are borne out by the relative condition of structures in blocks occupied by white, mixed, and nonwhite persons. Thus, 12.2% of the structures in 85,478 blocks occupied exclusively by white persons were in need of major repairs in 1934 or were unfit for use. In the 10,288 mixed racial blocks, 38.6 percent of the structures were in this poor condition, and in the 5,004 blocks occupied exclusively by nonwhite races, the proportion of such structures rose to 50.9 percent.[26]

This analysis suggests that rents were lower on mixed-race blocks because the housing quality was lower there. Had housing quality been the same but rents lower in the mixed blocks, Holt's conclusions about the perils of race mixing may have been defensible. Instead, Holt and subsequently the FHA went on to promulgate the notion that the presence of blacks lowered property values but without any sound analysis to support this assertion. And although *The Structure and Growth of Residential Neighborhoods in American Cities* may not have been a best seller, the *FHA Underwriting Manual* was *the* how-to guide for appraisers in the mortgage industry in this period.

By focusing on mixed neighborhoods as the locus of harm to property values, the government's policies may have appeared race neutral. However, given the population dynamics of the urban North, the negative rating of mixed neighborhoods was especially problematic. Hoyt was writing in the late 1930s, a time when the cities of the North were on the cusp of witnessing a migration of blacks from the South that was orders of magnitude greater than the migration heretofore. As blacks poured into northern cities, scores of neighborhoods would transition from white to black. The FHA and in future years the Veterans Administration (VA) would remain key in the financing of home purchases. But the federal government was writing off these neighborhoods as they went from white to black. Starved of capital, homeownership in these neighborhoods was more difficult, rehabilitation and new construction harder to come by, and existing properties appreciated more slowly. Given the influence of the FHA on the mortgage market, Holt's prognostications could not help but become self-fulfilling prophecies. If the FHA refused to underwrite mortgages in transitioning neighborhoods, these neighborhoods would indeed decline and become poor risks.

Eight decades later it is easy to criticize the FHA for its racist practices. Given the prevailing racial sentiment at the time, can we expect anything different? Perhaps not. Moreover, as discussed later, neither the HOLC nor the FHA originated the practice of redlining or discriminating in the allocation of mortgage capital.

But it is worth noting that there was a countervailing narrative to the notion that blacks destroyed property values and were poor credits risks. As early as 1920s, real estate specialists and financiers recognized the role of ignorance in shaping the ghetto housing market. The Chicago Commission on Race Relations reported in 1922, "The most formidable stumbling block in the way of home owning by Negroes is the unsalability of their mortgages. Except in a limited field these loans have no market." "The factors are similar to those in depreciation, often based on prejudice and erroneous beliefs concerning Negroes. Whatever depreciates real estate necessarily depresses its security value—whether the cause be fact or fiction."[27] The Chicago Commission, however, demonstrated that these beliefs were fiction. Interviews with real estate brokers and mortgage lenders revealed that "Negroes carry out what they undertake to do; . . . very few default in their payments, and when Negroes buy on the installment plan 'they pay out better than the whites do, as a rule.'" It noted that Negroes "are careful in assuming their obligations and make their payments promptly." The commission concluded that "most of the firms that had dealings with Negroes, whether as buyers, borrowers, or renters, expressed satisfaction with their transactions with them."[28] Nor were these the assessments of a group of idealistic or especially progressive real estate men. The vast majority of real estate persons spoken to by the Chicago Commission did not deal with Negroes. Sometimes this was because the realtors thought Negroes to be poor risks—"[Negroes have] not yet acquired the sufficient stability to carry on payments over a long term of years"—or because they did "not lend on the class of property purchased by Negroes."[29]

A study of fifteen cities in 1928, including seven in the North, concluded that real estate dealers who had experience with Negroes considered them "satisfactory clients if property is sold to them on correct principles, and if patience is exercised in helping them to keep up their payments." Even among those who did lend to Negroes, however, "the rates seem entirely too high when the character of the risk is considered."[30]

These studies suggest that ignorance led to the real estate industry falling back on common stereotypes of blacks as too poor or irresponsible to be good credit risks. Indeed, the Chicago Commission described how lenders who did lend to Negroes often found it hard to sell these loans on the secondary mortgage market.[31] Unfamiliarity with Negroes as credit risks and the belief that Negroes were poor credit risks constituted impediments to blacks who wished to obtain loans.

The Chicago Commission on Race Relations also examined the effect of "Negroes on Property [sic] depreciation," devoting a full twenty pages to the topic based on interviews with realtors and tracking land values in and around the black belt. Their basic finding was that due to discrimination and low incomes, blacks tended to move into neighborhoods that were already declining. Summarizing other studies in addition to the Commission on Race Relations study, a later study by T. J. Woofter concluded, "The areas that are usually penetrated by Negroes in their expansion are in neighborhoods that are already depreciating in value."[32]

Although real estate professionals often expressed the belief that property values would decline after an influx of Negroes, it seems most likely that any decline was due to panic selling by whites as well as to municipal authorities' proclivity to tolerate vice in black belts. For example, a Detroit study reported in 1926 that "the general deterioration of congested Negro areas cannot be attributed to Negro occupancy. For instance, other factors in the San Antonio District, such as the entrance of commercial buildings, factories and garages, the concentration of vice resorts, etc., had depreciated the values of houses for residential purposes before the Negro moved in. After the entrance of the Negro, further depreciation takes place because of the overcrowding on account of the effort to pay the rents charged."[33]

Some real estate professionals quoted in studies such as the one by the Chicago Commission on Race Relations, *The Negro in Chicago*, would often describe how "Negroes as a race do not keep their property up and so they soon make a community undesirable for a good class of white people" and how "property occupied by Negroes was more likely to run down."[34] Just as frequently, however, real estate professionals would describe how the restrictions placed on blacks often meant property values would *rise* after an influx of blacks because blacks had little choice but to pay inflated prices. One study reported, "Rents and selling prices have always been raised when Negroes moved into houses that formerly were occupied by whites."[35] Another described how "if the property is not already too high[ly priced] for the average Negro to purchase, the number of Negro prospective buyers tends to increase the prices after the first period of depreciation."[36]

A study of Negro migration to Detroit during World War I had painted a more complex relationship between neighborhood racial transition and property values. Interviews with ten white realtors showed six of them thinking that blacks lowered property values and four of them qualifying their conclusions. Interviews with ten black realtors showed six of them suggesting that the infiltration of blacks would actually increase property values. The report noted that

in the largest district in which Negroes live[,] that of the East Side, most of the houses into which Negroes move, are in the old district which is now in the process of becoming a becoming a business and industrial district whose white residents are in that intermediate stage where they lack or no longer take civic pride in their dwellings. In the West Side district, the second largest Negro section, rents and selling prices have always been raised when Negroes moved into houses that had already been occupied by whites and the raise averaged all the way from 25% to 50%.

The report had concluded that "in the last analysis, the great majority of objections to Negroes as neighbors are based on purely social grounds— namely to Negroes as members of a certain race. Very few whites or Negro real estate men thought that Negroes were more destructive on property than whites. It would appear that if property owners would not become so hysterical when one Negro family moved into a neighborhood, the so-called problem of a Negro invasion would never occur."[37]

This type of nuanced analysis is what one might expect from someone, such as Hoyt, committed to the "scientific analysis of city structure."[38]

Adjudicating between the simplistic notion that "blacks lower property values" and the more complex story in which blacks move into already declining areas and have variable impacts on property values depending on the context would not have been easy at the time *The Structure and Growth of Residential Neighborhoods in American Cities* was published, 1939. The point is that Hoyt did not appear to even try. Alternative explanations of why property might or might not decline when blacks moved into a neighborhood were not considered. Nor were the studies quoted here the work of obscure social scientists or left-wing propaganda. Indeed, only eight years prior to the publication of Holt's report, the federal government itself, albeit during a different administration, cited these same studies and their conclusions in the report *Negro Housing*.[39]

If ever there was a circumstance that cried "market failure," the treatment of blacks in the housing finance market was it. Faced with a new market in the form of black migrants from the South, lenders were hesitant. Given the minuscule population of blacks in northern cities prior to the Great Migration, many lenders had little or no experience with them. The prevailing views of blacks in the first decades of the twentieth century were that they were a race prone to criminality, less intelligent than whites, unable to save their money and instead tending to gamble it away on dice— hardly traits that would endear a people to mortgage financiers.[40]

Moreover, the housing market was unlike many other markets in terms of offering nondiscriminatory participants opportunities to profit. In a market for cars, a dealer who sold to blacks while others did not would be in a position to earn greater profits. In effect, there would be less competition, which would provide a disincentive for a car dealer to discriminate. A mortgage lender who loaned to blacks while his or her peers did not could possibly charge higher interest rates and would also be in a position to earn greater profits. But whereas the car dealer could wash his hands of the deal once the client drove away, the lender remained linked to the borrower for several years while the loan was being paid off. If other lenders refused to lend in the neighborhood, the neighborhood could decline, and the value of the lender's collateral would decline along with it. Thus, the lender's own prejudices, combined with his fears about discrimination by his competitors, could make mortgage funds especially scarce in neighborhoods with or anticipating a significant black presence.

During the Great Depression, instead of working to address this market failure, the federal government served to institutionalize it. Rather than addressing the inefficiency in the market that made investors skittish about investing in neighborhoods undergoing racial transition, the federal government canonized these beliefs in professional and scientific-sounding documents.

The discriminatory policies and practices of the HOLC and the FHA drew little attention, at least at first. The federal government's forays into the mortgage market were instead heralded. Even the black press counseled its readers to take advantage of the opportunities presented by these programs: "We are advising all who need [FHA] loans for the purpose herein described, to make the proper application to the proper department in your city."[41] Another black newspaper sought to provide "14 answers to your questions about modernization credits."[42]

Context is key in understanding the black press's actions. In encouraging its readers to take advantage of these housing programs, the black press was fulfilling its role as a "race organization." That is, the black press had an obligation not only to report noteworthy news but to also uplift the race. Giving its readers information that could help them to become or remain homeowners was consistent with that obligation. In addition, it was not immediately obvious that federal policy disadvantaged blacks vis-à-vis whites with regard to mortgage capital. More apparent was the relative increase in mortgage funds after the establishment of the HOLC and the FHA. During the depths of the Depression, banks were failing left and right, and mortgage financing was scarce. As a consequence, when federal funds made it possible to refinance, refurbish, or purchase a home, this possibility was welcome and noteworthy.[43]

For most blacks of the pre-Depression era, the frame of reference would have been a time when federal mortgage insurance did not exist and self-amortizing loans were rare. Blacks often had difficulty obtaining mortgages, and when they did, they paid usurious rates as high 25 percent.[44] Compared to the practices of that earlier period, the policies of the HOLC and the FHA would seem a step forward for blacks. These federal programs were visible manifestations of a government that was sympathetic to black concerns and helped shift black's political allegiance from the party of Lincoln (Republican) to the party of the New Deal (Democrat).[45]

Although the *Los Angeles Sentinel* began calling out the FHA for discriminating against black workers on FHA-financed projects as early as 1934,[46] it was not until several years after the HOLC and the FHA were initiated that their discriminatory lending policies were revealed. For example, in 1939

the Jamaica L.I. branch of the NAACP . . . investigated numerous complaints from colored people who sought to secure mortgages on new homes in or near Jamaica. Finally, the local administrators of the FHA admitted that no mortgages were guaranteed for colored people in any neighborhood which was less than 50% Negro. In a protest to Stewart McDonald, director, of the FHA in Washington the NAACP charges that the FHA is restricting Negro home buyers who wish to escape slum areas and improve their housing and health conditions. The NAACP also charges that the FHA, by enforcement of this rule, is creating segregation problems where none exist [sic]. Instances were cited where local builders, local banks and local community sentiment were not opposed to Negroes in the neighborhood.[47]

The *Los Angeles Sentinel* took its criticisms a step further, equating the FHA's policies with the ghettoization of Jews in Nazi Germany: "Fair minded Americans who have been protesting Hitler's despicable plan to herd German Jews into ghettoes will be surprised to learn that while they were venting their anger on the dictator their own government has been busy planning ghettoes for American Negroes through the Federal Housing Authority. . . . [The] FHA has a secret rule whereby it refuses to guarantee a loan for a Negro in a so-called 'white neighborhood.' In effect the rule means that Negroes must be confined to their 'own neighborhoods.'"[48]

Given what was at the time happening to the Jews of the Nazi ghettos, the *Sentinel*'s analogy is surely hyperbolic. However, the American ghettos, although much less lethal than the Nazi ghettos, were certainly more durable. Reinforced by government action in the 1930s, the black ghettos remain with us to this day.

The *Sentinel*'s charges notwithstanding, criticism of the federal government's policies was muted overall. The HOLC and the FHA still represented a relative improvement to what existed both prior to and during the Great

Depression. And redlining as it would come to be known was not yet fully transparent (note the *Sentinel*'s use of the term *secret*). The full implications of these policies would not be understood for decades to come. But as we shall see in coming chapters, the federal government's actions helped pave the way for the black ghetto to become a hell in later decades.

PUBLIC HOUSING

The segregated nature of the second major component of the Roosevelt administration's intervention into the housing market—public housing— might have been expected to evoke a different type of response from blacks than that evoked by the HOLC and the FHA. Contrary to the HOLC and FHA policies, which would be implemented behind closed doors and in obscure policy manuals, the erection of public housing was visible for all to see. Indeed, blacks' reaction to the discriminatory policies of public housing did differ from their reaction to the Roosevelt administration's mortgage-lending policies—they were at times downright enthusiastic about them.

Public housing represented the federal government's belated effort to deal with the problem of slum housing. By the time of the New Deal, housing reformers had been advocating for strategies to deal with slums for nearly a century.[49] America's reluctance to engage in the public provision of housing, however, made European-style "social housing" an unrealized dream of progressive reformers.[50] The suffering caused by the Great Depression, however, provided an opening for the federal government to act, for at least two reasons. First, people were receptive to government intervention no matter how unconventional because the private market economy was so obviously failing. Second, the development of public housing could and would be promoted as a jobs program that would put unemployed construction workers to work. In a further nod to commercial interests, public housing was also sold as a slum-clearance program. Public housing would replace slums, not compete with them.[51]

The choices confronting the federal government with respect to the northern ghettos were perhaps even more stark than those with regard to mortgage lending. Whereas the government could have a "secret" policy in approving loans, no such secrecy could be possible with public housing. The location and occupancy of the developments would be out in the open for all to see.

By the 1930s, ghettos in the urban North were becoming clearly demarcated. Because few integrated neighborhoods existed, if public housing were to replace existing slums, the housing would be either in black neighborhoods or in white neighborhoods. Thus, in the development of public housing, the issue of race could not easily be sidestepped.

Previously undeveloped sites would have been another option. If public housing were instead developed on greenfields rather than in already-existing black or white neighborhoods, there would have been no surrounding racially identified neighborhood to taint the project. The Greentowns developed by the United States Resettlement Administration in the 1930s are examples of such greenfield development. But, alas, public housing was limited to slum clearance to mollify the real estate industry's concerns. As a consequence, it had to be built in existing neighborhoods, which, given the high degree of segregation at that time, were almost always racially identifiable. The Roosevelt administration confronted the choice of either bucking local housing patterns or acquiescing to segregationists.

But in an instance of serendipitous yet deft political maneuvering, the administration adopted a "separate but equal" policy with regard to public housing, thereby reinforcing segregation yet at the same time winning praise from blacks.

The administration at least initially appeared to have no grand strategy for dealing with blacks' subjugated status in American society. And blacks themselves were decidedly lukewarm toward Roosevelt at first, a majority of them remaining loyal to Hoover and the Republicans in 1932. But a combination of factors predisposed the Roosevelt administration toward a more amenable relationship with blacks. Perhaps foremost, its aim to help "the forgotten man" could not help but provide some assistance to blacks, who fared worse than whites during the Depression. To be sure, southern congressmen erected all manner of roadblocks to prevent blacks from getting their fair share of the New Deal. The absence of Jim Crow in the North, however, meant blacks there were better positioned to take advantage of New Deal programs.

Second, key individuals close to President Roosevelt were instrumental in looking out for the interests of blacks. First Lady Eleanor Roosevelt's sympathy for black causes is well known. Secretary of the Interior Harold Ickes, a former president of the Chicago NAACP, also was an important supporter of black causes. With regard to public housing, this meant blacks would get a significant share of the public-housing units, albeit usually in segregated developments. Moreover, public housing was conceived as a public-works program, meaning that it was just as important for blacks to get their share of the jobs associated with public housing, including professional-level jobs, such as architecture and engineering.

The Roosevelt administration could then present to blacks a program that would provide new, decent, and affordable housing; provide construction jobs to unemployed laborers; and employ black professionals in the planning and construction of the developments—even though all the while reinforcing the walls of the ghetto. Indeed, this is how the program was sold to blacks, as one black newspaper explained:

Now what are the specific benefits of the program to Negroes? In the first place, because of the very insanitary and ugly housing now provided for Negroes through-out the country, they more than likely will receive about one-fourth of the total to be allotted by the Division for low-rent projects. Then too, it can be added here that continuous employment of the groups to be housed is essential to the success of the program. To date, a proportion of the housing payroll, equal to the occupational distribution as between white and colored workers of the building trades as shown by the 1930 census, has gone to Negro skilled and unskilled workers. Negroes . . . will be employed as architects, engineers, project analysts, social planners, project accountants and auditors, project managers and supervisors and re-housing engineers. This employment will mean that the program of the Housing Division is based on policies and practices of doing things *with* Negroes rather than *for* Negroes. Low-rent housing projects, which provide for Negro participation, have been announced in Atlanta, Chicago, Cincinnati, Cleveland, Detroit, Indianapolis, Montgomery and Nashville These projects will provide about 23,000 rooms for almost 6,175 Negro families, and about 9,500,000 direct man hours of labor.[52]

Given the relatively low expectations blacks had of the New Deal, it is perhaps not surprising that they generally welcomed the entreaties offered by the Roosevelt administration. Rather than viewing the new public-housing program as a bulwark of segregation, they viewed it as an opportunity for thousands of blacks to live in decent and affordable housing, for thousands to earn a living building these developments, and for hundreds more to practice as professionals building and designing these developments.

The black newspaper the *New York Amsterdam News* described the program as a "boon" to Negroes and opined:

The Roosevelt administration has not only gone ahead with the first federal housing program in the history of the nation, for both colored and white wage earners, but it has through Harold L. Ickes, Secretary of the Interior and PWA [Public Works Administration] administrator, refused to permit the construction of housing projects with federal funds for whites unless a similar project was constructed for Negroes wherever it was needed. The health, educational and financial benefits accruing to the Negro citizens of America as a result of the Roosevelt administration's enlightened housing and other building programs are enormous.

Furthermore, the editor argued, "none of the President's programs is of more lasting utility to the Negroes of America than his housing program."[53]

Upon announcement of the public-housing program, the *Pittsburgh Courier* described the program as one "that should be hailed by Negroes, who suffer more than any other citizens from bad housing."[54] The black press proudly reported the role blacks played in planning and developing government-sponsored projects: "The largest housing project in New Jersey for Negroes is being erected in the third ward of Newark. The manager will be a Negro college graduate and he will have Negro assistants in all six buildings."[55] Later headlines from the *Pittsburgh Courier* blared, "FOURTH OF 30,496 HOMES OPEN TO RACE" (see figure 3.2).[56] When it appeared that federal projects *might not* be targeted to black belts, as was initially the case in Philadelphia, the black press strongly objected. Early plans to erect public housing away from the heart of the Negro ghetto led the *Philadelphia Tribune* to level the accusation that the government was "leaving Negro slum dwellers in the slums."[57]

Even the militant and antisegregationist *Chicago Defender* presented segregated public housing as a positive for the race. On the one hand, the *Defender* counseled the race that "the federal housing project being instituted on the South side [*sic*] which is designed as a segregated institution should not be allowed to hamper free access of those who are capable of living in any section of the city where they can pay rent. Those who are prepared must continue to live in all sections of the city where their financial standing, character, and intelligence justifies it, regardless of race, color or creed."[58]

FIGURE 3.2 The black press positively reporting on government housing projects, 1938. *Source: Pittsburg Courier, August 6, 1938.*

On the other hand, the paper could not help but proclaim in a headline: "RACE GETS ONE-FOURTH OF BENEFITS FROM APPROVED FEDERAL HOUSING PROJECTS."[59] This headline is illuminating. Public housing was seen as a benefit more than as a bulwark of segregation.

Newspapers were not the only Negro institutions pushing for public housing. By the 1930s, grassroots organizations were cropping up in northern ghettos to combat discrimination across a number of fronts. They included groups such as the Consolidated Tenants League of Harlem, founded by the followers of Marcus Garvey, Donelan J. Phillips, and Vernal J. Williams, and, more prominently, the National Negro Congress (NNC). These groups were at the time viewed as "militant," with the NNC eventually attracting the FBI's interest.

Groups such as the NNC more than supported public housing: where public housing for Negroes was not being built, they often demanded it, calling for the federal government to undertake "slum clearance in the Negro areas." They pointed to the "more than $50,000,000 that has been expended on modern housing and slum clearance in Negro areas in other cities, [while] Philadelphia, with one of the largest Negro populations in the world, has been entirely neglected. We have come here to find out why this situation exists, and what we can do to remedy it."[60] In Los Angeles, the NNC was described as pushing "determinedly" for the cause of slum clearance and public housing in the Central Avenue district, then the heart of Negro Los Angeles.[61]

The Consolidated Tenants League of Harlem was indignant when initial plans for slum clearance and public housing in New York City overlooked Harlem. The league sent off a flurry of letters to the New York City Housing Authority, the mayor, and President Roosevelt demanding that Harlem be given top priority for new public housing. In mid-May, when New York City Housing Authority chairman Langdon Post still failed to make a commitment, the league announced plans for a rent strike by 30,000 residents and a neighborhood rally, at which Chairman Post, Reverend Adam Clayton Powell (future congressman for Harlem), and other local leaders were expected to speak.[62]

No doubt the abysmal housing conditions experienced by many blacks to that date prioritized the importance of decent housing over combating segregation. *The Negro in Chicago*, published in 1922, reported that among Negroes "there were about as many homes without as with bathrooms."[63]

As late as 1939, a land survey undertaken in Chicago found that only 58 percent of the structures in the Douglas section, which formed the heart of the black belt, had private bathroom facilities; 20 percent of the structures dated prior to 1885, compared to 8 percent for the city as a whole; and 52 percent of the structures either needed major repairs or were unfit for use, in contrast with only 8 percent for the entire city.[64] Madge Headley's survey of fourteen cities in 1928 found that only 33.6 percent of all black renters had inside toilet facilities.[65] Summarizing these and other studies, the Hoover administration's Conference on Home Building and Home Ownership concluded in 1931 that "there is no escaping the general [poor] aspect of this housing" and that only a small minority of housing in the urban North was in good condition.[66]

The desperate housing conditions and lack of jobs confronting most blacks probably contributed to how concerns about segregation now took a back seat. Even W. E. B. Du Bois, perhaps the most prominent agitator against segregation in the early twentieth century, spoke approvingly of segregated housing developments given the desperate need for such housing.[67]

For the common man, debates about integration were probably an abstraction of secondary concern. Although anyone would prefer to have the option to live where he or she wanted, segregated public housing offered an option much superior to segregated substandard housing. If we look to how people voted with their feet, then the nearly 10,000 applications for only 574 units in the Harlem River Houses in 1936 suggests that public housing, however segregated, was a popular proposition.[68]

Those fortunate enough to secure a place felt lucky and upwardly mobile. "We really moved to the projects because at that time Outhwaite homes was viewed to be something really special," one of Outhwaite's residents commented several decades later. "It's hard to believe that now. But it was *the* place to live. In fact, your friends would say 'you moved up in the world.'"[69]

As well they should. The first public-housing developments were far superior to what was available to folks of modest means at that time. As Hall of Fame pitcher Bob Gibson put it, "We moved to the government housing project and even though it was the ghetto, it was a step up in class because we had heat and electricity."[70] The new developments were clean and relatively spacious, with attractive landscaping, and had amenities such as refrigerators that were uncommon for that time.[71] Public housing had none of the stigma associated with late-twentieth-century "projects." Families applying for units were to be screened by both their "financial status" and "social desirability."[72]

Indeed, political support for dedicating one of the first public-housing developments to blacks stemmed in part from the uprising in Harlem on March 19, 1935. Like the study of the conditions leading to the Chicago riot of 1919 and anteceding the National Advisory Commission on Civil Disorder (Kerner Commission) report three decades later, a mayoral investigation of the causes of the disturbance identified poor housing conditions as one of the culprits.[73] The Harlem River Houses would be a balm to help soothe the burning anger that had led to the riot.

The positive tenor of the black community's attitude toward the first public housing does not mean there were no objections to the segregated nature of most developments. Not surprisingly, the NAACP, which remained "opposed to the principle and the practice of enforced segregation of human beings on the basis of race and color," also opposed the idea of segregated public-housing developments.[74] The Cleveland Committee, an interracial civic group in Cleveland, accused the federal government of segregating Cleveland developments by race, a charge the federal government denied.[75]

But the benefits encapsulated by the new public housing posed a dilemma. Consider that in 1942 the *Pittsburgh Courier* celebrated the fact that Sojourner Truth Homes, at one time targeted for white occupancy, were reserved for blacks after strong and organized protests from the black community,[76] yet only four years earlier the same paper had editorialized against public housing in a remarkably prescient piece:

It has long been apparent this is the purpose of Negro housing projects. As a general rule white people are barred from them while Negroes cannot usually rent apartments in buildings in so-called white neighborhoods. Negroes themselves are partly responsible for this condition because they have registered no strong and nationwide complaint against it. They have been hypnotized by eight or ten housing projects "exclusively for Negroes" and failed to note what this portended for the future. Segregation begets more segregation. First it was the all-Negro housing projects. Now it is the effective efforts of the FHA to keep Negroes living where prejudiced white folks think they ought to live. What will it be tomorrow if we continue to play ostrich?[77]

The *Courier* editorial confirms what the earlier evidence suggests—some Negroes clearly supported and even demanded segregated public housing. Was this simply a matter of realpolitik on the part of the race, settling for what was available? Whether blacks could have substantially altered the federal government's policies in the 1930s is debatable. Blacks had little success getting the federal government to pass antilynching legislation to stop that egregiously horrific practice, so there was even less chance that they could stop segregated public housing or discriminatory mortgage underwriting standards. As noted earlier, the relative ineffectualness of Negro protest had persuaded W. E. B. Du Bois, the once preeminent icon of militant integrationism, to rethink his stance on segregation.

To interpret the Negroes' enthusiastic response to segregated public housing as merely practical resignation to the racist times they lived in, however, would be a misreading. First, the 1930s were hardly a time when Negroes resigned themselves to accept segregation. The Great Depression caused more than abject suffering; it also made Negroes more receptive to leftist ideas and spurred many toward radical thought and active confrontation. It was during these times that militant grassroots groups such as the Consolidated Tenants League of Harlem and the NNC came into being.[78] Negro activists, including those in the NNC, organized dozens of "Don't Buy Where You Can't Work" campaigns in the 1930s to knock down Jim Crow in retail employment in the North. Tenants groups such as the Consolidated Tenants League of Harlem organized "rent strikes" whereby tenants would withhold rent until their landlord made repairs or stopped overcharging tenants for rent. This was the time when the "politics of respectability," whereby a refined "Talented Tenth" would advocate on behalf of the race, often took a back seat to "on the street" protests with picket lines and marches that included the working class.[79] Indeed, the entire civil rights movement moved left and became more confrontational during this time.[80]

Nor was black protest limited to small local matters such as being able to work in the local Woolworth's or not having to pay their landlords exorbitant rents. At the first NNC convention in February 1936, resolutions were passed against sundry injustices, including Italy's invasion of Ethiopia, laws that prevented Negros from voting in the South, antisedition laws, and segregated public schools, as well as resolutions encouraging the race to support black businesses and the recently unionized Brotherhood of Sleeping Car Porters.[81] Moreover, the resolutions that were passed show many activists within the race were aware of various matters affecting Negroes and were willing to go on record to speak out on these issues. Of note, however, the segregation of public housing that was being built by the federal government did not evoke a resolution against it.

Indeed, race leaders were willing to take their grievances to the highest office in the land. In 1940, civil rights leaders Walter White, T. Arnold Hill, and A. Philip Randolph requested and received an audience with President Roosevelt, demanding the desegregation of the military and a cessation in discrimination in military-procurement projects. Failing to secure significant action on the part of the Roosevelt administration, Randolph organized a March on Washington movement calling on Negroes to apply "pressure, more pressure and still more pressure" to secure their rights. The mobilization of thousands of Negroes to march on Washington, DC, in protest of discrimination in the armed forces and defense industries would be one means of applying pressure against discrimination. Although the march was called off and the armed forces would remain segregated until 1948, Randolph's threat did persuade President Roosevelt to issue Executive Order 8802, which forbade discrimination on the basis of "race, creed, color or national origin" by defense contractors and created the Committee on Fair Employment Practices, which served to ensure compliance with the order.

For our purposes here, more important than the successes of the aborted March on Washington were Negro mobilization and the threat to take action. By the early 1940s, Negroes were willing to take mass action to push the federal government to change discriminatory practices in one of its oldest and most important institutions—the military. The lack of vociferous protest against segregated public housing built in the ghetto thus speaks volumes.

Finally, we might also consider how the race reacted to the segregation of public schools in northern cities. Although the South has received the most notoriety for school segregation, schools in the North, too, were often segregated de facto if not de jure. Like public housing, schools represented important resources for the race as a community asset, a place to meet, education for black children, and professional jobs for colored teachers and principals. The reaction to Jim Crow schools in the North is thus instructive.

The resources embodied in segregated public schools and the idea that black teachers would better serve the interests of Negro students led many Negroes to prefer segregated schools. The NAACP often found little local support among Negroes when challenging specific instances of school segregation. Indeed, there were instances of Negro parents petitioning for school boards to establish separate schools. Negro teachers and principals, who typically had no chance of being hired in integrated schools, naturally had a vested interest in the maintenance of separate schools. In this way, Negroes' reaction to segregated public housing—enthusiastic—was akin to their reaction to segregated schools in the North.

But unlike the situation for public housing, against which protest was virtually absent, there were protests and work against school segregation, ranging from the activities of the national office of NAACP to the editorial columns of black newspapers to the protests of local parents' groups. In his book *Jim Crow Moves North*, the historian Davison Douglas references sixteen communities outside the South where Negro parents and their children held school boycotts as a means of protesting segregated schools during the 1920s and 1930s.[82] In Plainsboro, New Jersey, Negro parents successfully petitioned to halt the development of a separate Negro school.[83] One news article described colored citizens as "waging a bitter fight" and published pictures juxtaposing a dilapidated school for Negroes and a modern school for whites to underscore the injustice of an attempt to establish segregated schools in Berwyn, Pennsylvania. This same attempt to establish Jim Crow schools galvanized 1,200 colored citizens to stage a protest against school segregation.[84] In an editorial in June 1930, the *Pittsburgh Courier* lauded the integrated New York school system, where the Negro, "all in all, gets the same break as the Nordic," and pointed to the inferiority of the segregated schools in Washington, DC, despite the higher number of Negro teachers and principals there.[85] An editorial in the *Baltimore Afro-American* that same year likened Negroes in favor a separate schools to "slaves who thought slavery best." It described Negroes who fought the establishment of segregated schools in Indianapolis as "the better forces of the race" in contrast to the "short-sighted" and mere "job seeking" Negroes.[86]

Segregated schools thus stirred controversy within the race. Some saw advantages in segregation, whereas others spoke out and acted forcefully against such separation. Likewise, some Negros felt that segregated public housing provided concrete benefits to the race, whereas other contemporary observers noted that it introduced the stain of segregation to yet another sphere of public life. Notably absent but certainly conceivable, however, was a vociferous protest against segregated public housing.

The federal government's interventions in the housing market during the Great Depression thus presented blacks with a dilemma. Although they were opposed to segregation, both the mortgage insurance programs and the public-housing programs offered them something heretofore unthinkable: tangible benefits from the government for Negroes. Even if the government mortgage insurance programs were discriminatory, this was no different than what took place in the private mortgage market. Moreover, during the depths of the Depression, mere survival took precedence over concerns about segregation. For a race that was used to government indifference, brand-new housing allocated specifically for them was not something to scoff at. Indeed, the segregated nature of the first public housing played the ironic role of ensuring that the race got its due. Du Bois put the dilemma in the starkest of terms:

Out beyond me, where I write, lies a slum. . . . I have seen this slum now and again for thirty years: Its drab and crowded houses its mud, dust and unpaved streets; its lack of water, light and sewage; its crowded and unpoliced gloom. Just now it seems certain, that the United States Government is going to spend $2,000,000 to erase this slum from the face of the earth, and put in place, beautiful, simple clean homes, for poor colored people, with all modern conveniences. This is Segregation. It is Segregation by the United States Government. The homes are going to be for Negroes and only for Negroes; and yet I am a strong advocate for this development. . . . I take what I can get.[87]

The dilemma confronting Du Bois in 1934 would continue to haunt the race in the post–World War II era. For several reasons, however, the "half a loaf" offered by the federal government in the 1930s came to be seen more like quarter of a loaf as time progressed.

Writing seventy-three years ago, the sociologists St. Clair Drake and Horace Cayton aptly took measure of this paradox: "Although Negroes know that residential segregation has implications of inequality and inferiority—that it implies subordination—they do not oppose residential segregation with the same vigor that they display in attacking the job ceiling."[88] Perhaps because the sting of segregation was not as sharp when it came to neighborhoods as when it came to water fountains, public transportation, or the vote, or perhaps because the abject suffering during the Great Depression took precedence over concerns about segregation, Negroes reacted ambivalently while the federal government reinforced segregated spaces that have over time proved more durable than much of the segregation in the Jim Crow South.

The Great Depression ended the era of the New Negro, when the ghetto was a haven for blacks to advance their individual interests and the collective interests of the race. Concerns for survival crowded out other aspirations. But extreme hardship was common everywhere, so in this regard the ghetto was not particularly unique.

But the Great Depression era would still prove pivotal for shaping the role the ghetto would play as a haven or a hell in ensuing decades, for it was during this era that the federal government's resources came to bear on patterns of ghettoization, setting the mold for durable patterns of inequality that persist to this day. Blacks' reactions to the federal imprimatur, especially toward public housing, was at times celebratory—revealing the extent to which blacks had come to identify with the ghetto. Although the ghetto was not a haven in the sense of providing opportunity during the Depression, many saw it as an extension of the race and something to take pride in—even if it meant segregation, as was the case with public housing.

But just as the pre–Great Migration and New Negro eras were ended by epochal events, the Depression era, too, would end abruptly, this time due to actions around the globe.

Chapter Four

WORLD WAR II AND THE AFTERMATH

The Ghetto Diverges

World War II transformed the world, ushering in a new world order, and the ghetto was not immune to the epochal changes under way. Most significantly, the war triggered an even bigger wave of migration from the South to the ghettos of the North. Millions of Negroes migrated north, dwarfing the numbers that had migrated previously.

This second wave of migrants transformed American cities more dramatically than the previous one. The sheer number of migrants ensured this. Much larger swaths of the America's urban centers came to be included in the ghetto. The number of migrants meant that institutional and political power in urban America would be transformed. Blacks would begin to wield unprecedented power in the nation's largest cities. In many ways, the renewed migration of blacks to the ghettos of the North heralded the return of the ghetto as a haven for the race after the suspension of that role during the Great Depression. It was a place where blacks flocked to advance themselves and in doing so advanced the interests of the race as well.

But the ghetto was increasingly a hell as well. The offspring of the first wave of migrants came of age in the post–World War II era, and for these blacks the Jim Crow South was not their frame of reference. They looked around and saw whites moving into spacious suburban homes. To them, the ghetto, with its severe overcrowding and second-rate housing, was anything but a city on a hill. It was a hell that they were only too eager to escape.

This chapter chronicles the ghetto's continuing role as a haven for the millions of blacks fleeing the Jim Crow South. But it also tells how the ghetto's role as a city on a hill, an emblem of what the race could achieve, was eventually superseded by a much less promising role—as an underworld overcrowded, squalid, and full of despair.

A HAVEN ONCE MORE

After laying dormant during the Great Depression, the forces that pulled blacks out of the South reemerged during World War II. The war created a voracious appetite for able-bodied men and women to fight overseas, support the troops, and produce the hardware that made the United States the "arsenal of democracy." Manufacturing was still concentrated outside of the South, so the industrial centers of the North beckoned once again, as they had during World War I.

Southern blacks heeded the call in droves. In Baltimore, it was estimated that migrants were coming at a rate of 50 per day.[1] Detroit was described as receiving 1,200 to 1,400 migrants each week, the majority of them Negro. San Francisco witnessed an increase in its Negro population from 5,000 to 50,000 in a few short years. Seattle's Negro population tripled in a few years, and Los Angeles saw its Negro population increase 138 percent in a few months.[2] The second wave of migration would come to dwarf the World War I era migration that had preceded it. Whereas approximately 1.5 million Negroes migrated North from 1915 to 1940, it is estimated that roughly 4.5 million migrated between 1940 and 1970.[3] Approximately one in four of rural southern Negroes migrated to the urban North during the 1940s, and the South's share of the country's Negro population declined from 77 percent to 68 percent during this same time.[4]

Aside from differences in the size of the second wave of migration set in motion by World War II, this wave also differed in the destinations chosen by the migrants. As the figures quoted at the beginning of this section suggest, West Coast cities now figured prominently as destinations for southern migrants. Figure 4.1 depicts the dramatic rise in the number of southerners residing both outside the South and on the Pacific Coast (i.e., California, Oregon, and Washington).

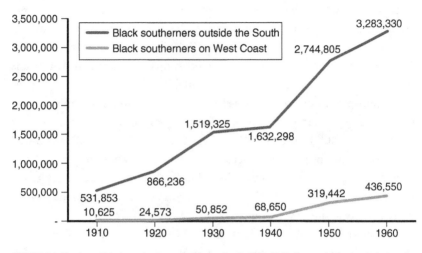

FIGURE 4.1 Number of black southerners outside the South, 1910–1960. *Source:* Author's tabulation of Integrated Public Use Microdata (Ruggles et al. 2010).

The arrival of Negroes on the West Coast in large numbers at first seemed to portend a different type of race relations and consequently different residential patterns as well. As the black sociologist Horace Cayton observed in 1943, in many West Coast cities there were "no segregated Negro areas," and the "race relations pattern [was] very liberal."[5] A report from the YWCA noted that before the war Negroes tended to be concentrated in certain neighborhoods in cities on the coast, such as the Fillmore District in San Francisco. Nevertheless, sizable numbers of whites, Filipinos, Japanese, and Chinese also lived in Fillmore.[6] Historians also note a lack of large-scale ghettos on the West Coast prior to the war.[7] Race relations there compared favorably to relations found in the rest of the country. Indeed, a survey of Negro residents who resided in Portland and Seattle prior to the war described places where "discrimination and prejudice existed" but went "unnoticed" or where race relations were generally "good" and "above average" compared to relations in northern cities.[8] The historian Josh Sides quotes a migrant to Los Angeles in the 1920s describing black southerners' view of the city: "It was a land of golden opportunities—orange groves and beautiful beaches—and life was all a matter of milk and honey."[9]

Although West Coast cities may have lacked the virulent racism of the South or of the big-city ghettos back east, they were hardly havens for interracial equality. The same survey quoted earlier noted that blacks were confined to the most menial positions with few opportunities to move up or into more skilled and remunerative jobs.[10] Sides also points out that "although housing and educational opportunities for African Americans in Los Angeles were superior to those available to blacks in other major cities, employment opportunities were not." He goes so far as to argue that black Angelenos had fewer opportunities to work in manufacturing than blacks back east.[11] In the pre–World War II era, racism was alive and well in the West, but the small numbers of blacks there meant they were not perceived as much of a threat by whites. Race relations were certainly much better than they were in the South. The racism in the West perhaps seemed more genteel and had yet to erupt into race riots.

Residential segregation patterns in West Coast cities on the eve of World War II reflect the nature of race relations at that time. Table 4.1 shows that with the exception of Portland in Multnomah County, in the counties encompassing Los Angeles, Oakland, San Francisco, and Seattle blacks experienced levels of segregation considered high as measured by the dissimilarity index (i.e., higher than 0.60). This pattern belies the notion that blacks lived interspersed with whites on the West Coast as if color did not matter and also dispels the view of the West as some type of racial nirvana. But the isolation indices, which tell us the average percentage of blacks in the census tracts where the typical black lived, are moderate or low, reflecting the lack of ghettos like those that had emerged in eastern cities by this

TABLE 4.1
Residential Segregation in West Coast Cities

County	1940			1960		
	Percentage of Blacks in Total Population	Dissimilarity Index	Isolation Index	Percentage of Blacks in Total Population	Dissimilarity Index	Isolation Index
Los Angeles	2.6	0.71	0.48	7.6	0.80	0.65
Alameda (Oakland)	2.6	0.64	0.20	0.12	0.70	0.58
Multnomah (Portland)	0.01	0.55	0.04	3.0	0.65	0.42
San Francisco	0.01	0.74	0.07	10.0	0.59	0.41
King (Seattle)	1.0	0.69	0.10	3.0	0.71	0.43

Source: Author's tabulation of 1940 U.S. census data available on Social Explorer.

time. The small number of blacks in western cities precluded the development of such ghettos. Moreover, many western cities had large numbers of other nonwhites (e.g., Chinese, Japanese, and Mexicans) that were also often excluded from white neighborhoods and tended to share residential space with blacks. In many ways, patterns of ghettoization on the West Coast prior to World War II resembled those on the East Coast and the Midwest prior to World War I. Blacks were segregated, but their small numbers meant they typically did not form the majority group of the neighborhoods in which they resided.

The arrival of tens of thousands of blacks during and after the war changed the dynamics of race relations on the West Coast. Blacks were now more visible and began competing with whites for a broader range of jobs. Race relations became more fraught as blacks advanced economically, gaining a toehold in industries and occupations formerly denied to them. Incidences of racial violence and blatant discrimination became more noticeable. Restrictive covenants, which appear to have been unpopular prior to the war, were adopted more widely. In 1944, the sociologist Charles S. Johnson and his colleagues reported some civic leaders openly advocating for increased residential segregation as a way of ameliorating racial tensions in San Francisco.[12] In 1947, the black writer Chester Himes published the semiautographical novel *If He Hollers Let Him Go*, based on his experiences in Los Angeles during the war. The protagonist, a skilled shipyard worker, finds racism omnipresent. Racism haunts his job, where he is treated unfairly and forced to endure being called a nigger by a white coworker. It is on the street, where police harass him when he is driving in white parts of town. And it rears its head when he eats in a nice restaurant but is forced to sit by the kitchen and is told never to patronize the restaurant again.[13]

Increasing discrimination in housing and a tendency for recent migrants to locate near other blacks and black institutions led to a "filling in" of neighborhoods where blacks were overrepresented prior to the war. In many West Coast cities, blacks took over the "Little Tokyos" that were empty due to the forcible internment of Japanese Americans during the war. In due time, West Coast Cities saw the emergence of segregated black neighborhoods, such as Albina in Portland, East Oakland, the Fillmore District in San Francisco, and Watts in Los Angeles, which resembled patterns of ghettoization experienced in the East. Table 4.1 shows how the isolation indices increased dramatically on the West Coast between 1940 and 1960. The ghetto patterns evinced on the East Coast would arise on the West as well, albeit with some differences—notably, the spatial isolation on the West Coast was never as intense as it was on the East Coast. Moreover, as we shall see in later chapters, West Coast ghettos have proved less durable due to immigration and gentrification. But during the middle decades of the twentieth century, ghettoization on the West Coast seemed to proceed in a manner that mirrored what was taking place in the older cities of the Northeast and Midwest.

Aside from the West Coast, a broader range of cities in the United States experienced an influx of southern migrants during the second wave of migration. Table 4.2 illustrates the number of cities that witnessed an increase of at least 10,000 in their population of Negro southerners between 1910 and 1930 and then between 1940 and 1960. A much larger number of cities experienced a significant influx of southern migrants by that metric.

TABLE 4.2
Increase in Numbers of Black Southern Migrants

1910–1930		1940–1960	
Baltimore	25,496	Baltimore	43,823
Chicago	123,679	Boston	13,312
Cincinnati	20,402	Buffalo	22,950
Cleveland	46,737	Chicago	179,394
Detroit	78,768	Cleveland	61,786
Los Angeles	25,293	Dayton	11,366
New York City	102,398	Detroit	136,923
Philadelphia	87,014	Flint	13,739
Pittsburgh	21,761	Gary	20,980
St. Louis	16,302	Los Angeles	128,780
Washington, DC	27,627	Milwaukee	26,020
		New York City	150,133
		Newark	24,763
		Oakland	36,880
		Philadelphia	65,631
		Rochester	10,420
		St. Louis	23,090
		San Francisco	29,160
		Seattle	10,860
		Washington, DC	63,098

Source: Author's tabulation of Integrated Public Use Microdata provided in Ruggles et al. 2010.

Note: The numbers presented here should be considered rough approximations of migration during certain years. The U.S. Census Bureau did not collect migration data in these years, so place of birth has to be used to infer migration. When city-level changes in migration are examined, however, this approach does not allow a distinction to be made between recent southern migrants and those who were born in the South but migrated between northern cities. Hence, the need for caution may exist when interpreting the results.

Patterns of ghettoization thus spread across a larger number of regions and cities in the country. Ghettoization, which had become a feature peculiar to big cities in the Midwest and Northeast, came to characterize the largest cities outside the South.

By "voting with their feet," the millions of migrants who streamed into the urban North and West after World War II showed the ghetto had returned to its role as a haven for the race. The segregated living environments that would await the migrants upon their arrival were no secret. By World War II, "Bronzeville" and "Harlem" were household names in black America. Most would have anticipated moving into the existing ghettos, such as these two in Chicago and in New York, or into budding ones that were taking shape in cities such as Buffalo, New York, and Gary, Indiana. For these new migrants, the ghetto would be a starting point, a place to become acquainted with their new environs. For example, chronicling three Negroes' flight from a potential lynching, the journalist Isabel Wilkerson describes how they "had to figure out where they knew somebody up North and the most direct route to wherever people they knew were located." Another migrant "landed in Milwaukee because her sister had migrated there."[14] Indeed, as figure 4.2 shows, by 1950 recent migrants from the South

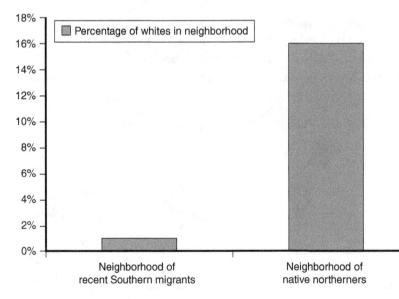

FIGURE 4.2 Percentage of whites in neighborhoods where blacks lived in 1950. *Source*: Author's tabulation of Integrated Public Use Microdata (Ruggles et al. 2010).

had significantly fewer white neighbors than blacks who were born in the North. Both recent migrants from the South and Negro northerners lived in neighborhoods relatively devoid of whites. Only 1 percent and 16 percent, respectively, of the neighbors of recent migrants from the South and of Negro northerners were white. This substantial difference suggests that recent migrants had more of a need to locate in the ghetto. Yet still they came.

The new migrants' motives were in many ways similar to the motives of those who had come a generation earlier, during and after World War I. Economic opportunity was a primary driver. Migrants just arriving in Baltimore told a news reporter in 1943 that they came for "big pay," "higher wages," and opportunities to "send money back home."[15] Although it was during World War II that the South began its long climb toward economic parity with the North, during the war and its immediate aftermath much of the South remained a relative economic backwater. World War II created an unquenchable thirst for manpower for the war industries, but much of the nation's manufacturing was outside the South, which facilitated the mass migration. Nor did the arrival of V-J Day stem the tide of Negroes pouring out of the South. When the war ended, Negroes, unlike many whites, refused to return to the South.[16]

For Negroes, economic opportunities were simply much greater outside the South than within it. Figure 4.3 makes clear the stark choice facing would-be black migrants. Census data on occupational prestige as measured by the Socioeconomic Indicator and average earnings by occupation show southern migrants were in significantly more prestigious and remunerative

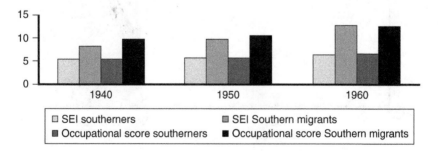

FIGURE 4.3 Comparison of blacks' occupational status in the North and the South, 1940–1960.
Source: Author's tabulation of Integrated Public Use Microdata (Ruggles et al. 2010).

occupations than their brethren who remained in the South. If anything, the gap in occupational earnings widened slightly between 1940 and 1960.

Moreover, the economists James Smith and Finis Welch found that southern black migration to northern cities increased black–white male wage ratios by 11 to 19 percent between 1940 and 1980.[17]

If the pull of better jobs were not enough, the mechanization of southern agriculture after the war provided an additional shove to migrants.[18] As one journalist wrote at the time, "The introduction of new farming machines and modern methods of scientific agriculture are rapidly cutting down the need for manpower. Tractors are taking the places of plows and mules. Cotton pickers are being laid off steadily because machines are more efficient. Since most of the Southern, colored people are farmers, they do not find it easy to survive on the plantations. They are leaving Dixie in droves."[19]

Indeed, some of the news reports in the late 1950s described the migrants as being "forced" to leave even though many preferred to stay put.[20] Hard numbers back up these impressionistic accounts. Smith and Welch report that in 1950 more than 90 percent of all cotton was picked by hand, but a mere twelve years later this number had dropped to less than 30 percent. The proportion of southern black males employed in agriculture dropped from 29.7 percent in 1950 to 8.5 percent in 1970.[21] Thus, in the 1950s the economic factors driving the migration may have been more "push" than "pull," but either way millions continued to leave the South.

Economic circumstances were not the only motives for the renewed migration, however. For some migrants, it might be more accurate to say that economic opportunities facilitated their acting on other more pressing reasons for leaving the South. Despite American rhetoric about fighting a war for freedom and democracy and subsequent Cold War propaganda about America leading the "free world," the South remained the land of Jim Crow. Some migrants left literally a few steps ahead of a lynch mob. Migrants preferred the North, where "a man is a man and can at least say what he thinks."[22] So strong was their antipathy for the southern caste system that one migrant preferred to "wash dishes in New York than be Superintendent of Schools in Anniston [Alabama]."[23] A news reporter quoted migrants during the war as wanting to escape a "hedged in" existence and as seeking "more freedom and to be able to vote."[24]

The ability to exercise one's constitutional right to vote was a lure for many migrants and a boon to the race. As was the case with the first wave

of the Great Migration, increasing numbers translated into increased political representation. In 1950, the *Afro-American* reported the election of
thirty-five black state legislators across the country, all outside the South.
Ghettoization continued to have the unintended consequence of giving
blacks a political voice.

By the late 1950s in Chicago, Detroit, New York City, and Philadelphia,
blacks translated their demographic growth into political power, each city
sending a black congressman to Washington. William Dawson, Charles
Diggs Jr., Robert N. C. Nix, and Adam Clayton Powell Jr. represented the
ghettos of the South Side of Chicago, the East Side of Detroit, North Philadelphia, and Harlem, respectively. Although these congressmen ostensibly
represented the interests of the residents in their districts, as black congressmen they represented the interests of the entire race. Black newspapers in
other cities referred to them as "our" congressmen and duly noted their
comings and goings and how they voted on pressing race issues. They were
expected to be and indeed were champions for the race.[25] Fred Poindexter
wrote a letter to the *Chicago Defender* in 1955 underscoring this very point:

This article may prove distasteful to some Negroes, but they cannot deny its truth.

I am very proud of *our congressmen* in Washington—Dawson of Chicago, Diggs
of Detroit, and Powell of New York.

The point I want to make is that these officials were elected to their office from
predominantly Negro areas. Our power and our political strength come from living together.[26]

Thus, southern migrants continued to stream into the ghettos of the North.
For them, the ghetto was still a promised land, a place where they could
walk with dignity, earn a better living, or simply survive. And as they poured
into the existing black belts, their numbers swelled the political power of
the race.

Of course, by the postwar era it was clear that the ghetto was no unal-
loyed promised land for all blacks. The steady stream of migrants into
northern ghettos led, as we shall see later, to severe overcrowding. Moreover, the impacts of redlining were being felt, starving the ghetto of the requisite capital to upgrade the physical structures there. Perhaps not surprisingly, the specter of slum clearance haunted many ghetto neighborhoods,
for they were often the most dilapidated and overcrowded neighborhoods

in northern cities. But, as discussed in the next section, Negroes' reaction to slum clearance, later referred to as "urban renewal," was complex and in some ways contradictory, reflecting diverse interests and viewpoints. The urban-renewal program of the postwar era thus provides a prism through which to see how the ghetto continued to be both a haven and a hell.

URBAN RENEWAL, NEGRO REMOVAL

Slum clearance, or what came to be known as "urban renewal," ostensibly replaced "slum" housing with affordable and decent housing. With the U.S. Housing Act of 1949, urban renewal entered its halcyon days. In subsequent decades, hundreds of thousands of "slum" housing units would be demolished and replaced with public housing, middle-income developments, and sundry other projects. As we saw in chapter 3, Negroes often celebrated slum clearance and viewed the public housing built on cleared sites as a boon to the race. In the postwar era, however, urban renewal proved a contentious policy dividing the race into three factions. The first two factions sought to preserve and protect the ghetto but differed on whether urban renewal could be instrumental to that end. The third faction saw the ghetto as an affront to American values that should be broken up as soon as possible, and, for them, urban renewal offered an opportunity to do just that.

Many of those who sought to preserve and protect the ghetto increasingly viewed urban renewal as a threat to their community. Indeed, as early as 1938 the *Baltimore Afro-American* reported "grumbling" over a proposed slum-clearance project in Northwest Baltimore by those who had "sentimental" attachment to their homes and had invested in their properties and by business owners who feared the loss of their clientele. Just as importantly, many in the proposed area did not view the entire area as a slum.[27] And in 1941 Negro businessmen in Cleveland also feared that their businesses, built up through hard-earned struggle, could not be reestablished elsewhere once they were displaced.[28]

By the late 1940s and into the 1950s, such "grumblings" would become commonplace. Rather than a help, slum clearance was seen as a hindrance. Rather than seeing the ghetto as merely a slum to be cleared, the people in this group saw it as a place they had invested in, developed relationships in, and wanted to preserve—a haven. Opposition to a slum-clearance project in St. Louis in 1948 epitomized the growing resistance. Spearheaded by the St. Louis Branch of the NAACP, opponents voiced concerns similar to those described a decade earlier in the *Baltimore Afro-American*. Homeowners objected that they would lose their hard-earned properties and attacked the project because they felt that "the heart and foundation of the colored population of the city," with "prominent colored doctors, lawyers, insurance offices, photographers, dentists, hotels and the Pine Street YMCA" as well as religious institutions, would be destroyed.[29]

In Indianapolis, a representative of the Negro Homeowners League summed up the fears of Negro property owners: "The plan is a 'big steal' and if carried out the owners would suffer irreparably in having to give up houses they had acquired at great sacrifice over the years. Restrictive covenants would make it practically impossible to relocate elsewhere, especially in view of the housing shortage."[30]

Indeed, in many of these so-called blighted areas lived Negroes who had overcome tremendous obstacles to become homeowners. These homeowners feared that they would not be justly compensated for their homes, that banks would be reluctant to finance their purchasing of another home, and that given the pervasiveness of housing discrimination they would not be able to find another home to purchase.[31] In Bedford-Stuyvesant, it was argued, "it has been a struggle for the people who were able to accumulate small savings over a period of years. They invested their life time savings in the homes they now own. These same people have deprived themselves of so many of the necessary things vital to healthful living, because of their inability to obtain loans to make necessary repairs on their home." To add insult to injury, their homes were now designated slums and slated for clearance. Illustrating the subjectivity of the term *slum*, another resident argued that "present plans involve the destruction of hundreds of perfectly sound homes." The Brower Park Civic Association opposed this approach, calling for authorities to "assist the small homeowner to improve his property."[32] Many of the property owners and their advocates certainly took the stance that theirs was not property in need of condemnation.[33]

Aside from business and property owners, poor renters also had reason for concern. Although substandard housing was often deplorable, it was better than homelessness. Those living in the slums were not guaranteed admission to the new housing. Quite often, those displaced did not qualify for the new housing for either economic or "moral" reasons. This was the case of a Harlem housewife, who in reaction to a proposed slum-clearance project admitted that "a new project will be nice but I can't see how it will help this community. Where are the people that are living in the houses going? I was turned down five years ago from a project because my daughter wasn't married."[34] Thus, a family's home was being demolished because of the putative horrors of their living in inadequate housing, yet the family might be ineligible for the new and improved housing and condemned to move into a slum elsewhere or be homeless!

Even the prospect of finding housing in another slum could be daunting. As noted earlier, the housing shortage reached emergency proportions after World War II. A Negro newspaper editorialized: "At the outset urban development plans were welcomed by Negro business and community leaders." But as time went on, doubts arose: "What provisions will be made for low wage and middle income tenants whose incomes may deny then tenancy in their redeveloped neighborhoods? What provisions will be made to relocate the thousands of Negro families 'cleared' from their home? Will they be forced into the already over-crowded ghettos? What consideration will be given uprooted churches, businessmen and property owners?"[35]

Chicago alderman William Harvey illustrated the conflict between the need for new housing and the tragedy of displacement when he described five families living in a building *with no windows* that was slated for clearance. Yet even with demolition imminent, the families had no place to go.[36] Windowless buildings were out of date by the 1950s, but with Negroes hemmed into Chicago's already overcrowded black belt, where could these families go? Indeed, Harvey cited the displacement of "too many people" as a reason for his long-standing opposition to the development of public housing on slum-clearance sites.[37]

Many "slums" or "blighted" areas were only such in the eye of the developer or planner, who ignored the social relationships in these neighborhoods and who judged the housing there from the vantage point of someone with a full range of housing options in the larger city. Old neighborhoods with flocks of people hanging outside, in particular the "wrong" kind of people, were often seen as little more than slums regardless of how satisfied the inhabitants or cohesive the community may have been.[38]

But more than pragmatic concerns over displacement motivated the Negro debate over slum clearance. There were those Negroes with a vested interest in the ghetto as well as those who saw the ghetto in nationalist terms. For black politicians who were voted into office by ghetto-dwellers,

black businessmen who profited from a captive clientele, and black clergy-
men who benefitted from having their congregants nearby, the ghetto was
the basis of their livelihood. The social reformer George B. Nesbitt quoted
a Chicago politician to make this point: "Sure I'm against covenants. They
are criminal. But I don't want Negroes moving all over town. I just want to
add little pieces to the Black Belt."[39]

Black real estate interests also stood to lose from dismantling the ghetto
via slum clearance. Removing the walls of the ghetto would mean increased
competition and the end of the exorbitant rents landlord could charge their
tenants. A few of these interests were large real estate companies that controlled multiple properties. A greater number of these interests were those
who owned two to four family homes and used the extra income from rent
to help pay their own mortgage.

Beyond the self-interest of those who were obviously tied to the ghetto
was an undercurrent of what the historian Andrew Wiese refers to as "ter-
ritorial nationalism."[40] Ghettoization not only confined blacks to certain
spaces but fostered ethnocentrism and a reflexive defensive posture not to
cede the ghetto to whites. This confinement was dynamic as the ghetto's
boundaries spread through the first half of the twentieth century. The dynamism of the ghetto was due to Negroes having to resort to all means short
of physical force to acquire additional space: subterfuge, with Negroes having a white person buy property for them; the will to stand up to bombing
and riots; and almost always the acceptance of having to pay more than the
whites who previously occupied the housing that was now considered part
of the ghetto. In this sense, the acquisition of space that would become the
ghetto was hard-earned.

Given the "battles" Negroes undertook to carve out the ghetto, or, as
George B. Nesbitt put it, the compulsion "to take space" from whites,[41] it is
perhaps not surprising that the race was suspicious of whites' desires to take
back these spaces. Nesbitt referred to this suspicion as the "legendary fear
of a day of wholesale ejectment" and a fear of the "conspiracy."[42] This was
a long-standing fear. As early as 1914, Du Bois had called the race's attention to an actual conspiracy by white real estate interests in Harlem, dis-
cussing "several sections to which they [the coloreds] could be removed that
afford adequate housing facilities equal if not better than those which they
now enjoy."[43] And in 1930 a Negro realtor predicted Harlem's passing as a

Negro mecca due to the neighborhood's convenient location.[44] In 1951, Harlem resident Arthur Madison wrote a poignant letter encapsulating the fears and interpretations of slum clearance:

Sir: Did you know that a most treacherous thing is happening here in Harlem? Has it occurred to you that we are gradually losing our cherished Harlem?

For 50 years and at great sacrifice and suffering, Afro-Americans largely from the South and West Indies, have given their life-blood and hard-earned money to establish a decent community for themselves and posterity. Overcoming strenuous opposition from every source, they now own valuable homes, churches, businesses, fraternities and social organizations in this world famous area called Harlem. Only because of rigid determination and perseverance has our community produced thousands of home owners[;] the refusal of mortgages, the extraction of exorbitant interest rates, the preying of loan sharks did not stop our onward march.

Now we are building financial institutions. . . . But lo: What it has taken us 50 long hard years to establish may be destroyed with a single, vicious prejudiced and damnable blow. Clothed in sheep's clothing and called community development, the total results will be a death blow to our financial, political and social gains.

Now under the guise of converting the area until beautiful buildings, all of our efforts and those of our forebears are to be wiped out by the City of New York in the name of "slum clearance." Why is the City of New York so suddenly solicitous of Harlem? Why? It's a military secret. I know the answer.[45]

Five years later another Harlem resident said in reaction to another proposed slum-clearance plan, "I can't see how it will help any. It looks like they are trying to run Negroes out of Harlem."[46]

These fears went beyond practical concerns about households being displaced without suitable replacement housing being available or being inconvenienced by the disruptions of clearance and rebuilding. Rather, the ghetto was seen as something "belonging" to Negroes, something whites aimed to take from them. This space had real meaning and value. The ghetto was a haven to be protected.

Of course, there were many Negroes who were both not eager to see the ghetto dismantled *and* supported slum clearance. To them, the program represented an opportunity to replace the deplorable housing that bedeviled many ghetto communities. The same St. Louis project opposed by the local NAACP in 1948 was supported by the local Urban League office, which thought it was urgent to replace the "90% of area that is blighted."[47] In many ghettos, conditions were truly bad, by almost any standard.

Consider conditions in the Hill District of Pittsburgh, where folks "live in a filthy, damp, two-room apartment and have to bathe in a wash tub, since there is no bathroom," where "sixty-four people share one bathroom," and where 6,000 of 11,500 units were substandard, lacking facilities such as a bathroom and hot and cold running water.[48] There was no question that housing like this and like what could be found across the black belts of the North needed to be replaced or upgraded. Many of these units were substandard in a way, however, that made upgrading or renovation impractical. Rooms sometimes lacked windows and ventilation, or the units as a whole lacked indoor plumbing or cooking facilities. In the early years of the urban-renewal program, the black press routinely celebrated the replacement of slums with new housing. The *Philadelphia Tribune* described one slum-clearance project in Philadelphia as "transforming a notorious dilapidated eyesore into a bright, modern living area."[49] In New York City, the Riverton housing development sponsored by the Metropolitan Insurance Company, which was the segregated version of Stuyvesant Town built downtown, was described as a "Harlem showpiece" replacing "old fashioned, run-down tenement houses and ramshackle garages." The new development, where "three of every four of the Riverton tenants own TV sets and more than 60 percent own cars," "disproved that Negro tenants destroy property and are poor rent risks."[50]

The black poet Langston Hughes even penned a poem singing the praises of the public-housing towers arising in Harlem in the early 1950s:

There's a new skyline in Harlem
It's tall and proud and fine.
At night its walls are gleaming
Where a thousand windows shine.

There's a new skyline in Harlem
That belongs to you and me
As the dark old ugly homes
Tumble into memory[51]

Thus, many Negroes saw urban renewal as a tool to do away with the dreadful housing conditions often found in the ghetto.

The third perspective on urban renewal is captured by what political scientist Preston Smith calls "African American policy elites."[52] George Nesbitt and Robert Weaver, who would become the first black cabinet member as head of HUD in 1965, are archetypes of this faction. As the descendants of the old integrationist civil rights leaders of the late nineteenth and early twentieth centuries, these elites viewed the ghetto, Jim Crow, and other forms of discrimination and segregation as betrayals of American democracy. Negroes were first and foremost American citizens and had the right to live wherever they wanted and could afford. The ghetto was the manifestation of these rights being denied.

For these policy elites, slum clearance represented an opportunity to break up the ghetto. To their way of thinking, this would be logical given the current circumstances in northern cities in the post–World War II era. Slum areas inhabited by Negroes would be demolished, and the displacees would be relocated to integrated housing developments outside the ghetto. Moreover, densities would be lessened in the ghetto, and the new housing built in the ghetto would be open to persons of all races. The end result would be fewer Negroes packed in the ghetto and integrated developments inside and outside the ghetto. Moreover, once the public witnessed the success of these integrated projects, resistance to integration would fade, further weakening the walls of the ghetto.

Such thinking was not far-fetched even in the late 1940s. Because slums were disproportionately in the ghetto, the ghetto was a natural target for slum clearance. Housing experts widely recognized that the ghetto was overcrowded, so it was logical to assume that displacees would have to be relocated outside the ghetto. It was also widely recognized that there was little vacant land to be found in the ghetto, which further reinforced the assumption that at least some of the displacees would have to be relocated outside the ghetto. Nesbitt called for the state to acquire tax-delinquent properties outside the ghetto and develop these sites for housing open for all. Because blacks' movement into a neighborhood had sometimes been accompanied by the subdivision of units and cutbacks on maintenance, Nesbitt called for occupancy standards and neighborhood-conservation agreements to assuage whites' fears of neighborhood decline.[53]

Finally, slum clearance and the ensuing federally financed public housing represented the opportunity to showcase the possibility of integrated housing. Indeed, several of the public-housing developments built in the 1930s were initially integrated.[54] The federal government could build housing open to persons of all races. The success of such interracial projects would illustrate the folly of those opposed to integrated housing.[55]

For folks such as Nesbitt and Weaver, the ghetto could never be viewed as a haven. Its very existence was an affront to the democratic ideals that Americans fought for during World War II.

In the end, urban renewal as implemented on the ground most likely satisfied none of the three factions. It was absolutely not used as an instrument to integrate American cities. The walls of the ghetto were instead reinforced with it. As has been aptly documented elsewhere, slum clearance ironically was used to manage the expansion of the ghetto.[56] Indeed, segregation appears to have peaked in 1960 at the zenith of the urban-renewal era.[57]

Those who championed the existing centers of black life as something to be preserved and protected were often, although not always, brushed aside. Many black communities were uprooted and destroyed by urban renewal.

Those advocating the replacement of slums may have come closest to seeing their aspirations realized. Some of the worst ghetto housing was indeed replaced. As discussed in the next chapter, by the 1960s there was a noticeable improvement in housing conditions in the ghetto. In that sense, those who advocated using urban renewal to improve the ghetto "won" the debate.

But theirs would be a pyrrhic victory. Although slum housing was cleared, the housing that replaced it, high-rise public housing, all too often became high-rise slums with social problems worse than those in the slum housing that preceded them.

Moreover, as Negroes gained their civil rights and continued a slow slog up the economic ladder, their continued confinement to the ghetto, whether gilded, federally constructed, or garden variety, would begin to drag the race back. The frustrations from this confinement would finally boil over across the ghettos in the 1960s.

JUST A GHETTO

Whether many blacks agreed with policy elites Nesbitt's and Weaver's prog-
noses for breaking up the ghetto is unclear. But it does appear that many
ordinary Negroes increasingly shared the elites' disdain for the ghetto.
Although the ghetto resumed its role as a haven during World War II, lur-
ing millions of blacks out of the South and helping to propel the race toward
equality, its darker role as a hell was also taking center stage at this time.
Several factors account for the ghetto's seemingly contradictory roles. First,
increasing numbers of ghetto dwellers grew up in or were born in the North.
For them, the ghetto was no promised land; they had been there all their
lives or the better part of their adult lives and thus had not seen the fulfill-
ment of this promise. Second, conditions in the ghetto, at least in a physical sense, worsened after World War II due to severe overcrowding. Third,
the war helped usher in changes in blacks' economic and social status that
were incommensurate with being confined to the ghetto. These first three
forces combined to create an almost irresistible force that would attempt
to break out of the ghetto. Finally, the suburban boom of the postwar era
provided the space for the ghetto to expand. This section of the chapter
addresses each of these points in turn.

For the increasing numbers of blacks who were either born or had spent
a significant amount of time in the North, their view of the ghetto con-
trasted sharply with the view of those fleeing the South during and after
World War II. Whereas recent migrants may have viewed the ghetto as a
place to escape the watchful eye of whites and to advance themselves and
the interests of their race, Negroes who had already been living in the ghetto
saw it differently. Figure 4.2, which shows black northerners in 1950 as having more white neighbors than recent black migrants, also suggests that
the ghetto was losing the allure for blacks who had long been in the North.
Blacks who had been born in the North and southerners who had migrated
to the North when they were young did not have the Jim Crow South as a
reference to contrast to their current conditions. Negroes who had been in
the North for a while or for all their lives would have had no need to acclimate to their new environs. The frame of reference for many Negroes of the
North, especially long-term residents, would have been white neighborhoods where housing conditions were considerably better than those in

the ghetto, not the shacklike homes typical on many southern plantations. As such, the higher proportion of white neighbors in northerners' neighborhoods depicted in figure 4.2 probably reflects a desire to move to the better housing typically found in white neighborhoods. The data in figure 4.2 are consistent with the findings by the sociologists Beverly Duncan and Otis Duncan, who found that in Chicago between 1940 and 1950 Negro migrants tended to be concentrated in established Negro areas, whereas those who had been in Chicago for longer were overrepresented among those moving into white areas.[58] Figure 4.2 shows that this phenomenon was not confined to Chicago.

Social realism, the literary genre that provided a window onto life in Great Depression black belts, also illuminates the way northern blacks were beginning to view the ghetto. The novel *The Street* by Ann Petry chronicles the experiences of a single mother living on 116th Street in Harlem at the end of World War II. This woman is a native New Yorker who had previously owned a home in Jamaica, Queens, when she was with her husband, so Harlem holds little allure for her. It is a place where she has wound up, "where colored people were allowed to live including anyone who could pay the rent, so some of them would be drunk and loud mouthed and quarrelsome, given to fits of depression when they would curse and cry violently, given to fits of equally violent elation. . . . [T]he good people, the bad people, the children, the dogs . . . would all be wrapped up together." She saw 116th Street as a place "full of young thin girls with a note of resignation in their voices, with faces that contained no hope, no life. She couldn't let Bub [her son] grow up in a place like this." Her greatest fear was that she and her son would become inured to the violence that episodically dotted the chronology of life in Harlem. She asked: "What reason did she have to believe that she and Bub wouldn't become so accustomed to the sight and sound of violence and death that they wouldn't protest against it—they would become resigned to it; or that Bub finally wouldn't end up on a sidewalk with a knife in his back?" The violence was happening again and again all through Harlem. "And it wasn't just this street that she was afraid of or that was bad. It was any street where people were packed together like sardines in a can. And it wasn't just this city. It was any city where they set up a line and say black folks stay on this side and white folks on this side, so that the black folks were crammed on top of each other—jammed and packed and forced in the smallest possible space until they were completely cut off from light and air." For her, 116th Street, Harlem—indeed, all black belts—were places "she and Bub had to get out of."[59] Increasingly, for those born in the North or who had resided there for a while, the ghetto was a place of restriction, where blacks were compelled to live and were packed into like sardines.

Indeed, ghettos across the country were bursting at the seams starting during the war and shortly thereafter. In 1953, the Negro picture magazine *Our World* described Chicago as "the nation's powder keg," where a lack of housing for the rapidly rising Negro population spelled danger. The article described a building on the South Side of Chicago where eleven children and five adults in three families shared one bathroom between them. Their bedrooms were windowless cubbyholes once used as storage bins.[60]

World War II, which created conditions that lured many more migrants North, also affected the housing market, both increasing the demand for housing outside the ghetto and restricting the supply of housing available to all. The supply of housing was restricted because wartime economic controls diverted all available resources to the war effort rather than to consumer items such as housing.

Although it was not universally the case, black belts had often suffered from overcrowding prior to World War II. This should come as no surprise. Negroes were relatively poor and typically paid more than whites for the same type of housing. One way to afford such housing was to take in roomers and thus cram more people into the same amount of space. Another way of making ends meet was to rent a unit smaller than what was actually needed for the family. Either way, the end result was overcrowding even before the war, which is amply documented by both contemporary and historical studies of the early-twentieth-century ghetto.[61]

World War II only made crowded conditions much worse. The Great Migration, which had ebbed during the Depression, picked up steam in response to the increased demand for workers in the burgeoning war industries. The usual way for the black belt to expand was through neighborhood change: Negroes would enter a block; in response, whites would shortly thereafter move to other, often new housing elsewhere, and additional housing would thus be available to the race. With the war on, however, resources that would have otherwise gone to the development of new housing were consumed by the war effort. Whites who might have fled with the arrival of Negroes increasingly had few places to run to during the war, which meant Negroes had to be kept out of whites' neighborhoods at all costs.

With white neighborhoods off-limits, the increasing Negro population had no choice but to pile into the existing black belt, crowding an already crowded situation. The ghetto literally began to burst at its seams. Negro districts were described as "the most congested in the nation."[62] A report on housing conditions in Milwaukee found that although the Negro population increased some 145 percent between 1940 and 1950, the number of dwellings occupied by Negroes increased only 79 percent, "intensifying an already crowded condition."[63] Likewise, the most crowded sections of the black belt in Chicago saw a 15.6 percent increase in population without a "corresponding increase in the supply of housing to accommodate the expanding population."[64] Even in Seattle, where, as in other West Coast cities, housing was newer and thus of higher quality, overcrowding was rife. The historian Quintard Taylor reports that by the end of the war, housing built for 3,700 families was now housing 10,000.[65] The South Side of Chicago was described as having a density of 90,000 persons per square mile, making it the "highest populated district in the world."[66] In 1946, the *Los Angeles Sentinel* blamed crowding in the Negro districts for creating "deplorable" conditions that led to crime and disease.[67]

The novelist Richard Wright captured the impact of World War II on overcrowding in Chicago in an article he wrote for *Ebony* magazine: "But where were the condemned empty buildings, the kind I had written about in *Native Son*? I looked in vain. There were no empty tenements! What had happened? Twelve years before the South Side had been full of them; they had constituted a danger to life and health and had often served as hideouts for criminals. Now I could find none." He reported that his friend and sociologist St. Clair Drake responded, "Man, don't you know what's happened? During the war so many thousands of Negroes flocked into the South Side to do war work that those empty buildings had to be used again!"[68]

The resulting crowding was what the protagonist in *The Street* feels is turning ghettos into places to be escaped.

Yet another element affected this situation: World War II and the postwar economic boom increased not only the size of the Negro population in the North but Negroes' earning power as well, leading to a second dynamic

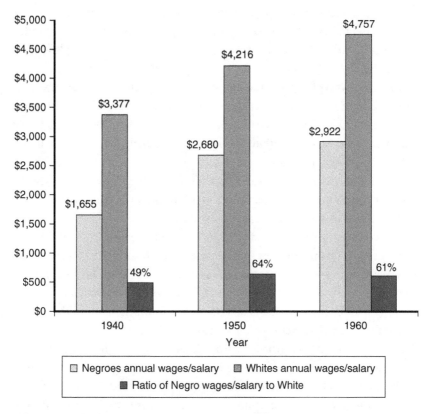

FIGURE 4.4 Blacks' income growth, 1940–1960. *Source*: Author's tabulation of Integrated Public Use Microdata samples (Ruggles et al. 2010). *Note*: The figures given here are in constant 1960 dollars.

that began to alter the ghetto's position—economic resources and aspirations that could not be satisfied in the ghetto.

Figure 4.4 shows that Negroes' real income between 1940 and 1960 more than doubled. With increased earning power, Negroes had the means to achieve their desires for better housing. These desires mirrored those of the burgeoning white middle class. In 1958, the scholar activists Eunice Grier and George Grier described Negro aspirations for "play space for children, good schools, safety and quiet, good property maintenance, and congenial neighbors of roughly equivalent income and educational background."[69] In *Places of Their Own*, the historian Andrew Weise describes how African Americans longed for "rustic" settings where they could have a "nice, clean place to raise a child."[70] Black belts had almost uniformly developed among the oldest and least-desirable sections of northern cities. Even in places that were initially physically appealing, such as Harlem, age and undermaintenance by landlords had over time made much of the housing less than appealing.

But even while Negroes' income increased rapidly during the war and its immediate aftermath, housing conditions in the ghetto did not improve commensurately. The discrepancy between Negroes' aspirations and their ability to meet those aspirations was most acute during the 1940s. The housing shortages due to World War II affected everyone but were especially painful for Negroes, who had a limited number of housing options to begin with. That many now had the means to afford better housing was like salt being rubbed in a deep and festering wound.

Concomitant with an increase in blacks' economic fortunes in the North was a gradual change in their social status. American society was evolving in ways that made ghettoization an anachronism. Through the Harlem Renaissance, the development of "black metropolises," and their participation in two world wars, blacks had proved their humanity and their right to fair treatment. The period after World War II was thus a period of rising expectations among Negroes. Negro soldiers had shed the same blood as white soldiers. For the second time in a generation, Negroes were asked to make the ultimate sacrifice to defend democracy abroad when they themselves could not experience democracy at home. The contradiction of being asked to fight fascism even while they were relegated to second-class citizenship was not lost on African Americans. Black newspapers readily likened segregationists to fascists and the black belts to the ghettos that confined Jews.[71] "The only difference between this legalized ghetto and the restrictions imposed on Jews in several European countries is that the American policy is hallowed by time," wrote the *Pittsburgh Courier* in 1940.[72] Blacks had already swallowed the bitter pill of making rest of the world safe for democracy in World War I and were not inclined to spill their blood without their own demands for equality being met.

President Roosevelt's executive order forbidding discrimination in war plants both contributed to the economic growth among blacks and lessened the social distance between the races. Negroes increasingly worked in semi-skilled and even skilled positions shoulder to shoulder with whites, belying the notion that the race was inferior and fit only for menial positions.

White America, too, particularly in the aftermath of defeating the monstrous Nazi ideology, began to face up to its failure to live up to the American creed. Racial barriers gradually began to tumble in the war's aftermath. Jackie Robinson broke into Major League baseball in 1947. The armed forces were integrated in 1948. Nat King Cole hosted his own television show in 1956. Particularly in the world of entertainment, there were black stars such as Sammie Davis Jr. and Fats Domino, whose fame and notoriety transcended race. Their stardom was owed as much to white America as to black America.

Given these changes in blacks' aspirations and status, the novelty of "black metropolises" or cities within a city wore thin for many blacks by the 1940s and 1950s. Whereas the notion of blacks adapting to urban life and living independently in cities might have been a major advance for the race in the first decades of the twentieth century, in the wake of World War II many Negroes yearned for more. They wanted access to the American dream that was being made available to whites.

Many Negro elites were in the vanguard of attempts to break out of the ghetto. Their experiences brought into sharp relief the incongruity between the Negro's rising status yet the near impossibility of breaking out of the ghetto. Even the same Negro stars who appeared on magazine covers and on television and who were heroes to black and white children alike found it almost impossible to escape the long reach of the ghetto. Consider the experiences of three stars of baseball, the American past-time: Jackie Robinson and Larry Doby, the first Negroes to play Major League baseball in the National League and American League, respectively, and Willie Mays, perhaps the most famous baseball player of that era, black or white.

When Jackie Robinson first entered the major leagues, he took up residence in a tenement in the then budding ghetto of Bedford-Stuyvesant in Brooklyn. As his career blossomed, he sought to translate his fame into a housing situation commensurate with his status, yet moves to Flatbush, Brooklyn, and Addisleigh Park in Queens were met with hostility from white neighbors. By 1954, Robinson had won several awards, including Rookie of the Year and Most Valuable Player, and was an ambassador for baseball, invited to speak at countless civic engagements both black and white. A search for a home in suburban Connecticut in 1954, however, required intervention by a group of local progressive ministers to engage realtors and to obtain a mortgage.[73] Robinson could integrate baseball, but that was no guarantee he could integrate a white neighborhood.

Playing for the Cleveland Indians but living in Paterson, New Jersey, Larry Doby experienced situations that paralleled Jackie Robinson's. After helping the Cleveland Indians win their first World Series in decades in 1948 and being greeted with a parade as a hometown hero, Doby could not buy a home on his own outside the burgeoning Patterson ghetto. The Dobys were instead steered to other parts of the ghetto, or houses were miraculously taken off the market after they inquired about them. It took the intervention of the mayor of Paterson, who used his influence to bully recalcitrant realtors, to enable the Dobys to pierce Paterson's ghetto walls.[74]

Jackie Robinson and Larry Doby could break baseball's color lines, but the barriers that kept Negroes hemmed in the ghetto were in many ways less pregnable. Nor would Willie Mays, truly an American hero, remain unscathed in his attempt to leave the ghetto. Mays initially lived in Harlem near the Polo Grounds when he began his illustrious career in 1951. When the Giants moved to San Francisco in 1958, and Willie tried to purchase a home in a lily-white planned community in that city, he ran into trouble. Upon learning the buyers were Negro, the owners refused to sell. By this time, Mays was perhaps the best player in baseball and had appeared on the cover of *Time* magazine. Only the intervention of the San Francisco mayor and a national firestorm of news controversy caused the seller to relent.[75] Most Negroes, of course, could not count on intervention by their local mayor or a national news controversy over the discrimination they experienced.

The experiences of Jackie Robinson, Larry Doby, and Willie Mays speak to the rigidity of the color line when it came to housing. Blacks could become public figures, celebrities even, but their race tainted them as unwanted neighbors among the mass of whites.

These sports heroes' experiences also speak to the evolving class relations within the Negro community. The ghettos that sprouted and expanded during World War I were havens in part because they gave rise to a new black elite who did not owe their status to whites. They were black entrepreneurs and politicians who built their fame and fortune providing goods or services to other blacks in the ghetto. They owed their status to the ghetto, whether they personally remained within it or not. As we saw earlier in this chapter, during and after World War II there remained many black elites whose status depended on the ghetto, but there was also a growing class of Negro pioneers who were making their way in white America and who sought to break out of the ghetto.

As such, the symbol of the ghetto of what the race could achieve began to fade into oblivion. It would seem the notion of the black metropolis no longer captured the imagination of Negro elites as it had decades earlier, when a young college-educated Negro migrant's greatest fear would be that "Harlem would be too wonderful for words." Instead, this same migrant, Arna Bontemps, would later note that

Harlem in 1942 and 1943 was another place. One of the first things to shock us was the revelation that the people who still give the area its reputation, the people by whom Harlem is favorably known, do not live there anymore. Paul Robeson and Marion Anderson are less familiar figures in Harlem than are Mrs. Roosevelt and Mayor La Guardia. Richard Wright and Countee Cullen live within shooting distance, more or less, but they are safely removed from the sounds of the streets. . . . Hazel Scott and Cab Calloway and Jimmy Lunceford and the rest would certainly not be moved by a poem which began, speaking of Harlem, *Let us roam the night together.* They live in Westchester.[76]

The Delany sisters, made famous by a book chronicling their century-long lives, had experiences in New York that poignantly captured the fading luster of the ghetto. Daughters of the first Negro Episcopal bishop elected in the United States and a teacher, the sisters became a teacher and the second Negro woman licensed to practice dentistry in New York. Their family appeared in Negro society pages as examples of Negro "firsts" and achievements, and they were firmly ensconced in the Negro elite. When the sisters moved to New York in 1916, they settled in Harlem, describing it as "heaven."[77] Upon retirement four decades later, however, they sought out the suburban Mount Vernon, New York.

The ghetto that once stood as a city on the hill symbolizing what Negroes could achieve was increasingly seen as just a ghetto. Bontemps concluded his article in the *American Scholar* by noting that although it might be "fun" for a while to self-segregate in the ghetto, it was no fun to be deprived of the freedom to move where one wanted and that Harlem and other black belts must go if America were to live up to its democratic creed.[78] Many of those at the pinnacle of black society were no longer content to be confined to the ghetto and drew little inspiration from living in a black metropolis.

Instead of Harlem and ghettos like it serving as symbols of racial advancement and as meccas drawing elite blacks such as the Delany sisters, the American Dream of a house with a white picket fence and a car in the garage came to be seen as symbols of racial progress.

The vast majority of Negroes, of course, were neither baseball stars nor Hollywood stars nor "elites." But rising aspirations, incomes, and social status (at least outside of housing) combined with the deteriorating conditions in the ghetto to create an almost irresistible force. Negroes could not be piled up on top of one another forever—something had to give.

Starting in the late 1940s, the walls of the ghetto would slowly begin to break, with the NAACP in the vanguard in the movement against government-sanctioned barriers that kept the Negro hemmed in the ghetto. The movement's first victory was the Supreme Court decision in *Shelley v. Kramer* (334 U.S. 1 [1948]), which opened the first crack in the physical boundaries of the ghetto. This ruling outlawed the enforcement of restrictive covenants based on race, rendering inert this popular tool for maintaining the color line in housing. Although segregation persisted and indeed increased in the wake of *Shelley v. Kramer*, the ruling did facilitate black movement out of the ghetto, allowing the physical space of the ghetto to expand. In perhaps the most sophisticated study of the impact of *Shelley v. Kraemer*, the social scientists Yana Kucheva and Richard Sander recently found that blacks moved into covenanted neighborhoods immediately after the court decision in 1948.[79] Without covenants, it became that much harder for whites to stay united and to refuse to sell to blacks. The temptation to sell to Negroes was great given the premium Negroes were willing to pay for housing outside the ghetto. With homes in the ghetto in short supply, white property owners could and did sell their homes to Negroes at inflated prices. Many a white homeowner took the money and ran, whatever their feelings about integration.

The NAACP's second prong of attack was against the FHA's discriminatory practice of refusing to insure homes in mixed or older neighborhoods, which had become obvious by the 1940s. Beyond that refusal, the FHA also encouraged the use of restrictive covenants in the properties it insured.[80] The NAACP and other civil rights organizations waged a lengthy battle to halt these discriminatory practices. Although FHA commissioner

Raymond Foley promised as early as 1946 that "Negroes may obtain FHA loans on property covered by restrictive covenants," and the *FHA Underwriting Manual* of 1947 no longer sanctioned the use of restrictive covenants, it would not be until the 1950s that the FHA followed this dictum consistently.[81] The FHA's discriminatory practices were like a shut-off valve on credit for would-be black homeowners because the FHA was the major insurer of mortgages. Any step that lessened discrimination by the FHA would thus make it easier for Negroes to purchase homes outside the ghetto. Given the overcrowded conditions in the ghetto, it was often only outside the ghetto that Negroes could find homes for purchase. The unenforceability of restrictive covenants and some increase in mortgage availability due to reforms at the FHA meant some Negroes were able to purchase homes outside the ghetto, although the number was still small and the change slow.

During the 1950s, a coalition of multiracial activists pushed against the remaining barriers that kept blacks hemmed inside the ghetto. These activists wrote articles and books denouncing the hypocrisy of segregated neighborhoods in a democratic America. Charles Abrams's book *Forbidden Neighbors: A Study of Prejudice in Housing* is an example of such efforts.[82] Activists also pushed local and state governments to enact fair-housing laws.[83] Their efforts paid off. In 1958, New York City became the first locality to enact an antidiscrimination law in housing, and starting in 1959 states outside the South began enacting fair-housing laws forbidding discrimination in housing transactions based on race.[84]

The final link in the chain hemming blacks in the ghetto was white flight to suburbia. Although the crumbling of state-sanctioned housing discrimination did not end discrimination and appears to have affected residential segregation only modestly, it did change the nature of the ghetto. The ghetto, which had previously been maintained through blatant discrimination, intimidation, and violence, was increasingly maintained through white flight. Rather than fighting the Negro invasion, many whites were only too happy to heed the clarion call of suburbia. In *Crabgrass Frontier*, the historian Kenneth Jackson chronicles this reaction aptly, describing how federally insured mortgages and the development of the interstate highway system put suburbia in reach for a wide swath of the white population.[85] David Cutler, Edward Glaeser, and Jacob Vigdor, using an economic model, describe how in 1940 blacks paid more for equivalent housing than whites, a pattern consistent with widespread discrimination through restrictive covenants and other mechanisms used to keep blacks in the ghetto. In contrast, by 1970 blacks were paying less for similar housing *even as segregation increased*, suggesting that white flight was now a major mechanism responsible for that segregation.[86] Thus, ghetto walls became more porous starting in the 1950s, with better-off blacks in the vanguard of out-migration from the ghetto.

To be sure, since the advent of the Great Migration, class sorting within the ghetto itself was pervasive. Those with the means to do so sought better housing and environs and to distance themselves from the lower classes. This infrequently meant making forays into white neighborhoods, which prior to *Shelley v. Kramer* and the outlawing of restrictive covenants was almost impossible for all but the most determined blacks. More typically, the miniscule black elite and middle classes carved out enclaves such as Harlem's Sugar Hill, described in the lifestyle magazine *Ebony* as home to "everybody who is anybody" in Harlem,[87] and certain blocks on the South Side of Chicago. These elite enclaves were small but still a part of the ghetto. The same *Ebony* article lauding Sugar Hill as a "haven for wealthy Negroes" and for "Harlem's most talked about men and women in law, sports, civil liberties, music, medicine, painting, business and literature" also noted that "keeping children out of trouble with juvenile gangs is a Hill mother's full time job" and that Hill Negroes were exploited by white landlords because "they can't move into any better place."[88] Indeed, a study of segregation in the first decades of the twentieth century concluded that "socioeconomic status was not an important determinant of residential integration for blacks in the pre–Civil Rights era. There is no evidence that higher socioeconomic status translated into more residential contact with whites during this time." However, "while class did not determine proximity to whites, it did play a role in determining the types of neighborhoods that blacks lived in. Higher-status blacks had higher-status neighbors and lived in neighborhoods with more homeowners."[89] Thus, prior to the 1950s elite and middle-class Negroes could distance themselves from the Negro masses somewhat, though they still tended to be spatially proximate.

By the 1950s, suburbanization was reaching its zenith. Whites who did not want black neighbors could simply move away. The historian Josh Sides describes how Compton, California, a suburb near the Watts ghetto went from 5 percent black in 1950 to 40 percent black in 1960. At first, whites reacted violently to the Negro encroachment, physically attacking white realtors who sold to blacks, picketing blacks' homes, and hurling racial slurs. Although sporadic acts of vandalism and violence continued, after a few years, "instead of resisting or cohabiting, many white homeowners decided to leave."[90]

By midcentury, members of the growing black middle class gradually began moving out of the ghetto. Their out-migration, however, did not signal an end to segregation. Their movement was instead into what the NAACP lawyer Thurgood Marshall called the "gilded ghetto,"[91] neighborhoods such as Addisleigh Park in Queens, New York, West Chesterfield in Chicago, and Chicago Boulevard and Boston Boulevard in Detroit.[92] These formerly white neighborhoods hardly resembled a ghetto—being neither rundown nor overcrowded—at least not initially. For some Negroes, the American Dream, albeit one devoid of whites, was now in reach. Negro lifestyle magazines such as *Ebony* and *Our World* came into being during the postwar era with the aim of "dealing with the positive things" accomplished by the race and covering subjects "that [Negroes] would be proud of" and would find "uplifting."[93] Toward these ends, glossy photos of Negro celebrities and stories heralding Negro "firsts" were mainstays of these publications. Typical fare included "Columbia University's first Negro Architecture graduate stepping out bravely into a man's world," Negroes spending "half a billion wheels," and the "Flying Horseman," a "Negro horseman [who is] among the top five riders in the country."[94]

Moving out of the ghetto and living the American Dream were also noteworthy. It was newsworthy when Pittsburgh Negroes moved out of the rundown Lower Hill ghetto and bought homes in residential areas.[95] Negroes were shown in what would now seem mundane poses: mowing the lawn, washing dishes, and watching television. But for a race that was typically portrayed only as victims of white racism in the black press or as criminals and buffoons in the white press or that was just plain ignored in the white press, these images were revolutionary. They provided proof that Negroes were not merely peasant folk, slum dwellers, or the victims of lynch mobs but upwardly mobile Americans availing themselves of opportunity and the latest modern appliances. In these pieces, Negroes were described as "living comfortably" in "ranch style homes" in Los Angeles in the 1950s,[96] enjoying the advantages of living in a mixed neighborhood in Hartford, Connecticut,[97] or "happy" that they now owned their homes, where their "kids could see grass and trees" and were no longer living in "the most crowded section of Cleveland."[98] Such stories abounded in the early years of *Ebony* and *Our World*.

More newsworthy still were Negroes who were truly "making it." One magazine described how in Philadelphia the "newest housing news among Negroes is the growing cult of 'good livers' who started a trickle to Germantown that is now a steady stream. Most, of course, are top-bracket professionals who can afford mansions costing as much as $50,000 like Dr. Jim & Mrs. Ruth Ramsay [who are pictured] in their new elaborately furnished Spanish-style house in Germantown."[99]

Only a generation earlier, merely surviving and taking on the accoutrements of modern city living were enough to count as progress for the race. Not dying out, as some late-nineteenth-century observers predicted, and handling the rigors of industrial life helped demonstrate the humanity of the black race. By the middle of the twentieth century, however, the race would take pride not in mere survival but in full participation in the American Dream. Acquiring homes outside the ghetto was a next step. In addition to the "firsts" accomplished by a few, the swelling population of Negroes in nice homes and with modern cars also served to cast doubt on notions of Negro inferiority. The pride inspired by Negroes moving out of the ghetto and achieving the American Dream of suburban single-family homeownership illustrates the way the ghetto evolved away from being a haven for all blacks, including elites.

At midcentury, the Negro's place in America was slowly evolving as full citizenship was gradually being ceded by white America. Yet the ghetto as a spatial institution appeared frozen in time. It was scarcely any easier for Negroes to locate outside the ghetto in the years following World War II than in the years following World War I, despite the lapse of a quarter of a century. Thus, the ghetto took on different roles for a changing and diversifying Negro America.

The ghetto remained a starting point for the Negro migrants who continued to stream out of the South in numbers that dwarfed the first wave of migrants during World War I. Hundreds of thousands of blacks escaped near servitude in the South to become part of the industrial proletariat in the North. For these Negroes the ghetto was an enclave, serving as a place for them to acclimate to the city. For a select few, the ghetto continued to serve as a springboard to economic and political success. These few were the Negro civic leaders, entrepreneurs, and politicians who owed their station in life to the mass of Negroes hemmed in the ghetto. Moreover, Negroes successfully elected several congressmen and scores of aldermen and councilmen to represent them in the cities of the North and to stand as champions for the race.

We might assume that as blacks knocked down barriers and became part of the American mainstream, they would also choose to live in integrated neighborhoods. If blacks were able to play integrated baseball, why shouldn't they be allowed to live in integrated neighborhoods? Although the idea of a black metropolis captivated the attention of black elites in the first decades of the twentieth century, by the 1940s that idea had lost its sheen. Many black elites increasingly owed their prominence to the larger society rather than to blacks in the ghetto. Moreover, for increasing numbers of ordinary Negroes, confinement to the ghetto served no real material purpose. These Negroes had either been born in the North or had been there long enough to have acclimated to life there. For blacks who came of age in the North, not having to step off the sidewalk in deference to whites or seeing a black policeman meant little. For these blacks, the ghetto did not represent the aspiration of what Negroes could achieve. Rather, confinement to the ghetto was a further reminder to them of what blacks could not obtain.

The evolving and differentiating status of Negroes in American life led to divergent views on the ghetto as an institution. There was unanimity among the race that Negroes should have the right to live wherever they could afford. But some Negroes felt the ghetto should be actively dismantled. Others were perhaps conflicted, not desiring the construction of additional ghettos but not ready to see the existing ones eliminated, either.

In the end, more powerful outside forces handed the "defend the ghetto" faction a victory, but one they perhaps would one day come to regret.

Chapter Five

THE GHETTO ERUPTS

The 1960s

Born in Philadelphia in 1945, Mel Dorn came of age in the North Philadelphia ghetto in the 1960s. Like other adolescents coming of age, he occupied his time dating and pondering the future. But unlike most Americans coming of age, he had another concern—the police. According to Mel, the police regularly rode around in patrol cars harassing people in his neighborhood, regularly "beat people upside the head for any reason," and even "lynched" people in the local precinct house.[1]

Nor was Mel's experience in North Philadelphia unique. In Detroit, a crew of plainclothes policemen known as the "Big Fo" regularly harassed and beat up residents of the ghetto, including Ike McKinnon, who later became Detroit's chief of police in the 1990s. As a teen, he had the misfortune of crossing paths with the Big Fo while coming home from school.

"They pulled me over. There I was, fourteen years old. This man was calling me all these vile and profane racist names as they beat me up. And I said, but sir what? And the more I asked questions the more they beat me up. I could see people standing, looking. And they're looking but they couldn't do anything because it was my turn to get my ass kicked."[2] These harrowing memories of wanton police brutality epitomize the further evolution of the ghetto from a haven in the early twentieth century to a more figurative ghetto with invisible walls and an occupying army—the police. The disrespect meted out by the police and the powerlessness of ghetto residents to stop the abuse left the ghetto simmering in the 1960s. More-over, it was not only the police but other institutions, including schools, and the decrepit physical fabric of the ghetto that cried out disrespect. These were the conditions that made the ghetto a hell.

But while dissatisfaction with ghetto confinement was reaching its apo-gee, the view of the ghetto as a place to establish black autonomy also reemerged. The ideology of black power influenced not only art, culture, and politics but also feelings toward the ghetto. For some, black power would resurrect the ghetto's role as a haven. This chapter traces the twists and turns of the ghetto's trajectory as it alternated between being a hell for those left behind and being the site for the race to achieve independence from whites.

TWO STEPS FORWARD, ONE STEP BACK

The 1960s would prove to be as pivotal a decade for the ghetto as it did for America and, indeed, much of the world. It was during this decade that the de jure and in many instances de facto relegation of blacks to second-class citizenship finally receded in tangible ways. Segregation in public accom-modations was outlawed. Millions of blacks in the South gained the fran-chise not only in theory but in practice with the full backing of the federal government. Harvard Sitkoff reports that between 1964 and 1968 the num-ber of southern black voters tripled.[3] The number of black elected officials skyrocketed both in the South and in the North. The list of "first black to" is long and inspiring. Blacks gained admission to elite institutions in unprec-edented numbers. Moreover, many elite institutions not only stopped bar-ring blacks from entry but actively began to seek out and recruit them through a policy known as affirmative action. Interracial marriage, once the greatest taboo, became legal across the entire country after miscegena-tion laws were struck down by the Supreme Court in *Loving v. Virginia* (388 U.S. 1) in 1967.

Blacks also began gaining widespread acceptance in American popular culture. Although black culture had always influenced American popu-lar culture, the 1960s witnessed this influence growing exponentially. The 1960s were the decade when black athletes not merely began playing the most popular American sports, baseball, basketball, and football, in larger numbers but also came to dominate them. In cinema and music, black individuals such as Sidney Poitier, Harry Belafonte, Diane Carroll, Jimi Hendrix, and others became stars above and beyond being *black* movie and music stars, owing a great deal of their success to the appreciation of them by white Americans. It was heretofore the best time for blacks in America.

Yet in some ways conditions in the ghetto worsened, and its role as a beacon for black America had rapidly diminished. Its role as a place of despair instead became more prominent. Kenneth B. Clark's book *Dark Ghetto*, published in 1965, was among the most poignant renderings of the ghetto's role in black life. After living in Harlem for forty years and serving as a consultant for Harlem Youth Opportunities Unlimited, a project set up to address juvenile delinquency, Clark penned what he called an "anguished cry" over conditions in the ghetto. For Clark, the ghetto was a place with "invisible walls erected by white society" for the purposes of "confinement and perpetuating the inhabitants' powerlessness."[4] He called his research method "involved observation," a form of participant observation wherein the observer is involuntarily a part of the process he observes. As a black man and native of Harlem, Clark could not of course isolate his lived experiences from his study of Harlem as a consultant. As a social psychologist working on a project to prevent juvenile delinquency, Clark was focused, perhaps not surprisingly, on the ghetto's pathologies. High rates of infant mortality, crime, disease, and family breakdown were among these pathologies, and in *Dark Ghetto* Clark set out to explain how the ghetto contributed to these maladies.

Dark Ghetto identified a number of culprits, including Negroes' denigrated status in American society, which inflicted feelings of inferiority and hopelessness. The menial, low-income jobs held by most ghetto residents were perhaps the most important cause of the pathologies plaguing the ghetto. With better jobs, Clark believed, ghetto dwellers' lives would necessarily improve. But Clark also implicated the ghetto itself in causing the pathologies among residents there. He pointed to the physical squalor of the ghetto and confinement to its space as damaging the Negro's sense of self-worth.

On the latter point, Clark could not have known the ghetto was in the midst of a mass exodus that would transform these spaces in a few short years—a point to which I return later in this chapter. But Clark's abhorrence of the ghetto's deplorable condition appears to be spot on. News accounts were replete with tales of a place with truly harrowing conditions.

The Reverend O. D. Dempsey described Harlem as a place where "our people . . . are paying the highest rent for the poorest services and the worst living conditions in the city."[5] Another news story in 1963 described a family with seven children, including a two-week-old, living in a Chicago flat with no heat, no gas, two glassless windows, and "rats as big as cats."[6] A tenant in the Bedford-Stuyvesant section of Brooklyn also complained of cat-size rats, no hot water for four months, and a hole in the kitchen ceiling.[7] The housing in the Hill District in Pittsburgh was described as "[50] percent defective, 30 percent deteriorating and 10 percent dilapidated."[8] The labor leader Clarence Coogins described the Potter section of North Edison as "the worst Negro ghetto in the United States," a place where the majority of Negroes lived in shacks without running water and floors.[9] Jack E. Wood Jr., associate executive director of the National Committee Against Discrimination in Housing, testified to the National Commission on Urban Problems that "survey after [s]urvey and observer after observer have warned that 70, 80, and even 90 percent of ghetto residents have reached the boiling point on impatience with housing discrimination and segregation, not just poor housing quality."[10]

Housing conditions were bad enough to spark tenant protests that included live rats caught in Bedford-Stuyvesant and Brownsville, two black neighborhoods in Brooklyn, New York, as a way of dramatizing the deplorable housing conditions there.[11] These conditions galvanized chapters of the Congress of Racal Equality (CORE) to organize rent strikes across northern ghettos in the early 1960s. In describing the motives for a rent strike, tenant organizer Roy Patrick said, "The tenants of Chicago's ghetto areas know of the cold that creeps in through their room by insufficient heating on the landlord's part, they know of the mice that develop into rats over a time span due to the neglect in care by the landlords. They know of the enormous prices paid for rent without any repairs, sufficient heat, or cleanliness on the part of the building owned by the landlord. They know of roaches, bugs, and other crawling insects that get into their food, their beds, their dishes,—their lives period."[12]

Another tenants' group in Chicago, the East Garfield Park Union to End Slums, picketed a landlord's suburban home over the deplorable conditions in his properties.[13] By withholding rent and picketing landlords' homes, tenant groups aimed to capture their attention and hit them where it would hurt—their pocketbook. Such actions would, it was hoped, push landlords to make much-needed repairs to their crumbling tenements. A Monroe County Human Relations Commission report posited that "housing [is] the most severe and central issue involved in the racial discrimination problem from every vantage point."[14]

The decline of the ghetto was such that one black observer described it in stark terms:

I'm more puzzled than ever as to how anyone can be happy while living in the ghetto. What I'm speaking of is the depressing, over-crowded, highly-restricted racial ghetto where, as in Chicago, some 700,000 people crowd into seven square miles, or less. They're crowded because unscrupulous real estate developers have converted apartments to hotels, because prejudiced bankers won't finance adequate housing for the ever rising tide of in-migrants, because (in some cases) they can't afford any better, because (in other cases) they don't have the gumption to move out.[15]

Surveys of residents in ghetto areas generally found dissatisfaction with housing quality. In a survey of New York City residents by John F. Kraft, Inc., in 1964, 49 percent of Negroes listed housing as "the biggest problem that Negroes in their part of the city had to worry about," whereas 54 percent listed economic complaints, and 39 percent listed crime.[16] Kraft's survey of Harlem residents' attitudes toward housing, rehabilitation, and urban renewal in 1966 found housing and dope addiction to be considered the two biggest problems in the community. One respondent summed up these two problems: "Problem? Poor housing. People live in rat holes. These houses aren't safe, and they need guards."[17] That same survey of Harlem residents reported finding "one overarching problem in Harlem—housing. Most other problems, such as dope addiction, crime and winos, and the rest, seem to be by-products of the basic problem." Moreover, an appreciable number of respondents couldn't describe one trait of Harlem that was an asset. "Most" welcomed tearing down and starting anew.[18]

Indeed, the violent unrest that would erupt in many ghettos in the late 1960s was frequently linked directly to poor housing conditions. The study of the causes of the urban unrest in 1967 by the presidentially appointed National Advisory Commission on Civil Disorder (Kerner Commission) looked at twenty cities outside the South, with the exception of Atlanta. The commission concluded there was a "reservoir of grievance" in these cities' ghettos, of which inadequate housing was a major tributary. Indeed, the commission reported that "forty-seven percent of the units in the disturbance areas were substandard and overcrowding was common."[19]

The contrast between the descriptions of the ghetto in this period and the glowing terms used to describe the northern "promised land" half a century earlier could hardly be starker. The changing attitudes toward the ghetto reflected more than just an absolute decline in physical conditions. On many absolute measures, housing for blacks and those residing in northern ghettos improved steadily in the post–World War II era. For example, the number of northern Negroes residing in substandard housing declined by roughly 50 percent between 1950 and 1960. Furthermore, as we encountered in chapter 4, white suburbanization allowed the ghetto to spread in size, thus reducing overcrowding somewhat. At the very least, conditions had basically remained the same: numerous descriptions of early-twentieth-century ghettos had also reported poor housing as a problem, with substantial portions of the Negro population residing in deplorable housing.[20]

Clearly, as the anecdotes given earlier attest, the physical condition of the ghetto was problematic in the 1960s. But the ghetto's transformation from a place of aspiration to one of denied dreams was not simply about a decline in physical conditions. Rather, the housing market of the ghetto and consequently its physical and spatial importance had changed in at least two significant ways by the 1960s. First, although the absolute condition of housing in the ghetto may or may not have declined in relative terms (I take up this question later), there can be no doubt that ghetto housing did decline. Take, for example, the South Side of Chicago, described in *The Negro in Chicago* in 1922 as "where most of the Negro population lives" and where "the low quality of housing is widespread."[21] But in 1922, when *The Negro in Chicago* was published, America in general was not especially well housed. The lack of hot water and even electricity was not uncommon in homes inhabited even by whites. Air-conditioning was unheard of in early-twentieth-century America. In 1937, President Roosevelt would assert that "one third of the nation [was] ill-housed."[22] Indeed, as late as 1950 roughly one-third of white Americans lived in substandard housing.[23] Living in substandard housing did not mark one as inferior when 44 percent of Americans lacked exclusive use of a tub or shower, 35 percent lacked a flush toilet, and 31 percent lacked running water, as was the case in the America of 1940.[24]

The feeling of living in substandard housing undoubtedly was greater in the wake of the post–World War II housing boom and suburban exodus that so dramatically improved housing conditions for millions of Americans. The postwar housing boom was responsible for providing millions of Americans access to new single-family housing units with modern amenities such as air-conditioning, dishwashers, and washers and dryers. Negroes, however, were for the most part denied access to this suburban bounty by both housing and mortgage discrimination. As described in chapter 3, banks, guided by federal mortgage insurance guidelines, refrained from lending in neighborhoods experiencing any racial transition. Indeed, until 1952, the FHA continued to insure homes that were covered by restrictive covenants. White realtors in 1917 had adopted "ethical" guidelines that forbade the introduction of Negroes into white neighborhoods, and this practice continued well into the second half of the twentieth century.[25] And if a prospective Negro homeowner somehow circumvented the banks and the realtors, many suburban developers simply excluded Negroes altogether from their newly built developments.[26]

That blacks were relegated to the oldest housing is underscored by the fact that in 1960 whereas 25 percent of whites in the Northeast and North Central regions lived in housing built in the previous ten years, only 9 percent of blacks lived in such housing.[27] Because blacks were largely excluded from newer housing in the suburbs, most of the housing they moved into as the ghetto expanded was older housing formerly occupied by whites.

Thus, the problem wasn't simply that housing in the ghetto was bad; that had always been the case with a few exceptions. Rather, the gap between deplorable ghetto housing and housing accessible to whites (i.e., modern suburban housing) had grown manifold. Outside of slum-clearance projects, relatively little in the way of new housing had been built in the ghetto in the half-century leading up to the 1960s. For example, between 1940 and 1950, only 100,000 of *9 million* new private housing units produced in the United States went to nonwhites.[28] By the 1960s, housing units that were already substandard in the 1920s and 1930s were still substandard but older. Yet all around the central city modern, spacious homes were being built.

The feeling of relative deprivation likely compounded the negative experience of living in bad housing. The stigma of living in slum housing is that much greater when only you and other ghetto dwellers are confined to such housing. Of course, not all of the urban unrest can be attributed to poor housing conditions. The explosion in Watts, Los Angeles, in 1965, one of the most lethal of the entire decade, occurred in a place where most housing was in decent condition relative to the housing of other ghettos. Because Los Angeles was a relatively new metropolis in the 1960s, not much of the housing stock was very old or severely deteriorated. Indeed, only 4 percent of Watts residents mentioned poor housing conditions when asked about the underlying causes of the unrest.[29] Yet it seems plausible that the much worse housing conditions in the older ghettos of the Midwest and Northeast may have helped set the stage for uprisings in those regions. Poor housing was one among several culprits of the violent unrest of the 1960s.

The way absolute housing conditions in the older ghettos changed in the 1960s presents something of a paradox at first glance. The anecdotes given earlier tell a story of rundown, decrepit ghetto housing. Yet housing conditions for urban blacks outside the South (and in the South, too, although it is not the focus here) improved steadily in the 1960s. For example, between 1960 and 1970 the proportion of housing units occupied by blacks that were overcrowded declined from 40 percent to 30 percent, and the proportion of housing units without complete plumbing declined from 15 percent to 3 percent among blacks outside the South.[30] Figure 5.1 shows that the neighborhoods blacks lived in became remarkably less dense through 1970. Whereas the ghettos of the years immediately following World War II were often described as "congested" or "tightly packed," these same spaces were losing people steadily over the ensuing decades.

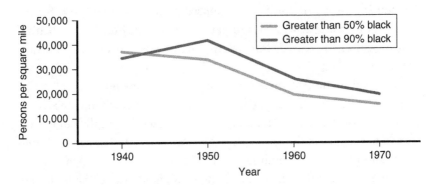

FIGURE 5.1 Persons per square mile in predominantly black neighborhoods outside the South, 1940–1970. *Source*: Author's tabulation of U.S. Census Bureau population-density figures for 1940, 1950, 1960, 1970, prepared by Social Explorer (accessed March 31, 2016).

Figure 5.1 is illustrative of a long trend that improved housing conditions for Americans black and white. A federal government report showed that for blacks outside the South, crowding and residence in substandard units declined dramatically during the 1950s.[31]

What accounts for the discrepancy between the overall improvement in blacks' housing and the tales of ghetto squalor that continued to proliferate? In the mid-1960s, Kenneth Clark saw confinement behind invisible walls as one of the hallmarks of the ghetto, but unbeknownst to him he was writing at a time when Harlem, like other northern ghettos, was in the midst of a massive depopulation—folks were indeed escaping the ghetto.[32] The trickle of blacks moving out of the ghetto in the 1940s and 1950s became a flood during the 1960s. The postwar housing boom allowing whites to move out of the central city freed up these units for blacks. This was by no means a smooth process. Often whole neighborhoods would transition from white to black in a matter of a few years as whites fled after the arrival of the first black family.[33] Panic-stricken whites often sold at rock-bottom prices to realtors, who then sold the same houses to unsuspecting blacks at inflated prices because of blacks' lack of alternative options. Denied mortgages by banks, blacks often had to finance their home purchase "on contract," whereby the seller financed the sale but retained title to the house. If the buyer missed a payment, he could be evicted immediately without a foreclosure process.[34] Nonetheless, white flight to the suburbs did provide better housing options to blacks.

Blacks' increasing ability to take the place of whites in formerly all-white neighborhoods reverberated in the ghetto by loosening the demand for housing there. In addition, options due to white flight and blacks' greater purchasing power (although that power continued to lag behind that of whites) increased dramatically in the postwar era, as shown in figure 5.2.

The combination of increased competition from formerly all-white neighborhoods and slackening demand due to rising Negro income meant the bottom of the housing market, which the ghetto typically composed, started to collapse in the 1960s. This collapse would have enormous implications for the physical condition of the ghetto.

When confronted with collapsing demand, landlords at the bottom of the housing market have few options for continuing to gain profit. They already are at the bottom of the market, so they cannot market their

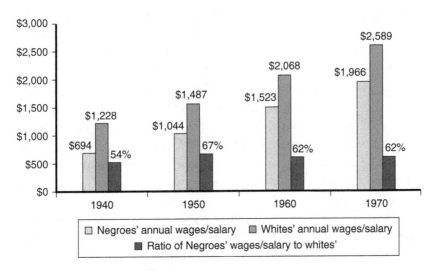

FIGURE 5.2 Annual wages/salary for male householders outside the South, 1940–1970. *Source:* Author's tabulation of Integrated Public Use Microdata (Ruggles et al. 2010).

housing to a poorer clientele. They can lower rents, and, indeed, rents increased more slowly than overall inflation during the 1960s.[35] But there are of course limits to how much rents can be lowered before this makes the operation unprofitable. Given that many costs for the landlord are fixed or likely to rise (e.g., property taxes, insurance, and utilities), the most obvious option would be to cut back on services or even to abandon the property if no amount of service cutbacks can render a profit.

This dynamic indeed appears to describe the paradox of ghetto housing in the 1960s. Rising incomes and white flight allowed blacks on average to move out of the tightly packed ghettos of the 1940s and 1950s and reside in better housing than ever before. But at the same time the ghetto housing market started to shrink. Faced with fixed or rising costs and declining revenue due to declining demand, landlords chose to cut the only expenses they could—maintenance. This led to the degradation of a significant component of ghetto housing even while housing for blacks on the whole was improving. The deplorable conditions described earlier in this chapter were one manifestation of this decline in housing maintenance.

Another manifestation was abandonment, which became widespread in American ghettos in earnest in the 1960s. Once deferring maintenance no longer allowed landlords to squeeze additional profits out of their buildings, many landlords simply walked away, leaving their buildings to deteriorate until uninhabitable. Extensive systematic data on abandonment in the 1960s do not exist, but anecdotes abound. As William Grigsby and his colleagues surmised in 1973, "Mounting evidence strongly suggests that the long-term upward trend in housing conditions in major metropolitan areas suddenly levelled off and reversed itself in the mid-1960s. Despite generally rising incomes and expanded Federal programs, the housing problems for lower income families in these areas is getting worse. The housing crisis . . . is occasioned by the deterioration and partial abandonment of large sections of the inner city."[36]

Moreover, a survey of Cleveland, Chicago, Detroit, Hoboken, New York, and St. Louis in 1973 concluded that "abandonment was found to be concentrated in low-income, all-black neighborhoods in which poverty and social pathologies have become worse since 1960."[37] Another study of abandonment in Newark found that increases in black poverty were associated with increased abandonment.[38] The abandonment that began in the latter half of the 1960s swelled to such proportions that news articles talked of a fear of "ghost towns" in the black inner city and likened abandonment to an "urban cancer" eating away at the vitality of many cities.[39]

The physical decline of the ghetto, both absolute and relative, during the 1960s was incongruent with the black progress described at the beginning of this chapter. As blacks fought their way into the mainstream of American society, their physical space was in many instances literally crumbling around them. Could the ghetto be viewed as the place where blacks would become full-fledged citizens, or was it only a reminder of their second-class status? The events of the 1960s would prove that the physical squalor of the ghetto would now become tinder for the volcanic rage that would erupt there.

THE GHETTO EXPLODES

The poor Negro citizens of Newark's South Ward feel that the city's politics and economics work against them. This has bred apathy . . . , and a state of deep frustration. Anger against the established powers can easily lead to violence and bloodshed.

DOROTHY HEIGHT, "SOUTH WARD NEWARK CHANGING; WHITES MOVE OUT, NEGROES MOVE IN: BUT THE POWER REMAINS THE SAME" (1966)

The riots of the 1960s stand out as *the* iconic events symbolizing dissatisfaction with the ghetto. The riots for the most part took place inside the physical space of the ghetto. They occurred for many reasons, but the ghetto as a place of confinement and mistreatment was undoubtedly among the major causes.

By the 1960s, urban riots and unorganized violence were hardly new to the United States. There were the infamous Draft riots of 1863, in which scores of blacks were attacked by whites who resented being drafted to fight in the Civil War while wealthy whites were allowed to purchase deferments. What might be more aptly described as pogroms, where whites attacked blacks, took place in Wilmington, North Carolina, in 1898; Atlanta in 1906; Tulsa, Oklahoma, in 1921; and Rosewood, Florida, in 1923, among other places. These violent outbreaks typically involved white mobs descending upon black individuals or communities and wreaking havoc. After both world wars, riots often occasioned Negroes' movement into all-white neighborhoods, which was followed by white mobs using intimidation and violence to chase the Negroes out.[40]

In the early twentieth century, however, the plotlines that heretofore characterized riots began to change. Rather than standing solely as victims, blacks often fought back. For the first time, blacks fought whites in the streets, most notably in Chicago and Washington, DC, during the "Red summer" of 1919. Fighting back was heralded as a sign of Negroes asserting their "manhood."[41] Moreover, it was in the early twentieth century that blacks began to act as the primary protagonists in these violent dramas. A case in point is the Harlem disturbance of 1935, when blacks took to the streets to protest perceived police brutality. The year 1943 would see a replay of these "black" riots, with disturbances occurring in Detroit, Harlem, and Birmingham. In each of these instances, blacks either battled with whites or were the primary actors in the riots.

By the 1960s, the die was cast for the nature of urban unrest. Blacks, often provoked by the actions of white authorities (e.g., the police), were the primary and often only actors rioting, and for the most part rioting took place within ghetto confines. The Watts unrest of 1965 was typical. A police stop for alleged drunken driving led to a scuffle, which attracted a crowd of onlookers that soon grew into an angry crowd. Spurred on by rumors of police brutality, the crowd lashed out at the police and the surrounding environs. Before it would all end six days later, 34 people lay dead, 1,032 had been injured, more than $40 million in property damage had been done, and the National Guard had been called in to restore order. Outbreaks on a similar scale would convulse both Detroit and Newark in the summer of 1967, and scores of smaller disturbances would happen in ghettos across the country before the end of the decade.

Police brutality was often the proximate cause of the riots—the experiences described at the beginning of this chapter suggest how chronic mistreatment by the police could have stoked the simmering anger that eventually boiled over. But as numerous post mortem reports attest, the roots of the unrest ran deeper. Discrimination outside the ghetto was certainly a cause, as were the discrimination that confined many to the ghetto and the deplorable conditions inside the ghetto, including police disrespect and crumbling housing. In post mortem assessments, rioters described their motives in terms of their anger and frustration with conditions in the ghetto. Consider the responses of participants in Buffalo disturbances from June 26 to July 1, 1967. Although a case of police brutality was cited as the immediate cause, participants also volunteered more deep-seated structural explanations: "The police push you off the street corners and off the sidewalks if you stand there. And where else you going to stand? You were probably pushed out of school and you can't get a job so you stand on the streets just hoping some money will come by or that you can get into some happening—something, something."[42] "We could sing 'We Shall Overcome' until doomsday and nobody would listen to us. Throw a brick and break a window and the whole world wants to know what's wrong—as if they didn't know already."[43]

The protests of the long hot summers of the 1960s were a revolt over what the ghetto represented as much as a revolt over other types of Negro disenfranchisement. As such, these summers provide further evidence of the ghetto's evolution from a place of aspirations to a place of despair.

Interpreting the urban unrest of the late 1960s as evidence of ghetto dissatisfaction and the loss of the ghetto's role as a beacon for black progress rests on several pillars. First, consider where the riots took place. The violence—setting buildings on fire, sniping at police, and looting commercial establishment—took place within the most disadvantaged sections of the cities: the ghettos.[44] In lashing out, people congealed into mobs and often took out their frustration on the buildings around them, literally burning down and looting the structures in their midst. Lest we think that all mob violence simply lashes out at the nearest, most convenient target, we should recall that many of the urban riots described at the beginning of this section entailed white mobs seeking out and destroying black neighborhoods. White mobs, acting on the rumor of a black man attacking a white woman and of Negroes arming themselves to attack whites, armed themselves and attacked the black Greenwood section of Tulsa in 1921. The mob targeted and acted on the source of their rage—Negroes who needed to be "put in their place." The mobs acting on their passions nearly half a century later would also target their rage at commercial establishments and the police. Housing and black-owned stores were less often the target.[45] Snippets of the riots in progress relate that "around noon, extensive fire bombing began. Few white persons were attacked; the principal intent of the rioters now seemed to be to destroy property owned by whites, in order to drive white 'exploiters' out of the ghetto." In another instance, "grocery stores and liquor stores, clothing and furniture stores, drug stores and cleaners, appliance stores and pawnshops were the principal targets."[46] Thus, the riots, although often appearing to be utter chaos in form and self-destructive to the communities where they occurred, did have a certain logic. Homes were not destroyed as often because of the obvious utility of housing, even if dilapidated and owned by someone else. Moreover, there was less to be gained by looting other poor people's homes.

Second, consider the words of the people living in the riot-torn communities, such as those quoted in historian Max Herman's oral history of the unrest in Detroit and Newark in 1967:

People were already feeling that something was gonna happen in the City of Newark in those days. Because a lot . . . , too may unemployed, not representation, and at the same time, what happened was, people try to get better living conditions. And that what created frustration, people starting to get upset.

We had a rebellion, because of police conditions, health conditions, employment conditions, people didn't know how to express the rage that was in them but it boiled to a point where it had to explode, and it exploded.

What it felt like in the streets, in the years before hand was that literally people were gonna rise up, that they were gonna get to the point where that had just had enough and no matter what it cost them, they were going to do something dramatic to protest.[47]

Opinion surveys taken in the 1960s generally found that although most blacks did not approve of the disturbances, they were sympathetic to the animus that motivated the disorder. For example, one survey found that two-thirds of blacks thought the disorder "served a purpose."[48] Another survey found the majority of blacks thought riots were caused by maltreatment of the race, including by means of prejudice (36 percent), a lack of jobs (29 percent), and ghetto conditions (28 percent) in general.[49] A survey of blacks living in the area affected by the Watts riots in 1965 found that 50 percent of respondents held an unfavorable view of the riot. Nevertheless, 46 percent of these same respondents thought the terms *revolt*, *rebellion*, and *insurrection* were appropriate for describing what happened, and 62 percent saw the disorder as a form of "Negro protest."[50] To the extent that the locals affected by the disorder disapproved, it was often because of the violent outcomes and the destruction of property rather than because they did not understand the rioters' motives. Summarizing the evidence, the Kerner Commission—established by President Lyndon B. Johnson to study the riot—concluded: "[There was] . . . a great deal of tacit support for the rioters among the non-rioters. Apparently many of them also saw the rioting as a protest, and a successful one at that, against the grievances of the Negro ghettos[,] . . . [w]hich means that the 1960s riots were a manifestation of race and racism in the United States, a reflection of the social problems of modern black ghettos, a protest against the essential conditions of life there."[51]

The riots were thus an explosion of pent-up anger at conditions in the ghetto and specific institutions, notably the police and retail commerce. For many, the ghetto was like an internment camp with an occupying army (the police) and retail merchants who exploited rather than served the community. This mass protest against conditions in the ghetto speaks volumes about the evolution of the ghetto in black life. At a time when blacks were defeating Jim Crow in the South and achieving notable "firsts," the ghetto itself was now seen as an intolerable millstone around the race's neck.

The latter point does not speak to the long-standing debate over rioting as an act of mass criminality versus a form of political protest. Supporters of the view of the rioters as criminals pointed to the widespread looting and the lack of coherent political objectives that characterized most of the disturbances. In a chapter of *The Unheavenly City* entitled "Rioting Mainly for Fun and for Profit," Edward C. Banfield argued in 1970 that the unrest of the 1960s was a form of rampaging and pillaging and, as the chapter title suggests, "mainly for fun and for profit." He pointed to rising living standards among blacks to buttress his view.[52] Conversely, rioting as political protest is seen an expression of dissatisfaction with living conditions in the ghetto.

The political interpretation seems more persuasive. The timing of the riots, during a decade of rebellion against authority across the Western world, is consistent with this perspective.[53] The political protest perspective is also consistent with the sparks that precipitated most of the riots in this period. It is true that people coalescing into mobs engage in arson, looting, and violence not only over outrageous acts but over joyous ones as well. Witness the riots that often occur around sporting events. But the ghetto riots of the 1960s almost always arose from perceived or real police mistreatment of blacks—a long-standing grievance in the ghetto. If people were mobbing just to loot, pillage, and have "fun," why did the riots occur only on the occasion of police brutality?

My sympathies aside, *both* interpretations support my thesis that the riots were the exclamation points signaling the death of the ghetto as a symbol of black progress. Most obviously, the riots as political protest confirms the notion that blacks were protesting the wretched conditions of the ghetto. If, in contrast, the ghetto still served mainly as a haven, a place for aspiration and of inspiration, protesting the conditions found there would be unlikely at best.

Viewing riots as mass criminality, however, is also consistent with the fall of the ghetto. Rather than a place for blacks to establish their humanity, prove themselves capable of adapting to modernity, and achieve upward mobility, the ghetto was now a place where baser motives prevailed. It was a place where people engaged in mass criminality, burning, and looting. In the riots-as-protest view, there is a compelling inference of the decline of the ghetto, whereas in the mass-criminality view the riots themselves serve as direct evidence of the decline of the ghetto.

The 1960s were thus the fulcrum point for the ghetto's evolution from a space of uplift to one of desolation. And yet it can still be claimed that although economic and social forces had coalesced to make the ghetto a place to escape, also rising at this time was an ideology that promised to utilize the ghetto as the place where blacks could finally achieve full independence.

BACK TO THE GHETTO

If the riots were a means of expressing anger and frustration at conditions in the ghetto, a contemporaneous attitude and ideology represented an alternative way for blacks to achieve full equality—black power. This alternative perspective had enormous implications for the meaning of the ghetto to black America.

Black Power

The long civil rights struggle, which in some sense began once the Thirteenth Amendment of the Constitution was passed, is remembered as a struggle for blacks to become fully incorporated into the civil, economic, and political life of America. Once slavery ended, blacks wanted to be equal, to be treated fairly, and to be given the same opportunities that white Americans had. Black Americans opposed the Black Codes adopted in southern states because the codes singled blacks out for conditions that differed little from slavery. They bitterly opposed disenfranchisement and the ensuing Jim Crow segregation because full citizenship was denied with them. In the North, too, blacks struggled for equality during the nineteenth and twentieth centuries, fighting de facto and occasionally de jure segregation.[54] And, of course, the civil rights movement of the post–World War II era fought against segregation, which was ubiquitous in the South. The history of African Americans is a history of fighting for the rights and privileges promised all Americans.

But there was always a competing approach for achieving racial equality. Given the ubiquitous maltreatment of blacks at the hands of whites, some blacks questioned if true equality within a white-dominated polity was possible or even desirable. In the nineteenth and early twentieth centuries, whites almost uniformly thought the Negro inferior. Even whites opposed to slavery or later to de jure segregation seldom thought blacks as the biological or social equal of whites. In the words of one Negro, "Very few white people have ever seriously considered the Negro as entitled to complete citizenship and equality."[55] Perhaps Negroes would be better off on their own, where "the millions of black folk could be free to till the fields and get the benefit of their toil; where they could find and keep jobs in industry and commerce, in transportation and other utilities, in the building trades, in editing daily newspapers, where, in all the affairs in our civilized life, Negro women and men could advance as far as their abilities permit."[56] These statements from Oscar C. Brown, leader of the 49th State Movement, aptly capture the thoughts of black nationalists before and after he wrote his manifesto "What Chance Freedom?" in 1935. According to this view, rather than integration and full inclusion into American society, a separate Negro society might be the best way for blacks to achieve equality.

A Black Nation Where?

The various strands of black nationalism that arose over the years differed in many ways, but a common theme among them was the notion of a physical space that blacks could control without interference from whites. Early black nationalists in the eighteenth and nineteenth centuries often thought in terms of recolonizing part of Africa so that American blacks could create their own nation-state. Some free blacks, with British and American assistance, respectively, did indeed establish free colonies in Sierra Leone and Liberia. Sierra Leone was established in 1787 by the blacks who fought with the British during the American Revolutionary War and Liberia in 1821 by free American blacks.

After the Civil War, blacks with a nationalist inkling looked closer to home to achieve their dreams of creating a black "promised land." Fleeing white terrorism and searching for a place to become economically self-sufficient, thousands of blacks moved to Kansas, famous as the home of the fierce abolitionist John Brown. Some migrants viewed their move in millenarian terms, calling their migration an "exodus" to freedom.[57]

During the first wave of the Great Migration during World War I, black nationalism as an ideology blossomed, as noted in chapter 2. This time, both Africa and the incipient big-city ghettos served as spaces where black nationalists' dreams might be realized. Black groups for whom Africa beckoned as the place to realize Negro redemption included the Moorish Science Temple and the United Negro Improvement Association founded by Marcus Garvey.

Although lacking the visibility and emotional inspiration of the United Negro Improvement Association, the black ideology that was most pervasive and long lasting was the dream of a "black metropolis" that would result in political power and separate black-owned and run institutions—as in the

Bronzevilles arising in American cities. Without retreading the same ground as chapter 2, it is sufficient here to recall the durability of the Negro cultural, economic, and political institutions as well as the ghetto spaces created during the first wave of the Great Migration. Many of these institutions and the ghetto, too, are still with us some one hundred years later.

The Great Depression squashed dreams of completely realizing a black metropolis, and the Garveyite dream of a black homeland was hampered by opposition from other black leaders (e.g., W. E. B. Du Bois), mismanagement, federal investigations, the eventual conviction of Garvey for fraud, and the sheer impracticality of Garvey's vision. The ideology of black nationalism, with the exception of the small 49th State Movement, which pushed for a forty-ninth state carved out of one of the less densely populated states,[58] would lie dormant from the 1930s to the 1960s.

The Ghetto as a Home of Black Nationalism

During the 1960s, however, there was a resurgence of black nationalism, especially outside of the South. Whereas Jim Crow segregation and enfranchisement made civil rights and integration goals that virtually all blacks could get behind, the subtler racism of the North inspired a cynicism that caused many blacks to turn inward in their search for equality.

Former African and Asian colonies successfully shaking off the yoke of their European masters during the 1950s and 1960s also served to inspire black political activists in the United States. The success of black and brown peoples abroad dispelled the myth of white superiority and pointed the way forward for American blacks to achieve independence. If Africans in Africa could free themselves of the great European empires, surely black Americans in America could free themselves from the hegemony of white supremacy. Inspired by events abroad, black nationalists would issue calls for independence that ranged from the establishment of independent nation-states to local control of institutions in the ghetto.[59]

Echoing the words of Oscar C. Brown, who had advocated a "black state" three decades before him, Malcolm X argued that "twenty million ex-slaves must be permanently separated from our former slave master and placed on some land that we can call our own. Then we can create our own jobs. Control our own economy. Solve our own problems instead of waiting on the American white man to solve our problems for us."[60] Further distinguishing the aspirations of nationalists like himself and the integrationists, he argued: "[The] only kind of revolution that's nonviolent is the Negro revolution. The only revolution based on loving your enemy is the Negro revolution. The only revolution in which the goal is a desegregated lunch counter, a desegregated theater, a desegregated park, and a desegregated public toilet; you can sit down next to white folks on the toilet. That's no revolution. *Revolution is based on land. Land is the basis of all independence. Land is the basis of freedom, justice, and equality.*"[61]

The Black Panther Party, too, would make land point ten of its Ten Point Program: "We want land, bread, housing, education, clothing justice and peace."[62]

Provocative as these words were, Malcolm X and other nationalists were short on details specifying where the land that would serve as the basis of the revolution was to be. At best, one can glean references from Malcolm X calling for "a separate nation for ourselves, right here in America" or asserting that "we must and insist upon an area in this land that we can call our own" or, more concretely, asking, "[If] the United States can subsidize Israel to start a state[,] . . . Why can['t] the Black Man in America have a piece of land with technical help and money to get his own nation established?"[63]

One exception to this vagueness was the Republic of New Africa (RNA), which called for South Carolina, Georgia, Alabama, and Mississippi to serve as the locus of a new black nation-state. Founded by the brothers Milton and Richard Henry in Detroit in 1968, the RNA sought to have a black nation created in the black belt where the bulk of the slaves' labor was stolen, the most exploitative form of sharecropping took place, and large numbers of blacks still lived. With startup funding from the U.S. federal government in the form of reparations, blacks would have the wherewithal to choose their own destiny free from interference from whites.

But although some argued for the creation of a nation-state in the South or among an amalgamation of unnamed states, it would be the ghetto where dreams of a black nation would come closest to fruition.

The Ghetto as a Black Nation

Dreams of a separate land controlled by blacks had emotional appeal and captured media attention, but the realization of this dream encountered the same problem faced earlier by the Garveyites—sheer impracticality. By the 1960s, few if any places on earth were not already claimed by modern nation-states. This meant the continental United States was the only real possibility for a black nation-state. But where? Consider the RNA's proposal that this state be formed by a combination of South Carolina, Georgia, Mississippi, and Alabama. In 1970, these four states had more than 8 million whites.[64] Would these whites be incorporated into the new black nation-state? Would they be "encouraged" to leave in a form of ethnic cleansing on a Stalinist scale? Given that the federal government had fought a war a century earlier to prevent these same states, along with several others, from leaving the union, it is hard to imagine the federal government not only allowing but actively facilitating the creation of a separate nation-state there. It is ironic that those who were most skeptical about white intentions and hence viewed separation as the only realistic solution in turn expected the most from whites—to cede a substantial portion of the nation to a sovereign black state.

Perhaps because of the sheer fantasticalness of the idea, support for a separate nation-state was never more than marginal. One survey in 1968 showed that only 6 percent of blacks supported the notion.[65] Even the RNA, one of the most ardent proponents of a separate nation-state, estimated that less than half of the approximately 22 million blacks in America would wish to live in such a state.[66]

Instead of in a separate nation, black nationalism would manifest itself in what Robert Brown and Todd C. Shaw refer to as "community nationalism."[67] Community nationalism garnered much greater mass appeal and would indeed come to shape the landscape of the ghetto for decades. Nationalism in this flavor meant black sway over institutions in the ghetto and was thus more palatable to the masses. Whereas only 6 percent of blacks favored a black nation-state according to the same survey done in 1968, 96 percent were in favor of more Negro businesses, banks, and stores, and 70 percent felt Negroes should shop in Negro-owned stores whenever possible. Nationalist sensibilities were reflected in another survey where a respondent said, "Negroes are becoming more conscious of the need for making their communities better. For that reason I can't see that it would be entirely necessary to move to white areas to find better housing."[68] Nationalist sentiments also lurk beneath some of the comments made by respondents in Clark's book *Dark Ghetto*, questions such as "Why in the hell—this is more or less a colored neighborhood—do we have so many white cops? We don't need them here." and "Why don't more colored business places open? This is our part of town."[69]

Although the term *black power* was coined in the South by Stokely Carmichael, it was in the black ghettos of the North that black power was most prominent. For example, the most influential mosques of the Nation of Islam in the United States were typically in the northern ghettos.[70] When groups of young blacks began forming branches of the Black Panther Party outside of Oakland, California, they did so in the urban North. Only four of the sixty-seven branches listed in a congressional investigation in 1971 were in the South.[71] Moreover, it was at "the center of low-income areas of African American communities,"[72] specifically the ghettos of the urban North, that Panther offices were located. Although the majority of blacks still lived in the South, and large numbers had started to escape the ghettos of the urban North by the late 1960s, it was in the urban North that the ideology of black power took root. The message of the original Black Panther Party in Oakland—self-defense and self-determination—resonated most among everyday working-class and poor blacks who lived in the ghettos.

Similar to the black nationalism that had manifested decades earlier in dreams of a black metropolis, the black nationalism of the late 1960s had impacts on black culture and economic and political institutions. The Black Arts Movement represented the artistic and cultural facet of the black power ideology of the 1960s and indeed was considered by some a precursor to the rise of black power in the late 1960s and early 1970s. Like the Harlem Renaissance of several decades earlier, the Black Arts Movement had powerful political overtones. Broadly speaking (and running the risk of oversimplification), the Harlem Renaissance had aimed to prove the Negro's humanity through the production of world-class art by Negroes, whereas the Black Arts Movement aimed to produce black art that was independent of white control and not governed by white sensibilities. Black Arts Movement artists were not looking to prove the race's humanity. Rather, they sought to craft and refine a cultural aesthetic independent of whites. Indeed, artists operating in this movement saw oppressed blacks, not whites, as their primary audience. As one proponent of the movement put it, "The Black Arts Movement eschews 'protest' literature. It speaks directly to Black people."[73]

The ultimate aim of black art of course varied from artist to artist. For Leroi Jones (who later chose to be called Amiri Baraka), sometimes called the father of the Black Arts Movement, black art was to be the vanguard of the black revolution, creating a new black aesthetic and identity that would supplant prevailing white and Western ways of knowing and viewing the world among blacks. This new black aesthetic would elevate the consciousness of the black masses and prepare them for revolution.[74] Art for art's sake that did "not respond positively to the cause of black mental and physical liberation was irrelevant."[75] Some black artists were influenced by Pan-African ideals and sought connections with African culture. Others such Maulana Karenga argued that there was a unique African American aesthetic born of the experiences of African ancestry, slavery, and living in America that should be cultivated.[76] Whatever their differences, there was near unanimity among black nationalists that blacks should create and curate their own art and that such art would be critical for elevating black consciousness and pride.

The rhetoric of community nationalism spoke of raising black consciousness and pride, using this new consciousness to gain economic and political power, protecting such power where it existed, and using that power to benefit blacks. Malcolm X argued that blacks should use their numbers in the cities to control municipal governments for the benefit of blacks.[77] Some writers took up this ideology to question the quest for integrated housing. Decrying calls for integrated housing, one writer said: "One example must suffice to illustrate the incompatibility of the assimilationist ideologies with the new needs and priorities of black people. . . . [H]ousing is one of the most fundamental internal affairs and also the fact that, for black people, internal affairs are power affairs." The writer concluded, "A leadership whose ideologies lead it to think in terms of literally tearing down black communities for the sake of integration, whose actions—whatever the intent—threaten the political and economic base of the black community, is not the leadership to occupy the dominant position."[78] Others, such as members of the Black Panther Party, whose ideology and tactics evolved considerably over the years, equated the ghetto to a third-world colony that needed liberation:

In our struggle for National liberation, we are now in the phase of community liberation to free our black communities from the imperialistic control exercised over them by the racist exploiting cliques within white communities, to free our people, locked up as they are in urban dungeons, from the imperialism of the white Suburbs. Ours is a struggle against community imperialism, our black communities are colonized and controlled from outside, and it is this control that has to be smashed, broken, shattered, by whatever means necessary. The politics in our communities are controlled from outside, the economics of our communities are controlled from outside, and we ourselves are controlled by the racist police who come into our communities from outside and occupy them, patrolling, terrorizing, and brutalizing our people like a foreign army in a conquered land.[79]

"Foreign army" indeed. The Black Panther biweekly newspaper regularly featured images and stories likening the ghetto to third-world colonies.

The Black Panther Party's support for the incorporation of North Richmond is another instance of its attempt to wrest political control for the black community. Referring to the travails of North Richmond, an unincorporated ghetto outside of Richmond, California, that had petitioned for annexation to that city, "The Black Panther Party for Self Defense, in cooperation with other concerned residents of the area, have decided in the interest of black people to incorporate the area into an independent city that will not be at the cruel mercy of the racist swine, the bloodsucking parasites."[80] Some activists in Watts also sought to secede from the City of Los Angeles as a way of allowing for self-determination and a system that would better serve the residents of Watts; it was felt that the "people can take care of their community better than congressmen in Washington, assemblymen in Sacramento and Councilmen downtown."[81]

Children, the seeds of the next generation, also figured prominently in the visions of community nationalists. Blacks' lack of control over their children's education was a glaring reminder of the lack of black power. One activist observed that the residents of Harlem "do not control policy or direction, and are powerless to bring about meaningful changes. In New York City, as in the segregated schools of the South, the people of Harlem have no control over their schools. As in the South, we have a situation where white overlords are overseeing the education of black children."[82] It was felt that this lack of control, besides leading to bad education, "is at the root of the anguish in black communities across the country." Ghetto schools were seen as being staffed by "white middle-class teachers who bring preconceived notions about the inability of the 'culturally deprived' to learn," resulting in a situation where "[black] kids cannot possibly learn."[83] Cultivating and nurturing black children in a way that would allow them to grow up to be proud and successful black adults was something that should be in the hands of the black community, so it could hold schools accountable.

The Black Panther Party was initially conceived as a program for self-defense, so it should come as no surprise that its rhetoric included notions of self-defense. The party would "require many facets," and "armed defense guards would have to be organized within the confines of the law. They would function as defense units to safeguard life, limb and property in the ghetto communities."[84] Beyond checking the power of the police in the ghetto, the Black Panthers also sought control of the community's housing: "We believe that if the white landlords will not give decent housing to our black community, the housing and the land should be made into cooperatives so that our community, with government aid, can build and make decent housing for its people."[85]

Community nationalists thought that the local retail economy, too, could and should be controlled by blacks as a means of ameliorating the poverty prevalent in the ghetto: "Economically, African-American nationalism demands that we use collective economic power, wherever it is feasible, as a means to improve our group's economic position. . . . [T]he small businesses, such as grocery stores, laundries, clothing stores, restaurants, must be owned by black people on a collective basis,"[86] and, "economically, we are at the mercy of the exploiters, businessmen, storeowners, merchants, who have turned our communities into market places out of which they make huge profits, through high prices and high rent, draining off all the prosperity, and leaving our communities to deteriorate into desolate, poverty-stricken, dirty slums."[87] In Boston following the death of Dr. Martin Luther King Jr., at a rally of more than 8,000 people, the Black United Front issued twenty-one demands to the mayor and city of Boston, including turning over all of the white-owned and controlled businesses in Roxbury to black people and naming all schools in the black community after black heroes.[88]

Finally, black power meant land reform and redevelopment in both the North and the South as well as collective black ownership of land resources to provide food, community services, and meaningful employment.[89]

Roy Innis of CORE succinctly made the case for black power in the ghetto: "Large densely populated black areas, especially in urban centers, must have a change in status. They must become political sub-divisions of the state, instead of sub-colonial appendages of the cities. Blacks must manage and control the institutions that service their areas, as has always been the case for other interest groups."[90]

Thus, in the rhetoric of community nationalism, blacks would create cultural institutions and assume control of the economic, educational, and political institutions of the ghetto. Economic control would allow black firms to hire other blacks and keep profits in the community, thereby enriching the ghetto. Educational control would produce schools accountable to the community and ultimately better-educated children. Finally, political control would give ghetto residents a voice in how they were governed along with all the benefits that voice would entail. That was the rhetoric of community nationalism.

The Reality of Community Nationalism

In the late 1960s, ghetto nationalist rhetoric was easy to find. But what of the reality? Was the ghetto a space where black power could actually be put into practice?

In the cultural realm, putting black power into practice increasingly meant creating and disseminating black art in the ghetto. During the early twentieth century, Negroes were routinely excluded from many cultural venues, and so Harlem provided a necessary space for the renaissance to flower. By the 1960s, however, there were several bohemian districts in major cities, such as Greenwich Village in New York, Venice Beach in Los Angeles, and the area around Wayne State University in Detroit, where blacks had an opportunity to be creative in relatively racially tolerant spaces.[91] Some blacks went on to achieve great acclaim in these bohemian milieus— Leroi Jones perhaps being the most notable. Beyond bohemian neighborhoods, many black artists and black power intellectuals got their start in predominantly white institutions, such as Wayne State in Detroit, where the Black Student Union served as a font for the Black Arts Movement in Detroit. Similarly, the Afro-American Association at the University of California at Berkeley, whose nationalist work included community organizing and the sponsoring of artistic events and cultural centers, was where founding members of the Black Panther Party and the cultural nationalist group US got their first introduction to an organized black nationalism.[92]

Nevertheless, for several reasons the ghetto would serve as a haven for the Black Arts Movement. First, there were relatively few bohemian districts in only a few cities, so in many cities black artists had to create their own spaces if they wanted to hone their craft. Second, many participants in the Black Arts Movement were inspired by a desire to connect with the black masses, hoping to raise consciousness among them and inspire a revolution. Finally, black art, in keeping with black power ideology, was to be crafted free of white influence. These last two ambitions could best be achieved in the ghetto, where the masses of blacks still resided and where there were few if any whites.

Leroi Jones's move from Greenwich Village to Harlem and the splitting of the downtown-based Negro Ensemble Company to create the National Black Theater in Harlem are illustrative of the ghetto's role as a haven for the Black Arts Movement. By 1965, Leroi Jones was a well-respected playwright and poet whose work had achieved critical acclaim in the white arts media. Based in the East Village and Lower East Side, he had earned the moniker "King of the Lower East Side." After the murder of Malcolm X in 1965, however, Jones felt that living the life of a true revolutionary meant living among the black masses, so he left the East Village and moved to Harlem to found the Black Arts Repertory Theatre in 1965, whose aims were to expose the black masses to their artistic heritage and to provide space for black artists to develop their craft.[93]

In a similar fashion, Barbara Ann Teer, one of the original founders of the Negro Ensemble Company, based in the Theater District of Manhattan, left the Theater District to create the National Black Theater in Harlem in 1968. Although both of these theater companies sought to create black-inspired theater for black audiences and to provide opportunities for black artists to develop, the National Black Theater placed much more emphasis on connecting with the masses of black people and the ideology of black power—hence, Teer's insistence that the theater be located in the ghetto and include the word *black* rather than *Negro* in its name.[94]

Both Jones and Teer were established black artists who had achieved a modicum of success in the white theater world downtown. Yet they sought out the ghetto as the space to accomplish their dreams—using black art to raise the consciousness of black people and inspire revolution. For Jones and Teer, the ghetto provided a haven for black art, unlike what was available downtown. Other art institutions founded in Harlem around this time, such as the Lafayette Theater and the Studio Museum, allowed the race a greater voice in the curation of black art than was available in the institutions downtown.

Unlike in the Harlem Renaissance, when Harlem was the unchallenged epicenter of an arts movement, in the Black Arts Movement ghettos in other cities were more than bit players. Indeed, the cultural historian James Smethurst argues that Chicago, Detroit, and the cities of the West Coast were in some ways more important than Harlem in this later period.[95]

As was the case in Harlem, the ghettos within these cities provided space for artists to hone and ply their craft and to build a community of artists that fostered communication, collaboration, and inspiration essential to artistic endeavors. In Chicago, the Ebony Museum (later renamed the DuSable Museum) provided a space for blacks to consider the black art they deemed significant, nurture budding young artists, and educate the masses of the race on black art. In Detroit, the Vaughn bookstore served as a space for the dissemination of leftist and Black Arts Movement literature, for readings, and for people to come together to discuss the challenges confronting Detroit's black community.[96] The Boone House, a community arts space started by Margaret Danner in a vacant house owned by the Solomon Baptist Church in Detroit, played a similar role as a space for black artists to come together and showcase their work. The Concept East Theater was started in Detroit in 1962 by performing artists who wanted a permanent space for blacks to showcase their work as well as to give black actors, writers, directors, and other theater professionals an opportunity to work.[97]

Black Arts West in the then heavily black Fillmore section of San Francisco was a locus of black performing artists and provided a space for blacks in the Bay Area to conceive, create, and perform their art. Farther south, in the Watts ghetto of Los Angeles, Jayne Cortez and James Woods set up Studio Watts, which they conceived of as a space to use art to affect social change. The performing and visual artists and writers were welcomed and encouraged to use the space to develop and disseminate their art as well as to mentor Watts residents with artistic aspirations.[98]

Outside the hubs of Chicago, the Bay Area, Detroit, Los Angeles, and New York, similar spaces were created or evolved in other ghettos across the country. Karamu House in Cleveland, which was initially a multiracial settlement house built by whites in 1915, had by the 1940s come to reflect the predominantly Negro character of the surrounding neighborhood and by the 1960s was a space for black artists in Cleveland. In Newark, the Spirit House founded by Amiri Baraka (formerly Leroi Jones) and the Cellar were spaces for black artists to create, perform, commune, and educate.[99]

Despite the inroads into white America made by some black artists, for the Black Arts Movement as a whole the ghetto was a haven where the ultimate goal of this movement—to raise the consciousness of the race—could best be achieved. Many of the cultural traditions and institutions that began as part of the Black Arts Movement, such as Kwanzaa and the Studio Museum in Harlem, remain with us to this day. The change in race consciousness as reflected by the switch from the terms *colored* and *Negro* to *black* and *African American* and by the wearing of natural hairstyles is part of the legacy of the Black Arts Movement.

Political power was a second dimension where black power ideology sought to make a dramatic break from the status quo in the 1960s. The ideology of black power coalesced with the increasing size of the black population in America's ghettos to set the stage for real political power to emanate from the ghetto. In cities where alderpersons or councilpersons were elected through an at-large system, black political representation had been stymied. As a relatively small portion of the population even when voting as a bloc, blacks seldom had enough votes to elect black politicians in cities with this system.[100] In cities with district-based voting, such as Chicago or New York, blacks had achieved elective office shortly after the onset of the Great Migration.

By the 1960s, the black population had grown so large in many northern cities that black political power was inevitable regardless of the electoral system in place. The cities of Baltimore, Camden, Cleveland, Detroit, Gary, Newark, Oakland, and Washington, DC, had populations that were at least one-third black. If blacks supported black candidates, which the prevailing black power ideology helped ensure, this meant black political power could and did shape and win elections. Starting with the elections of Carl Stokes in Cleveland and Richard Hatcher in Gary, Indiana, in 1967, blacks began winning the mayoralty of the nation's largest cities. Having a black mayor would prove no panacea, but there were tangible benefits. There was the symbolic pride of having a black person as the chief executive of cities that were among the largest in the country. Black public officials in such high-profile positions no doubt helped pave the way for blacks to be elected to other high-profile political positions, such as senator, governor, and ultimately president of the United States.

Aside from the symbolic benefits of a black chief executive, black mayors also brought economic benefits to the black communities that elected them. Beyond the usual patronage that all politicians dole out, many black mayors adopted specific affirmative-action programs to boost black businesses contracting with local government. Black mayors followed Atlanta mayor Maynard Jackson's establishment of set-aside programs stipulating that a portion of city contracts be awarded to minority-owned firms. Kenneth Gibson, elected Newark's first black mayor in 1970, created a program that set aside 25 percent of contracts for minorities.[101]

The quest for community control manifested not only in the election of black politicians but also in the development of community-based organizations that would address the socioeconomic problems confronting the ghetto. Ghetto residents would be mobilized and organized, and they themselves would marshal the requisite resources to confront the challenges in their communities.

The manifestation of black power into the community control of local resources was given a boost, perhaps unwittingly, by federal urban policy shifts in the 1960s. Chastened by the failure of urban-renewal programs to arrest urban decline and by the backlash against the demolition and displacement that often accompanied these programs, which we encountered in the previous chapter, the federal government sought new ways to address urban decline. Federal policy makers were influenced by Chicago community organizer Saul Alinsky, who wrote, "It is the most common human reaction that successful attainment of objectives is much more meaningful to those who have achieved the objective through their own efforts."[102]

Thus, through components of the War on Poverty, such as the Special Initiatives Program (SIP), which required portions of the programs be directed to "locally initiated community corporations," and the Community Action Program (CAP), which called for "Maximum Feasible

Participation," the federal government perhaps unintentionally provided tools for the realization of black power in the ghetto. SIP provided one impetus for the creation and strengthening of community-based organizations. CAP required that poor local residents play a major role in running federal antipoverty programs and, indeed, in determining how federal resources should be used, and further amendments to the CAP stipulated the degree to which community involvement was required. Taking advantage of the federal largesse was a new type of community-based organization: the community-development corporation (CDC).

At least a majority of CDCs' governing boards were made up of local residents, and CDCs frequently hired neighborhood residents to staff their programs. These corporations saw themselves as employing a holistic approach to the challenges facing their community and to that end were involved in business development, community organizing, housing development, and social service provision. The Bedford Stuyvesant Redevelopment Corporation and the Hough Area Development Corporation, both started in 1967, are examples of early CDCs that came into being at the beginning of the black power era. Most notably, many of the CDCs would prove durable, continuing to exist today. The track record of CDCs has been highly contested, however. Detractors claim that CDCs, including ones dating to the black power era, have done little to arrest the decline of the ghetto and act just like any other profit-maximizing institution.[103] Conversely, others have acknowledged the Sisyphean task of community development but point to successful affordable-housing and social service programs as evidence of CDC success.[104] To be sure, black power ideology was not solely responsible for the successes (or failures) of the CDC movement. But the existence of the ghetto did provide a space for community nationalism and consequently for the CDC movement to take root and flourish. When thinking about the role the ghetto played for blacks in the 1960s, the ghetto as a place to create durable community-based institutions has to be included.

The ideology of community nationalism sought more than political power, however; economic power was also a goal. In this dimension, the successes were perhaps less concrete. As we saw in chapter 2, the ghetto as a distinct and separate space seemed to offer the opportunity for blacks to carve out their own economy. This could mean black economic self-sufficiency or autarky, as articulated by Malcolm X:

The Honorable Elijah Muhammad teaches us that on our own land we can set up farms, factories, businesses. We can establish our own government and become an independent nation. And once we become separated from the jurisdiction of this white nation, we can then enter into trade and commerce for ourselves with other independent nations. This is the only solution. The Honorable Elijah Muhammad says that in our own land we can establish our own agricultural system. We can grow food to feed our own people. We can raise cattle and use the hides, the leather, and the wool to clothe our own people. We can dig the clay from the earth and make bricks to build homes for our people. We can turn the trees into lumber and furnish the homes for our own people.[105]

Or as Talmadge Anderson put it, "If black people are to be liberated under capitalism . . . black people must control the land and the institutions affecting the black community. In order to achieve this objective, it might mean the temporary, but strategic separation on an economic basis."[106]

As an alternative to or in conjunction with autarky, community nationalism might mean a rejection of capitalism altogether. Black power in this view meant "the primitive accumulation of capital by black people in a collective or co-operative ownership fashion for the benefit of the masses of black people and not just a few individuals."[107] Or community nationalism might mean practicing the principal of Ujaama, or cooperative economics. Ujaama is one of the seven principles of Kwanzaa, which was conceived in 1966 by the US organization. Ujaama stresses a cooperative and communal economy that will prevent individuals or groups from amassing undue wealth and power or from experiencing extreme poverty. As distinguished from "European communism," the collective approach practiced by blacks was to be "voluntary" and thus "communal."[108]

Whatever emotional appeal autarky or communal socialism may have had, neither idea came to fruition. Autarky would have required blacks to form a self-contained economy, which, of course, would have been impractical even if the majority of blacks had desired to do so. Moreover, for the same reason that economic isolation makes nations poorer, autarky would likely have made blacks poorer. Economic growth typically occurs from economic specialization that allows a region or group to use trade to its advantage. Autarky would have required blacks to provide all goods and services in their self-contained economy. Most likely, blacks would have had to do without goods and services or pay much higher prices for these items.

"Model minorities" that are typically held up as economic success stories typically achieve such success by specializing in a particular "ethnic niche."[109] Communities that have attempted to practice a limited form of autarky (e.g., the Amish) are typically not known for their economic dynamism. Likewise, communal socialism would be impractical to implement in the midst of the largest and most developed capitalist nation on earth and, based on the experiences of other socialist nations, would likely have increased economic inequality between blacks and whites.

Indeed, during the black power era and thereafter, black economic success came outside the ghetto. The most successful black individuals and business enterprises for the most part owed their success to their operation in the wider economy. The economist Timothy Bates writes,

Traditional Black businesses catered to a minority clientele, tended to be small, generated few jobs, and were rarely owned by college graduates. Throughout most of the twentieth century, typical Black firms in urban areas were mom-and-pop food stores, small restaurants, barbershops, and beauty parlors. These traditional personal service and retail businesses located in Black residential areas and served neighborhood clienteles rather than breaking into larger-scale lines of business because of constraints deeply rooted in American society.[110]

In contrast, successful black business in the post–civil rights era tended to "serve racially diverse or largely nonminority clienteles," according to Bates, and were more likely to be located outside the ghetto.[111] Indeed, social scientists have found that higher rates of residential segregation are associated with lower rates of self-employment for various racial and ethnic groups.[112] Although nationalists viewed the ghetto as the bedrock on which to build the black economy, the irony is that integration would prove more lucrative for black entrepreneurship.

This is not to deny the influence that black nationalism had on economic development in the ghetto. Indeed, even President Richard Nixon would at least pay lip service to notions of black power, calling for "black ownership . . . black pride, black jobs, black opportunity, and yes, black power in the best, the constructive sense of that often misapplied term."[113] Some ideas planted the seeds for policies and programs that remain with us today. CORE's Community Self-Determination bill, which called for federally chartered, community-controlled development corporations that would partner with outside investors to develop enterprises in the ghetto and whose profits would be reinvested in the ghetto, anteceded the rise of the CDC model described earlier as well as programs such as the New Markets Tax Credit, which uses tax incentives to encourage investment in poor neighborhoods. Overall, however, history would prove that the ghetto would not serve as the springboard for black economic development in the 1960s.

This failure stands in stark contrast to the role the ghetto played in black economic development when the first wave of nationalism swept the ghetto in the "New Negro" era. During that era, modern economic institutions controlled by blacks were created in larger numbers than ever before in U.S. history. Moreover, the ghetto was instrumental in this development. Despite the aspirations of nationalists, the ghetto of the 1960s would not play a similar role. Unlike in the Black Arts Movement, for which the ghetto would provide a space for transformational art and politics and for which the ghetto indeed served as an incubator, in the economic sphere the ghetto no longer served to propel the race forward.

THE GHETTO AND THE 1960S

The 1960s witnessed the almost complete eclipsing of the ghetto's role as a haven, when the ghetto shackled black progress and served as a font of black anger. This eclipse was driven by the changing status of blacks in America and changes in the ecology of central cities that rendered the ghetto more marginal than ever before.

Despite the persistence of racism, blacks' status improved steadily over the course of the first six decades of the twentieth century, and with that improvement the ghetto's role changed as well. By the 1960s, blacks no longer needed to prove that they could survive in the city, create art, or establish modern urban institutions—as was the case in the early twentieth century, when many questioned blacks' ability to achieve just these things. Moreover, the ghetto as a place to take advantage of economic opportunities afforded by a dense concentration of urban blacks was being superseded by the opportunities outside the ghetto. Put succinctly, the enclavelike functions of the ghetto had receded dramatically by the 1960s. Yet many blacks were still confined to the ghetto. Adding insult to injury, physical conditions in the ghetto were also declining both relatively and absolutely in many cities.

The decline of the ghetto as a place of aspiration and blacks' growing resentment at being confined there were underscored by the urban unrest experienced in ghettos across the country in the latter part of the decade. This anger and frustration also fed a nationalistic ideology that raised the ghetto once more as a place for aspirations—this time as a place to create a black nation where blacks would control their own economic and political institutions.

Although the ghetto did facilitate the achievement of some black nationalist dreams, notably in the political arena and in the creation of some cultural and community-based organizations that endure to this day, its overall trajectory remained unaltered. In the wake of the civil rights movement, the ghetto's role as a haven would largely be overshadowed by its role as a hell in the life of African Americans.

Chapter Six

THE LAST DECADES OF
THE TWENTIETH CENTURY

The dawn of the 1970s marked the end of the long civil rights struggle. Blacks' civil rights—including the right to vote, to use public facilities unimpeded, and to marry outside of their race—were now enshrined in law. Discrimination based on one's race, both in employment and in housing, which had been the bane of blacks' existence in the urban North, were now illegal. Blacks' cultural and social acceptance, too, was increasing. Started in the 1950s, the trend of blacks becoming national cultural icons, as exemplified by Muhammad Ali, Sammy Davis Jr., and Aretha Franklin, was becoming commonplace. Prejudicial attitudes among whites had declined as well. For example, an analysis of survey questions from 1942 to 1983 that asked white respondents various questions about their openness to integration concluded that "the change over the past four decades has been away from both the principle and, to an extent, the practice of absolute segregation—and in this sense it has been a genuine and large change."[1]

The easing of America's racial caste system transformed the ghetto's role in black America. First, its role as a haven for those fleeing the Jim Crow South, as a space for blacks to adapt to the modern industrial economy, and as a space to develop and nurture black institutions receded. The changing migratory patterns of blacks could provide no clearer evidence of the ghetto's changing status. Blacks stopped flocking to the ghetto by the 1970s, and many who were already there left as fast as they could.

Second, the demise of the racial caste system made the ghetto's walls more porous, allowing increasing numbers of blacks to leave and remain outside of the ghetto. Much as the Great Migration created and shaped the ghetto, this out-migration, often unheralded, would also dramatically affect the ghetto, draining it of the vitality that young, hungry migrants provided.

The easing of blacks' castelike status also changed the definition of the ghetto. For much of the twentieth century, the ghetto could be defined as where black people lived. There were few blacks with the means to escape the ghetto, and white flight and the small size of the black middle class meant those escaping the ghetto were soon followed by their poorer brethren. But in the post–civil rights era, the number of middle-class black neighborhoods soared. When combined with easing of white flight and fair-housing laws that made housing discrimination illegal, some blacks had more choices about where to live than ever before—even if their options were still much more limited than those of whites.

The ghetto did not disappear; it simply evolved. And in many ways it would evolve to make life there qualitatively worse. Indeed, the ghetto of the late twentieth century would barely resemble the ghetto of the early twentieth century that was a place for aspirations. Social conditions deteriorated, and for many the ghetto served not as a springboard for improvement but as an impediment to opportunity.

This chapter chronicles the evolution of the ghetto in the last decades of the twentieth century and the first decades of the twenty-first. After illustrating the demographic changes that sapped the ghetto of its vitality, the chapter focuses on the forces that buffeted black neighborhoods in this period. It concludes on a more optimistic note, however, illustrating that despite the ghetto's fall from grace, there remain many blacks who still view it as a haven and put forth considerable effort to improve life there.

THE PROMISED LAND NO MORE

Perhaps the most compelling evidence of the change in the ghetto's status comes from the actions of blacks themselves. The civil unrest of the 1960s symbolized the race's anger over ghetto conditions, but by the 1970s folks were registering their discontent with those conditions in another way—migration. People voted with their feet and stopped migrating to the northern ghettos, and those who could escape did so. Thus, the ghetto, which was a creation of two great migrations, the first commencing during World War I and the Roaring Twenties and the second from World War II through the 1960s, would again be transformed by two more demographic waves. The first was the near cessation of blacks migrating to the ghettos of the urban North.

After eight decades of streaming north in search of a promised land, blacks increasingly stayed put or even moved to the South from other parts of the country. The 1970s were the first decade in the twentieth century to witness a positive net-migration of blacks into the South.[2] Indeed, the trend appears to have begun in the late 1960s in the wake of the civil unrest wracking ghettos at that time. The report *One Year Later*, issued as a follow-up to the Kerner Commission's report in 1967, stated that "the rate at which the Negroes are coming into the central cities decreased even more dramatically. From 1960 to 1966, Negro population in central cities grew an average of 370,000 per year. In the past two years [1968–1969], however, growth has dropped to only about 100,000 per year."[3]

Nor was this shift in migration simply a case of fewer black southerners migrating to the ghettos of the North. Rather, fewer black southerners were being drawn to the North, *and* many blacks who were already living in the North decided that the South offered greener pastures.[4] The cessation of the Great Migration and the increasing number of northern blacks moving to the South occurred for several reasons, but most prominent was the declining and in some instances reversing of the opportunity gap between the North and the South. As *Ebony* magazine wrote in 1973, "Many young blacks who have traveled in, lived in, or gone to colleges in the North have been convinced by big-city unemployment, frustration and fear, that the grass is greener in the South."[5] A return migrant from Chicago said much the same: "I didn't see any reason to stay up there in that madhouse when all I found was just as much discrimination and poverty, and even more crime, than there is down here."[6] The mayor of Fayette, Mississippi, hosted a "Mississippi Homecoming" in 1974 to welcome blacks fleeing the cruelty and poverty of northern ghettos.[7] In 1974, the *Chicago Defender* summed up the trend: "Whatever your view, it is clear that the major cities in the North today do not represent a sanctuary for blacks who seek to escape poverty and human cruelty. Some blacks who are recent migrants in the North have concluded that they 'jumped out of the frying pan into the fire.'"[8] The *Chicago Defender*, that champion of the Great Migration six decades earlier, was now effectively counseling black southerners to stay put.

In the late twentieth and early twenty-first centuries, the black media gave their imprimatur to the rise of the South as the new promised land. An informal survey of influential blacks in 1997 found Atlanta to be ranked the "best" city for blacks ahead of the Great Migration–era meccas Chicago and New York.[9] By 2004, in ranking the ten best cities for African Americans, the black business lifestyle magazine *Black Enterprise* would include only one city outside the South—Columbus, Ohio.[10] A follow-up survey three years later again ranked only two cities outside the South, suggesting the initial ranking in 2004 was no fluke.[11] Indeed, in 2015 *NewsOne*, reporting on a *Forbes* ranking of the metropolitan areas where blacks were doing best economically, noted that "one of the most noticeable trends of the report is that the South is comprised of [*sic*] cities and metropolitan areas that offer the best opportunities for Black residents. In the *Forbes* survey, 13 of the 15 metro areas captured were in the South."[12]

The great advances achieved by blacks during the civil rights era—ending Jim Crow, gaining the franchise, and the like—all served to make the South relatively more attractive vis-à-vis the North. Although racial animus between southern blacks and whites lingered well beyond the 1960s, the disparities between the North and South were no longer as great. Lynchings, a most egregious example of whites' subjugation of blacks in the South, had almost disappeared by the 1960s.[13] Relative to southern whites, the economic status of southern blacks improved, as evidenced by the dramatic increase in the ratio of black earnings to white earnings in the South.[14] Beyond the easing of blacks' castelike position in the South, regional economic disparities between the South and the rest of the United States also began to recede.[15] Thus, two key draws of the northern ghetto, as a place to exercise one's civil rights and to achieve upward mobility, were fading fast by the 1970s.

The second demographic wave felt in the wake of the civil rights era was a second migration—out of the ghetto. Whole swathes of black central-city neighborhoods emptied out. The trickle that had made abandonment noticeable in the late 1960s continued apace during the 1970s. One news article in 1970 reported that "abandonment of housing that could be rehabilitated at reasonable cost is occurring almost exclusively in poor minority neighborhoods" and that "blacks, when they have the means and opportunity, are migrating to the suburbs or outer areas of the city to escape blighted neighborhoods. For example, Negroes are moving from Anacostia, the Southeastern section of Washington, into Prince Georges County, MD., leaving behind vacant units."[16] Central Harlem saw its population decline from approximately 233,000 in 1950 to 102,000 in 1980, losing one-third of its black population between 1970 and 1980 alone.[17] Neighborhoods in Chicago's black belt also emptied out. Bronzeville saw its population decline from 79,000 to 36,000 between 1950 and 1980, losing one-quarter of its population between 1970 and 1980. Grand Boulevard went from a maximum population of 115,000 in 1950 to 54,000 in 1980, losing one-third of its population between 1970 and 1980.[18] The Central Cleveland neighborhood, the disembarkment point for black migrants from the South through much of the twentieth century, witnessed a plummeting of its population. Peaking at nearly 70,000 in 1950, the Central Cleveland neighborhood lost more than half its population over the next twenty years and continued to decline to only 12,000 residents by the end of the twentieth century.[19]

If we consider all neighborhoods outside the South that were at least 50 percent black in 1970, we see that on average their black population declined over the next decade. Figure 6.1 plots the change in the black population for neighborhoods that were at least 90 percent black in 1970. Clearly, many more neighborhoods lost blacks than gained blacks.

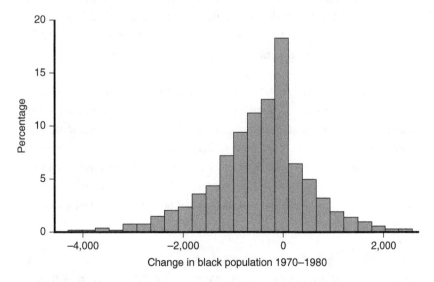

FIGURE 6.1 Change in the black population in majority-black neighborhoods, 1970-1980.
Source: Author's tabulation of Longitudinal Tract Database data (Logan, Xu, and Stults 2015).

Figure 5.1 in chapter 5 showed that overcrowding among blacks decreased dramatically during the 1960s. "Black belts," which in the 1940s were described as having "alarmingly high" densities and "no vacancies,"[20] were by the 1970s becoming "ghost towns."[21]

The change in the ghetto that accompanied its depopulation often evoked a nostalgia for the way things used to be. A black professional in Chicago reminisced that "during the 1960s and 1970s—the last period before affluent blacks finally moved downtown or out to the suburbs altogether, we had such a strong black professional class [because] segregation pushed us into just a few areas."[22]

In *The Warmth of Other Suns*, the journalist Isabel Wilkerson poignantly describes a Harlem in the aftermath of the exodus: "The Harlem that George Sterling fled to in 1945 no longer exists. The Savoy Ballroom closed its doors in 1958. Small's Paradise closed in 1986, its patrons now frail and the children of the Migration not dressing up and dancing the Lindy Hop late into the night. The Sunday stroll died off with the top hat. The black elites—the surgeons and celebrities who would have made their homes on Sugar Hill in previous generations—can now move wherever they want. Many of them live in Westchester or Connecticut now."[23]

The continued out-migration also accelerated the pace of housing abandonment noted in the previous chapter. Housing abandonment created not only eyesores but also breeding grounds for all manner of vermin and vice.[24] In 1976, a letter to the editor of a well-known black newspaper described the void left by abandonment:

Approximately 10 years ago we had the convenience of a beautiful shopping area, with well-known banks, nice apparel shops, supermarkets, bakery shop, and a neighborhood theater, and much more. The area was clean and within walking distance of our homes. There were no boarded-up homes and stores as evidence as they are today. Since that time all of the original stores, supermarkets, and banks have relocated. Boarded-up buildings exist along Ogontz Avenue from 72nd Avenue to Cheltenham Avenue. The residential areas have been damaged with vacant and abandoned homes.[25]

Blacks' movement out of the ghetto did not suddenly occur in the 1970s after the passage of fair-housing laws. As noted in chapter 4, some middle-class blacks had been able to move to suburban environs as early as the late 1940s and in the 1950s. What was different in the post–civil rights era, however, was that hardly anyone was migrating *to* the ghetto to replace the fleeing middle class or anyone else who had left it. The cessation of the Great Migration was part of the dramatic change that emptied out the ghetto. Like any dynamic entity, the ghetto needed new folks to replace those who died or moved away. This replenishment dried up in the 1970s. In the 1950s and 1960s, although blacks were fleeing the ghetto (with it typically snapping at their heels), their ranks were replaced somewhat by new migrants from the South. Southern migrants, as is typically the case with migrants anywhere, were relatively ambitious, capable, and upwardly mobile even if they were relatively poor at the beginning of their sojourn.[26] They migrated with a desire to build a new life and hence lent the ghetto an aspirational quality—at least into the 1960s.

Contemporary observers of the decline of the ghetto in the 1970s were cognizant of this demographic shift. *Ebony* magazine captured the spirit of this view:

The big cities of the North seemed to produce an endless supply of talented blacks to move away to help other communities. But it wasn't just because the ghetto was a proficient horn of plenty. The ghetto itself was constantly being replenished with fresh brains and brawn through the migration of ambitious blacks from the rural south. Today the migration of blacks to the big city ghettos of the North has slowed somewhat. The ghetto is not getting as great a flow of fresh brains and brawn as it did during the height of the migration. The ghetto becomes a wilderness. The ambitious and successful are moving out and no one is moving in. Slum housing is allowed to completely deteriorate, the wreckers come and block after block of vacant land appears.[27]

Furthermore, the article stated,

the black ghetto of 20 years ago was a vibrant, creative area. There was poverty, yes, and there was crime. There were people on welfare and there were marginally employed families who miraculously eked out enough to feed clothe and educate sometimes six or eight children. There were pimps, prostitutes, gamblers, hustlers and con men. A Malcolm X, a James Baldwin and a Floyd Patterson could come out of that kind of a slum ghetto. They had hope and they had strength and they had ambition.

The ghetto of today is a different story. It still has many of the people it had before but today it is a bitter place and, in many cases, the ambition to escape has been clouded in the euphoria of drugs. The ghetto consumes itself.[28]

Thus, two demographic shocks, the cessation of the Great Migration and flight from the ghetto, dramatically changed this place. Moreover, the destinations of blacks leaving the ghetto in the wake of the civil rights movement were changing as well. As already noted, many blacks were returning to the land of Dixie. But even among those remaining in the North, residential patterns were changing in a way that transformed the role of the ghetto in black life. First, blacks were increasingly residing in nonblack neighborhoods. Second, the number of desirable, middle-class black neighborhoods exploded.

From the late nineteenth century through the 1960s, black movement out of the ghetto and into white neighborhoods was almost always followed white flight. As one social scientist put it, summarizing the midcentury consensus on black movement into white neighborhoods, "The residential integrating of whites and blacks is an inherently unstable situation and . . . racial segregation is the norm. Once blacks move into a previously all-white neighborhood, the neighborhood is predicted to shift rapidly and irreversibly from white to black dominance."[29] Thus, the ghetto expanded, following blacks wherever they moved. Middle-class blacks fled the ghetto in the middle decades of the twentieth century but could seldom remain out of the ghetto's reach for long. Because the black middle class had been relatively small, the first blacks moving into white neighborhoods, who tended to be middle class, were usually followed by poorer blacks. In time, the formerly middle-class black enclave would resemble the older black ghetto that the middle-class blacks thought they had left behind. The ghetto simply expanded as the black population shifted outward from the older core areas of the ghetto. A number of studies have chronicled the history of black in-movement, white flight, and subsequent neighborhood decline.[30] In these chronicles, a familiar story unfolds. Along with whites escaping a neighborhood into which middle-class blacks moved, investment capital and other resources also fled the neighborhood. Banks stopped lending in these neighborhoods. Stores shuttered or were replaced by others offering inferior merchandise. The rapid demographic change that accompanied white flight contributed to social instability and rising crime and disorder.

Although physical conditions in the "new" ghetto were perhaps better than those in the "old" ghetto, many of the same social problems (e.g., crime, unemployment) arose there. In this sense, the ghetto spread wherever blacks moved.[31]

By way of illustration, consider Compton, California, which began experiencing white flight in the 1950s and was at that time a beacon for upwardly mobile blacks. Ads in the black press boasted about new housing developments open to blacks, with central air-conditioning, hardwood floors, and proximity to golf courses.[32] By 1975, however, Compton was being described by its own residents as a place where "nothing is ok" and "crime was unbearable" and where nearly 60 percent of the residents were receiving public assistance.[33]

After the 1960s, however, movement out of the ghetto did not always mean movement into an existing or incipient ghetto. Increasingly, white neighborhoods did not experience white flight or rapidly become all black after the entry of blacks.[34] The ceasing of the Great Migration meant there was less demographic pressure from a rapidly swelling black population. As a consequence, the entry of one or two blacks into a neighborhood did not always translate into dramatic black in-migration or white flight. The easing of white racism also meant whites were more tolerant of a few black neighbors.

The growing ethnic and racial diversity resulting from the Hart–Celler Act of 1965, which liberalized U.S. immigration policy, also changed the dynamics of black out-migration. In the last decades of the twentieth century and the first decade of the twenty-first, integration was no longer synonymous with living among whites. Increasingly, blacks moved into diverse neighborhoods with Latinos, Asians, and whites.[35] Thus, there was a glacial yet persistent decline in segregation experienced by blacks.[36] As figure 6.2 shows, whereas in 1960 fully two-thirds of blacks outside the South lived in majority-black neighborhoods, by the time of the American Community Survey in 2009–2013 most blacks in the North no longer lived in neighborhoods where they were the majority.

Finally, many middle-class blacks moved to neighborhoods that were predominantly black but solidly and stably middle class and away from the older ghetto neighborhoods that had formed in the early twentieth century.

In most instances, in the early and mid–twentieth century when middle-class blacks fled the ghetto into higher-status neighborhoods, they were

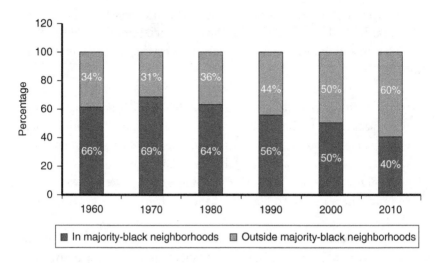

FIGURE 6.2 Proportion of northern blacks in majority-black neighborhoods, 1960–2013. *Source:* Logan Xu, and Stults 2015.

usually followed by their poorer brethren once white flight commenced. The small size of the black middle class in earlier decades meant that after the initial encroachment by middle-class blacks into white neighborhoods, poorer blacks would be the ones to replace the whites who fled.

As blacks began to benefit from the economic growth of the post–World War II era, and as civil rights legislation knocked down many barriers for them in the workplace, however, the black middle class and the number of black middle-class enclaves grew as well. Increasingly, in the post–civil rights era middle-class blacks who left the ghetto moved into black middle-class neighborhoods. Moreover, because the size of the black middle class itself was increasing, a steady supply of black middle-class households kept these neighborhoods from declining in socioeconomic status, as would have likely occurred in the past.

Figure 6.3 illustrates the growth in predominantly black census tracts with median incomes above the median household income for the entire nation. Defining black neighborhoods as those at least 50 or 90 percent black, the figure shows a dramatic increase in the number of middle-class black neighborhoods after the 1960s. In 1960, a black middle-class household seeking a predominantly black neighborhood outside the South with above-average incomes had only forty-two such tracts to choose from. By

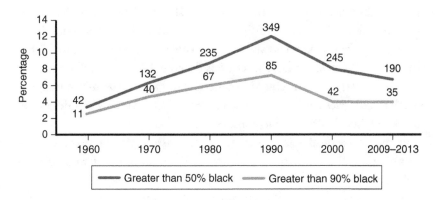

FIGURE 6.3 Number of black neighborhoods with median incomes higher than the national average, 1960-2013. *Source*: Author's tabulation of National Historic Geographic Information Systems data (1960) (Manson et al. 2017) and Longitudinal Tract Database data (1970 to 2009-2013) (Logan, Xu, and Stults 2015).

1980, there were 342 such neighborhoods. The increase is just as dramatic if we focus on neighborhoods at least 90 percent black.

In *Blue-Chip Black*, sociologist Karyn Lacy distinguishes the "core" black middle class from the more solidly "elite" middle-class blacks.[37] Comprising two-thirds of the black middle class, the core black middle class might accurately be called lower middle class and typically resides in neighborhoods on the edge of the ghetto, where problems such as crime and poor schools are a constant concern.[38] In contrast, members of the elite black middle class are typically found in "placid suburban subdivisions," where they don't have to worry about dubious characters congregating on their stoops or their cars getting broken into and vandalized when night falls.[39] Needless to say, these black neighborhoods, although segregated, lack the stigmatization associated with the ghetto.

Economically above-average black neighborhoods such as those depicted in figure 6.3 or featured in *Blue-Chip Black* include predominantly black communities such as Mitchellville, Maryland, described in 1999 as a "neighborhood of sumptuous houses studded with huge picture windows, two- and three-car garages filled with BMWs and Mercedes, and lushly manicured emerald green lawns ringed with colorful flower beds."[40] *Ebony*, the leading black lifestyle magazine, describes neighborhoods such as Jackson Park Highlands in Chicago and Ladera Heights in Los Angeles as black neighborhoods for those with money and status.[41] These neighborhoods lack the stigma that is a typically associated with black neighborhoods.

Although elite blacks had always carved out spaces for themselves within the ghetto, the post–civil rights era was different because the black middle and upper classes had grown dramatically, and so the size and number of black middle-class neighborhoods had grown, too. Although middle-class black neighborhoods in this era may have lacked some of the amenities and resources of similarly situated white neighborhoods, these same neighborhoods were distinctly different from poor or lower-middle-class neighborhoods.

In the wake of the civil rights movement, middle-class black neighborhoods differed from their earlier counterparts in another significant way. Their residents increasingly *chose* to live in these types of neighborhoods. A hallmark of the ghetto from the late nineteenth century to the end of the civil rights era was that it was a space of confinement. Blacks may have celebrated these spaces and used this confinement to their advantage, but few could escape it. As Robert Weaver, author of the classic book *The Negro Ghetto*, wrote in 1948, the cities of the North shared one "universal characteristic"—the near impossibility of moving out of the already established ghetto.[42] After the 1960s and 1970s, this was increasingly no longer the case.

In the wake of federal fair-housing legislation passed in these decades, blatant housing discrimination declined.[43] Middle-class blacks in particular appeared to face less discrimination than poorer blacks, and those middle-class blacks encountering discrimination often had resources to overcome discriminatory barriers. An article in the *Urban Affairs Review* in 2001 found landlords could distinguish middle-class blacks from other blacks based solely on diction and were more likely to discriminate against poorer blacks.[44] Moreover, the elite blacks chronicled in *Blue-Chip Black* used a variety of means to move where they wanted, such as searching for a home without the aid of a realtor when they felt the realtors of an area were discriminating against them. Surely, blacks, whatever their means, faced obstacles in their housing choices. And for some, especially the poor, moving out of a black neighborhood was nigh impossible. But for elite middle-class blacks determined to move out of predominantly black neighborhoods, this option became increasingly available in the late twentieth century.

Some blacks declined this option. As David Dent wrote in a widely read article in 1992, "As an increasing number of black Americans head for the suburban dream, some are bypassing another dream—the dream of an integrated society. These black Americans are moving to black upper- and middle-class neighborhoods, usually pockets in counties that have a white majority."[45] They didn't want to deal with the hassle of being told there were no units for rent or sale, or they didn't want to worry how their neighbors would react to them, or they preferred to live among other blacks.

"I don't want to come home and always have my guard up," said David S. Ball, a senior contract administrator who worked on railroad projects in the Washington, DC, area. Ball and his wife, Phillis, moved from Washington to a predominantly black subdivision in Fort Washington, Maryland. "After I work eight hours or more a day," he stated, "I don't want to come home and work another eight."[46] The existence of segregated black middle-class neighborhoods could be due in part to the constrained choices of black residents themselves. Although neighborhoods such as Mitchellville might be segregated and inferior in terms of amenities in comparison to white middle-class neighborhoods, these neighborhoods still appealed to many middle class blacks.

Thus, in the late twentieth century black neighborhoods were no longer synonymous with the ghetto in a pejorative sense.

THE OUTCAST GHETTO

After the demographic shift discussed in the previous section occurred, there remained a set of black neighborhoods for whom the term *ghetto* in its most stigmatizing form continued to be an apt moniker. The stigma associated with living in these ghetto neighborhoods was worse than in earlier times when the vast majority of blacks were confined to such spaces. The critical social scientist Loic Wacquant, who has written much on the outcast nature of the ghetto, quotes one ghetto-dweller as saying, "Friends from other places don't want really to come here. And you yourself, you wouldn't want to invite intelligent people here."[47] Another study of residents of high-poverty, segregated neighborhoods in Buffalo found residents being stigmatized by people within their own social networks: "I get the feeling some people feel uncomfortable visiting me, because of the crime that's been in the area."[48]

Rap songs, one voice of those marginalized in the ghetto, often portrayed the ghetto as a forlorn place. As Melle Mel rapped in the late 1970s,

You'll grow in in the ghetto living second-rate
And your eyes will sing a song of deep hate
The places you play and where you stay
Looks like one great big alleyway[49]

The hyperstigmatization of the ghetto that began in the late twentieth century persists to this day. The online forum City-Data, which serves as a bulletin board for people seeking information about places to live, has a plethora of opinions about various neighborhoods. "Ghetto" neighborhoods are typically described as bad, and neighborhoods with undesirable qualities are called "ghettos." One post queried, "What are the ghetto parts of Columbus? I'm looking to avoid people with less than desirable moral values."[50] As Wacquant writes, the ghetto has come to be viewed as a "a mere receptacle for the stigmatized and superfluous fractions of the black proletariat: the un-employed, welfare recipients, criminals and participants in the booming informal economy."[51]

In addition to stigma, confinement or barriers to exit are also hallmarks of the ghetto. Although fair-housing laws have made discrimination a less-potent force, there remain powerful forces that hem many poorer blacks in the ghetto. The sociologist Patrick Sharkey provides an elaborate description of this phenomena in his book *Stuck in Place*. Sharkey's research shows that blacks growing up in poor black neighborhoods as children are likely to reside in poor black neighborhoods as adults. More precisely, Sharkey found that 67 percent of black children whose parents lived in the bottom twenty-fifth percentile of neighborhoods in terms of median household income also live in the bottom twenty-fifth percentile of neighborhoods in terms of median household income when they become adults.[52] Notably, Sharkey found this intergenerational transmission of residence in low-income neighborhoods to be much higher among blacks than among whites. White children whose parents lived in poor neighborhoods are not that likely to live in poor neighborhoods as adults. Moreover, the evidence presented by Sharkey suggests the experience of growing up in such poor black neighborhoods is a significant factor in predestining the children to repeat the experiences of their parents. In other words, growing up in the ghetto makes children more likely to live in the ghetto as adults. Across generations, families are "stuck in place" and unable to escape the ghetto.

Thus, although the forces that created the ghetto in the early twentieth century—state-sanctioned housing discrimination and pervasive white racism—waned, the ghetto did not disappear. There remain black spaces that are stigmatized and whose residents are often unable to escape. The next section describes the forces that make poor black neighborhoods places that trap its residents and considers how they altered the role of the ghetto from a haven to a hell.

To utilize neighborhood-level statistical data, I define ghettos as majority-black census tracts with poverty rates above the poverty rates for all blacks nationwide. Although these thresholds are admittedly arbitrary, they do capture neighborhoods that are predominantly black and disadvantaged. High-poverty black neighborhoods have been found to map onto disadvantage in a number of studies.[53] When qualitative evidence (e.g., eyewitness accounts, news reports) is used, neighborhoods that have been historically part of the ghetto, such as Bronzeville in Chicago and North Philadelphia, and those neighborhoods that seem to fit my definition of stigmatized, predominantly black spaces are considered part of the ghetto.

The ghetto thus persisted in the wake of the civil rights era. The demographic shocks described earlier, along with changing race relations, altered the ghetto's status in black America. But as an entity the ghetto persisted. Conditions inside the ghetto, which changed as well, are the focus of the remainder of this chapter.

THOSE REMAINING

Despite the increasing ability of blacks to live in integrated neighborhoods and the increasing availability of black middle-class neighborhoods, many blacks remained in disadvantaged, predominantly black neighborhoods. For purposes of illustration, the second column of table 6.1 lists the number of blacks living in census tracts that were majority black and with poverty rates above the average for all blacks in the United States. The third column lists the number of all blacks living in metropolitan areas.

Between 1970 and 1980, the number of blacks in predominantly black tracts with above-average poverty rates soared much more quickly than the

TABLE 6.1
Northern Blacks in Disadvantaged Neighborhoods, 1970–2013

	Number of Blacks Living in Disadvantaged Neighborhoods	Number of All Metropolitan Blacks
1970	903,186	10,223,178
1980	3,151,009	13,555,287
1990	3,244,936	15,109,963
2000	4,646,061	17,022,424
2009–2013	3,077,057	18,866,704

Source: Decennial Census, American Community Survey 2009–2013 (U.S. Census Bureau 2016).

growth in the overall black population, whereas the number of blacks in the North as a whole grew modestly. After 1980, the number of blacks in predominantly black tracts with above-average poverty rates grew steadily, peaking both in absolute numbers and as a proportion of the northern black population in 2000. At the time of the American Community Survey of 2009–2013, 16 percent of northern blacks lived in these disadvantaged neighborhoods.

By the end of the civil rights era, the social ecology of these ghetto neighborhoods had been completely transformed. Whereas before this point the ghetto had served as a stepping stone, a place for the race to acclimate to modernity and achieve economic mobility and a modicum of cultural and political power, now the ghetto had become a trap. Residing in the ghetto seemed to lessen one's life chances. At least one empirical study supports the notion that the ghetto's aspirational role ceased after the 1960s. The economists William Collins and Robert Margo examined the relationship between the level of residential segregation and idleness,[54] single motherhood, and wages and income for the period 1940–1990. They found that a greater degree of segregation was consistently associated with higher rates of idleness, single motherhood, and lower wages and income, but only starting in 1980 and later.[55] Although Collins and Margo could not definitively explain their observation, these results are consistent with the notion that the ghetto had lost its aspirational character in this period.

In the 1950s and even the 1960s, with upwardly mobile and capable migrants still arriving from the South and the depopulation not yet complete, the social fabric of the ghetto had not yet frayed. By the 1970s, however, the ghetto was a place where the disadvantages of being black were amplified. *Social conditions worsened in the ghetto.* In three social domains in particular—crime, employment, and family composition—the situation worsened in ways not seen during the era of state-sanctioned discrimination. In a fourth domain, the state enacted a policy that was perhaps more harmful than any since the institutionalization of redlining in the Great Depression: mass incarceration. These four shifts at the end of the twentieth century interacted with one another, compounding the disadvantages of the ghetto and illustrating the ways that the ghetto was no longer a haven. This chapter summarizes three of these trends, and the next chapter addresses the fourth.

Crime

Since the Industrial Revolution, crime among the poorer classes has always been viewed as a problem among city dwellers. The black ghetto is no different in this regard. Studies of Negro ghettos in the early twentieth century never failed to mention vice and the "vicious" classes.[56] In the mid-1960s, however, crime in the ghetto seemed to escalate; letters to the editors and news articles of black newspapers became replete with tales of crime and violence. A brutal slaying of a seventy-two-year-old woman in Chicago public housing in 1964 was described as "part of everyday living in Chicago's jungle of high rise, low-income projects."[57] Conditions for Negroes were described as "catastrophic" and "social chaos."[58] Black neighborhoods were "becoming virtually jungles of crime and violence."[59] Residents in Harlem protested the lack of police protection, demanded more foot patrols, and lamented how they "were afraid to leave their homes in the day and fearful of walking the streets at nights."[60] Another ghetto resident described the ghetto as a place where "our people are being killed wholesale by their own people."[61] Thirty-nine percent and 47 percent of respondents to surveys of New York City Negroes in 1964 and 1966, respectively, identified crime as *the* single biggest problem.[62]

By the 1970s, anecdotal reports about rising crime in the ghetto were commonplace. The *Chicago Defender* would report that the rising crime had reached "tidal wave proportions," that "fear pervades black ghettos," and that twelve Illinois state legislators were proposing a two-day summit on "how best to deal with the rising crime rate in the black community."[63] The *New Pittsburgh Courier* wrote that "black women are assaulted by young black gangsters who terrorize the so-called 'ghetto.' Burglars and robbers prey upon hard-working black folks who oftentimes were the true fountain of black power."[64] And the elderly lived in "constant fear" due to increasing ghetto crime, claimed the *Philadelphia Tribune*.[65] A survey of residents in nine black Chicago neighborhoods in 1972 found crime to be the number one problem ahead of jobs or housing discrimination.[66]

The popular black lifestyle magazine *Ebony* ran several full-length articles chronicling the rise of crime. An article published in 1976 described an elderly woman who "was 79 years old and lived alone in Chicago's Woodlawn area. Home invaders broke into her apartment, tied her up and placed her in a bathtub of water." In harrowing detail, this same article also chronicled an incident "in Detroit, [where] two armed young men held up a man returning from shopping. This, too, was during the Christmas season. When the man stepped forward to say 'Look, man, it's Christmas. Why don't you give me a break,' one gunman fired a bullet through his heart." The magazine summed up the carnage as "from neighborhood to neighborhood, from city to city and from state to state, a cult of violence is taking its' toll. This has been particularly true in black neighborhoods." To the writer, this was a new phenomenon, a difference in degree and kind: "There is little doubt that black ghetto residents are more concerned about crime today than they were several years ago because crime has changed. It has become uglier, more deadly. Blacks in many areas now find themselves living in fortress homes and the busiest businesses in ghettoes are those dealing in locks and alarms."[67] In 1979, the magazine devoted an entire issue to crime, with John H. Johnson (the magazine's founder) writing, "It is our belief, and it is the basic premise of this issue, that Black on Black Crime has *reached a critical level that threatens our existence as a people.*"[68] In harrowing detail, this same issue chronicled the sad story of a Harlem family who had two teenaged sons murdered in four years. The story showed how the family suffered not only the loss of two young men, but an emotional and psychological fallout that would stagger the family for years to come.[69] Another story described how crime was driving people away from the ghetto: "I can't blame her. They broke into her house. They took two of her cars off the street so she moved to the suburbs."[70] The depopulation described earlier in this chapter was linked to the steadily rising wave of crime. That *Ebony*, a magazine started with the intent purpose of uplifting the race by telling positive stories (as we encountered in chapter 4) would devote so many pages to the topic of crime is especially telling.

Although this evidence is anecdotal, we do know that after declining for several decades, the homicide rate, the most reliable crime indicator, spiked dramatically among blacks during the 1960s, rising from 50.7 in 1965 to 83.1 in 1972.[71] Rates remained high for several decades before starting to tumble in the 1990s.[72] Homicide arrest rates for nonwhite males doubled between 1960 and 1970, and arrests of blacks for violent crimes rose from 500 per 100,000 to 800 per 100,000 between 1965 and 1974.[73] Both patterns confirm the impressionistic accounts of surging crime.

We don't know for sure that increasing crime among blacks was taking place in what would be considered the ghetto. Neighborhood-level crime statistics prior to 1970 are not immediately available. Aside from the evidence of an anecdotal type, such as that given earlier, we can also draw on a slew of ethnographic works that describe a ghetto besieged by crime. Ethnographic and journalistic works such as *There Are No Children Here*, *Code of the Street*, and *American Project* describe ghetto life as one where crime figures prominently in the day-to-day life of residents.[74] Moreover, surveys of former ghetto residents who participated in government-sponsored mobility programs and received housing vouchers to move out of the ghetto almost uniformly reported lower exposure to crime as a chief benefit of their new environs.[75] A resident of Mount Laurel, New Jersey, who had moved there from Camden, New Jersey, described her previous neighborhood as a place where "people was getting killed in front of my door," and another Mount Laurel resident, originally from New York, described her former neighborhood as a place with "drugs, fights" and how she did "not really want[] my kids to grow up over there."[76]

Intertwined with increasing crime was an increase in the use and distribution of illegal drugs. Rising drug use, especially highly addictive ones such as cocaine and heroin, fueled the increase in crime in several ways. First, highly addictive and incapacitating drugs made users virtually unemployable. Supporting themselves and their habit meant resorting to petty crime. Addicts burgled, robbed, and committed all manner of larceny to finance the next fix.[77] These problems would only worsen in the ensuing years as drug addiction spread.

Second, although selling drugs by definition was criminal, the illegal nature of the market meant conventional methods businesses use to market their product, expand market share, and settle disputes with employees, suppliers, and competitors were unavailable in the drug market. Drug dealers often had to resort to violence to resolve disputes. This became all the more prevalent when crack became the dominant drug in many inner-city communities in the 1980s. Crack markets, unlike heroin markets, were highly decentralized, with many players providing more opportunities for disputes that could most easily be resolved using violence. Drug dealers, in a cash-intensive business with no recourse to the police, made tempting targets for robbery. To protect themselves, they hired bodyguards and weapons. Rising crime made people distrustful of their neighbors. Even law-abiding folks might have seen carrying a weapon as a prudent precaution.

Adding to this combustible mix were the actions of the police. The police have never had a stellar reputation in the ghetto, dating even back to the late-nineteenth-century black belts. Numerous late-nineteenth- and early-twentieth-century commentators observed how black belts were places where vice was allowed to flourish. Excepting the most egregious crimes (e.g., murder), it seemed the police took a hands-off, see-no-evil approach to crime in the ghetto. For example, in *The Condemnation of Blackness* the historian Khalil Muhammad describes how Philadelphia mayor Rudolph Blankenburg's antivice campaign in 1912 virtually ignored black neighborhoods.[78] Nor was Philadelphia unique in allowing vice to flourish in the local black belt, with one observer noting as early as 1913 that "the segregated black district is almost invariably the region in which vice is tolerated by the police."[79]

Fast-forward several decades, when a black journalist in Philadelphia wrote in 1965, "Some people dreamed that with the coming of boasted reform our street corners would be free of loafers; dens of vice would be closed, and a new condition of things would be seen. All, however, have been disappointed."[80] Police neglect remained. Another journalist noted in 1970: "Nearly every youngster in the ghetto knows who the local pusher is, but he continues at his stand day after day, without ever being picked up. There are plenty of stories about payoffs to policemen and even instances of policemen involved in the trade."[81]

The police were seen as abdicating their responsibility to provide safety for ghetto residents and sowing the seeds of mistrust within the ghetto. Providing security, a core function of any state, was thus compromised, and residents often felt scores could be settled only by taking matters into their own hands. Robert Sampson and Dawn Bartusch found that blacks living in the most disadvantaged black neighborhoods were relatively cynical about the law and distrustful of the police.[82] Mistrust of the police and other state institutions (e.g., civil court) meant disputes had to be settled outside the state's legal system. An indigenous apparatus for settling disputes arose in its place. Particularly among young men, violence was a part of that apparatus. Cynicism toward the criminal justice system left ghetto residents with a form of do-it-yourself justice. Scores would be settled not by filing lawsuits or by contacting the police but by protecting one's self and reputation, with force as necessary. Thus, high rates of interpersonal violence became a defining feature of the ghetto starting in the late 1960s and continuing thereafter. In *Code of the Street*, the sociologist Elijah Anderson chronicles the way residents of the North Philadelphia ghetto carry themselves with an aura of danger to ward off those who might harm them.[83] With regard to crime, it does seem things got worse in the ghetto. It is not completely clear that things worsened more in the ghetto than elsewhere—crime rose across the board in the United States during the 1960s—but the ghetto's already higher-than-average crime rate might have been more noticeable.

The dramatic increase in crime from the 1960s through the 1990s contributed to the more definitively changed status of the ghetto from a haven to a hell. High rates of crime only served to exacerbate the flight from the ghetto chronicled earlier in this chapter. Rather than being a place to take steps toward full inclusion in America, the ghetto became a place to avoid or escape.

As we shall see in the next chapter, the crime and danger that came to characterize the ghetto in the last decades of the twentieth century began dropping around the turn of the twenty-first century—leading to a further evolution of the ghetto's status. But before the decline in crime could become evident, policy makers adopted a policy that, although perhaps well intentioned, served in many ways to further weaken the social fabric of the ghetto—the policy of mass incarceration.

The rise in ghetto crime, perpetrated mostly by black males, was also inextricably linked to another dramatic shift in the ghetto—the rise in joblessness. Because those not gainfully employed are more likely to commit crime, those incarcerated cannot hold employment, and employers look askance at hiring former felons, the contemporaneous rise in crime has led many to connect these two phenomena in the late twentieth century ghetto. Although the direction of causality is not always clear, the change in the ghetto from an oasis of economic opportunity in the early twentieth century to a desert bereft of jobs was one of the most striking transformations of the post–civil rights ghetto.

Joblessness

The restructuring of the urban economy, a process that began in the post–World War II era, was having a devastating impact on ghetto residents by the 1970s. Employment, especially manufacturing employment, was increasingly being dispersed away from central cities and the ghetto.[84] Manufacturers moved to suburbia, out of the North, and eventually overseas to take advantage of less-expensive land with which to implement more efficient horizontal production processes and to escape the power of organized labor.[85] The construction of the interstate highway system served to facilitate the manufacturing exodus. Manufacturers also sought out less costly, nonunionized labor in "right to work" states outside of the North or in other countries. As a result, job opportunities were locating farther and farther away from ghetto residents.

Technology also exacerbated employment problems in the ghetto. We have already seen how automation displaced many blacks in agriculture in the South after World War II. The displacement impacts of automation would again be felt in the manufacturing sector in the postwar era.[86]

Because low-skill manufacturing jobs were one of the original lures that had sparked the Great Migration and offered some of the best opportunities for upward mobility for the race, the decline of manufacturing was especially devastating in the ghetto. The service sector expanded significantly, but the best opportunities in this sector often required high levels of credentials and skills—things that were in short supply in the ghetto.

The work of historians and contemporary social scientists, surveys of ghetto residents, and the available empirical evidence tell the same story—joblessness was becoming problematic as early as the late 1950s in some places and was wreaking havoc on inner-city ghettos by the 1970s.

Chronicling the flight of automobile manufacturing out of Detroit in the 1950s, Thomas Sugrue shows how manufacturers frequently moved to locales where union labor was weak as a way of evading the unions' demands.[87] This tactic exacerbated technological trends that made suburban and exurban sites less expensive for manufacturing due to the greater availability and lower cost of land there. The ancillary industries that supplied automobile manufacturers often moved as well to be near their primary customers—the auto plants. Automation also weakened the power of unions—machines don't strike. Concessions that were made by unions typically fell on the backs of the newest workers, who were disproportionately black. Whereas blacks could obtain reliable factory employment up to the 1950s, albeit often in the worst jobs, thereafter few could count on steady employment in manufacturing or elsewhere. In Detroit, the black male labor-force participation rate plummeted from 83 percent in 1950 to 56 percent in 1980.[88] Joblessness and the ensuing social problems were being felt in Detroit by the late 1950s. Sugrue writes that "for those who cared to listen there were rumblings of discontent in the late 1950s and 1960s."[89] The hollowing out of Detroit's manufacturing industry played out over the next several decades as that city became the poster child for urban unrest, depopulation, and inner-city decline.

William Julius Wilson, undoubtedly the most famous proponent of pointing to joblessness as an explanation of the inner city's woes, chronicled the devastation wrought by prolonged joblessness in Chicago in the 1970s and 1980s.[90] The technological changes and geographic dispersion of industry were not limited to Detroit, although perhaps happening there earlier. Much of the industrial Midwest and Northeast hollowed out in a similar fashion and with similarly devastating impacts on black male employment. Cities such as Buffalo, Gary, and Camden experienced equally calamitous declines. In other cities with more diversified economies (e.g., Chicago, New York, Pittsburgh), deindustrialization still affected the ghetto, but the surrounding city and blacks who were no longer in the ghetto felt the impact much less harshly.

Figure 6.4 provides a compelling picture of how joblessness changed in the past half-century in the ghetto. The blue line represents neighborhoods at least 50 percent black and with poverty rates higher than the nationwide black poverty rate. The red line is all other majority-black neighborhoods. In 1960, male labor-force participation rates in the lowest-income black neighborhoods stood at 74 percent and was only five percentage points below the labor-force participation rate in other black neighborhoods. By 2000, the disparity between the poorest black neighborhoods and other black neighborhoods had ballooned to twenty percentage points. Moreover, only a little more than half of black males (54 percent) in the poorest black

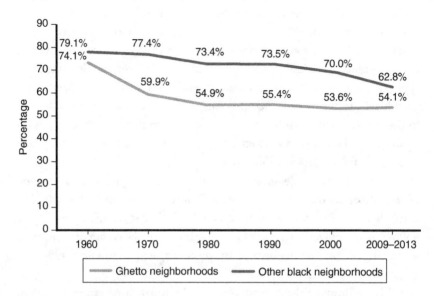

FIGURE 6.4 Males age 18–64 labor-force participation rate in black neighborhoods, 1960–2013. *Source*: Author's tabulation of National Historic Geographic Information Systems data (Manson et al. 2017). *Note*: Because poverty rates are not available for census tracts in 1960, majority-black neighborhoods with average family incomes lower than the twenty-fifth percentile are used for 1960.

neighborhoods in 2000 were in the labor force. The gap between the poorest black neighborhoods and other black neighborhoods narrowed considerably by 2009–2013, but economic dislocations caused by the Great Recession (discussed in chapter 7) suggests caution before interpreting the latter data points as harbingers of a new trend.

The changes in employment opportunities in the ghetto over the course of the twentieth century are among the most dramatic of all changes. It was, after all, employment opportunities that sparked the Great Migration and ensuing ghetto formation during World War I in the first place. The contrast with the early-twentieth-century ghetto is striking. A survey of North Philadelphia in 1926, the densest concentration of Negroes in the city at that time, would find "little unemployment."[91] A half-century later, lack of employment would be one of most pressing problems there and in other American ghettos. The decline in employment opportunities would prove disastrous.

In a modern society, employment largely defines one's social status. Conversely, joblessness has been found to be associated with a host of both physical and psychological maladies,[92] and in this regard residents of the ghetto were no different. The persistent and prevalent joblessness wrought havoc in the ghetto.

Increasing joblessness meant less-steady income in the ghetto, which would reverberate among businesses serving this market. Less jobs meant less money to patronize retail shops and to pay landlords. When combined with the dramatic depopulation of the ghetto described earlier, it is easy to understand why many ghetto neighborhoods came to be bereft of basic retail options such as full-service grocery stores in the post–civil rights era. Faced with a poor and shrinking customer base, many businesspersons closed up shop or declined to open businesses in the ghetto in the first place. Stores, jobs, and the economic life they bring to a neighborhood often disappeared too. A lack of stores and services only served to make a neighborhood less attractive, and the cycle of abandonment and decay thus continued. The decline of the housing market chronicled earlier in this chapter is probably due in part to the worsening economic conditions in the ghetto. Residents with low and unstable incomes make poor tenants from the vantage point of a profit-maximizing landlord.

Increasing joblessness probably played some role in the rise in crime in the 1960s and 1970s. Young men are the most criminally prone, and it is this population that first experienced the brunt of automation and deindustrialization in manufacturing industries. As jobless young men of the 1960s and 1970s became jobless middle-aged men of the late 1970s and 1980s, the repercussions of this trend would be felt among their offspring. Without employment, these men frequently lacked employment connections to pass on to the next generation. As the sociologist Elijah Anderson puts it, these "old heads" without stable employment could hardly mentor the youth or guide them to fulfilling life choices.[93] The underground economy would become an attractive alternative. And, indeed, some studies have linked joblessness among older black males to crime and violence among young black males.[94]

Rising crime and economic restructuring only fed upon themselves and served to accelerate the trends of depopulation. Few potential migrants wanted to migrate somewhere where crime was high and jobs were few. Many already living in these places didn't want to stay there, either.

Joblessness among males also appears to have affected one other dimension often held up as a symbol of the ghetto's decline—the family.

The Ghetto Family

Starting in the 1960s, the popular image of the ghetto family was one in which stable two-parent households were disappearing and being replaced by households headed by single females. Indeed, as figure 6.5 shows, the proportion of families with children headed by single females in ghetto neighborhoods marched steadily upward in the post–civil rights era. By 2010, more than two-thirds of families with children in the ghetto were headed by a woman. Although some commentators interpret this trend as being driven by teenagers increasingly having children out of wedlock and as prima facie evidence of social disintegration in the ghetto, the reality is more complex. There are a number of moving pieces behind the rise of female-headed households.

In the United States, fertility has been declining across the board, among young and old, rich and poor, with unmarried white women perhaps being the exception. For blacks, fertility rates have declined among teenagers and unmarried women. But these rates declined even faster for married black women. Thus, an increasing share of black births were to unmarried women. In addition, after 1960 marriage rates also declined more quickly for blacks than for any other group.[95] Thus, proportionally speaking, there were more unmarried black women to have babies than married black women, even if both were experiencing declines in fertility.

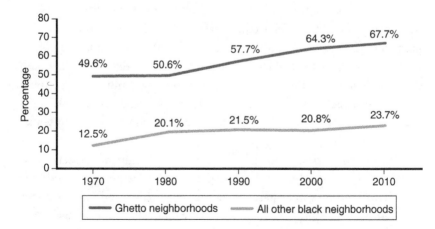

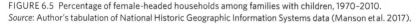

FIGURE 6.5 Percentage of female-headed households among families with children, 1970–2010.
Source: Author's tabulation of National Historic Geographic Information Systems data (Manson et al. 2017).

The decline in marriage and fertility among blacks of all classes was in some ways a harbinger of things to come for whites and indeed for much of the Western world as the Second Demographic Transition swept across Europe, North America, Australia, and New Zealand. Declining fertility, later ages for first marriage and first child births, longer periods of single adulthood, and alternative arrangements for childrearing, including cohabitation and single parenthood, are the hallmarks of this transition.[96] The rise in female-headed households and out-of-wedlock births in the ghetto in many ways only preceded what has happened in the rest of the Western world in the past few decades.

But for several reasons it would be a mistake to view the ghetto as simply being in the vanguard of new types of family arrangements. First, the changes have been more dramatic in the ghetto. For example, the rate at which whites are born out of wedlock has increased dramatically, hovering at about 29 percent as of 2014. But that is roughly where the rate for blacks was *half a century ago*.[97] At nearly 70 percent, the rate of female-headed households for blacks far exceeds the rate for whites. Moreover, in some ghetto neighborhoods, the rate has at times exceeded 80 percent. In the Cherry Hill and Old Town/Middle East neighborhoods of Baltimore, the rate soared past 80 percent by 2014. These neighborhoods are more than 90 percent black, with poverty rates of 40 percent.[98] In the Central neighborhood of Cleveland, the rate of female-headed households was *90 percent* in 2000.[99]

Second, although out-of-wedlock births are increasing among whites and in Europe, too, a greater proportion of these births are to cohabiting couples who behave more or less as though they are married (i.e., they have lived together for years and even decades).[100] In poorer ghetto communities, out-of-wedlock births occur for couples who also often start out as though they are married, but over time these unions have proven more fleeting than the unions of white and European couples having out-of-wedlock births. These unstable unions in ghetto communities are associated with poorer developmental outcomes for children.[101]

Finally, although the Second Demographic Transition has manifested across all population groups, the causes of the increase in female-headed households among blacks appears to be more strongly linked to a lack of marriageable males. The joblessness described earlier translated into a dearth of employed black males who could stably help support a family. The advent of mass incarceration in the 1980s physically removed many black males from black communities, making them a scarce commodity in the ghetto. Black males in the ghetto were increasingly not only jobless but locked up to boot. In contrast to much of the rest of the Western world, where increases in female-headed households are due substantially to *increasing economic opportunities for women*, the growth in female-headed households in the ghetto has been driven to a large extent by *declining opportunities for men*. The consequences of the rise in out-of-wedlock births and female-headed households in the ghetto, therefore, have been more deleterious. The argument being made here is not that the rise of female-headed households *caused* the ghetto to decline. Rather, the rise of female-headed households in the ghetto is a symptom of the lack of opportunity there.

Taken together, the increases in crime, joblessness among men, and female-headed households are indicative of the wholesale transformation of the ghetto's role in black America. Although there are ongoing debates about the causes of these transformations and the way these changes have affected the lives of ghetto residents, it would be hard to argue with the notion that the ghetto of the post–civil rights era was a different type of place than the ghetto before that era, and perhaps the most important difference was the loss of its aspirational character.

Moreover, poor blacks were not merely confined to the ghetto. Their life chances were made worse by residing there. The social bonds of the ghetto were often such that they served to literally bond the poor to their depressed environments and impede the way forward. A social ecology dominated by disadvantaged households meant fewer connections to people with access to resources that could enhance upward mobility. Better-off neighbors are an advantage in that they offer ties that are more "leverageable"—that is, ties that foster upward mobility or offer access to important social and economic resources. For example, employed neighbors are more likely than unemployed residents to have information about employment. Likewise, a neighbor with an important position in the local school system has the potential to assist in extracting the best education from the system. Poorer neighbors may provide important social ties, but they may be less likely to contain the type of resources that lead to upward mobility. To paraphrase the urban-planning academician Xavier de Souza Briggs, ties of the type that bridge social worlds are less common in the ghetto.[102] Bridgeable ties might help an aspiring adolescent navigate the college admissions process or provide the recommendation needed for a stable job with opportunities for upward mobility.

The concentration of poverty in the ghetto did more than obstruct opportunities for the individuals living there. These communities' collective efficacy, or their ability to collaborate to achieve ends for the benefit of the whole, was sapped as well. Poorer neighborhoods often have a more fragile social structure for several reasons. First, the poor often have more residential instability because they are more frequently renters and thus usually have a greater need to move more often for economic reasons.[103] This greater residential mobility among the poor makes it more difficult for them to establish strong social ties in any one place, hence undermining neighborhood cohesion. Second, poor communities often lack the political power to keep destabilizing forces such as liquor stores outside of their neighborhood.[104] Finally, poorer residents lack the time and financial resources to contribute to social organizations that are often requisite for a strong social structure.[105]

In a series of innovative studies that tapped into the willingness of individuals to come together to address community-wide problems, Robert Sampson and his colleagues show that segregated, high-poverty neighborhoods suffer from a dearth of collective efficacy. Residents of these communities are less willing to intervene when they see someone acting disorderly and have less confidence in working with their neighbors to solve community-wide problems such as crime, social disorder, and low-performing local public schools.[106] Put more concretely, neighborhood order and safety depend not only on the local police but also on the willingness of neighborhood residents to intervene if they witness something amiss. Likewise, good schools require not only good teachers but also parents who can both contribute resources and demand resources from the public authorities. In cohesive communities, residents will feel more confident intervening if they witness a crime, and their voices will be amplified if multiple voices speak together to achieve a desired end. Thus, safe streets and good schools are but two locally consumed items that often require the community's collective efforts to achieve.[107]

Lacking the collective efficacy to protect their communities, ghetto residents often find their neighborhoods besieged by sundry social ills, pockmarked by unused land, and deprived of resources that will enhance their quality of life. Social scientists have documented the myriad ways that the disadvantages plaguing poor neighborhoods become cumulative and worsen the quality of life in those same neighborhoods. For example, amenities provided by the market—for instance, by means of grocery stores—are often absent or in short supply in disadvantaged neighborhoods because these neighborhoods are perceived as risky places to do business. One result is that food deserts, or neighborhoods that present obstacles to accessing healthful food, become more prevalent in disadvantaged communities.[108] Thus, because amenities, environmental hazards, socioeconomic status, and political power are not evenly distributed across space, the neighborhood one resides in can profoundly affect one's life chances. In contrast to those living in "good" neighborhoods where access to a variety of stores, safety from crime, and good schools for one's children are taken for granted, disadvantaged neighborhoods provide fewer amenities and present roadblocks to opportunity at nearly every turn. Higher crime rates pose not only the threat of bodily harm and loss of property but other pernicious side effects as well. In high-crime neighborhoods, even law-abiding residents may be tainted with suspicion by police and outsiders and as a result be subjected to police harassment or experience difficulty in finding employment outside of their neighborhood. With criminals lurking in their midst, there may be a tendency for residents to hunker down to avoid being victimized. Such hunkering down weakens social ties and makes it difficult for neighbors to come together to achieve collective ends, such as good schools. The lack of good schools in turn inhibits future opportunities for children and adolescents who grow up in this community.

In contrast, disamenities such as environmental hazards are often found in abundance in disadvantaged communities both because, in a catch-22, these toxins depress property values, making it relatively affordable to live near such hazards, and because disadvantaged communities often lack the political power to keep these unwanted wastes out of their neighborhoods.[109] Recently released neighborhood data by HUD show that predominantly black neighborhoods with extremely high levels of poverty have on average greater exposure to environmental toxins than 80 percent of other neighborhoods.[110] Thus, to the burdens of residing in the ghetto we must add environmental hazards, which can adversely affect one's health and consequently the opportunity to prosper.

This, in a nutshell, is the theory of neighborhood effects that explains why living in a disadvantaged neighborhood such as the ghetto can deprive individuals of the opportunity to maximize their full potential.[111] These theories help explain how the ghetto became a hell in the post–civil rights era.

A Haven for Some Nonetheless?

The chapter thus far paints a picture of a ghetto that is anything but a haven—rather, it is a place where only those with no other options remain. But although the preceding discussion makes clear that the ghetto's role as a haven for blacks was severely diminished in the wake of the civil rights era, it would be mistaken to assume that no one valued the neighborhoods many had written off. Perhaps the most compelling evidence of the ghetto's ongoing, albeit diminished, role as a haven is evinced by the community-development movement.

Consisting of neighborhood-based grassroots organizations dedicated to improving their neighborhoods, the community-development movement shows flight was not the only response to the catastrophic forces engulfing the ghetto in the late twentieth century. Rather than fleeing the ghetto, the institutions and people at the core of the community-development movement chose to stay put and invest substantial resources in the ghetto. For them, the ghetto was something worth fighting for, not fleeing from at the earliest opportunity.

To some extent, it should be expected that many ghetto residents would cherish these spaces, notwithstanding the considerable challenges that came with living there. These much-maligned neighborhoods were also the sources of friendships, the location of loved ones, the spaces for networks of support, and home where comforting everyday routines were carried out. Even in the Robert Taylor Homes of the South Side Chicago ghetto, one of the poorest and physically decrepit public-housing developments in the late-twentieth-century United States, a sizable proportion of residents wanted to remain in the development to be close to their relations and support networks.[112] Folks who participated in community development were not merely attached to the ghetto because they happened to live there but also willing to act on these feelings by devoting considerable resources to improving life there. Their actions illustrate the extent to which the ghetto remained a haven for many blacks in the late twentieth and early twenty-first centuries.

To be sure, some members of the community-development movement had little choice but to stay in the ghetto and to work to improve it. Housing discrimination persisted long past the passage of the Fair Housing Act of 1968, limiting the options of would-be migrants from the ghetto. Many ghetto residents were too poor to afford to move anywhere else, and conditions had deteriorated to such an extent that action was required for their very survival. Consider the tenants of many Harlem buildings during the 1970s and 1980s who found themselves de facto landlords after their landlords abandoned their buildings. Tenants had to figure how to maintain those buildings, pay taxes, and take on the role of property manager. Some would form cooperative organizations with assistance from city government.[113] Most would have been too poor to afford housing outside of Harlem. This scenario was repeated numerous times in ghettos across the United States as the private and public sectors withdrew resources from the ghetto. Ghetto residents became de facto community organizers, property managers, and officers of public safety because no one else would step in to provide these goods and services. They became community-development practitioners because they had no other choice.

But other members of the community-development movement surely had other options. Indeed, in the example cited in the previous paragraph, some of the tenants who formed cooperatives in response to their landlords' abandonment of buildings in Harlem did have the option to move to the suburbs. Sometimes their grown children offered to support such a move and even begged them to do so. But as one of the respondents put it in explaining why she did not move in with her son on Long Island, "I'd be moving away from the people I see all the time. . . . [I]t's as different as from daylight to dark from where he lives to here."[114] Ernest Gates, a native resident of Chicago's West Side ghetto, chronicled in historian Alexander von Hoffman's book *House by House, Block by Block*, is another example of someone with options who nevertheless decided to stay in the ghetto. After developing a successful trucking business, he considered moving his family out of the ghetto into a luxurious condominium. But he decided to stay put, troubled by the notion that if folks like himself left, the ghetto would never rebound. Instead, he rehabilitated the house he grew up in and then the surrounding houses, hoping to serve as a catalyst and inspiration to the surrounding neighborhood. He eventually became active in the community, organizing to help influence the redevelopment occurring as part of the new United Center Arena, and eventually helped found the Near West Side Community Development Corporation.[115]

Tenant cooperatives in Harlem and the case of Ernest Gates are two anecdotal accounts of community-development practitioners in the ghetto, but they are emblematic of a large and significant trend in the ghetto. In the wake of the abandonment and depopulation of the ghetto in the 1970s and 1980s, community-development corporations such as the Near West Side CDC and black churches were virtually the only major indigenous institutions left in the ghetto. The typical CDC was founded by local neighborhood residents, who organized themselves to address a pressing community need, such as affordable housing or a lack of social services. During the 1960s, CDCs were a manifestation of black power ideology and were a response to the quest for community control. Over time, CDCs proliferated, coming to number in the thousands and spreading beyond black neighborhoods to neighborhoods representing virtually every race and ethnicity in America.[116]

After the cessation of the War on Poverty under President Nixon, the development of affordable housing became the primary mechanism through which funds flowed into the ghetto. In cities that had experienced widespread housing abandonment, such as New York, CDCs turned shells into rehabilitated affordable housing by using both government funds and sweat equity. Starting in 1986, the Low Income Housing Tax Credit, which provides a subsidy for affordable housing, became a major source of funds for the development of affordable housing. Moreover, in the 1990s stricter enforcement of the Community Reinvestment Act of 1977, which requires banks to meet the credit needs of areas where they take in deposits, led banks to increase investment in ghetto neighborhoods. Using government subsidies, foundation support, and investment from the banking sector, CDCs developed thousands of affordable-housing units in the ghetto. Indeed, in many instances CDCs were the *only* developers in ghetto communities.

Faith-based organizations played an outsize role in the CDC movement in the ghetto. Faced with declining population, rising crime, and overall deteriorating conditions in the ghetto, black churches had three options:

activism, flight, or resignation.[117] Some black churches did follow their congregants to greener pastures. A larger portion simply resigned themselves to the worsening conditions, focusing on saving souls one at a time. But some ghetto churches decided to focus on "giving voice to and working on the problems of the neighborhood," according to the political scientist Michael Leo Owens.[118] Many black churches, surrounded by poverty and social problems, saw their immediate environs as places in which to do the Lord's work. Joblessness, the crack epidemic, and other challenges confronting the ghetto were seen as calls for the black church to follow biblical commands to help the needy. Political scientist Michael Owens's interviews with pastors of activist black churches reveal a clergy often motivated by biblical teachings and Jesus's example. The gospel compels empathy for the poor and describes how Jesus regularly preached to prostitutes, thieves, and other sinners. The Book of Luke 4:18 proclaims:

> The Spirit of the Lord is on me,
> because he has anointed me
> to proclaim good news to the poor.
> He has sent me to proclaim freedom for the prisoners
> and recovery of sight for the blind,
> to set the oppressed free,

Where else besides their very neighborhoods, the ghetto, could black churches follow this biblical command? To relocate to greener pastures would be to turn their back on brethren in need and to ignore the Lord's command. As a consequence, a number of black churches formed CDCs and were actively engaged in neighborhood revitalization and stabilization in the ghetto. Organizations such as the East Brooklyn Churches in Brownsville and East New York and the New Communities Corporation in Newark, New Jersey, were among the largest housing developers and social service providers in the ghetto.

As CDCs of all types matured, they became sophisticated affordable-housing developers and providers of an array of social services. CDCs built and maintained housing, provided social services, and even operated charter schools. Competently providing such an array of goods and services required great skill and tenacity. These CDCs had to master the intricacies of real estate development, social service provision, and human-resource management that are part of any large organization. Moreover, they needed to maintain relationships with funders outside the community and government regulators, all while advocating on behalf of and remaining connected to their constituents. Successful CDCs truly had to balance competing interests on a razor's edge and became highly capable organizations. Many failed, but there were some notable successes, especially in cities where the surrounding economy and housing market were strong. In many instances, CDCs have had to grapple with too much success in revitalizing the ghetto when ensuing gentrification has threatened to displace long-term residents, an issue I discuss in the next chapter.

The CDC movement illustrates the extent to which the ghetto remained a haven because a desire, a willingness, and, most important, a capacity to work to reshape the ghetto environment show the agency and capabilities of the people involved. By spending their resources on the ghetto, folks involved in the community-development movement were putting their money where their mouths were, so to speak. Their actions indicate the extent to which the ghetto remained a haven despite its many hellish characteristics—a place that many wanted to remain in and even invest in. Given the considerable effort and ultimately many successes of the community-development movement in the ghetto, it would be a mistake to characterize the ghetto only as a hell. To be sure, in spite of CDCs' efforts, in many instances neighborhood conditions continued to worsen. CDCs could not always counter the forces of deindustrialization, depopulation, disinvestment, and mass incarceration. Moreover, some CDCs proved corrupt or ineffectual or both. But there can be no doubt that CDCs, taken as a whole, had a positive impact on the quality of life in the ghetto. Their persistence and success, limited as it may be, show that the ghetto was not merely a receptacle of society's outcasts. It was not a space that everyone clamored to escape at the first opportunity, nor was it merely the place that those with no other options wound up or had to stay in. The capacity to create and successfully operate CDCs and the accomplishments of these organizations prove that institutions internal to the ghetto had and continue to have the capacity and efficacy to effect change.

The CDC movement thus elucidates a second point of this chapter: even during its nadir, the ghetto remained a haven for many blacks. Beyond that and perhaps more importantly for residents of the ghetto, CDCs improved the quality of life in many ghetto communities.

LATE-TWENTIETH-CENTURY HELL BUT STILL A HAVEN

After the civil rights era, social trends that began in the late 1950s and 1960s crystallized and completely recast the role of the ghetto. The cessation of migration from the South, the out-migration of working-class and middle-class blacks, the rises in crime and female-headed households, and joblessness fed off of each other and combined to create what some called the "underclass ghetto." Whether this label is apt or the harm caused by the stigmatization associated with its use outweighs the analytical clarity it lends is open to debate. But the term does denote a stage in the history of the American ghetto—a time when the ghetto no longer served as a vehicle for upward mobility for the race, when the majority of blacks outside the South were no longer its residents, and when the life chances of those left behind seemed increasingly grim.

Despite the overall decline in the ghetto's fortunes, it remained a haven for a significant number of blacks in the late twentieth century. Like residents of any other neighborhood, residents of the ghetto would often become attached to their home environs. They would view these places as the locus of their social support systems and as the home where they felt most comfortable. Moreover, the vernacular culture of the ghetto, unique in its own way, served to strengthen residents' attachment to their neighborhoods. If they could not be at home in the ghetto, where could they be at home?

The strength of residents' attachments can be seen in the community-development movement. By not only staying put but also fighting to improve their community, ghetto residents participating in community development contradicted stereotypes of them as passive victims to outside forces. Like anyone else, ghetto residents have agency, and those participating in the community-development movement used that agency to help create a durable movement that had important and lasting impacts on the quality of life in the ghetto. Thus, the strength and pervasiveness of the community development movement in the ghetto are indicative of many residents' attachment to the ghetto and the extent to which the ghetto remained a haven.

Chapter Seven

THE GHETTO IN THE TWENTY-FIRST CENTURY

An incident at midday on August 9, 2014, in Ferguson, Missouri, would set in motion a chain of events that in many ways seemed to mirror the "long hot summers" of the 1960s that we encountered in chapter 5. One minute past noon on that day, an unarmed eighteen-year-old black male was stopped by a lone white male police officer while walking down the street because he fit the description of the suspected perpetrator of a robbery that had occurred minutes earlier. During an ensuing altercation, the police officer shot this black male twelve times and killed him.

The deceased suspect, Michael Brown, would lie on the street for four and a half hours. The apparent callousness of leaving a man's body on the street for several hours and rumors that he was shot with his hands up merged with long-simmering resentment over police maltreatment of blacks in the community to spark protests in the immediate aftermath of the shooting. The heavily militarized police response, complete with armored vehicles, assault weapons, and tear gas, served to further antagonize the protesters. Many of the protests were peaceful, but some turned violent, involving clashes with the police, arson, and looting in ways reminiscent to the wave of urban unrest that wracked the ghetto half a century earlier.

In many ways, the unrest on the nights following the killing of Michael Brown followed the script that dictated events across scores of ghettos in the 1960s. An unarmed black male, check. An altercation with the police, check. Long-simmering resentment over police maltreatment, check. Economic marginalization, check (with the black population suffering a poverty rate of 27 percent and a staggering unemployment rate of 24 percent among black males).[1] A low ratio of black men to women in the 25–54 age bracket, check (with only sixty black men for every one hundred black women in this age bracket in 2014, an indicator of black men falling to early mortality, incarceration, and a life on the margins and thus outside the notice of U.S. Census Bureau, and all worse in Ferguson than in any other American city in 2015).[2] Finally, federal policy acting to concentrate low-income blacks in certain neighborhoods within Ferguson, check.

Nor would Ferguson be an isolated incident. The sad story of Freddie Gray, whose death while in police custody on April 12, 2015, sparked several days of urban unrest, offers another parallel to the ghetto unrest of the 1960s. Like Michael Brown, Freddie Gray died at the hands of the police under questionable circumstances. Gray lived in a ghetto perhaps even more disadvantaged than the one where Michael Brown lived. The census tract where Freddie Gray was arrested, which was 99 percent black in 1970, saw its population decline from 5,218 in 1970 to 2,699 in 2010—a decline of 48 percent. Data from the American Community Survey for 2010–2014 reveal a poverty rate of 33 percent for the surrounding Sandtown–Winchester/Harlem Park neighborhood, a level far exceeding the 20 percent threshold used by HUD to designate high-poverty neighborhoods.[3] The arrest rate for adults in Gray's tract ranked sixth out of fifty-five Baltimore neighborhoods and was more than twice the citywide average.[4] Schools in the area were very segregated—Gray's high school was 99 percent black, filled with underperforming students, and until recently did not offer options for high-achieving students, such as Advanced Placement courses.[5] Environmental toxins were close to home: the house where Freddie Gray lived in as a child was littered with flaking, lead-based paint chips.[6]

The summer of 2014 reminded America of the distress that persisted in many ghetto communities. Ferguson itself had only recently experienced an influx of poor blacks. The daunting challenges that gave rise to the urban unrest half a century earlier and that made the ghetto a hell in the last decades of the twentieth century were still with us in the twenty-first century—even though there was a black family in the White House.

But a new time brought new trends that reinforced some extant patterns in the ghetto while introducing new ones. This chapter discusses three major trends that came to the fore in the twenty-first century and the implications of these trends for the ghetto's role as a haven or hell: mass incarceration, the subprime crisis, and gentrification.

MASS INCARCERATION IN THE GHETTO

Created as an instrument of the state for maintaining order, penal systems date back centuries, and their primary objectives have vacillated among reform, revenge, and safety. Whatever the emphasis, the use of incarceration was typically reserved for the most extreme outcasts of society. In the last decade of the twentieth century, however, the ghetto would bear witness to a policy of mass incarceration that left virtually no one there untouched. The origins of mass incarceration as a policy continue to be debated, with some pointing to the war on drugs of the 1980s and the draconian laws that were passed in the latter part of that decade to address the crack-cocaine mayhem consuming the ghetto. Still others consider the rise in crime during the turbulent 1960s as the impetus for increased incarceration over the ensuing decades.[7] As noted earlier, Khalil Muhammad traces back to the late nineteenth century the linking of blackness with criminality and a concomitant urge to penalize the race.[8]

There is no debate, however, about the dramatic rise in incarceration starting in the 1970s or over the fact that this increase in incarceration did not parallel changing crime rates. Between 1970 and 2000, the incarceration rate quadrupled, according to one source.[9] By the beginning of the twenty-first century, the United States had the highest incarceration rate in the world.[10] Among no group were the impacts of mass incarceration felt more intently than among African American males. Their incarceration rate reached a staggering 3,457 per 100,000 in 2000, a rate nearly six times higher than that for white men.[11]

And among blacks specifically, those residing in the ghetto would bear the brunt of the fallout from the policy of mass incarceration. Beyond the obvious direct impact of putting hundreds of thousands of blacks under the supervision of the criminal justice system, the policy of mass incarceration also altered the role of the ghetto in black life. In many ways, mass incarceration worsened conditions in the ghetto and further sapped the ghetto's autonomy.

How Mass Incarceration Affected the Ghetto

The *schwerpunkt* of mass incarceration was felt most keenly in the ghetto because the poor, uneducated blacks disproportionately housed there were the ones most likely to become enmeshed in the criminal justice system. It was in the ghetto that the police engaged in a type of policing that often seemed to presume entire populations (i.e., young men) of communities guilty until proven innocent. In *The New Jim Crow: Incarceration in the Age of Colorblindness*, Michele Alexander reports the experience of an incredulous law student on a police ride-along in Chicago: "Each time we drove into a public housing project and stopped the car, every young black man in the area would almost reflexively place his hand up against the car and spread his legs to be searched. And the officers would search them. The officers would then get back in the car and stop in another project, and this would happen again."[12]

In *Locking Up Our Own*, former public defender James Forman Jr. describes how Operation Ceasefire, a police action, used frequent, routine traffic stops to search for guns and other contraband. He emphasizes that this practice was most often targeted at the poor black neighborhoods of Southeast Washington, DC. Predominantly white neighborhoods and even middle-class black neighborhoods were spared.[13] Numerous studies of incarceration and of the prevalence of having a felony conviction or currently being under the supervision of the criminal justice system tell a similar story—those in the ghetto have disproportionately been affected by mass incarceration. This is the case in the Chicago ghettos, where the incarceration rate per 100,000 persons 18–64 years old was between 2,000 and 4,500 in the years 2000 to 2005. In contrast, in predominantly white Chicago neighborhoods, rates of incarceration were lower than 500 per 100,000 persons.[14] A Pew Research Center study in 2009 found that one in seven black male adults was under correctional supervision in the East Side Ghetto of Detroit; for all males in the United States, the rate is one in eighteen.[15] In 2008, zip code 11918, encompassing the North Philadelphia ghetto, had an imprisonment rate of 18 per 1,000 adults, whereas the predominantly white suburban zip code in adjacent Montgomery County had an imprisonment rate of *zero*.[16] At the start of the twenty-first century in the ghetto of South-east Washington, DC, *the majority* of black men older than eighteen were under some type of correctional supervision.[17]

The concentration of people cycling in and out of the criminal justice system would profoundly affect ghetto neighborhoods, as the sociologists Donald Braman and Alice Goffman have ably shown.[18] Spending time in two ghetto neighborhoods in Washington, DC, and Philadelphia, respectively, these ethnographers describe several ways in which mass incarceration has corroded the social fabric of the ghetto.

First, consider that being sent to jail or prison can be thought of as a type of residential move. Moving away weakens existing ties, and it takes time for new ties to develop and strengthen. Neighborhoods with high levels of mobility, whether voluntary or not, have weaker social ties for that reason. The cycling of people in and out of jail and prison thus destabilizes the social fabric of ghetto communities. Incarcerated people cannot create or nurture social bonds in the neighborhood. People who move to the neighborhood while the incarcerated person is away do not have the chance to connect with that person. Poor neighborhoods such as the ghetto already have high rates of residential turnover,[19] so mass incarceration layers an additional degree of residential instability on neighborhoods that are already unstable.

Second, the long arm of the carceral state reaches into the social ties of ghetto communities. Braman details the emotional and financial impact that incarceration has on the families and friends of those incarcerated. Bail money, money for commissary purchases, and visits to those imprisoned are the burdens imposed on those with loved ones enmeshed in the criminal justice system. For ghetto residents with meager resources to begin with, their woes are made worse by the loss of income and other resources that those now incarcerated formerly provided. Young men, albeit poor, would still likely contribute some income to their household or provide help around the house as a caregiver. Once they are incarcerated, this contribution stops. The prisoner's household is thus hit with a double whammy of declining income and increased expenses. Moreover, the economic hit endured by households of the incarcerated is likely to be enduring: even after release from prison, those with felony convictions will find it hard to find employment.

The way incarceration blocks the incarcerated from reciprocating to help those who help them is perhaps the most pernicious impact of mass incarceration on social ties. Virtually all social ties are built on some notion of reciprocity—you scratch my back, I scratch yours. Indeed, one anthropologist calls reciprocity the "central moral formula for interpersonal conduct."[20] Incarceration interrupts the flow of reciprocation, however, with assistance flowing one way only—from those who are not incarcerated to those who are. Over time, people become wary of associating with the incarcerated for fear of being called on to supply bail money and make costly visits, knowing they will receive nothing in return. Braman chronicles the way many social ties between family members fray under the weight of repeated incarcerations. He observes how family members experiencing the "slow grind of unreturned assistance and care . . . begin to pull back from the relationships and norms that usually bind them together."[21] The social glue that binds people together thus becomes brittle under the pressure of mass incarceration.

Yet this is not the only way mass incarceration undermines social ties in the ghetto. In *On the Run*, Alice Goffman focuses on young men attempting to evade incarceration. She shows that even places that one might think to be beyond the probing eye of the law, such as funeral homes and maternity wards, serve as sites for police to canvass for young black men with outstanding warrants. The police stake out these locations, and the young men, in turn, learn to approach these places warily, if at all. Young men take to leading a life in the shadows, not sleeping in the same place twice, not sharing their last names with friends, and giving friends and acquaintances fake names—all to make it difficult for the police or others who might inform the police to know their whereabouts. In perhaps the most tragicomic parts of Goffman's tales, some men even resort to "do it yourself healthcare," pulling their own teeth or paying health-care workers for pilfered antibiotics, all to avoid having contact with hospitals and ultimately the police.[22]

The police, however, do not confine their searches to funerals, hospitals, and the like. More typically, they lean on family and friends to find suspects. "Cops may exert significant pressure on a man's relatives or partner to provide information about him. Out of frustration and anger at his failures as a father, spouse, brother or son, his partner or family members may freely call the police on him, taking advantage of his wanted status to get back at him or punish him. . . . [H]e comes to regard those closest to him as potential informants."[23] The life "on the run" becomes one imbued with cynicism toward the state, family, and friends. Goffman makes this point clearly: "As long as a man is at risk of confinement, staying out of prison and routine participation in family, work, and friendships become contradictory goals—doing one reduces his chance of achieving the other."[24]

The ghetto, which residents at one time saw as a refuge from white America, has become a place that allows no refuge if you are young, male, and black. But mass incarceration has likely eroded the ghetto's role as a haven in at least one more important way. As Michelle Alexander notes, almost all states restrict the voting rights of prisoners, with only Maine and Vermont allowing inmates to vote.[25] Voting rights return to those released from incarceration in only fourteen states (all outside the former Confederacy).[26] This means that those imprisoned lose their voice in the political system for the duration of their conviction, and most of them lose it for several years thereafter. Even when not legally restricted from voting, many former felons are reluctant to interact with the government in any capacity, including voting. As noted earlier, former felons are wary of places police might stake out for fear of being in violation of some aspect of their parole or probation, which includes polling places.

But barriers to civic participation are not limited to restrictions on voting. Most states, including twenty-four states outside the former Confederacy, bar former felons from jury service.[27] The right to a trial by one's peers is of course enshrined in the U.S. Constitution and is considered one of the pillars of an accountable system of government that prevents tyranny. But this important civic opportunity and responsibility, participating in jury services, is withheld from many former felons.

The resulting civic incapacitation due to a loss of voting rights and the duty of jury service is concentrated in the ghetto because the policy of mass incarceration is disproportionally manifested there. In the public sphere, ghetto residents are fighting for their interests with one arm tied behind their back—current former felons in their midst cannot vote or serve on juries. Ghetto communities needing to make their voice heard in the political arena, secure public resources, protect the community's interests, or advocate for local needs find their voices muffled by the fact that sizable numbers of people in their communities are enmeshed in the criminal justice system.

The policy of mass incarceration, enacted in the wake of the civil rights era, has thus had a devastating impact on the ghetto. And although it may have contributed to the decline in crime, this gain must be weighed against the devastating losses incurred by such a large segment of the ghetto's population cycling in and out of jail and prison. For this large segment of the ghetto, in particular young black males, mass incarceration serves to further compound the disadvantages of the ghetto.

THE SUBPRIME CRISIS

It is more than just losing a house. It is like losing a part of yourself, like a part of you died. My home was where my children and grandchildren came.

—CAROLYN HOLBROOK, FORMER MINNEAPOLIS HOMEOWNER, QUOTED IN
BARBARA REYNOLDS, "MINORITIES FALL VICTIM TO PREDATORY LENDERS" (2012)

Even while the most marginalized black neighborhoods have borne the brunt of mass incarceration, the first decades of the twenty-first century also witnessed another disaster that fell disproportionately on the black middle class—the subprime mortgage crisis.

In the first decade of the twenty-first century, the subprime mortgage crisis precipitated the worst economic debacle in eighty years. The fallout spread across the globe, and people from all walks of life were affected. The subprime crisis had important implications for the role of the ghetto in black life because it threatened to erase the differences between the ghetto and black middle-class neighborhoods where blacks had "made it." This section briefly describes the origins of the subprime crisis in black neighborhoods and describes the fallout in terms of its impact on the role of the ghetto as an institution.

Subprime loans are high-cost loans designed to reflect the borrower's higher risk. To the extent subprime loans are merely priced higher to reflect the borrower's greater risk, such loans are not necessarily problematic. These loans provide a means for economically marginal or nonconventional (e.g., the self-employed) borrowers to access credit. The popularity of subprime lending mushroomed after the deregulation of the financial industry in the 1980s removed usury ceilings on lenders. The financial industry developed new ways to package subprime loans as investments with high returns— the higher interest rates meant higher returns to the owner of the mortgage. The financial industry became more variegated, with mortgage brokers and other intermediaries arising to make and sell mortgage loans. Investment-rating companies and investment banks used putatively sophistical tools

that convinced them that subprime mortgages were safe. Financial regulators for the most part looked the other way, assuming the "discipline of
the market" would prevent any excesses. And almost everyone got caught in
the mania of the housing bubble, assuming housing prices would continue
to rise.

Black neighborhoods, whether those historically part of the ghetto or
new middle-class enclaves, proved an attractive target for subprime lenders. Lenders marketed their products in black-oriented media, made connections with local black institutions, and hired black mortgage brokers to
hawk their products.[28] After decades of limited access to the mortgage market, many black borrowers were eager to take advantage of the newly pro-
miscuous lending by banks. Rather than shopping for the best interest rates,
some black borrowers were lured solely by the prospect of being approved.
The long history of underservice by the financial industry also left some
black borrowers less familiar with financial instruments and susceptible to
costly and risky adjustable-rate mortgages. They would prove unwitting
prey for unscrupulous lenders, who steered many of them to subprime
loans, even when their financial history qualified them for conventional-
rate mortgages.

The end result was that black neighborhoods received a disproportionate share of subprime loans.[29] Moreover, several studies have shown that
even after accounting for the riskiness of predominantly black neighborhoods, banks were more likely to offer the residents of these neighborhoods
subprime loans.[30]

Several court cases corroborate the scholarly evidence. For example, Emigrant Savings Bank was found guilty of targeting black neighborhoods in
New York City for subprime loans.[31] Both Countrywide Savings Bank (since
acquired by Bank of America) and Wells Fargo agreed on nine-figure settle-
ments for targeting black neighborhoods for subprime loans, with one
employee of Wells Fargo going as far as to call these products "ghetto loans."[32]

For a while, the increasing availability of mortgages did enable more
blacks to become homeowners, with the black homeownership rate peaking at 49 percent in 2004.[33] As one former Citigroup executive said, "As long
as the music kept playing"—that is, as long as housing prices kept rising—
the downside of these expensive loans were masked somewhat.[34] Troubled
borrowers could refinance their loans or if necessary sell their house to pay
off their mortgage.

Eventually, however, the music did stop. Housing prices could not rise forever. The bubble popped. Lenders became skittish, and buyers hesitated to plunk down ever-increasing amounts for a house. Many of the subprime loans had low "teaser" rates that reset to a higher rate after a year or two. Eventually, more and more borrowers could not make their mortgage payments or refinance their loans or sell their houses. Foreclosure loomed for many. The subprime market imploded, imperiling the global economy.

The targeting of subprime loans to black neighborhoods made the fallout in these same neighborhoods especially severe. Perhaps counterintuitively, the fallout was worse in middle-class black neighborhoods. In very poor black neighborhoods, homeownership was relatively rare, and housing prices appreciated only modestly there, if at all. There were thus few opportunities for subprime lenders to make loans in these neighborhoods and few borrowers relative to the size of the neighborhood population. The sociologists Derek Hyra and Jacob Rugh studied the fallout from the subprime crisis in Bronzeville in Chicago, Harlem in New York City, and the Shaw–U Street area in Washington, DC. Whereas Bronzeville was hard hit by the crisis, with property values falling 20 percent and the foreclosure rate reaching 9 percent of all loans, Harlem and Shaw–U Street emerged relatively unscathed, with property values holding steady and foreclosure rates not rising higher than 2 percent. The low homeownership rate and gentrification inoculated these ghetto neighborhoods from the worst ravages of the subprime debacle. Borrowers in Harlem and Shaw–U Street tended to be upwardly mobile gentrifiers, not the typical target for subprime lenders. Even Bronzeville, which was relatively hard hit, did not fare as bad as predominantly black neighborhoods closer to the suburbs, where homeownership was more prevalent.[35]

In contrast, several formerly stable black middle-class neighborhoods were hard hit by the fallout from the subprime debacle. Consider the South Shore neighborhood of Chicago. Just southwest of the Bronzeville ghetto, South Shore had been a locus of Chicago's black middle class in the latter part of the twentieth century. The Great Recession and subprime crisis combined, however, to leave a trail of disorder in their wake. Alden Loury, director of research and evaluation at Chicago's Metropolitan Planning Council, likened the impact to "a bomb dropped on vulnerable communities." The once proud bastion of black middle-class stability now ranked eighth out of seventy-seven community areas in Chicago in terms of foreclosures in 2007.[36] Moreover, the increase in foreclosures led to an increase in homes being boarded up and in owner-occupied units being converted to rentals. The ranking of the South Shore neighborhood climbed in more than the number of foreclosures: by 2017, the neighborhood ranked sixth among the city's seventy-seven community areas for incidents in which one or more people were killed.[37]

Southeast Queens, New York, was another black middle-class bastion hard hit by the fallout from the subprime crisis. Starting in the 1940s, this section of Queens became home to such luminaries as Count Basie, James Brown, W. E. B. Du Bois, Lena Horne, Jackie Robinson, and LL Cool J. In both 1994 and 2005, Queens County was the only large county in the United States where median black income actually surpassed that of whites, largely because of middle-class blacks in Southeast Queens.[38]

Despite this prosperous past, Southeast Queens was at the epicenter of the fallout from the subprime crisis. Like other black middle-class neighborhoods, this area attracted peddlers of subprime loans like a carcass attracts vultures. By 2009, the Jamaica Community District, which encompasses most of Southeast Queens, had the second-highest rate of subprime lending and the fourth-highest foreclosure rate in New York City in 2009.[39]

Even some of the neighborhoods in Prince George's County, Maryland, the richest majority-black county in the nation, could not escape the plague of subprime lending, subsequent foreclosure, and financial distress. In 2015, the *Washington Post* ran an article on the Fairwood subdivision in the county, a majority-black neighborhood with a median annual income of $173,000, where homes once sold for seven figures. By 2015, *half* of the loans on homes built in 2005 and 2006 were in foreclosure.[40]

Foreclosures, although perhaps the worst and most obvious sign of distress, were not the only sign. Many subprime borrowers held on to their homes through tremendous sacrifice, taking on extra work, skimping on other necessities, and sometimes going deeper into debt. Through this ordeal, the black middle class collectively witnessed the evaporation of millions of dollars of wealth, wealth that could not be used to cushion them from the shock of unexpected financial trauma or be passed down to future generations. The stress from the subprime crisis and ensuing fallout surely had incalculable costs. Indeed, a systematic review of empirical studies on foreclosure and health outcomes concludes that "most of the 35 identified studies showed that foreclosure has adverse effects on health, mental health, and health behaviors." Moreover, these studies revealed that "degradation of the neighborhood environment and increase in community stressors also had indirect, cross-level adverse effects on health and mental health."[41]

Although the subprime crisis hit many neighborhoods that might not fit our conceptions of a ghetto, the neighborhoods hardest hit were often meccas for the black middle class and elite. Because of the overwhelming importance of race, the crisis links these neighborhoods to poorer black neighborhoods for at least three reasons. First, as several studies have shown, it was the race of the borrowers and the racial composition of the neighborhoods specifically that made these spaces attractive targets for subprime lenders. Several court cases revealed that black neighborhoods specifically were targeted for riskier loans. Second, the redlining of the ghetto in the twentieth century made these neighborhoods especially susceptible to predatory lenders. Like parched ground that quickly absorbs the rain, the scarcity of credit in the ghetto made residents eager to snatch up new opportunities to borrow. The long history of scarce credit was seared into the collective memory of the ghetto. As a consequence, borrowers had little or no history of accessing loans from conventional lenders, and some didn't even think to approach such lenders.[42]

Finally, some black neighborhoods that were swamped with subprime loans found themselves drowning in foreclosures. Foreclosures often led to rapid residential turnover or vacant property, serving to destabilize neighborhoods. Indeed, several systematic studies have linked increases in foreclosure to rising crime.[43] For example, in a study of crime in Chicago, Johanna Lacoe and Ingrid Gould Ellen found that additional foreclosure increases total crime by a factor of 1.011.[44] Although this study did not focus specifically on black or ghetto neighborhoods, there is little reason to doubt that similar impacts will be found there. Several formerly middle-class black neighborhoods, such as the South Shore neighborhood in Chicago, staggered under the weight of the foreclosure crisis and began to experience the types of social problems more typically associated with the ghetto in the late twentieth century. The subprime crisis thus threatened to completely obliterate the already thin line between the ghetto and putatively stable black middle-class neighborhoods.

The subprime crisis illustrates that the dividing line between poor black neighborhoods, which are more typically considered "ghettos," and middle-class black neighborhoods can be ephemeral. Although middle-class black neighborhoods do not suffer from the same range of challenges as poor neighborhoods and their residents have a greater degree of choice about where to live, during the subprime bonanza they were still vulnerable to discriminatory practices in the form of predatory lending. Moreover, these neighborhoods could not escape the long reach of history because redlining during the twentieth century left these neighborhoods vulnerable to predatory lending in the twenty-first.

In the early twenty-first century, the persistence of race as a determinant of life chances meant that both poor and middle-class black neighborhoods, despite seemingly vast differences in status, were susceptible to the effects of racism. Neighborhoods such as the Fairwood subdivision of Prince George's County were surely different from the poorest sections of Southeast DC, but both neighborhoods found themselves disadvantaged for an important reason—the race of the inhabitants. Thus, the forces of ghettoization, which manifested themselves in different ways throughout the early twentieth century—racial zoning, redlining, white flight, and urban renewal—now reemerged in a different form: subprime lending. The tactics were different, and the racism motivating these tactics was not as virulent, but, broadly speaking, the outcome was the same. Even middle-class black neighborhoods were disadvantaged because of their inhabitants' race. That these neighborhoods were havens for the black middle class made little difference, in the same way that the ghetto's role as a haven for blacks in the early twentieth century did not protect the ghetto from redlining, urban renewal, and disinvestment then, either.

At the dawn of the twenty-first century, the ghetto could be conceived as existing on a continuum. At one end were poor, disadvantaged black neighborhoods of the type chronicled as home of the underclass and consistent with the pejorative use of the word *ghetto*. At the other end were solidly middle-class black neighborhoods seemingly worlds apart from the former in terms of status, wealth, and appearance. But the subprime crisis reminds us that the overarching force that made the ghetto, race, could affect middle-class black havens as well. Although blacks could seek refuge in havens, whether the historical ghetto of the twentieth century, the underclass ghetto of the late twentieth century, or the middle-class enclaves of the twenty-first century, these havens could not completely inoculate them from the ravages of racism in America.

GENTRIFICATION

In 2016, the *New York Times* published an article titled "The End of Black Harlem." The article described how Harlem was experiencing an "influx of tourists, developers and stroller-pushing young families," along with "high-end housing and hip restaurants, and various public improvements, like new landscaping and yoga studios."[45] Given the social disasters that had wracked Harlem and other ghettos in the late twentieth century, an unfamiliar reader-observer might have expected a celebratory tone in the article; however, its tone was anything but that. Instead, the article lamented the loss of Harlem's black identity, echoing an earlier complaint expressed in the *New African*. This earlier article, published in 2014, made note of the same types of changes under way in Harlem. And as in the *New York Times* article, its tone was not celebratory. Noting that unlike in the 1900s, when Harlem was a haven for blacks fleeing terrorism in the South or in the 1920s for West Indians or in the 1950s for Puerto Ricans or in the 1980s for the Senegalese, the changes under way made it "clear Harlem is no longer a local black people's haven."[46]

Sentiments such as those expressed in these two articles are surprisingly common. This chapter shows that despite depopulation, disinvestment, and mass incarceration, some blacks still viewed the ghetto as a haven. Although that role was not as prominent as it had been decades earlier, two factors—place attachment, or the close feelings people develop toward their neighborhood, and the perception of the ghetto as a homeland—caused residents and some blacks outside the ghetto to see it as a haven. This section examines how gentrification provides a lens through which to see how the ghetto was still considered a haven in a number of cities across the country. This examination is important because it allows for a more complete description of the ghetto's role in black American life and because of the implications for planning and policy discussed in the concluding chapter.

Gentrification, or the process whereby older, inner-city neighborhoods that have suffered from disinvestment experience an influx of residents of higher socioeconomic status and investment, is illustrative of the ghetto's role as a haven for at least two reasons. First, the ghetto residents' reactions to the gentrification of their neighborhoods belie the notion that the ghetto is a hell to all. Second, the motives of black gentrifiers, who are often overlooked in discussions of gentrification, show that this group viewed the ghetto as a haven.

The sociologist Ruth Glass first coined the term *gentrification* in 1964 to describe professionals moving into older, dilapidated London flats and renovating these units,[47] and the process has been observed in cities across the globe. Casual observations of gentrification in the United States date back at least to the late 1960s, when it was referred to as "brownstoning" because dilapidated brownstones in neighborhoods such as Park Slope and Boerum Hill in Brooklyn were attracting upwardly mobile artists and professionals.[48]

The ghetto, having experienced redlining, decades of white flight, and depopulation, was the epitome of the disinvested inner-city neighborhood. In the late nineteenth and early twentieth centuries, many ghettos were located in the oldest sections of cities, near concentrations of commerce and industry. In these earlier times, such proximity was often a drawback because of the congestion and pollution of the early industrial city. Those with means moved to early suburbs or to quieter, more tranquil environs, thus leaving the inner city to the poor, including blacks. By the late twentieth century, however, deindustrialization and urban renewal had transformed many downtowns into gleaming office towers replete with museums, restaurants, and other cultural amenities. Many ghetto neighborhoods, formerly disdained for their proximity to the dirt and grit of industrial-era downtowns, were now conveniently located near these resurgent downtowns. For these reasons, the ghetto seemed ripe for gentrification.

The stigma and fear of the ghetto, however, meant that, with a few exceptions notwithstanding, gentrification did not happen in the black ghettos during the late 1960s and 1970s. High crime rates, drug trafficking, and public housing kept would-be gentrifiers at bay. Indeed, a profile of a white gentrifier who moved to Harlem in 1979 included this note: "one reason Jeffrey Rouault is the only white Harlem lawyer named is his experience as a pioneer. He has been hit with a bottle, clubbed with a two-by-four, and robbed."[49] Such experiences served to reinforce existing stereotypes about danger in the ghetto. And as we saw in the previous chapter, crime was high in the ghetto in the 1960s, 1970s, and 1980s. This fear of the dark ghetto led two authors of an early study of the potential for gentrification in Harlem to surmise that the "white gentry was less squeamish about moving into white working-class areas."[50] Echoing this point, one Harlem resident was quoted as saying in the late 1980s, "White people . . . they're not going to come here [to Harlem]."[51] Indeed, a recent study of gentrification in

Chicago found gentrification happening more slowly in black and Hispanic neighborhoods than in poor white ones.[52] The gentry might be attracted to the authenticity and grit of the inner city, but they apparently like their grit lighter complexioned and not too "real."

But although gentrification has connotations of race, it is by definition about class. While observers were concluding that gentrification would not occur in the ghetto, gentrification in "blackface," or with the black middle class as the protagonists, was occurring right under the noses of those who argued it would not occur.[53] As discussed in more detail later in this chapter, during the 1980s and 1990s members of the black middle class often remained or moved into ghetto neighborhoods, helping to arrest the decline that was happening there. Following on the heels of and perhaps in part due to the actions of these black gentrifiers and the community-development movement described in the previous chapter, a number of neighborhoods in the ghetto experienced full-scale gentrification that eventually came to include gentrifiers of all races, even whites. By the 2000s, whites moving into the ghetto was a newsworthy trend.

News stories in black-oriented periodicals blared titles such as "Invasion of the 'Hood Snatchers': How Black Neighborhoods Are Being Gentrified" and "The Whitening of Black Neighborhoods."[54] The appearance of middle-class whites in the ghetto starting in the 1990s would underscore what the black middle class had shown a decade or two earlier—the ghetto was not impervious to the forces of gentrification.

Neighborhoods previously described by outsiders as "sketchy," "war zones," and "ghetto" were suddenly home to professional whites, artisanal retail shops, and the now ubiquitous coffee shops. A *New York Times* real estate column in 2000 quoted a realtor describing Harlem as "being on everybody's lips . . . [and] no longer a no man's land." (Apparently, the tens of thousands of people residing in Harlem before gentrification were literally "nobodies.") The column concluded, "That fact has not been lost on whites, who seem to be moving into Harlem, the country's center of African-American culture, as fast as they can label their cardboard boxes."[55]

In 1994, one street in Harlem was described variously as "the other America, the America of the black underclass. It is a place—and it could be in Chicago, Miami or Los Angeles—with its own values, rules and economy. . . . [G]enerations live and die on this block, a world apart." It was a street where "almost everyone . . . is related to someone who has been shot, is addicted to drugs or dying of AIDS." It was a block that "looks like a city after a war, with its vacant lots, abandoned buildings and four-to-seven-story dowager buildings of ornate ironwork, tiled hallways and marble stairways, long in decline."[56]

But a mere seven years later, the block had "black, white and Hispanic young professionals secure in the information economy" and rehabilitated brownstones being sold for $400,000 dollars and up.[57] In Washington, DC, the site of the disturbances in 1968 in the wake of the murder of Martin Luther King Jr. that left twelve people dead and caused $354 million dollars in damage was by 2008 hosting a "yuppie farmers market" and had become in the words of the *Washington Post* "one of the trendiest hubs in the region."[58] In North Philadelphia, a woman whose family were the first blacks on the block in the 1950s, who had lived through white flight, and who had witnessed the pockmarking of the block with abandoned buildings and lots now experienced unsolicited offers to buy her home from whites looking to move into the neighborhood.[59]

Indeed, in perhaps the clearest sign of advancing gentrification, the first decade of the twenty-first century witnessed what was likely the largest influx of whites into black neighborhoods since blacks began urbanizing in large numbers in the late nineteenth century. When compared to the 1980s or 1990s, the proportion of black neighborhoods experiencing at least a 5 percent increase in their white population in the 2000s was at least twice as high. Figure 7.1 shows there was a dramatic increase in the number of

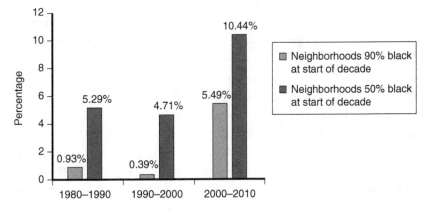

FIGURE 7.1 Proportion of black neighborhoods experiencing influx of whites, 1980–2010.
Source: Freeman and Cai 2015.

TABLE 7.1

Number of Black Neighborhoods Experiencing a White Influx by Decade

	1980–1990	1990–2000	2000–2010
New York City	15	13	89
Washington, DC	16	2	52
Philadelphia	0	4	32
Chicago	4	6	25
New Orleans	3	3	23
Atlanta	2	9	20
Oakland	5	2	15
Richmond, VA	6	4	15
Indianapolis, IN	4	2	12
Savannah, GA	2	5	11

Source: Author's tabulation of Longitudinal Tract Database data (Logan, Xu, and Stults 2012; see also Logan, Xu, and Stults 2015).

black neighborhoods experiencing an influx of whites, defined as an at least 5 percent increase in the white population, in the past decade.[60]

Table 7.1 lists the ten cities with the largest number of census tracts experiencing a white influx between 2000 and 2010. Six of the ten cities are outside the South, and the four cities with the most neighborhoods experiencing an influx are in the North. Although New York City ghettos such as Harlem and Bed-Stuy and Washington, DC, ghettos have captured the lion's share of media attention for the gentrification occurring there, as table 7.1 makes clear, the pattern is by no means limited to these cities. Gentrification, including an influx of whites, had arrived in the ghetto throughout the country in general by the 2000s.

At first glance, gentrification might seem a God-sent antidote to what ailed the ghetto. After decades of depopulation, disinvestment, and flight by the middle class, gentrification represented a reversal of these trends. Instead of white flight and the exodus of the middle class that we encountered in the previous chapter, the middle class was returning to the ghetto, investing their own capital and sweat equity and eventually enticing outside investment as well. But as any student of urbanism knows, gentrification has hardly been welcomed with open arms in the ghetto.

As early as 1985, when gentrification was still a relatively rare phenomenon, *The Crisis*, the organ of the NAACP, asked if gentrification were "a new form of oppression" for inner-city blacks. The article pointed out how Harlem politician William Dawkins opposed a rezoning that would contribute to gentrification because it "promises to revitalize the neighborhoods, but not for the benefit of the indigenous families."[61] Indeed, as described in *Ebony* magazine that same year, many blacks viewed gentrification as evidence of a "plan" to evict blacks from choice locations and replace them with whites.[62] More recently, when protesting against a rezoning plan in Harlem that might facilitate gentrification, the architectural historian Michael Henry Adams likened gentrification in Harlem to the British colonization of South Asia.[63] In my former neighborhood in West Harlem, residents hold an "antigentrification" block party every summer. To working-class homeowner Shirley Parnell in Washington, DC, gentrification is something that "kind of kicks some of us to the back of the bus."[64] By the second decade of the twenty-first century, negative associations with gentrification had been cemented, prompting the well-respected current affairs journal, the *Atlantic*, to publish an article titled "Why Is Gentrification Such a Bad Word?"[65]

A post on a the City-Data Forum in 2015, a website where people looking to move or relocate inquire about various neighborhoods, succinctly summed up the everyday fears of gentrification:

When white people come, more white people tend to follow, then next thing you know Grandma is cashing out and moving down south LOL, long time renters get priced out, the nature of the policing changes in a way that is pretty ignorant of who is actually a problem and who's not, all your favorite local eateries and small businesses start closing because they can no longer afford the rent, and all your normal practices (like the cookout you have every year) become a "problem." Your music is too loud, hanging out with you friends is now threatening, your clothing is too "low rent," and everything changes. People you've known your whole life are gone. The neighborhood is "better," but not for you and yours.[66]

The oft-expressed antagonism toward gentrification has many roots, but this antagonism also reveals the extent to which the ghetto has remained a haven for some blacks. Although many blacks did flee the ghettos starting in the late twentieth century, not everyone left. Many remained in these neighborhoods, some because they had nowhere else to go, but some because they wanted to stay put. The ghetto was their home, and they were attached to these spaces for reasons described in the previous chapter. Beyond attachment due merely to familiarity and social ties, the ghetto has a vernacular culture that, as we shall see, is threatened by gentrification.

Indigenous residents often express the threat to their vernacular culture as a fear of gentrification "pushing them out" both literally and figuratively. In my interviews with residents of Clinton Hill and Harlem for *There Goes the 'Hood*, a common refrain was a feeling of being "pushed out." One interviewee said, "They're taking over, we're being pushed out." Even homeowners, such as one long-term Harlem resident, expressed this fear: "I don't wanna be pushed out. You know what I'm saying? Because I truly believe there's a conspiracy, in trying to push people, black people, that own homes in Harlem."[67]

The fear of being literally being pushed out is well known. After the initial entry of a few gentrifiers, who may be more highly educated but have incomes not much higher than the original residents—hence their seeking housing in the ghetto in the first place—the news of the ghetto's suitability spreads by word of mouth. Other would-be gentrifiers hear that living in the 'hood is perhaps not so bad, and they also seek out housing there. New stores may open to cater to the new population. Residents more affluent than the first gentrifiers are eventually drawn to the neighborhood. The influx of gentrifiers soon translates into increased demand and rising housing prices. Original renters might find their rents increasing far beyond what they can afford. Original homeowners might find their property taxes, which are often based on the market value of homes in the neighborhood, rising dramatically. Soon many of the original residents and blacks in general can no longer afford to live in the neighborhood. This is the common understanding of how gentrification affects communities.

The evidence on whether gentrification actually forces many people out of their homes is mixed. A number of studies have found little difference in mobility rates between the poor or renters living in gentrifying neighborhoods and the poor or renters residing in low-income neighborhoods that do not gentrify.[68] At least two studies found that those in gentrifying neighborhoods are more likely to move due to reasons we associate with displacement.[69] But, overall, the empirical evidence on widespread physical displacement is surprisingly thin.

What empirical studies of physical displacement do consistently show, however, is that when neighborhoods gentrify, the poor and nonwhites are less likely to move into these same neighborhoods.[70] As the original residents move, which happens in any neighborhood, gentrifying or not, they are replaced by more affluent and often white residents, changing the neighborhood's demographic, economic character, and perhaps ultimately its cultural character as well.

Residents' fears of being displaced or "pushed out" thus extend beyond the literal definitions of these terms. They also encompass being displaced or pushed out culturally and even politically. The "culture" in cultural displacement refers to the customs and norms that govern life in ghetto neighborhoods. How people make use of public space, whether they greet strangers on the street, and the types of clientele local retailers cater to are examples of culture vulnerable to displacement from gentrification. Political power is vulnerable to displacement because the types of politicians elected in the ghetto may change when gentrification occurs. The notorious conflict over African drumming in Marcus Garvey Park in Harlem illustrates the strain associated with cultural displacement all too well.

Beginning in the 1970s, drummers began gathering in Marcus Garvey Park in the heart of Harlem to drum every weekend. The drummers practiced African-influenced drumming styles and apparently did so without incident for several decades. This practice seems to have become an accepted part of the cultural fabric and rhythms of Harlem, befitting a neighborhood known as the "black capital of America."

In the 1990s, however, gentrification began changing the demographic complexion of the neighborhood. Perhaps most surprisingly, whites began moving in, including near Marcus Garvey Park. To at least some of the white newcomers, the drums were a nuisance, not a cultural tradition to be cherished. In 2007, one white resident, Sid Miller, stated, "I wished [sic] they weren't there. It's annoying, it's very annoying. I don't like it, none of the homeowners like it."[71] Some of the newcomers went as far as to call the police because of the "noise" the drummers were creating. After several tense standoffs between the police and drummers, protests against police involvement, and numerous consultations between community groups, an uneasy "cold war" was established between the drummers and their supporters, on one hand, and nearby residents, many of whom were gentrifiers, on the other, whereby the drummers would play in a part of the park farther away from homes in the area.[72]

The conflict over the drumming reveals the extent to which Harlem was viewed by at least some of the drummers and their supporters as a haven for black culture and people. Although the park is a public space open to people of all backgrounds and races, many of the drummers and their supporters were quick to articulate black cultural norms and traditions to defend the practice of drumming. Implicit in their arguments is the notion that the Harlem ghetto belongs to black people, and their culture "belongs" in Harlem. The anthropologist Khadijah White describes how black drummers were drawn to the drumming circle by a sense of belongingness, even if they did not live in Harlem. In this sense, blacks belong in Harlem—"even (or, perhaps, especially) . . . individuals who do not necessarily have a previous connection to that space."[73] African-style drumming was for some a black cultural custom and therefore belonged in the Harlem ghetto. As one drummer put it, "The drums belong here . . . this is our church."[74] Agnes Johnson, a frequent spectator of the drumming, related how "African women in traditional dress all started to dance, do you know how glorious that is for our children to see that? They don't have to wait for black history month, they can see it and touch it and be part of it. Everyone starts to smile; everyone starts to relate to it."[75] The drumming was a reminder of Harlem's role as a haven for black culture in America. But gentrification posed a definite threat to this practice, and this incident is illustrative of black residents' fears of being pushed out.

Several studies of gentrification in the ghetto report conflicts paralleling the conflict over African drumming in Marcus Garvey Park. *There Goes the 'Hood* describes conflicts over cooking out in Fort Greene Park in New York City and drinking on one's stoop in Harlem. Residents of Clinton Hill frequently used Fort Greene Park to cook out during warm weather. Starting in the early years of the twenty-first century, however, as the neighborhood surrounding the park experienced gentrification, residents began complaining about the cookouts, pointing out that they were against park rules. In Harlem, a respondent noted in the wake of gentrification, "If we on the corner or stoop with a beer the police is coming. Meanwhile Danelo's [a new restaurant in the neighborhood] put a patio out and people is sitting out there drinking wine. But I can't have a beer?!"[76] The anthropologist Sabiya Prince chronicles a clash over how loudly a teen could play his music on a Saturday afternoon in a gentrifying black neighborhood in Washington, DC. Whereas long-term residents had learned either to tolerate the music or to negotiate some type of truce with the teen, a white newcomer resorted to calling the police after an argument over the music became confrontational.[77] Chronicling gentrification in the Shaw–U Street neighborhood of Washington, DC, sociologist Derek Hyra tells of black congregation members being evicted from parking in a school parking lot and then being ticketed by the police for double parking on Sundays while attending church.[78] These parking troubles arose with the gentrification of the neighborhood and complaints by gentrifiers about these practices. In predominantly black sections of Oakland, California, including parts of the East Oakland ghetto, gentrification brought jittery whites to the 'hood, who called the police on "suspicious"-looking blacks who were doing no more than walking in the street.[79]

In all of these instances, as in the case of the African drumming in Marcus Garvey Park, long-standing practices were being challenged by newcomers to the neighborhood. Long-term black residents of these neighborhoods had customarily cooked out in the park, shared a beer on their front stoop, or doubled-parked in front of their church. These actions may technically be illegal but were long tolerated. Gentrification brought newcomers who were white, did not find these practices acceptable, and were willing to use the police to enforce their standards of public behavior. That these white newcomers tried to use the power of the state to enforce their vision for the neighborhood is the dynamic that leads longtime residents to associate gentrification with being "pushed out."

The filmmaker Spike Lee's angry tirade against gentrification makes the case:

You just can't come and bogart. There were brothers playing motherfuckin' African drums in Mount Morris Park for 40 years and now they can't do it anymore because the new inhabitants said the drums are loud. My father's a great jazz musician. He bought a house in nineteen-motherfuckin'-sixty-eight, and the motherfuckin' people moved in last year and called the cops on my father. He's not—he doesn't even play electric bass! It's acoustic! We bought the motherfuckin' house in nineteen-sixty-motherfuckin'-eight and now you call the cops? In 2013? Get the fuck outta here!

Nah. You can't do that. You can't just come in the neighborhood and start bogarting and say, like you're motherfuckin' Columbus and kill off the Native Americans. Or what they do in Brazil, what they did to the indigenous people. You have to come with respect. There's a code. There's people.

You can't just—here's another thing: When Michael Jackson died they wanted to have a party for him in motherfuckin' Fort Greene Park and all of a sudden the white people in Fort Greene said, "Wait a minute! We can't have black people having a party for Michael Jackson to celebrate his life. Who's coming to the neighborhood? They're gonna leave lots of garbage." Garbage? Have you seen Fort Greene Park in the morning? It's like the motherfuckin' Westminster Dog Show. There's 20,000 dogs running around. Whoa. So we had to move it to Prospect Park!

I mean, they just move in the neighborhood. You just can't come in the neighborhood. I'm for democracy and letting everybody live but you gotta have some respect. You can't just come in when people have a culture that's been laid down for generations and you come in and now shit gotta change because you're here?[80]

For residents of the ghetto, gentrification often poses a threat to long-standing customs and traditions, the threat of being pushed out. As one ghetto resident put it in a student-produced documentary on YouTube, "You're displacing us and a place that we created a culture for."[81]

Although political displacement is evolving more slowly, incumbent politicians have electoral advantages that often allow them to remain in office even as their constituency changes, but there's evidence that gentrification is threatening the political power associated with the ghetto. As of 2018, blacks no longer hold a majority of the Oakland City Council, and the same can be said for "Chocolate City," Washington, DC. As gentrification ensues in ghetto neighborhoods, newcomers begin to flex their political power, and this often means that nonblack politicians are elected to represent these neighborhoods. The ghetto, which was the font of black political power for much of the twentieth century, will see its political currency in black America decline, at least in those ghetto neighborhoods experiencing gentrification. Reporting on the election of Adriano Espaillat, the first non–African American to represent Harlem in seven decades, the New York Times found current residents lamenting, "It's the end of a culture," and "We have no more face. It's a perpetual loss of ground, a loss of the black community having identity."[82] Harlem no longer being represented by an African American was only indirectly due to gentrification—the decline in the black population occasioned a redrawing of the congressional district's boundaries to include largely Dominican Washington Heights. But the sentiments expressed by these residents capture the feeling of political displacement.

These examples of cultural and political displacement show it is not necessarily the physical displacement of residents but the displacement of the vernacular culture and the loss of political power that contribute to feelings of being pushed out. These neighborhoods have long been black and relatively poor and part of what is considered the ghetto. The customs and practices there may differ from what is acceptable in suburban middle-class neighborhoods, but to many of the long-term residents these customs are part of what make these neighborhoods home.

Indeed, it is the fact that these neighborhoods are not solidly middle class that has allowed them to play the role of a haven for long-term residents. Perhaps just as important as the availability of cheap housing is the space to engage in customs and practices that might raise eyebrows or not be tolerated elsewhere. In the ghetto, such practices as drumming, drinking on one's stoop, and cooking out in the park are acceptable and even cherished.

There is great irony that these "ghetto" (in the adjective sense) customs are often viewed as "authentic" and draw some gentrifiers to these older, poorer neighborhoods in the first place. Sharon Zukin has written about the draw of "authentic" neighborhoods with ethnic restaurants, funky shops, and working-class culture for gentrifiers.[83] In the Shaw–U Street neighborhood of Washington, DC, some gentrifiers are even drawn to the most negative stereotypes of the ghetto—its danger and violence. The danger gives the neighborhood an edge and makes it cool, hip, and desirable to young millennials.[84] Others are attracted to the mythical heyday of the ghetto, the early-twentieth-century Negro Renaissance, when this part of DC was known as the "Black Broadway." "Swagger jacking" is the phrase used in DC to describe the appropriation of black culture by young white gentrifiers.[85]

Whatever the allure of the original culture of the ghetto, however, it is clear that gentrification often spawns conflict between the gentrifiers and long-term residents. This conflict, which many long-term residents perceive as a threat to push them out, is illustrative of the ghetto's role as a haven for some to this day.

BLACK-ON-BLACK GENTRIFICATION

Gentrification also elucidates the continuing role of the ghetto as a haven for some when we consider the actions and motives of a group often overlooked in the gentrification sagas: black gentrifiers. As noted earlier, it was members of the black middle class who were among the first to engage in activities associated with gentrification.

Monique Taylor's book *Harlem Between Heaven and Hell* chronicles the experiences of the black middle class moving into Harlem, renovating brownstones, and becoming politically active in their community—all of the hallmarks of gentrifiers—in the 1980s and 1990s.[86] In *Jim Crow Nostalgia*, Michelle Boyd tells a similar tale of middle-class blacks working to restore the Chicago South Side neighborhood of Bronzeville to its former glory in the 1990s.[87] If we look at empirical data of black gentrification, in both the 1980s and 1990s poor black neighborhoods witnessed an influx of educated blacks. These neighborhoods were poorer than average at the beginning of this period but experienced an increase in the number of college-educated blacks greater than in the average neighborhood.[88] Middle-class blacks, or the black gentry, were moving to and remaining in the ghetto.

During the 2000s, however, there was a noticeable decline in black gentrification by this measure. A much smaller proportion of neighborhoods experienced black gentrification (figure 7.2). The decline may be attributable to the Great Recession, which decimated the fortunes of the black middle class—including those who might have chosen to gentrify ghetto neighborhoods.

In the wake of the civil rights revolution and the passage of fair-housing laws, middle-class African Americans had more options than ever before when choosing where to live. To be sure, their choices were "constrained,"

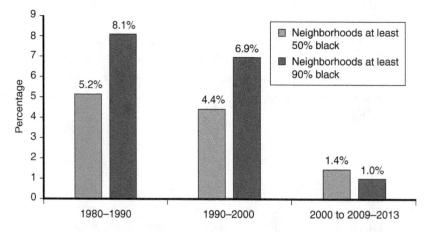

FIGURE 7.2 Proportion of poor black neighborhoods experiencing black gentrification, 1980–2013.
Source: Author's tabulation of 1980, 1990, 2000 census data and 2009–2013 American Community Survey data (U.S. Census Bureau 2016).

as the sociologist Mario Small puts it.[89] They might have faced discrimination in trying to rent in a predominantly white neighborhood, might have found their financing options more limited if they wished to purchase a home, or, if successful in moving out of segregated black neighborhoods, would often have found the complexion of their new neighborhood indistinguishable from their old one in a matter of a few years as their arrival triggered white flight. Nevertheless, middle-class blacks were increasingly able to escape the poorest black neighborhoods, to which the depopulation of the ghetto attests.

Black gentrifiers made a choice, however much constrained, to live in the ghetto. Feelings of nostalgia for the ghetto that birthed modern black American culture compelled some black gentrifiers to see the ghetto as a homeland of sorts. "There's a lot of people out in the suburbs who are anxious to come back home," said then congressman Charles Rangel in describing the incipient gentrification in Harlem in the 1980s.[90] Emory Moore, whose story was chronicled in *New York Magazine*, represents another case of a black gentrifier returning "home." After growing up and leaving Bed-Stuy for college and thereafter traveling abroad for his career, he returned to Bed-Stuy at age forty-three because "it's a place where I feel I belong."[91] Laina Dawes, a black Canadian blogger raised by white parents in overwhelmingly white settings, admired African American popular culture as a child. She envisioned herself moving to the United States to find her true identity as a part of the black diaspora and so sought out one of the largest black ghettos in the United States: Bed-Stuy.[92] May Dixon, a southerner described in *Harlem Between Heaven and Hell*, came to Harlem because it reminded her of family, her culture, and her home.[93] The blogger Erin Parks, who moved to Bed-Stuy from Georgia, says, "It was not just about I want to come to your neighborhood because it is cool now. It's about this is where I want to live. Coming from Georgia, Brooklyn for me felt like home. If you are struggling with it, be a part of it, because at the end of the day we all have to stick together."[94]

For Laina Dawes, May Dixon, Erin Parkes, and other black gentrifiers, the black ghetto was home, even though they grew up elsewhere—another country and another region of the United States. For many blacks, the ghetto had come to supplant Africa as a mythic homeland. As discussed in chapter 5, at various points in their history American blacks looked to Africa as an ancient homeland where the race accomplished great things. It was a way of inspiring the race and developing pride in their blackness. In the nineteenth century, former slaves, some having never set foot in Africa, traveled to Liberia to establish their new home. In the early twentieth century, Marcus Garvey sought to uplift the African diaspora and instill pride in the race, and a key component of his strategy was developing their homeland—Africa—into a powerful and prosperous nation from which blacks across the diaspora (e.g., the Caribbean, the United States, and Europe) could draw pride and respect. Malcolm X started the Organization of African Unity in 1963 with the aim, among others, of restoring connections to the African homeland. Rap music had its Afrocentric phase in the 1980s, when groups such as Brand Nubian, A Tribe Called Quest, and the Jungle Brothers donned kente cloth and black, Africa-shaped medallions and rapped about the motherland. The common thread from early settlers in Liberia to Marcus Garvey, Malcolm X, and the late-twentieth-century rappers is a reference to Africa as a homeland, a place that Africans Americans are connected to in spirit. Folks might be "three centuries" removed but yet the continent is a "fount of pride," as the Harlem Renaissance poet Countee Cullen wrote in *Heritage*.[95]

The aspirations and motives of some black gentrifiers in the late twentieth century in many ways mirrored the sentiments regarding Africa held by blacks earlier in the century. Like Countee Cullen's connection to a place he had never been, Laina Dawes, May Dixon, and Erin Parkes had an affinity for or sense of belonging in Bed-Stuy and Harlem, despite having grown up in vastly different settings in the southern United States and Canada. Just as Marcus Garvey sought to advance the race by developing Africa into a prosperous place, many a black gentrifier saw redeveloping the ghetto as a way to advance the race. According to sociologist Kesha Moore, some 90 percent of the black middle-class residents involved in gentrifying the North Philadelphia ghetto reported "giving back" or "helping our people" as reasons for moving there.[96]

As described in chapter 2, the early-twentieth-century ghetto was at that time a symbol of black modernity and what the race could achieve. Decades later, many black gentrifiers looked at this past proudly and drew inspiration from it. Black gentrifiers sought to re-create the age of the enclave in the ghetto. In her study of a redevelopment plan in the Douglas–Grand Boulevard neighborhood of Chicago, sociologist Michelle Boyd discusses how black gentrifiers renamed the area "Bronzeville" and in doing so resurrected a label commonly used for the neighborhood in the early part of the twentieth century, during the age of the black enclave. "We want to acknowledge that it's Bronzeville, because it means that what once was can be. . . . That's why we're restoring it, not building it, not creating it." Another pro-redevelopment middle-class black said, "Bronzeville carries with it the whole struggle of black people. . . . And it is a clear tool for us as African Americans to claim a turf. To claim a turf and to redevelop that from us, who care nothing about our struggle, historically."[97]

The Hill District of Pittsburgh was once a bustling black community that housed the influential *Pittsburgh Courier*; served as the base of the National Negro League baseball team, the Black Crawfords; was the home of the first black-owned and black-built baseball park in America, Greenlee Field; and spawned such luminaries as playwright August Wilson. Like scores of ghettos across the nation, it had fallen on hard times by the last decades of the twentieth century. But memories, real and imagined, of what the Hill once was has inspired some middle-class blacks to make it their home. "When I look around here, I don't see it as it is," said Mr. Radney, a twenty-nine-year-old designer and engineer standing in front of an abandoned brick row house that he hoped to renovate. "I see it as it could be, because I know what it was." The news article quoting Mr. Radney contained the familiar refrain about a time when blacks of all classes lived side by side—"The Hill was a conglomeration of everything and everybody," recalled an eighty-six-year-old interviewee for the article. The decline of the Hill was due in part to the flight of the black middle class, which "diluted our strength," according to recent in-migrant Justin Laing, thirty-two, a program director at a nonprofit organization who grew up in Silver Spring, Maryland, and who had recently bought a house in the Hill with his wife, Bonnie, and two children. "The remedy was to rebuild *our* communities from a position of strength."[98] Although native to another state, Mr. Laing still felt a sense of attachment to the Hill ghetto, claiming ownership of the space.

Some of the black gentry see themselves, in the words of early-twentieth-century sociologists St. Clair Drake and Horace Cayton, as "advancing the race" by turning the ghetto of dilapidation and disinvestment into one with rehabilitated homes—a physical space the race can be proud of.[99] A neighborhood rife with abandoned buildings, crime, and dirty streets is not one to inspire youth, so improving the physical condition of the community is part and parcel of the black gentry's mission to advance the race.

William Ingram, one of the participants in the study featured in the book *Jim Crow Nostalgia*, recalled the pride he felt as a young man in seeing office buildings built and owned by blacks on the South Side of Chicago. Knowing that blacks could create and own something as substantial as an office building provided a psychological boost. He later sought to restore these majestic buildings as a way of restoring the heyday of the ghetto in order to inspire pride in the community today.[100]

Physical improvements to the ghetto would also bring ancillary benefits as well. By refurbishing dilapidated housing units, longtime homeowners in the ghetto would see their property values rise as well, providing them with increased wealth. The success of black gentrifiers in renovating neighborhoods and illustrating the viability of the housing market in the ghetto would attract private developers interested in constructing new middle-class housing. Private developers in turn would pressure city government to invest in police protection, street cleaning, and other public services as a way of protecting their investment. The growing purchasing power of the ghetto would lure new stores, thus not only increasing shopping options for long-term ghetto residents but also adding another group of stakeholders to demand better police protection and cleaner streets from city government. Studies of the actions and motives of black gentrifiers, such as *Harlem Between Heaven and Hell* and *Black on the Block*, found black gentrifiers viewing their investment in the ghetto as benefitting not only themselves financially but also the entire community.[101]

Beyond the physical and quality-of-life improvements that would benefit and inspire ghetto dwellers, the black gentrifiers themselves would also inspire as role models. Harkening back to the mythic age of the ghetto, when blacks of "all classes lived side by side," some black gentrifiers see themselves as playing the same role that the black middle class played in the early and mid–twentieth century. Whether by coincidence or some other means, William Julius Wilson's notion of the black middle class stabilizing poor ghettos and serving as role models is now part of the folk wisdom.[102] Just as the black middle class of yesteryear uplifted the race merely by their achievements, today's black gentry with their education, middle-class mores, and professional careers serve as role models for disenfranchised ghetto youth. Moreover, having often been educated in or working for white institutions, the black gentry have the wherewithal to force local politicos to improve amenities and services in the ghetto. Malcolm Balderidge, a professor whose story is chronicled in *Harlem Between Heaven and Hell*, expressed his motivation thus: "I thought that I could help, or lend whatever abilities I had and provide whatever kind of role model I could for some of the males, African American males, who I thought were hopelessly gone in another direction."[103]

By their presence in the ghetto, the black gentry help return the ghetto to its former glory. In doing so, they preserve the ghetto as a haven for black Americans—"our Israel," as a woman interviewed by Monique Taylor put it—and create a powerful symbol of black uplift—a refurbished, thriving black community that is home to all classes.[104]

For many black gentrifiers, the ghetto is a haven—one that needs investment and refurbishment, to be sure, but a haven nonetheless. Like those who had the resources to leave but decided to stay put, black gentrifiers could also have chosen to remain outside the ghetto—and, indeed, many of them arrived there from elsewhere. Nor does it appear that these black gentrifiers are drawn merely by a desire to live with other blacks; instead, they seem to be drawn to the ghetto because it stands as a haven for the entire race. By the late twentieth and early twenty-first century, there were solidly middle-class black neighborhoods in cities where black gentrification was occurring. The ghetto, however, provides an opportunity to commune with blacks of all backgrounds, to connect to the past, and to "give back" to the community. The ghetto is thus a haven that continues to lure some middle-class blacks.

Gentrification in the ghetto thus provides a lens through which to see the ghetto's continuing role as a haven. For long-term residents, gentrification threatens to upend their environment, which, although much maligned, is also cherished and unique in many ways. The vernacular culture of the ghetto is one that many long-term residents value, and the attachment that comes with living in a place over time causes many to continue to see the ghetto as a haven. For middle-class black gentrifiers, gentrification provides an opportunity to return "home," to connect with the ghetto's vernacular culture, to uplift their race, and to re-create the mythic golden age of the ghetto, when "blacks of all classes lived side-by-side."

As an aside, it is worth noting that the reality of gentrification is messier than either long-term residents' complaints or some black gentrifiers' motives would suggest. Some ghetto residents appreciate the improved amenities and services associated with gentrification. And not all black gentrifiers are looking to uplift the race or connect with a mythic past; some are just looking for inexpensive housing that is conveniently located. Even among those moving to the ghetto because they view it as "returning home," the actual experience might be far different. Drawn to Harlem because of its rich history and to follow in the footsteps of Josephine Baker and Langston Hughes, blogger Morgan Jenkins notes how she felt out of place from the moment she walked up 125th and Lenox. She came to realize that despite her blackness and kinky hair, she was not "of the community" and felt more like a parasite.[105]

In some instances, the aspirations and foci of black gentrifiers do not overlap with and even contradict those of their poorer brethren. In their studies of gentrification in Bronzeville and Harlem, respectively, both Michelle Boyd and Derek Hyra found conflict and disagreement over what was of import. Whereas the black gentrifiers were more interested in improving and maintaining property values and attracting higher-end retail to the ghetto, poorer residents were more focused on affordable housing, job opportunities, and daycare. Given these two groups' class differences, their different foci are not surprising. The material differences in life circumstances between the black gentry and poorer residents of the ghetto meant their interests often did not align.

A further caveat should be added regarding gentrification in the ghetto. Gentrification has been most common in older neighborhoods, with distinctive architecture in cities where the local economy is growing and where the neighborhoods' black identity date to the early part of the twentieth century. As noted earlier in this chapter, it is these older ghetto neighborhoods' proximity to the downtowns that makes many of these neighborhoods attractive to gentrifiers in the first place. Black gentrification, to the extent it is sparked by nostalgic feelings for a time when "blacks of all classes lived side-by-side" and the ghetto spawned a host of black institutions, will most typically occur in those ghetto neighborhoods where this is the historical reality. Bronzeville in Chicago and Harlem in New York City, of course, are the iconic ghettos exemplifying this pattern. Other ghetto neighborhoods that can boast of rich histories may also attract black gentrifiers or, as in the case of U Street in Washington, DC, white gentrifiers. Newer ghetto neighborhoods, especially those without a particularly glorious past, such as the now demolished Robert Taylor Homes in Chicago, are less likely to evoke the nostalgic feelings that might lead to gentrification.

Finally, it should be kept in mind that the vast majority of black or ghetto neighborhoods have not experienced gentrification of any type. For example, in an earlier study I found that only 10 percent of majority-black neighborhoods in 2000 would experience at least a 5 percent increase in their white population over the ensuing decade.[106] Given the much smaller size of the black middle class and gentry, black-led gentrification is almost certainly an even less frequent occurrence.

These caveats notwithstanding, black gentrification is nevertheless illustrative of the way the ghetto remained a haven in the late twentieth century and continues to be one in the early twenty-first century.

STILL A HAVEN?

The early twenty-first century witnessed a landmark event in race relations with the election of the nation's first black president—Barack Obama. Yet in many ways the ghetto's role in black America continued to be what it was at the end of the twentieth century: hell for many but still a cherished haven for others.

The ghetto continued to be a hell for much the same reasons it had been previously, but the policy of mass incarceration in many ways served to make things worse. Layered on top of concentrated disadvantage, mass incarceration and its implementation turned ghetto communities into quasi–police states, so that private and public actions could be taken only after considering risk of arrest. The civic capacity of these communities would be retarded by the sprawling reach of the carceral state, leaving them undeveloped participants in the political life of the country.

The subprime crisis that hit black middle-class enclaves in the first decade of the twenty-first century blurred distinctions between these neighborhoods and those more typically associated with the ghetto in its pejorative sense, for at least three reasons. First, the subprime crisis illustrated the persistent power of race in shaping neighborhood trajectories—much the same way the ghetto was created and shaped because of race in the twentieth century. Second, the historical legacy of the ghetto—redlining specifically—made it more likely for the subprime crisis to hit harder there. Finally, the fallout from the subprime crisis—an epidemic of foreclosures and rising crime—threatened to push many black middle-class neighborhoods down the same spiral of decay that had enveloped poorer black neighborhoods.

Whereas black-led gentrification demonstrated how many middle-class blacks still viewed the ghetto as a haven, white-led gentrification kindled fears of blacks losing the ghetto. Yet both types of gentrification in truth underscore the continuation of the ghetto's role as a haven. To be sure, some fears of gentrification stem from the fear of being physically displaced from the neighborhood. But this chapter presents evidence showing that fears of the loss of the ghetto's vernacular culture and of its political power are just as important in animating fears of gentrification.

The persistent attachment to the ghetto in the late twentieth and early twenty-first centuries shows that long after the heyday of the ghetto during the Negro Renaissance and the ghetto's prominence in the black power era, its role as a haven had not yet completely disappeared.

CONCLUSION

How to Have a Haven but No Hell
in the Twenty-First Century

This book traces the arc of the ghetto's role in black American life from the late nineteenth century to the present. In doing so, the book makes clear that a view of the ghetto as merely the object of wider, white, institutional, and societal forces aiming to subjugate blacks is incomplete. Black agency was important in creating the ghetto and shaping how the ghetto influenced blacks' lives. The ghetto's role in black life was thus multifaceted, as a haven reflecting blacks' role in creating and shaping it and as a hell created by discrimination and racism. The prominence of these respective roles waxed and waned through different eras. This conclusion briefly summarizes these evolving roles and considers the implications of this finding both for our thinking about the ghetto and for any policies that we might undertake to address the persistence of ghettos in the United States.

In the late nineteenth century prior to the Great Migration, ghettos as we know them today—agglomerations of virtually all-black neighborhoods with tens of thousands of people—did not exist in the North. The small number of blacks in the urban North precluded this type of development. Nevertheless, blacks experienced the forces of ghettoization. Housing discrimination was rampant. Black spaces were stigmatized, with both native whites and recent nonblack immigrants reluctant to move into areas occupied by blacks. The condition of much of the housing occupied by blacks was deplorable. Contrary to the arguments of some historians and social scientists, late-nineteenth-century blacks were highly segregated. They were not scattered about randomly or in a manner commensurate solely with their differing economic statuses. The small number of blacks meant they never dominated an entire section of a city or even a neighborhood, perhaps leading some later observers to assume ghettoization was not a problem in this period. But the first chapter makes clear that ghettoization characterized the late-nineteenth-century black experience in the North.

The small number of blacks in the urban North precluded the incipient ghettos from functioning as havens. Blacks' numbers were too small to wield independent political power or to support significant black commerce. Their small numbers and lack of economic opportunity meant blacks as a race did not see the incipient ghettos of the North as a haven. When alternate places to the white terror reigning across the South were considered, it was the western states, the Caribbean, or even Africa that beckoned.

The first decades of the twentieth century witnessed changing contexts that would both create the modern ghetto and transform the ghetto into a haven for the race. By the turn of the twentieth century, the first generation of Negroes were coming of age with no experience of slavery and chafing at the repression of the Jim Crow South. World War I provided the catalyst for the New Negro sentiment to manifest itself. The war halted migration from Europe and increased demand for American manufacturing, and southern blacks provided the necessary labor.

With a means to support themselves, the New Negroes moved North in search of opportunity. The experience of fighting in the war, where Negro soldiers were asked to put their lives on the line to protect democracy and where many were exposed to decent treatment in Europe as soldiers, only served to make the New Negroes more militant.

Economic opportunity and the New Negro mentality spurred the Great Migration northward. Hundreds of thousands of blacks left the South in heretofore unprecedented numbers. Virulent white racism restricted where the migrants could live, but economic opportunity fused with the New Negro mentality swamped any concerns folks might have had about being relegated to the ghetto. They instead viewed the ghetto as a haven and an opportunity to create the black metropolis, where economic and political power could be consolidated and where an artistic movement, the Negro Renaissance, could be nurtured.

Blacks proved their humanity by surviving and thriving in the city. Although the belief seems preposterous now, there were many, including some black leaders, who were doubtful that the race could in fact survive in the city.

In many ways, the early-twentieth-century black ghetto functioned like an enclave for immigrants to the United States, with two distinctive differences: the black ghetto would prove much more durable and would be more homogenous and isolated than the ethnic enclave.

The catastrophe that was the Great Depression during the 1930s extinguished dreams of a black metropolis and made mere survival the paramount objective for blacks everywhere. The ghetto was not immune in this regard, as blacks there struggled mightily. Relative to other parts of the country, the ghetto was neither a haven nor a hell because blacks everywhere were "catching hell."

The federal government's foray into the housing market to resuscitate the moribund housing market, however, provides a lens to see how blacks viewed the ghetto. Blacks objected vociferously to anything that restricted their right to live where they wanted, such as federally sanctioned redlining, but they welcomed segregated public housing. By the 1930s, the ghetto had become not merely a space where blacks were relegated but a homeland of sorts to develop and protect. The infusion of federal dollars in the form of public housing was seen as a boon, and most blacks did not oppose this form of government-sanctioned segregation as they did other types of segregation, such as in public schools.

World War II shifted the economic context such that the ghetto became a haven once again. The wartime economic boom lured hundreds of thousands of southern Negroes northward and, for the first time in significant numbers, westward as well. For migrants, the ghetto offered an opportunity to acclimate to the urban North and offered a stepping stone toward the American mainstream.

After the war, the ghetto continued to play the role of haven for the millions of blacks who continued to stream out of the South searching for freedom and opportunity. The ghetto was instrumental in helping change blacks' status, and the role of the ghetto itself changed during this time as blacks' status changed. As blacks slowly broke into the wider American society, the ghetto's role as a springboard slowly receded. In many instances, blacks would gain acceptance to other all-white institutions before being able to break out of the ghetto. Thus, the ghetto persisted and even grew after de jure segregation was outlawed. There was thus a time, especially during the 1950s and 1960s, when blacks were achieving many "firsts" (e.g., becoming the first black cabinet secretary, the first black Supreme Court justice, and so on) and civil rights were being expanded, yet ghettoization was intensifying and physically expanding. Now the ghetto's role as hell became more prominent, especially among blacks who were born in the North or who had already acclimated to life there. For these blacks, the ghetto seemed less promised land than dead end.

During the 1960s, America reached the zenith of postwar prosperity, and black "firsts" steadily accumulated. The ghetto, however, seethed as physical conditions worsened and the relative deprivation there became starker still. The ghetto's role as a hell burst into national consciousness as scores of ghettos burned in perhaps the largest wave of civil unrest in the nation's history.

Rekindled in these fires was a growing affinity for black nationalism. It would be in the ghetto where black nationalists' dreams came closest to achieving the ideal of black power. As such, the ghetto remained a haven despite the anger evinced by the widespread and continuing exodus of many blacks from there.

The post–civil rights era witnessed the opening of unprecedented opportunities outside the ghetto for blacks and a simultaneous collapsing of economic opportunities for those without advanced skills or high levels of education. The cessation of the Great Migration and the continuing exodus of blacks from the ghetto reflect these changes. These demographic trends changed the character of the ghetto. Before the 1970s, blacks had been leaving the ghetto for decades, but the ones who left had largely been replaced by aspiring migrants from the South, allowing the ghetto to maintain its vibrancy into the 1960s. Without the continuing influx of migrants, who are typically the most able and motivated in a population, the ghetto was sapped of the vital energy that had made it a springboard for upward mobility for decades. Without that energy, the ghetto's role as a haven receded, leaving the modern conception of the ghetto as a hellish place.

The ghetto's role as a haven did not completely disappear, though, because the very durability of ghetto neighborhoods, some dating back nearly a century, had instilled them with the properties of a symbolic "homeland." The ongoing community-development movement and early instances of black-led gentrification attest to the ghetto's continuing role as a haven. But in the last decades of the twentieth century and the first decades of the twenty-first, this role grew much smaller.

Key factors in shaping the ghetto's role as a haven or hell can be distilled when we look back at the evolution of the ghetto over time. These factors include blacks' status relative to the larger white-dominated society, economic opportunity, and prevailing cultural and political ideologies among blacks. Economic opportunity has of course been of paramount importance and might be considered a precondition for the ghetto serving as a haven for other reasons as well. When economic opportunities were great in northern and western cities, such as during World War I, World War II, and the post–World War II economic boom, the ghetto could serve as a haven for the race, so millions of blacks migrated there in search of these opportunities. Conversely, it should come as no surprise that prior to World War I, when blacks were largely excluded from the Industrial Revolution taking place in American cities, the budding ghettos did not serve as any type of haven or inspire large-scale migration. Likewise, the economic restructuring of urban America starting in the 1970s changed the nature of economic opportunity to favor the skilled and those with post-secondary education, and so the ghetto's role as a haven receded in the last few decades of the twentieth century.

During the resurgence of white supremacy in the early twentieth century, when blacks' very humanity was questioned and their fitness for surviving in the modern world was up for debate among even so-called enlightened whites, the budding ghettos provided an opportunity for blacks to prove themselves and instill pride in the race. When black political representation had been decimated in the South, these ghettos provided an opportunity for blacks to achieve some representation. Later in the twentieth century, as ghettos grew and white flight ensued, the ghettos again served as a font for black political power.

Whereas mere survival in the ghetto was a significant milestone for the race in the 1920s, by the 1950s the notion of surviving in the city held little import. Instead, achieving the American Dream of single-family home in suburban-like settings symbolized the race's advancement. Likewise, the gradual receding of white supremacy as a core belief of white Americans in the latter half of the twentieth century lessened the importance of the ghetto. As blacks were able to access neighborhoods and resources previously denied them, the importance of the ghetto as a space to create and support black institutions diminished.

Cultural and political attitudes also influence whether the ghetto is seen a haven for the mass of black Americans. Most significantly, when and where sympathies toward black nationalism are in vogue, the ghetto's role as a haven reemerges. As an ideology, black nationalism reached its apex during the New Negro era of 1910–1930 and during the black power era of 1965–1975. During these eras, many blacks turned away from seeking acceptance from whites and inward toward building black institutions and cultural movements within the black community. The ghetto served as a haven where such ideas and cultural expressions could flower and serve to benefit the entire race. In the post–civil rights era, when some degree of integration became an option for many blacks, there remained a small but significant number of blacks who still subscribed to nationalist tendencies. These blacks thought it was important for blacks to invest resources in the ghetto and to retain some degree of control over these same spaces. The community-development movement, in part an outgrowth of the nationalist-fused calls for community control of the 1960s, became the institutionalized mechanism for blacks to invest in and retain control of the ghetto. Later, many black gentrifiers saw their presence and efforts to invest in the ghetto as a form of self-help consistent with black nationalism.

Broadly speaking, when the broader society closed or limited opportunities to blacks, the ghetto offered a space for black institutions to flower. This process can be seen most concretely in the cultural and political spheres. When blacks' very humanity was questioned and their ability to survive modernity in doubt, the ghetto showed that blacks could survive and thrive in modern life. When it was asserted that Negroes could create high art and when blacks wanted to create art that spoke to the black masses, the ghetto provided a haven for these artistic movements to manifest.

Thus, the dual roles of the ghetto as both a haven and a hell have waxed and waned, oftentimes competing for prominence, as during the post–World War II era, when millions of blacks used the ghetto as a springboard into modern America even while hundreds of thousands of upwardly mobile blacks chafed at being relegated to second-class housing in the ghetto. Understanding this duality provides us with a more complete picture of the ghetto as an institution in black American life and has implications for policies that might redress the problems endemic to the ghetto.

POLICY IMPLICATIONS

If we accept the duality of the ghetto, that it has been both a haven and a hell, what are the implications for collective action either by the government or by grassroots community groups? One obvious goal would be to limit one side of the duality, the ghetto as hell. Less obvious but potentially important is to consider whether there is a need for the ghetto to be a haven and if so, how.

There are at least two powerful social justice arguments for improving conditions in the ghetto. First, the life chances of ghetto residents are in many ways made worse by their residence in the ghetto. As shown in chapter 7, not only are conditions in the ghetto bad, but the opportunity to escape these conditions is hindered by residing in the ghetto.

Second, current conditions in the ghetto are due in part to past actions by those outside the ghetto. In particular, policy makers, including the federal government, are heavily implicated in buttressing the walls of the early-twentieth-century ghetto. The infractions are too numerous to list here, but they include institutionalizing the practice of redlining, which served to starve the ghetto of credit from the 1930s through the 1980s; sanctioning lending discrimination against blacks seeking to move into white neighborhoods; employing land-use regulations to restrict poor blacks' access to richer neighborhoods; and developing and operating a segregated public-housing program for several decades. Although blacks sometimes wanted to live in the ghetto, they always wanted the option to leave if they could and so desired. The policies described here often denied blacks that choice. Most blatantly, by sanctioning housing discrimination in federally sponsored housing until 1962 and in private housing until 1968, the federal government stood by while blacks were denied their constitutionally guaranteed civil rights.

Government action and inaction in the case of sanctioned discrimination helped cast the durable patterns of ghettoization that persist in American cities to this day. It is not merely the case that blacks in the 1940s or 1950s were restricted to the ghetto because of government policies. The ghetto that was created and that endures is in part a product of those policies. Because of the durability of the ghetto, current residents are living in environments created in part by government policy of the past.

As such, the ghetto is not merely a historical transgression against people long dead. Rather, the bitter fruits of ghettoization are still being harvested to this day. Thus, social justice aims and the goal of redressing past wrongs animate the call for reducing the hellish conditions in the ghetto.

There is also a practical justification for "gilding the ghetto." As earlier chapters have shown, many blacks have in the past and continue to see the ghetto as a haven—that is, a space where black culture and institutions can be nurtured and thrive. As a consequence, a policy approach that centers solely on mobility out of the ghetto would likely receive a lukewarm reaction at best. Even if such a policy were politically feasible, it seems unlikely that all blacks would welcome it. Thus, improving the current conditions in the ghetto is imperative.

Prospects for Gilding the Ghetto

Can the ghetto's role as a hell be diminished? In 1993, in response to a question about the efficacy of Empowerment Zones, a federal initiative to revitalize ghettos and other poor neighborhoods in the wake of the Rodney King unrest, Andrew Cuomo, then assistant secretary at HUD, said, "If you expect to see Harlem as gentrified and mixed-income, it's not going to happen."[1] Writing about these efforts, journalist Nicholas Lemann commented, "For three decades, Administration after Administration [sic] has pondered the ghettos and then settled on the idea of trying to revitalize them economically—even though there is almost no evidence that this can work."[2]

History has proven this sentiment to be too pessimistic. Chapter 7 describes the evolution and maturation of the community-development movement into a sophisticated industry capable of significantly improving the quality of life in many ghetto communities. By the late 1990s, one could find a number of neighborhoods that once resembled bombed-out war zones but had now been transformed into relatively stable working-class neighborhoods. In *House by House, Block by Block*, the historian Alexander von Hoffman describes several of these neighborhoods, including the West Side of Chicago and the South Bronx in New York City.[3] Similar rebirths happened in many ghetto neighborhoods across the country and have been chronicled in books such as *Upon This Rock: The Miracle of a Black Church*, which features some of the revitalization work done in Brownsville, Brooklyn; *Streets of Hope*, which describes the rebirth of the Dudley Street area in Roxbury, Boston; and *The Roots of Urban Renaissance*, which tells the story of the revival of Central Harlem.[4]

Some key ingredients emerge in these success stories. Typically, a strong community-based organization often led by a charismatic leader is in the vanguard of the revitalization process. The Harlem Congregations for Community Improvement and the Dudley Street Initiative in Roxbury are examples of such organizations, and the Reverend Johnny Ray Youngblood operating in Brownsville, Brooklyn, is an exemplar of the charismatic leader.

Community developers have married together resources from state and local government, foundations, and the federal government to bring significant infusions of money into their communities. Geography matters, too. Community development in cities with strong local economies or an influx of immigrants or both helps keep local housing markets resilient because a strong economy and immigration can help stem and even reverse population decline. Newcomers to a city have to live somewhere, and so ghetto neighborhoods, where housing is cheapest, become their destination. In a strong housing market, it becomes profitable to invest in ghetto neighborhoods.

Groups such as the Enterprise Foundation, the Local Initiatives Support Corporation, and NeighborWorks America acted as intermediaries between community-based organizations working in the ghetto and corporations and investors with funds to invest. The intermediaries greased the skids for investment by informing the corporate sector of the types of opportunities available in the ghetto and providing technical assistance to community-based groups so they could package themselves and their work in a way that would attract outside investors.[5]

Also noted in chapter 7 was the increasing prevalence of gentrification in ghetto neighborhoods. Indeed, judging from the approach taken in news media stories, gentrification has almost come to rival decay and disinvestment as the greatest threat to the ghetto. The gentrification oftentimes followed on the heels of decades' long efforts by the community-development movement to stabilize neighborhoods, and black gentrifiers saw themselves as "giving back" to the community.

The pattern of gentrification and revitalization in many ghetto neighborhoods is a stark contrast to the prevailing gloom-and-doom sentiment of a generation ago. Whereas Andrew Cuomo, Nicholas Lemann, and others could realistically question if meaningful community development in the ghetto were even possible, the challenge now is to scale up the successful initiatives. We have blueprints for improving conditions in poor, disadvantaged neighborhoods, and there is no reason to believe these efforts cannot be replicated elsewhere. To be sure, there are some ghetto neighborhoods, in particular those in areas with declining regional economies, that may have little realistic chance of returning to vibrancy even with substantial investments in resources. In those instances, the option of helping people to leave may be more important. This is not to say these communities should be written off, but the quality of life in declining communities will need to be enhanced with investment in infrastructure and public and commercial services for the local population. But facilitating movement to areas with more opportunity might be the best route and is a way of providing additional opportunity.

Both the successes of the community-development movement and gentrification offer proof that the physical space of the ghetto can be improved and that the middle class can be drawn to live there. Less clear is the extent to which community development or gentrification enables the poorer, long-term residents of ghetto neighborhoods to achieve upward mobility. Interviews of residents of gentrifying neighborhoods indicate that they appreciate some aspects of gentrification—the improved choice of retail options, better public services demanded by and provided to the gentry, and rising property values for those who own their homes.[6] But these outcomes do not necessarily mean poor residents will be lifted out of poverty.

A recent study of New York City Public Housing residents comparing those in developments in gentrifying neighborhoods with those in developments in other low-income neighborhoods suggests those in the gentrifying neighborhoods fared somewhat better.[7] Residents in the developments in gentrifying neighborhoods had annual incomes between $1,600 and $3,500 higher and had attended college at a slightly higher rate. These results are not definitive, being limited to New York City and not ruling out other possible explanations for the patterns observed—such as more advantaged public-housing residents being more likely to live in gentrifying neighborhoods. Nevertheless, the results are suggestive that gentrification has a positive impact on upward mobility. Moreover, bigger impacts might be expected for children who grow up in gentrifying neighborhoods, whose trajectories are more malleable and who have more exposure to any benefits that gentrification may bring.

Beyond the challenge benefitting long-term residents by improving neighborhoods is the challenge of these residents being able to afford to remain in those same gentrified neighborhoods. In both gentrifying neighborhoods and those where the neighborhood is simply improving without gentrifying, housing prices will likely rise. This is especially the case in cities with hot real estate markets. Indeed, in hot real estate markets, the difference between community development and gentrification might be a distinction without difference—especially with regard to housing affordability. Thus, any strategy relying on gentrification or community development to improve the lives of long-term residents in these neighborhoods would likely need a robust affordable-housing component that helps existing residents be able to afford to remain in the neighborhood as well as a component in which poorer residents are allowed to continue to move into the neighborhood. Such strategies might include the preservation of public housing in gentrifying neighborhoods, which New York City has managed to do, or zoning that incentivizes developers to incorporate affordable housing in new developments in gentrifying neighborhoods.[8] Other affordable-housing programs could be tweaked so as to target resources to neighborhoods undergoing gentrification.

For example, law professor Rachel Godsil suggests creating housing vouchers specifically for residents in neighborhoods where housing prices are rising rapidly. The vouchers would go to those who have lived in the neighborhood for at least five years and would last for a certain period of time, perhaps five years.[9] Such vouchers would help residents in gentrifying neighborhoods "stay put" without having to bear undue housing-cost burdens. Another idea would be to adapt Tax Increment Financing to create a source of funding for affordable housing in gentrifying neighborhoods. Tax Increment Financing programs are typically used to fund infrastructure, wherein a locality invests in public infrastructure in a given neighborhood in anticipation of a rise in property values resulting from that investment. The increase in property tax revenues, or increment, arising from rising property values is then used to pay for the infrastructure improvements. But a locality can also anticipate rising property values in a gentrifying neighborhood. After property values rise, the increment in property taxes in the gentrifying neighborhood might be dedicated to affordable housing—whether in the form of new units or vouchers. This type of targeted affordable-housing strategies could go a long way toward keeping gentrifying neighborhoods accessible to ghetto residents.

Even if affordability in gentrifying or revitalizing neighborhoods is maintained, is it realistic to expect the benefits to somehow rub off on existing and in-moving poor residents in such a way so as to foster upward mobility? It may be in some cases, but quite often a comprehensive investment in the people living in poor neighborhoods is necessary.

There is a long history of attempts to uplift the poor through neighborhood-based programs in the slums and ghettos of America and other industrialized countries. The Settlement Houses of the late nineteenth and early twentieth centuries sought to inculcate the poor with middle-class norms, to teach immigrants the local language, and to provide educational and recreational activities for children. The National Urban League worked with recent migrants to the ghetto to help them adapt to modern life by securing housing, providing job training, and locating employment opportunities. During the War on Poverty of the 1960s, programs such as Head Start and Upward Bound sought to improve the educational attainment of disadvantaged preschoolers and high school students, while other programs such as Food Stamps addressed needs such as hunger. Many of these efforts shared a belief that a holistic approach to addressing the needs of the disadvantaged in the ghetto or slums is *the way* to help those trapped in disadvantaged neighborhoods such as modern ghettos.

Geoffrey Canada utilized this approach in his Harlem Children's Zone (HCZ) initiative. The premise behind the HCZ is that if provided all-encompassing services from cradle to adulthood, poor children can succeed in school, avoid incarceration, and go on to live productive lives. Starting in the 1990s, the HCZ, originally encompassing twenty-four blocks in Harlem, grew to include sixty blocks in the neighborhood. The HCZ includes preschool programs, charter schools, after-school programs, job-training programs, support services to improve parenting, community organizing, college training, and public-health campaigns. HCZ staff go door to door to make sure residents are aware of various programs and services, and these efforts appear to pay off, with some 80 percent of the children in the zone involved in at least one HCZ program.[10]

Measuring the impact of the HCZ on the entire neighborhood is difficult because the program lacks a "control group" of neighborhoods with which to compare outcomes. Moreover, contemporaneous with the arrival of the HCZ were unprecedented declines in crime, the ebbing of the crack epidemic, widespread gentrification, the reform of welfare, and sundry educational reform initiatives—all factors that can influence children's educational attainment and social outcomes regardless of whether the HCZ has had any impact. Nevertheless, several rigorous social science studies suggest the HCZ has achieved positive outcomes for children and their life chances. For example, the HCZ Asthma Initiative reduced absences from school and visits to the emergency room due to asthma-related problems.[11] Students attending one of the HCZ charter schools were found to perform better on standardized tests, to be more likely to graduate from school on time and to enroll in a four-year college, to be less likely to report a pregnancy (among girls), and to be less likely to be incarcerated (among boys).[12]

The HCZ approach provides a blueprint for tackling the social problems of low educational attainment, poor public health, and lack of job skills often found in many ghetto communities. President Obama seemed enamored with the HCZ approach, rolling out two federal programs modeled specifically after the HCZ approach during his tenure—the Promise Neighborhoods Program and the Promise Zone Program. Neither program has been as ambitious as the original HCZ, however, and we might expect any impacts they may have to be commensurately smaller as well. But a HCZ-like approach combined with investment of the type occurring through community-development efforts and gentrification in some low-income neighborhoods is likely to be transformative for youths growing up in ghetto communities.

Before attempting to implement the HCZ model or something like the Promise Zones approach at scale, a pilot program would be a wise first step. A few neighborhoods across the country could be selected, perhaps through competitive bidding. Although the focus of this book is on ghetto neighborhoods outside the South, it would be politically impractical and perhaps unethical to target only those neighborhoods. The first round of pilot neighborhoods should also include black ghettos in the South, Latino barrios, and predominantly white pockets of poverty in places such as Appalachia. The pilot would still focus on a handful of neighborhoods, perhaps five to ten, but would select from an array of neighborhood types aside from black ghettos in the North.

A pilot approach would be less costly initially and would have the advantage of providing opportunity to draw lessons from the first wave of implementation. The program could thus be tweaked as necessary to address any shortcomings identified or to amplify any unanticipated strengths revealed. An attempt to move the effort to scale would be buttressed by evidence and practical experience on what works.

Finally, it should not be forgotten that perhaps the most pressing problem of the poor, whether in the ghetto or anywhere else, is a lack of money. At a time when the economy does not produce enough jobs to lift everyone out of poverty, it is perhaps not surprising that some are calling for some type of universal guarantee of income. Some call for a basic-income guarantee; others, such as the economists Mark Paul, Sandy Darity, and Darrick Hamilton, suggest a federal job guarantee;[13] while yet others are reviving the idea of a negative income tax, as advocated by Milton Friedman. Whichever approach is taken, these schemes would provide an income floor to support everyone, including ghetto residents. With this, the problems of desperate poverty would be ameliorated. The aforementioned efforts to strengthen community-based development, encourage investment in the ghetto, and provide supportive services for ghetto residents would still be called for, but we would be starting from a point where we know everyone's basic economic needs are addressed.

Taken together, the continuing efforts of the community-development movement, the lure of central cities triggering gentrification, and some type of universal income program could go a long way toward remedying the type of desperate conditions still persisting in many ghetto communities from the late twentieth century to this day. The most important and perhaps insurmountable obstacle is the political will to redistribute wealth in a way to fund the initiatives described here. I profess no keen insight on solving this seemingly intractable political problem.

But let's assume the policies outlined here were implemented and done at scale. The quality of life in the ghetto would generally be better, and it would no longer be a hell or would certainly be less hellish. But would the ghetto then be a haven?

THE GHETTO AS A HAVEN IN
TWENTY-FIRST-CENTURY AMERICA

Improving the quality of life in the ghetto in the manner described in the previous section would likely result in two countervailing forces affecting the ghetto's role as a haven in black life. First, improved living conditions in the ghetto would make "escape" unnecessary as a way of achieving upward mobility. Unlike circumstances now, when many blacks feel compelled to move to more-integrated neighborhoods to achieve a higher standard of living, if ghetto conditions were improved, more ghetto residents could stay put and still achieve upward mobility. Ghettos in cities where the local economy is booming might even witness an in-migration of blacks from elsewhere, with these blacks moving there to take advantage of the opportunities in the surrounding city and choosing to live in the ghetto to be close to institutions and organizations (e.g., black churches) with which they might have more familiarity. It is unlikely that we would see anything on the scale of the Great Migration—interstate migration is down in the United States, and the interregional economic and social disparities that drove that migration have largely disappeared (see chapter 6). But with an influx of ambitious, younger blacks, more ghetto neighborhoods would recover their long-lost vibrancy. In addition, the policies described would help longtime residents participate in revitalizing the ghetto. Ghetto neighborhoods would no longer be synonymous with disadvantage and might thrive as other predominantly black institutions, such as historically black colleges and universities, have in the post–civil rights era. In this way, the ghetto could be more of a haven than it is today.

But improving conditions in the ghetto would also make these places more attractive to nonblacks, too. The increasing prevalence of gentrification in the ghetto illustrates that many nonblacks will move there if these neighborhoods have desirable amenities (e.g., accessible locations, distinctive architecture, etc.). In some and perhaps most cities, an improvement in ghetto neighborhoods would not necessarily mean a wholesale transformation of black neighborhoods into predominantly white or nonblack neighborhoods. In most cities with a sizable black population, where there is no housing shortage and housing prices are not skyrocketing, an improvement in ghetto conditions might attract more nonblacks to ghetto neighborhoods, but not enough to radically transform the racial composition there. A city such as Philadelphia, for example, has a strong enough local economy to attract nonblacks to some ghetto neighborhoods, but the housing market there has not heated up to an extent that the entire city is likely to become unaffordable.

Improving the ghettos of a city would make these neighborhoods more attractive to upwardly mobile blacks as well as to more nonblacks. But these neighborhoods would likely retain a black identity for the foreseeable future.

There are some ghetto communities where a substantial improvement in living conditions would ultimately lead to an influx of nonblacks, a loss of black identity, and the cessation of the ghetto's role as a haven. Especially in cities with a very strong economy, an overheated housing market, and a relatively small black population to begin with, significantly improving conditions in the ghetto will not only attract nonblacks to these neighborhoods but eventually lead to the loss of black identity in these same neighborhoods. In cities where the black population is relatively small to begin with, any neighborhood that attracts residents from a broad swath of the population will over time come to resemble the larger population. And with demographic change, cultural and political changes will likely follow. As we saw in chapter 7, an influx of nonblacks would likely result in clashes over the prevailing vernacular culture. The norms for public behavior, the types of shops in the community, and political power might all be contested between blacks and nonblacks. This countervailing force might dampen the extent to which the ghetto remains a haven for some blacks. The friction arising from disputes over the vernacular culture and the prospect of the black culture being supplanted by another—the white hipster culture, for example—might make the ghetto anything but a haven for blacks. If political power is lost, shops begin catering to newcomers, and the everyday practices of community residents are questioned, in what way would such a neighborhood remain a haven for blacks?

Even the provision of affordable housing in ghetto neighborhoods experiencing rapid and widespread gentrification might not be enough for the ghetto to remain a haven for blacks. Affordable housing would ensure that low- and moderate-income households can remain in and continue to move into a neighborhood. But affordable housing does not prevent the rest of the housing market from turning over. Nor does affordable housing necessarily mean that long-term residents will retain political power. One can imagine a diverse neighborhood in which blacks are confined primarily to affordable housing. Such an outcome is not the worst possible one, but this type of neighborhood would not be a haven for blacks.

The scenarios described (absent a concentrated effort to make these neighborhoods better for low-income blacks) are already playing out in some formerly black neighborhoods, such as the Fillmore District in San Francisco and the Central District in Seattle. Consider the decline in San Francisco's black population from 84,857 in 1980 to 43,448 in 2015. This dramatic decline is not being driven by blacks fleeing San Francisco—blacks are not leaving the city any more quickly than whites[14]—but by fewer blacks moving into the city. As a result, neighborhoods such as Fillmore have witnessed a plummeting of their black population.

Some do and will bemoan the fading away of some ghetto neighborhoods for reasons articulated throughout this book—especially that the ghetto has often been a haven for many blacks. This role as a haven arose because of the economic opportunities in the cities, the critical mass of blacks concentrated in the ghetto, the relative autonomy blacks had there, and the choking off of opportunities elsewhere. With this relative autonomy, blacks could acquire political power, develop cultural awareness, and build economic and social institutions in ways unlikely if the ghetto did not exist. To a large extent, this role as a haven was necessitated by blacks' exclusion from the larger society.

When some ghetto neighborhoods cease being a haven, whether because of declining opportunities, gentrification, or rising crime, blacks will stop migrating to those places, and those neighborhoods will either become hollowed out, as has happened in many shrinking Rust Belt cities, or become predominantly nonblack, as is happening in some West Coast cities. The loss of a neighborhood's black identity will no doubt feel painful to some residents living through it, much the way some whites bemoaned the loss of their ethnic communities during the heyday of white flight in the mid–twentieth century.[15]

For the ghetto to continue to be a haven, it would have to be a place that serves the needs of blacks from all walks of life. It would have to be a place where the benefits of concentrating together with other blacks would outweigh any negatives. When and where white supremacy recedes, the need for such spaces will recede, too. If America ever achieves Martin Luther King Jr.'s dream of a society where race does not color the judgment of one's character, the ghetto's role as a haven may become superfluous.

The election of Barack Obama as the nation's first black president seemed to portend a time when Dr. King's dream was in reach. The persistence of interracial economic disparities and ongoing inequities in the criminal justice system, however, attest to the remaining distance to be traveled to a "postracial" America.

If persistent racial inequality in the Obama era was indicative of how far we have to travel to reach the promised land of racial equality, the election of Donald Trump suggests the promised land may be moving farther away. President Trump has regularly trafficked in racism, misogyny, and xenophobia in attempting to roll back progressive policies. It is too early to tell if the election of Trump will lead to a long-term reversal in the trend toward racial equality. But his election, the rise of highly polarized politics, and the increasing popularity and visibility of extreme right-wing politics both in the United States and abroad certainly causes one to question which way the arc of the moral universe is bending right now.

If the notion of an inclusive American Dream dims and the prospects for a nation completely free of white supremacy fade, we might see the niche of black-led gentrification become a mass movement and blacks of all classes again looking inward as a way of advancing the race. In that case, the ghetto's role as a haven would expand and perhaps rival its achievements in that role in the early twentieth century.

But neighborhood revitalization might result in some ghetto neighborhoods losing their black identity. If insufficient blacks are drawn to these spaces, that is the likely outcome. These spaces will no longer serve as a haven for the race. Just as black agency was responsible for creating the role of a haven in the first place, it will ultimately be up to the race to decide if the ghetto will continue to be a haven for blacks in the twenty-first century and beyond.

NOTES

INTRODUCTION

1. Cantey 1927.
2. Taitt 1925.
3. 1909a; 1910.
4. 1909a.
5. 1931a.
6. 1911.
7. 1909b.
8. 1912.
9. Osthaus 1973.
10. Osthaus 1973.
11. 1931c; Osthaus 1973.

1. THE EMBRYONIC GHETTO

1. Dunbar 1902, Kindle edition, location 1356.
2. Dunbar 1902.
3. Du Bois 1901, 13, 14, 15.
4. 1892b.
5. Du Bois [1899] 1996, 166.
6. Du Bois [1899] 1996, 152.
7. 1946a. See also Badger 1943 and Hall 1943.
8. Small 2008.
9. Small 2008, 389.
10. Marcuse 1997, 231.

11. Massey and Denton 1993.
12. Spear 1967, 6–7, emphasis in original.
13. Katzman 1973, 69.
14. Kusmer 1978, 42.
15. Lane 1986, 20.
16. Abrams 1966, 67.
17. Sacks 2006, 72.
18. R. Weaver 1948, 21.
19. R. Weaver 1948, 21.
20. Myrdal 1944.
21. R. Weaver 1948, 6.
22. Massey and Denton 1993.
23. Massey and Denton 1993, 20, my emphasis.
24. Cutler, Glaeser, and Vigdor 1999, 462–465.
25. 1883a.
26. 1886.
27. 1889a.
28. 1892c.
29. 1892a.
30. 1883b.
31. R. Johnson 1984.
32. Baker 1908, 120.
33. Riis [1890] 1971, 115.
34. Du Bois [1899] 1996, 295.
35. Du Bois [1899] 1996, 347.
36. 1915a.
37. New York Association for Improving the Condition of the Poor 1856, 46.
38. Reed 2005, 238.
39. Middlesex Real Estate Association 1887.
40. Massey and Denton 1993, 20.
41. Cutler, Glaeser, and Vigdor 1999.
42. Du Bois [1899] 1996, 296.
43. United Kingdom Board of Trade 1911.
44. Ovington 1911, 36.
45. Riis [1890] 1971, 152, emphasis added.
46. 1891.
47. See, for example, R. R. Wright 1908, 601; Spear 1967, 24; Sacks 2006, 76–77.
48. Krysan, Farley, and Forman 2009.
49. Veiller 1903, 86.
50. Riis [1890] 1971, 116.
51. Lane 1986, 122, 152.
52. Kusmer 1978, 48.
53. Spear 1967.
54. R. R. Wright 1908, 602.
55. See, for example, Massey and Denton 1993 and Cutler, Glaeser, and Vigdor 1999.
56. Cutler, Glaeser, and Vigdor 1999.

57. U.S. Census Bureau 1977.
58. Freeman 2010.
59. Farley and Frey 1994.
60. Ruggles et al. 2010.
61. Roof, Vanvaley, and Spain 1976.
62. Massey and Denton 1993.
63. Logan et al. 2015, 31.
64. Osofsky 1971.
65. Lane 1986, 140–142.
66. Reed 2005, 190–200.
67. Davis 2011, 145.
68. Davis 2011, 134.
69. Blackmon 2009.
70. Davis 2011.
71. Lane 1986, 136.
72. Davis 2011.
73. Katzman 1973.
74. Buckley 2016, 67.
75. 1889c.
76. Ohio History Connection 2016.
77. 1880.
78. Katzman 1973, 158.
79. Katzman 1973, 83.
80. Du Bois 1909.
81. Du Bois [1899] 1996, 317.
82. 1898a.
83. 1898b.
84. 1884.
85. Kusmer 1978, 99.
86. Buckley 2016.
87. See Du Bois [1899] 1996, 316–319.
88. Reed 2005.
89. Du Bois [1899] 1996, 58–61.
90. 1880.
91. 1909c.
92. 1889d.
93. Baker 1908, 199.
94. Woodson 1918, 163.
95. Du Bois [1899] 1996, 328.
96. F. Washington 1920, 25.
97. Ovington 1911, 79.
98. 1889e.
99. 1889a.
100. 1889b.

2. THE AGE OF THE BLACK ENCLAVE

1. "Policy" was an illegal game of chance similar to the lottery.
2. Lindsay 1929, 193.
3. Chicago Commission on Race Relations 1922, 131.
4. Drake and Cayton [1945] 1993, 63.
5. According to the 2010 U.S. census, the tract encompassing Jesse Binga's former home, track 8345 in Cook County, Illinois, is now 98 percent black.
6. Letters from Nina Du Bois, his wife, and Yolande Du Bois, his daughter, written in March 1921 list 94 Johnson Street, Brooklyn, New York, as their home address. By August 1921, however, their home address is listed as 108 Edgecombe Avenue in Harlem (W. E. B. Du Bois Papers, 1803–1999 [bulk 1877–1963], University of Massachusetts Amherst, http://credo.library.umass.edu/view/collection/mums312). The Brooklyn address was located in a tract that was between 10 and 25 percent black in 1920 (Kings County Census Tract Map, 1920, prepared by Social Explorer, January 15, 2015, https://www.socialexplorer.com/).
7. Du Bois 1934b.
8. Marcuse 1997, 228.
9. The data given here are from the tables in Gibson and Jung 2005.
10. In E. Scott 1919a, 337, 339.
11. Chicago Commission on Race Relations 1922, 89–92.
12. Grossman 1989, 1330.
13. E. Scott 1919a, 1919b.
14. B. Washington 1907b.
15. J. Calloway 1917, 410.
16. Douglass 1880.
17. 1915b.
18. Douglass 1880; Woodson 1918.
19. Woodson 1918, 176.
20. Grossman 1989, chap. 4.
21. E. Scott 1920, 24–35.
22. 1915c; 1916.
23. 1917.
24. B. Washington 1913.
25. E. Scott 1919a, 1919b.
26. Letters in E. Scott 1919b, 432, 434, 435, 436.
27. Letter in E. Scott 1919b, 461.
28. Jackson and Wylie 1966, 46.
29. Quoted in Osofsky 1971, 99.
30. B. Washington 1912, 55.
31. See, for example, Du Bois 1914a.
32. Quoted in Chicago Commission on Race Relations 1922, 510.
33. Quoted in 1911b.
34. Gatewood 1990, 145.
35. E. Scott 1920, 28.
36. C. Lewis 1914.
37. C. Johnson 1928, 359.

38. 1925a; 1925b.
39. Hartt 1921, 334.
40. Quoted in Chicago Commission on Race Relations 1922, 439.
41. Woodson 1918, 179.
42. Boas 1905, 87.
43. Devine 1905, 2.
44. Brandt 1905, 7.
45. C. Johnson 1923.
46. D. Lewis 1979, 121.
47. Waldron 1978, 24.
48. See, for example, D. Lewis 1979, 120; Robeson 2001, 43.
49. Calloway and Rollins 1976, 68.
50. Caroll 1920; Freeman 2006b, 22–23.
51. Bone 1986.
52. 1920.
53. 1918.
54. C. Johnson 1924, 323.
55. Biles 1992, 112.
56. Spear 1967; Reed 2011.
57. *Chicago Defender*, April 5, 1924, quoted in Gosnell 1925, 63.
58. B. Washington 1907a, 269–270.
59. Hope 1899, 60.
60. Escridge 1899, 61.
61. Du Bois 1899, 7.
62. B. Washington 1905, 19.
63. Crowe 1906.
64. Caroll 1920, 434.
65. Hartt 1921, 335.
66. W. White 1920, 113; Frazier 1929, 71.
67. Haynes 1924, 304.
68. Lindsay 1929.
69. Woodson 1929.
70. Grossman 1989, chap. 3.
71. R. Boyd 1998, 606.
72. The phrase "Negro market" comes from R. Boyd 1998.
73. C. Johnson 1930, 264.
74. Ruggles et al. 2010.
75. See, for example, F. Washington 1920; Chicago Commission on Race Relations 1922; Mark 1928; Woofter 1928a; Spear 1967; Osofsky 1971; Kusmer 1978.
76. Delany, Delany, and Hearth 1993, 145.

3. THE FEDERALLY SANCTIONED GHETTO

Some of the material in this chapter will also appear in Freeman 2018.

1. 1935a.
2. 1938a.

3. U.S. Department of Housing and Urban Development 2008.

4. R. Weaver 1948, 52.

5. D. Lewis 1979.

6. 1931b.

7. 1930a; 1931b.

8. 1930d.

9. 1930a.

10. Reich 2009.

11. Himes 2000.

12. R. Wright 1940, Kindle edition, location 2393.

13. R. Wright 1940, Kindle edition, locations 624, 3575, emphasis in original.

14. Gregory 2005.

15. The one exception was the provision of housing for munitions workers during World War I. However, according to Kenneth Jackson, less than twenty-five thousand units were built under these efforts (1985, 192).

16. Massey and Denton 1993, chap. 2.

17. See, for example, 1933c and 1933d.

18. Jackson 1985, 200.

19. Hillier 2003.

20. Woods 2012.

21. Jackson 1985; Crossney and Bartelt 2005.

22. *FHA Underwriting Manual* (1938), quoted in Jackson 1985, 208.

23. Woods 2012.

24. Hoyt 1939.

25. Hoyt 1939, 54.

26. Hoyt 1939, 71.

27. Chicago Commission on Race Relations 1922, 220, 216.

28. Chicago Commission on Race Relations 1922, 219, 220.

29. Chicago Commission on Race Relations 1922, 221.

30. Headley 1928b, 146, 147.

31. Chicago Commission on Race Relations 1922, 223.

32. Woofter 1928b, 74.

33. Detroit Bureau of Governmental Research 1926, part V, 32.

34. Chicago Commission on Race Relations 1922, 203.

35. Commonwealth of Pennsylvania Department of Public Welfare 1927, 40.

36. Mark 1928, 28.

37. F. Washington 1920, 22–23.

38. Hoyt 1939, iv.

39. President's Conference on Home Building and Home Ownership 1931.

40. Chicago Commission on Race Relations 1922, 436–445.

41. 1934c.

42. 1934a.

43. 1936b; 1939c.

44. Headley 1928b.

45. Sitkoff 1978.

46. 1934b.

47. 1939a, 54–55.
48. 1938b.
49. Grisom 1845.
50. Bauer 1934.
51. It is unclear whether demolishing slums made a big difference in public housing's impact on the housing market. The number of units built was relatively small, at least initially.
52. Murchison 1935, 210, emphasis in original.
53. Winston 1936.
54. 1933a.
55. Du Bois 1933.
56. 1938a.
57. Gay 1938.
58. 1935b.
59. 1938d.
60. Roster 1936.
61. 1939b.
62. Schwartz 1986.
63. Chicago Commission on Race Relations 1922, 191.
64. Cited in Works Projects Administration 1942.
65. Headley 1928a, 118.
66. President's Conference on Home Building and Home Ownership 1931, 12.
67. Du Bois 1934a, 149.
68. 1936c.
69. 2010, unpaginated interview.
70. Gibson 1968, 5.
71. 1937; Plunz 1990.
72. 1936d.
73. 1935a.
74. Du Bois 1934a.
75. Simmons 1937.
76. 1942.
77. 1938c.
78. Gelman 2016.
79. Wolfinger 2009; Gelman 2016.
80. Sugrue 2008.
81. National Negro Congress 1936.
82. Douglas 2005, 330.
83. 1930c.
84. 1933b.
85. Schuyler 1930.
86. 1930b.
87. Du Bois 1934c, 147.
88. Drake and Cayton [1945] 1993, 113–114.

4. WORLD WAR II AND THE AFTERMATH: THE GHETTO DIVERGES

1. A. Weaver 1943.
2. 1943; Cayton 1943.
3. Alexander 2006; Heinicke 2006, 239.
4. Heinicke 2006, 240–241.
5. Cayton 1943.
6. Johnson, Long, and Jones 1944.
7. See Broussard 1993; Q. Taylor 1994; Sides 2003.
8. Colbert 1946, 697.
9. Quoted in Sides 2003, 15.
10. Colbert 1946.
11. Sides 2003, 21–22.
12. Johnson, Long, and Jones 1944, 30–32.
13. Himes 1945.
14. Wilkerson 2010, 185, 243.
15. A. Weaver 1943.
16. 1945b.
17. J. Smith and Welch 1986, 4–7.
18. Fligstein 1983.
19. Bibb 1950.
20. See, for example, 1957.
21. Smith and Welch 1986, 77.
22. Quoted in Lyons 1945.
23. Quoted in Lyons 1945.
24. A. Weaver 1943.
25. 1950a; 1950c; 1954a.
26. Poindexter 1955, emphasis added.
27. 1938e.
28. 1941.
29. 1948b.
30. Quoted in 1947a.
31. 1947a; 1950b.
32. 1963.
33. 1953b; 1954b.
34. Quoted in Mallory 1956.
35. Jarrett 1952.
36. 1953b.
37. 1954b.
38. Gans 1962.
39. Quoted in Nesbitt 1949a, 52.
40. Wiese 2005, passim.
41. Nesbitt 1949b.
42. Nesbitt 1949a, 50.
43. Du Bois 1914b, 174.
44. 1930e.

45. Madison 1951.
46. Quoted in Mallory 1956.
47. 1948a.
48. Jones 1950.
49. 1953d.
50. White, Gardener, and Young 1953b.
51. Hughes 2001, 207.
52. P. H. Smith 2012, Kindle edition, location 52.
53. Nesbitt 1949b.
54. 1936a.
55. R. Weaver 1948.
56. A. Hirsch 1983; Jackson 1985; Bauman 1987; Massey and Denton 1993.
57. Cutler, Glaeser, and Vigdor 1999.
58. Duncan and Duncan 1957, 132.
59. Petry 1946, 3, 188, 204–205.
60. 1953a.
61. See, for example, F. Washington 1920, 190; Chicago Commission on Race Relations 1922; Osofsky 1971.
62. 1945a.
63. Rinder 1955, 11.
64. Duncan and Duncan 1957, 143.
65. Q. Taylor 1994, 169.
66. Durham 1945.
67. 1946c.
68. R. Wright 1951.
69. Grier and Grier 1958, 7.
70. Wiese 2005, 153.
71. 1938b; 1940c.
72. 1940b.
73. Rampersad 1997, 180, 205, 272–275.
74. J. Moore 2011, chap. 8.
75. J. Hirsch 2010, 274–279.
76. Bontemps 1945, 171.
77. Delany, Delany, and Hearth 1993, chap. 15.
78. Bontemps 1945, 171.
79. Kucheva and Sander 2014.
80. 1940a.
81. 1946d; 1947b; Spraggs 1949.
82. Abrams 1955.
83. Pritchett 2002b.
84. The nature of these laws varied, with some exempting small owner-occupied housing. See Collins 2004.
85. Jackson 1985.
86. Cutler, Glaeser, and Vigdor 1999.
87. 1946e.
88. 1946e.
89. Freeman 2010, 247, 251.

90. Sides 2003, 127.
91. Quoted in 1958.
92. Graham 1999, 309.
93. National Visionary Leadership Project 2004; J. Johnson 2004, recorded interview.
94. 1955b.
95. White, Gardener, and Young 1954.
96. 1955c.
97. 1955a.
98. 1953c.
99. White, Gardener, and Young 1953a.

5. THE GHETTO ERUPTS: THE 1960S

1. Dorn 2011, recorded oral history.
2. Oral history in Herman 2013, 68.
3. Sitkoff 1993, 182.
4. Clark 1965, 11.
5. Quoted in 1960.
6. Stome 1963.
7. 1960.
8. Werner 1964.
9. Quoted in 1966a.
10. Quoted in 1967a.
11. 1964.
12. Quoted in 1964.
13. 1966c.
14. Quoted in Vacca 1991, 45.
15. Young 1960.
16. John F. Kraft 1966a, table titled "New York Times Survey July 27, 1964: Major Problems"; respondents were allowed to list more than one item.
17. John F. Kraft 1966b, 19.
18. John F. Kraft 1966b, cited in 1967a.
19. National Advisory Commission on Civil Disorders 1968, 472.
20. Chicago Commission on Race Relations 1922.
21. Chicago Commission on Race Relations 1922, 240.
22. Roosevelt 1937.
23. United States Housing and Home Finance Agency 1963, 13.
24. U.S. Census Bureau 1992, 1.
25. Helper 1969.
26. Jackson 1985.
27. United States Housing and Home Finance Agency 1963, 18.
28. Schwulst 1956, 128.
29. John F. Kraft 1966a, 10.
30. Author's tabulation of Integrated Public Use Microdata for 1960 and 1970 (Ruggles et al. 2010).

31. United States Housing and Home Finance Agency 1963. This report analyzes housing condition for nonwhites in the United States, 92 percent of whom were Negro in 1960 (2).
32. Clark did note that Harlem's population declined roughly 10 percent between 1950 and 1960. But he did not make much of this decline and thought this trend was limited to New York (1965, 59).
33. Duncan and Duncan 1957; Taeuber and Taeuber 1965.
34. *Inside the Battle for Fair Housing* 2014.
35. Zelder 1972.
36. Grigsby et al. 1973, 44.
37. National Urban League 1973, 39.
38. Sternlieb et al. 1974.
39. 1971; Claytor 1971.
40. Chicago Commission on Race Relations 1922, 8; 1946b.
41. 1919.
42. Quoted in Johnnson 1967.
43. Quoted in T. Johnson 1967.
44. National Advisory Commission on Civil Disorders 1968, 172–184.
45. Much of the property damage during the disturbances in the 1960s was to commercial property. Detroit was the major exception to this pattern. But even in Detroit, where 274 houses were destroyed, we can infer that the overwhelming majority of the property damage was to nonresidential property. According to the 1970 U.S. census, in the Detroit metropolitan area the median home value for blacks was $15,000, meaning residential property lost (274 * 15,000 = $4,110,00) accounted for a small portion of the estimated total damage of $45,000,000 cited in the Kerner Report (National Advisory Commission on Civil Disorders 1968, 115–116)
46. National Advisory Commission on Civil Disorders 1968, 40, 64.
47. Quoted in Herman 2013, 77, 76.
48. Campbell and Schuman 1968, 242.
49. Erskine 1967, 663–667.
50. Sears and Tomlinson 1968, 489.
51. Campbell and Schuman 1968, 243.
52. Banfield 1970, 185.
53. Marwick 1998.
54. Sugrue 2008.
55. O. Brown 1935, 134.
56. O. Brown 1935, 137.
57. Painter 1976.
58. O. Brown 1935, 137.
59. Joseph 2006.
60. Malcolm X 1963b.
61. Malcolm X 1963a, emphasis added.
62. Newton and Seale 1966, unpaginated pamphlet.
63. Elijah Muhammad and Malcolm X quoted in Lincoln 1994, 90–92.
64. A. Hirsch 1983.

65. Campbell and Schuman 1968, 16.
66. "The Anti-Depression Program" 1997, 199.
67. Brown and Shaw 2002.
68. Quoted in S. Washington 1966.
69. Clark 1965, 4, 27.
70. Clegg 1997.
71. U.S. House of Representatives 1971.
72. Bloom and Martin 2013, 196.
73. Neal 1968b, 30.
74. Neal 1968a.
75. Donaldson [1969] 1997, 219.
76. S. Brown 2003.
77. Cited in Boggs and Boggs 1966, 40
78. Tolbert 1968, 10.
79. E. Cleaver 1968.
80. Quoted in 1967b.
81. 1966b.
82. Solomon 1968, 41.
83. Innis and Solomon 1967.
84. R. Williams 1968.
85. 1968.
86. Bailey 1967.
87. E. Cleaver 1968.
88. 1969.
89. R. E. Wright 1969.
90. Innis [1969] 1997, 177.
91. Smethurst 2005.
92. S. Brown 2003; Smethurst 2005.
93. Ellis 1965; Baraka 1997; Maurer 2014.
94. Smethurst 2005.
95. Smethurst 2005, 179–246.
96. Hunter 1997.
97. Smethurst 2005, 202–208.
98. Widener 2010.
99. Smethurst 2005, chaps. 4 and 5.
100. Biles 1992.
101. Biles 1992, 120–121.
102. Alinsky 1969, 175; see also Rohe 2009.
103. See, for example, Lemann 1994 and Stoecker 1997.
104. See, for example, Bratt 1997.
105. Malcolm X 1963b.
106. T. Anderson 1970, 14.
107. R. E. Wright 1969, 27.
108. S. Brown 2003, 15.
109. Waldinger 1996.
110. Bates 2006, 230.
111. Bates 2006, 230; see also Bates 1989.

112. Fischer and Massey 2000.
113. Quoted in Kotlowski 1998, 411.

6. THE LAST DECADES OF THE TWENTIETH CENTURY

1. Bobo, Schuman, and Steeh 1986, 163.
2. Frey 2004.
3. Urban America 1969, 111.
4. Frey 2004.
5. 1973.
6. Quoted in Hayes 1974.
7. Martin 1974.
8. Martin 1974.
9. 1997.
10. C. Brown and Padgett 2004.
11. C. Brown et al. 2007.
12. Chandler 2015.
13. 2015.
14. J. Smith and Welch 1986.
15. Kim 1998.
16. Herbers 1970.
17. Beveridge 2008.
18. Rob Paral and Associates 2015.
19. City of Cleveland 2011.
20. R. Weaver 1948, 100, 106.
21. 1971.
22. Quoted in Graham 1999, 203.
23. Wilkerson 2010, 491.
24. Cassell 1973.
25. Farris 1976.
26. Long 1975; Long and Heltman 1975.
27. 1972.
28. 1972.
29. Lee and Wood 1991, 610.
30. Pritchett 2002a.
31. Jargowsky 1994.
32. 1959; Snides 2003.
33. J. Cleaver 1975.
34. Lee and Wood 1991; Ellen, Horn, and O'Regan 2012.
35. Logan and Zhang 2010; Farrell and Lee 2011.
36. Glaeser and Vigdor 2012.
37. Lacy 2007.
38. See, for example, Pattillo 1999.
39. Lacy 2007.
40. Stewart 1999.
41. Bennett 2002; Collier 2002.

42. R. Weaver 1948, 100.
43. Turner et al. 2002.
44. Massey and Lundy 2001.
45. Dent 1992.
46. Quoted in Dent 1992.
47. Quoted in Wacquant 1993, 372.
48. Quoted in Richardson, Glantz, and Adelman 2014, 83.
49. Grand Master Flash and the Furious Five 1979.
50. Poger 2016.
51. Wacquant 2008, 114.
52. Sharkey 2013, 41.
53. Sampson, Raudenbush, and Earls 1997. Some scholars, such as Paul Jargowsky (1994), a leading scholar on poverty concentration, defined ghettos as those neighborhoods where the black poverty rate was at least 40 percent. HUD picked up this 40 percent threshold to identify areas of racial and ethnic poverty concentration. It was based, however, on field observations attempting to identify the most problematic neighborhoods in several cities. In other words, it was an outcome-based measure with visible signs of disorder and a bad reputation. Similarly, Erol Ricketts and Isabel Sawhill (1988) use certain behaviors (e.g., not participating in the labor force) to define underclass neighborhoods that many construe as the ghetto. The central argument of this book, however, is that the ghetto can have different types of outcomes, good and bad, and can be a haven or a hell. For that reason, I have not used the 40 percent threshold or other outcome-based measures here.
54. Collins and Margo define idleness as being neither in school nor employed (2000, 240).
55. Collins and Margo 2000.
56. Chicago Commission on Race Relations 1922; Detroit Bureau of Governmental Research 1926, chap. 9.
57. General 1964.
58. AR 1967.
59. Sorrells 1972.
60. General 1964.
61. G. Montgomery 1973.
62. John F. Kraft 1966a, 1966b.
63. 1970; Guilmant 1970.
64. Robinson 1970.
65. P. J. Smith 1977.
66. A. Weaver 1972.
67. 1976.
68. Johnson 1979, 32, emphasis in original.
69. Harris 1979, 57–62.
70. 1979.
71. Latzer 2017, Kindle edition, locations 2055–2142.
72. Roth 2009.
73. Latzer 2017, Kindle edition, locations 2077–2664.

74. Kotlowitz 1992; E. Anderson 2000; Venkatesh 2002.
75. Rubinowitz and Rosenbaum 2002; Briggs, Popkin, and Goering 2010; Massey et al. 2013.
76. Quoted in Massey et al. 2013, 133.
77. Fortner 2015.
78. Muhammad 2010, Kindle edition, location 4138.
79. 1913.
80. Keber 1965.
81. W. Young 1970.
82. Sampson and Bartusch 1998.
83. E. Anderson 2000.
84. Kain 1968; Sugrue 1996.
85. Sugrue 1996.
86. Stierholz 2014; Zimmermann 2014.
87. Sugrue 1996.
88. Author's tabulation of Integration Public Use Microdata (Ruggles et al. 2010).
89. Sugrue 1996, 241.
90. Wilson 1987.
91. 1926.
92. McKee-Ryan et al. 2005.
93. E. Anderson 2000.
94. Parker and Reckdenwald 2008; Parker and Maggard 2009.
95. Wang and Parker 2014.
96. Lesthaeghe 2010.
97. Child Trends 2015.
98. Baltimore Neighborhood Indicators Alliance 2016.
99. Center on Urban Poverty and Community Development 2016.
100. Edin and Kefelas 2005.
101. McLanahan and Sandefur 1994.
102. Briggs 1998.
103. Kan 1999; Freeman 2005; Freeman, Cassola, and Cai 2015.
104. Sampson 2012.
105. Galster and Killen 1995; Sampson 2012.
106. Sampson 2012.
107. Sampson, Morenoff, and Gannon-Rowley 2002.
108. Neckerman et al. 2009.
109. Northridge and Freeman 2011.
110. Based on my tabulation of HUD's Affirmatively Furthering Fair Housing data (U.S. HUD 2015). HUD defines extremely high-poverty neighborhoods as census tracts where the poverty rate is greater than 40 percent or is three or more times the average tract poverty rate for the metropolitan/micropolitan area, whichever threshold is lower (9).
111. For more on this relationship, see Galster and Killen 1995 and Sampson 2012.
112. Venkatesh 2002.
113. Saegert 1989.
114. Quoted in Saegert 1989, 306.

115. Hoffman 2003, 149–154.
116. Bratt and Rohe 2007.
117. Owens 2007.
118. Owens 2007, 88.

7. THE GHETTO IN THE TWENTY-FIRST CENTURY

1. U.S. Census Bureau 2016, tables B17001B and C23002B.
2. Wolfers, Leonhardt, and Quealy 2015.
3. Baltimore Neighborhood Indicators Alliance 2014a.
4. Baltimore Neighborhood Indicators Alliance 2014b.
5. Gross 2015.
6. McCoy 2015.
7. M. Alexander 2012; Fortner 2015.
8. Muhammad 2010.
9. Sentencing Project 2015.
10. Mauer 2006, 10.
11. Humphreys 2016.
12. Quoted in M. Alexander 2012, 125.
13. Forman 2017, 197–201.
14. Sampson and Loeffler 2010, 24.
15. Pew Center on the States 2009, 9.
16. Justice Mapping Center 2010.
17. Braman 2004, 3, citing Washington, DC, Department of Corrections data.
18. Braman 2004; Goffman 2014.
19. K. Lee 2014.
20. J. Scott 1977, 167.
21. Braman 2004, 162.
22. Goffman 2014, 37.
23. Goffman 2014, 37.
24. Goffman 2014, 196.
25. M. Alexander 2012, 158–161, 192–193.
26. 2016.
27. Kalt 2003.
28. Powell 2009.
29. Bunce et al. 2001; Been, Ellen, and Madar 2009; Hwang, Hankinson, and Brown 2015.
30. Calem, Gillen, and Wachter 2004.
31. Jean Robert Saint-Jean and Edith Saint-Jean v. Emigrant Mortgage Company, 11-CV-2122 (SJ), U.S. District Court Eastern District of New York, 2016.
32. Powell 2009 (quote); Savage 2012.
33. Reynolds 2012.
34. 2007.
35. Hyra and Rugh 2016.
36. S. Young 2008, 17, including the quotation of Alden Loury.

37. Bergen, Caputo, and Lee 2017; Dworkin and Wittekind 2010.
38. Roberts 2006.
39. Armstrong et al. 2010, 123.
40. Kelly, Sullivan, and Rich 2015.
41. Tsai 2015, 14.
42. Botein 2013.
43. Zhang and McCord 2014; Payton, Stucky, and Ottensmann 2015; Boessen and Chamberlain 2017.
44. Lacoe and Ellen 2015.
45. Adams 2016.
46. Goffe 2014.
47. Glass 1964.
48. Goodman 1969.
49. Unger 1984.
50. Schaffer and Smith 1986, 351.
51. Quoted in M. Taylor 2002, 97.
52. Hwang and Sampson 2014.
53. K. Moore 2009.
54. M. Montgomery 2002; Watson 2003.
55. M. Williams 2000.
56. F. Lee 1994.
57. Waldman 2001.
58. Risen 2008.
59. E. Young 2014.
60. Freeman and Cai 2015.
61. Lawrence 1985.
62. F. White 1985.
63. Adams 2016.
64. Quoted in Tavernise 2011.
65. Bodenner 2015.
66 Tinawina 2015.
67. Quoted in Freeman 2006b, 74, 112.
68. Freeman and Braconi 2004; Freeman 2005; McKinnish, Walsh, and White 2010; Ellen and O'Regan 2011; Freeman, Cassola, and Cai 2015.
69. Freeman 2005; Martin and Beck 2016.
70. Freeman and Braconi 2004; Freeman 2005.
71. Quoted in Adler 2007.
72. T. Williams 2008.
73. K. White 2015.
74. Quoted in Adler 2007.
75. Quoted in Adler 2007.
76. Quoted in Freeman 2006b, 137–138, 106.
77. Prince 2014, 121.
78. Hyra 2017, 136.
79. Levin 2015.
80. As given in 2014.

81. OhNeeksTV 2015.

82. Quoted in Neuman and Schmidt 2016.

83. Zukin 2009.

84. Hyra 2017.

85. Crockett 2012.

86. M. Taylor 2002.

87. Boyd 2008.

88. Black-gentrified neighborhoods are defined here as neighborhoods that (1) were at least 50 percent black at the start of the decade; (2) had an above-average poverty rate at the start of the decade; (3) experienced an increase in the number of college-educated blacks (at least four years of college), one standard deviation or greater than the increase in the number of college-educated blacks in all neighborhoods.

89. Small 2008, 394.

90. Unger 1984.

91. Quoted in Coplon 2013.

92. Dawes 2015.

93. M. Taylor 2002, 150.

94. Quoted in Gabreyes 2015.

95. Cullen 1925.

96. K. Moore 2009, 129.

97. Quoted in M. Boyd 2008, 73, 74.

98. All quoted in Clemetson 2002, emphasis added.

99. Drake and Cayton [1945] 1993, 716.

100. M. Boyd 2008, 76.

101. M. Taylor 2002; Pattillo 2007.

102. Wilson 1987.

103. Quoted in M. Taylor 2002, 132.

104. M. Taylor 2002, 35.

105. Jenkins 2015.

106. Freeman and Cai 2015.

CONCLUSION: HOW TO HAVE A HAVEN BUT NO HELL IN THE TWENTY-FIRST CENTURY

1. Quoted in Lemann 1994.

2. Lemann 1994.

3. Hoffman 2003.

4. Freedman 1994; Medoff and Sklar 1999; Goldstein 2017.

5. Liou and Stroh 1998.

6. Freeman 2006b.

7. Dastrup, Ellen, and Jefferson 2016.

8. Dastrup, Ellen, and Jefferson 2016.

9. Godsil 2013.

10. Harlem Children's Zone 2017.

11. Spielman et al. 2006.
12. Dobbie and Fryer 2015.
13. Paul, Darity, and Hamilton 2017.
14. Kopf 2016.
15. For a compelling example, see Rosen 1999.

REFERENCES

1880. "Wealthy Colored People in New York." *People's Advocate*, September 18.

1883a. "Prejudice." *Gazette*, August 25.

1883b. "The Renting Problem." *People's Advocate*, December 1.

1884. "The National Capital." *New York Globe*, February 2.

1886. "Southern Domestic Help: Conditions in Louisville." *New York Freeman*, September 11.

1889a. "Enough of Georgia." *Detroit Plaindealer*, October 4.

1889b. "An Invitation to Genuine Americans to Move Into the Northwest." *Detroit Plaindealer*, October 18.

1889c. "No Color Caste in California—a Splendid Field of Labor for the Negro." *Indianapolis Freeman*, September 28.

1889d. "Seales and Epps." *Cleveland Gazette*. January 12.

1889e. "Want to Leave the South: Afro-American Baptists Think Negro Should Go West." *Detroit Plaindealer*, September 20.

1891. "Social and Personal News." *Cleveland Gazette*, April 25.

1892a. "Northern Jim Crow, South." *Indianapolis Freeman*, August 20.

1892b. "Old Rounders Observations." *The Freeman*, June 11.

1892c. "Rental Agents Versus Northern Negroes." *The Freeman*, August 20.

1898a. "All Negroes Look Alike." *Baltimore Afro-American*, April 9.

1898b. "Business and the Color Line." *Baltimore Afro-American*, November 19.

1909a. "Chips." *Broad Axe*, February 27.

1909b. "Exterior and Interior Views of Jesse Binga's Bank Commercial Department." *Broad Axe*, December 25.

1909c. "That 'Blue-Vein' Society Again." *Wichita Searchlight*, June 19.

1910. "Block of Stores and Flats Leased for 30 Years: Jesse Binga Takes from Henry Botsford." *Broad Axe*, October 29.

1911a. "Chicago's Only Banker." *Chicago Defender*, December 23.

1911b. "Rousing Celebration of the Emancipation Proclamation at John Wesley Church: Rev. Ernest Lyon Scores Segregation by Law but Says It Is Good for the Race When Self-Imposed." *Baltimore Afro-American*, January 7.

1912. "The Defender's Summary of Great Negroes." *Chicago Defender*, February 3.

1913. "Along the Color Line." *Crisis: A Record of the Darker Races* 6 (1): 9.

1915a. "The Negro District in Springfield." *The Southern Workman* 44, no. 9: 475.

1915a. "Sticking to the Farm." *Chicago Defender*, January 15.

1915c. "St. Louis Notes." *Chicago Defender*, October 9.

1916. "Vital Principle." *The Appeal*, May 13.

1917. "A Great Victory." *Washington Bee*, November 10.

1918. "A Colored Congressman." *Philadelphia Tribune*, February 9.

1919. "Where Is He 'At'?" *Baltimore Afro-American*, August 1.

1920. "Southerners Make Good in the North." *Baltimore Afro-American*, October 22.

1925a. "Harlem Should Have a Negro Judge." *New York Amsterdam News*, April 8.

1925b. "Negroes to Ruin Harlem Hospital." *New York Times*, June 24.

1926. "Colored Population Shifts to Northern Part of City." *Philadelphia Tribune*, January 30.

1930a. "City Still Haven for Migrant Jobless." *Baltimore Afro-American*, March 15.

1930b. "Fight Segregation of Indiana Students." *Chicago Defender*, September 30.

1930c. "Halt Proposed Jim Crowing of New Jersey Schools." *Pittsburgh Courier*, June 14.

1930d. "Jobless, He Ends Life with Rope." *Chicago Defender*, October 25.

1930e. "Realtor Foretells Passing of Harlem." *Chicago Defender*, June 14.

1931a. "Banker Binga in Jail Hospital." *Chicago Defender*, March 14.

1931b. "Hungry Marchers Raid Grocery Store." *Negro Star*, February 6.

1931c. "Jesse Binga." *Pittsburgh Courier*, March 21.

1933a. "Federal Housing." *Pittsburgh Courier*, October 21.

1933b. "How Berwyn, PA, Would Spread School Segregation." *Pittsburgh Courier*, June 10.

1933c. "How to Get Federal Help Under Home Owner's Loan." *Chicago Defender*, July 15.

1933d. "Relief Ahead for Home Owners." *New York Amsterdam News*, July 19.

1934a. "14 Answers to Your Questions About Modernization Credits." *Chicago Defender*, September 22.

1934b. "Discrimination Policy Pursued by Social Agency." *Los Angeles Sentinel*, December 13.

1934c. "The Housing Loan." *Chicago Defender*, September 1.

1935a. "$4,700,000 for Housing Here: New Project Will Provide Rooms for $8." *New York Amsterdam News*, July 6.

1935b. "Live Where You Can Afford It." *Chicago Defender*, February 9.

1936a. "17 of 50 Housing Projects for Race; Two to Be Mixed." *Chicago Defender*, January 11.

1936b. "Old House Turns Swank After Face Lifting." *New York Amsterdam News*, October 24.

1936c. "Rush in Harlem for PWA Houses." *New York Times*, November 8.

1936d. "Would Pick Tenants by Point System." *New York Times*, January 29.

1937. "U.S. Government Installs 1853 Westinghouse Refrigerators in Low Rent Housing Projects." *Cleveland Plain Dealer*, June 6, 1937.

1938a. "Fourth of 30,496 Homes Open to Race." *Pittsburgh Courier*, August 6.

1938b. "Ghettoes American Style." *Los Angeles Sentinel*, December 29.

1938c. "Perpetuating Segregation." *Pittsburgh Courier*, October 22.

1938d. "Race Gets One-Fourth Benefits from Approved Federal Housing." *Chicago Defender*, August 6.

1938e. "Slum Clearance Displeases Many." *Baltimore Afro-American*, June 18.

1939a. "Housing Authority Draws Mortgage Color Line." *The Crisis: A Record of the Darker Races* 46 (2): 54–55.

1939b. "Negro Congress Says Slum Project Here Assured." *Los Angeles Sentinel*, October 12.

1939c. "Park Gardens." *New York Amsterdam News*, September 9.

1940a. "FHA Urges Jim Crow in Loans." *Los Angeles Sentinel*, August 1.

1940b. "Perpetuating the Ghetto." *Pittsburgh Courier*, February 24.

1940c. "The Plight of Sharecroppers." *Chicago Defender*, June 29.

1941. "Cleveland Negroes Protest Home Project Extension; Say Colored Business Will Be 'Wiped Out.'" *Philadelphia Tribune*, September 6.

1942. "The Lesson of Sojourner Truth." *Pittsburgh Courier*, May 9.

1943. "Housing Crisis Looms for Negro Workers." *Pittsburgh Courier*, September 11.

1945a. "Battle of the Ghettos." *Chicago Defender*, August 4.

1945b. "Negro Migrants Intend to Stay in Northwest." *Chicago Defender*, January 6.

1946a. "Fascist Wednesday." *Chicago Defender*, February 9.

1946b. "Long Island Mob Shoots Up Mixed Project." *New York Amsterdam News*, September 21.

1946c. "Overcrowding, Sanitation Lack, High Rents in 'Ghetto' Districts Create Scandalous Situation: BREEDING GROUND FOR DISEASE, EPIDEMICS, CRIME." *Los Angeles Sentinel*, January 3.

1946d. "Race Pacts No Bar to FHA Loans." *Chicago Defender*, June 8.

1946e. "'Sugar Hill: All Harlem Looks Up to 'Folks on the Hill.'" *Ebony*, November.

1947a. "Condemnation of Indianapolis Slum Area Termed 'Big Steal.'" *Atlanta Daily World*, December 31.

1947b. "Restrictive Covenants, Bias No Longer Sanctioned by FHA." *Chicago Defender*, May 24.

1948a. "Citizens Group Opposes St. Louis Slum Clearance." *Atlanta Daily World*, September 28.

1948b. "What the People Say." *Chicago Defender*, September 4.

1950a. "35 Legislators Elected in 13 States Tuesday." *Baltimore Afro-American*, November 18.

1950b. "City Council Ignores Complaints of Citizens; Approves Home Project." *Los Angeles Sentinel*, November 30.

1950c. "Rep. Dawson's New Year Message to the Public." *Cleveland Plain Dealer*, January 6.

1953a. "Chicago Housing: The Nation's Powder Keg." *Our World*, April.

1953b. "Hunt for Homes on in Chicago." *Chicago Defender*, October 10.

1953c. "The Mischals of Cleveland: How the Negro Lives No. 2." *Our World*, April.

1953d. "Norris Homes Open Today, Slum Area Got Facelifting." *Philadelphia Tribune*, August 18.

1954a. "Charles Diggs Jr., Our New Congressman, Talks to AFRO." *Baltimore Afro-American*, November 13.

1954b. "Chicago Approves $26 Million Housing Project." *Atlanta Daily World*, December 29.

1955a. "The Borders of Hartford: How Negro America Lives." *Our World*, April.

1955b. "Half a Billion on Wheels." *Our World*, March.

1955c. "The Mills of Los Angeles." *Our World*, March.

1957. "Drought, Machines, Force Migration." *Chicago Daily Defender*, February 7.

1958. "What the Negro Wants Now." *Ebony*, March.

1959. "Compton Associated Brokers: Live in Smog-Free Compton—10 Minutes to Downtown L.A. by Frwy." *Los Angeles Sentinel*, February 5.

1960. "Dempsey Wages War in Housing." *New York Amsterdam News*, June 18.

1963. "Residents Nix B'klyn Housing." *New York Amsterdam News*, April 27.

1964. "Rent Strike Hits Chicago!" *Chicago Daily Defender*, January 9.

1966a. "Charge Edison 'Worst Negro Ghetto' in USA." *New York Amsterdam News*, September 10.

1966b. "Opposition Shown to Freedom City." *Los Angeles Sentinel*, July 28.

1966c. "Rent Strike Brews: Landlord Picketed at Suburban Home." *Chicago Daily Defender*, September 12.

1967a. "Harlem's Biggest Problem? Housing Survey Reveals." *New York Amsterdam News*, January 21.

1967b. "Panthers Demand Independence for N. Richmond Area." *The Black Panther*, June 20.

1968. "Black Panther Party Platform and Program." *The Black Panther*, May 18.

1969. "United Front Tackles Problems." *Bay State Banner*, November 27.

1970. "Crime in the Ghetto." *Chicago Daily Defender*, April 1.

1971. "Inner City 'Ghost Towns' Feared in Most Cities." *Atlanta Daily World*, April 22.

1972. "Photo-Editorial: Let's Keep the Inner-City Black." *Ebony*, March.

1973. "Atlanta: New Mecca for Young Blacks." *Ebony*, September.

1976. "Photo-Editorial: Our Hope—New Values in the Ghetto." *Ebony*, March.

1979. "The Destruction of Cities." *Ebony*, August.

1997. "Which City Is Best for Blacks?" *Ebony*, December.

2007. "City Chief on Buyouts: 'We're Still Dancing.'" *New York Times*, July 10.

2010. *Outhwaite Homes: Growing Up at Outhwaite*. Cleveland: Cleveland State University Center for Public History + Digital Humanities.

2014. "There Goes the Neighborhood." *Reid Report*, MSNBC, February 27.

2015. "Lynchings by Year." Charles Chestnutt Digital Archive. http://www.chesnuttarchive.org/classroom/lynching_table_year.html.

2016. "State Felon Voting Laws." ProCon.org, April 22. http://felonvoting.procon.org/view.resource.php?resourceID=000286.

Abrams, Charles. 1955. *Forbidden Neighbors: A Study of Prejudice in Housing*. New York: Harper and Brothers.

——. 1966. "The Housing Problem and the Negro." *Daedalus* 95 (1): 64–76.

Adams, Michael Henry. 2016. "The End of Black Harlem." *New York Times*, May 27.

Adler, Margot. 2007. "Drumming Up a Protest in a Harlem Park." *Weekend Edition Sunday*, NPR, September 2.

Alexander, J. Trent. 2006. "Demographic Patterns of the Great Black Migration (1915–1940)." In *The Great Black Migration*, edited by Steven A. Reich, 236–239. Westport, CT: Greenwood Press.

Alexander, Michelle. 2012. *The New Jim Crow: Incarceration in the Age of Colorblindness*. New York: New Press.

Alinsky, Saul. 1969. *Reveille for Radicals: A Practical Primer for Realistic Radicals*. New York: Vintage Books.

Anderson, Elijah. 2000. *Code of the Street: Decency, Violence, and the Moral Life of the Inner City*. New York: Norton.

Anderson, Talmadge. 1970. "Black Economic Liberation Under Capitalism." *Black Scholar*, October, 10–14.

"The Anti-Depression Program of the Republic of New Africa." 1997. In *Modern Black Nationalism from Marcus Garvey to Louis Farrakahn*, edited by William L. Van Deburg, 198–202. New York: New York University Press.

AR. 1967. Letter to the editor. *Chicago Defender*, June 17.

Armstrong, Amy, Vicki Been, Caroline K. Bhalla, Ingrid Gould Ellen, Josiah Madar, Simon McDonnell, Claudia Sharygin, and Max Weselcouch. 2010. *State of New York City's Housing and Neighborhoods 2009*. New York: Furman Center, New York University.

Badger, John Robert. 1943. "World View: Hitlerism in America." *Chicago Defender*, July 3.

Bailey, Peter. 1967. "What African American Nationalism Means to Me." *Negro Digest*, December.

Baker, Ray Stannard. 1908. *Following the Color Line: An Account of Negro Citizenship in the American Democracy*. New York: Doubleday, Page.

Baltimore Neighborhood Indicators Alliance. 2014a. "Percent of Family Households Living Below the Poverty Line." University of Baltimore. http://bniajfi.org/indicator/census demographics/.

——. 2014b. "Spring 2016 Vital Signs." http://bniajfi.org/wp-content/uploads/2016/04/VitalSigns14_Crime.pdf.

——. 2016. "Vital Signs by Community." http://bniajfi.org/mapgallery/gallery-vs16-census/.

Banfield, Edward C. 1970. *The Unheavenly City: The Nature and Future of Our Urban Crisis*. Boston: Little, Brown.

Baraka, Amiri. 1997. *The Autobiography of Leroi Jones*. Chicago: Lawrence Hill Books.

Bates, Timothy. 1989. "The Changing Nature of Minority Business: A Comparative Analysis of Asian, Nonminority, and Black-Owned Businesses." *Review of Black Political Economy* 18 (2): 25–42.

——. 2006. "The Urban Development Potential of Black-Owned Businesses." *Journal of the American Planning Association* 72 (2): 227–237.

Bauer, Catherine. 1934. *Modern Housing*. New York: Houghton Mifflin.

Bauman, John F. 1987. *Public Housing, Race, and Urban Renewal: Urban Planning in Philadelphia 1920–1974*. Philadelphia: Temple University Press.

Been, Vicki, Ingrid Ellen, and Josiah Madar. 2009. "The High-Cost of Segregation: Exploring Racial Disparities in High-Cost Lending." *Fordham Urban Law Journal* 36 (3): 362–393.

Bennett, Lerone, Jr. 2002. "Blacks in Chicago." *Ebony*, November.

Bergen, Kathy, Angela Caputo, and William Lee. 2017. "South Shore, Once Thriving, Struggles Amid Economic Erosion and Crime." *Chicago Tribune*, May 2.

Beveridge, Andy. 2008. "Harlem's Shifting Population." *Gotham Gazette*, September 2.

Bibb, Joseph D. 1950. "They Leave Dixie." *Pittsburgh Courier*, July 1.

Biles, Roger. 1992. "Black Mayors: A Historical Assessment." *Journal of Negro History* 77 (3): 109–125.

Blackmon, Douglas A. 2009. *Slavery by Another Name: The Re-enslavement of Black People in America from the Civil War to World War II*. New York: Anchor.

Bloom, Joshua, and Waldo E. Martin. 2013. *Black Against Empire: The History and Politics of the Black Panther Party*. Berkeley: University of California Press.

Boas, Franz. 1905. "The Negro and the Demands of Modern Life." In *The Negro in the Cities of the North*, edited by Edward T. Devine, 85–87. New York: Charity Organization Society.

Bobo, Lawrence, Howard Schuman, and Charlotte Steeh. 1986. "Changing Racial Attitudes Toward Residential Integration." In *Housing Desegregation and Federal Policy*, edited by John M. Goering, 152–169. Chapel Hill: University of North Carolina Press.

Bodenner, Chris. 2015. "Why Is Gentrification Such a Bad Word? Your Thoughts." *The Atlantic*, June 27.

Boessen, Adam, and Alyssa W. Chamberlain. 2017. "Neighborhood Crime, the Housing Crisis, and Geographic Space: Disentangling the Consequences of Foreclosure and Vacancy." *Journal of Urban Affairs* 39 (8): 1–16.

Boggs, Grace, and James Boggs. 1966. "The City Is the Black Man's Land." *Monthly Review*, April, 35–46.

Bone, Robert. 1986. "Richard Wright and the Chicago Renaissance." *Callaloo* 28 (Summer): 446–468.

Bontemps, Arna. 1945. "The Two Harlems." *American Scholar* 14 (2): 170–171.

Botein, Hilary. 2013. "From Redlining to Subprime Lending: How Neighborhood Narratives Mask Financial Distress in Bedford-Stuyvesant, Brooklyn." *Housing Policy Debate* 23 (4): 714–737.

Boyd, Michelle R. 2008. *Jim Crow Nostalgia: Reconstructing Race in Bronzeville*. Minneapolis: University of Minnesota Press.

Boyd, Robert L. 1998. "Residential Segregation by Race and the Black Merchants of Northern Cities During the Early Twentieth Century." *Sociological Forum* 13 (4): 595–609.

Braman, Donald. 2004. *Doing Time on the Outside: Incarceration and Family Life in Urban America*. Ann Arbor: University of Michigan Press.

Brandt, Lilian. 1905. "The Make-Up of Negro City Groups." In *The Negro in Cities of the North*, edited by Edward T. Devine, 7–10. New York: Charity Organization Society.

Bratt, Rachel G. 1997. "CDCs: Contributions Outweigh Contradictions—Reply." *Journal of Urban Affairs* 19 (1): 23–28.

Bratt, Rachel G., and William M. Rohe. 2007. "Challenges and Dilemmas Facing Community Development Corporations in the United States." *Community Development Journal* 42 (1): 63–78.

Briggs, Xavier de Souza. 1998. "Brown Kids in White Suburbs: Housing Mobility and the Many Faces of Social Capital." *Housing Policy Debate* 9 (1): 177–221.

Briggs, Xavier de Souza, Susan J. Popkin, and John Goering. 2010. *Moving to Opportunity: The Story of an American Experiment to Fight Ghetto Poverty*. New York: Oxford University Press.

Broussard, Albert S. 1993. *Black San Francisco: The Struggle for Racial Equality in the West, 1900–1954.* Lawrence: University of Kansas Press.

Brown, Carolyn M., and David Padgett. 2004. "Top 19 Cities for African Americans." *Black Enterprise*, July.

Brown, Carolyn M., David A. Padgett, Tennille M. Robinson, and Stephanie Young. 2007. "Top 10 Cities for African Americans 2007." *Black Enterprise*, May.

Brown, Oscar C. 1935. "What Chance Freedom!" *The Crisis: A Record of the Darker Races* 42 (5): 134–149.

Brown, Robert A., and Todd C. Shaw. 2002. "Separate Nations: Two Attitudinal Dimensions of Black Nationalism." *Journal of Politics* 64 (1): 22–44.

Brown, Scott. 2003. *Fighting for US: Maulana Karenga, the US Organization, and Black Cultural Nationalism.* New York: New York University Press.

Buckley, Gail Lumet. 2016. *The Black Calhouns: From Civil War to Civil Rights, with One African American Family.* New York: Atlantic Monthly Press.

Bunce, Harold L., Debbie Gruenstein, Christopher Herbert, and Randall M. Scheessele. 2001. *Subprime Foreclosures: The Smoking Gun of Predatory Lending?* Washington, DC: U.S. Department of Housing and Urban Development.

Calem, Paul S., Kevin Gillen, and Susan M. Wachter. 2004. "The Neighborhood Distribution of Subprime Mortgage Lending." *Journal of Real Estate Finance and Economics* 29 (4): 293–310.

Calloway, Cab, and Bryant Rollins. 1976. *Of Minnie the Moocher and Me.* New York: Thomas Y. Crowell.

Calloway, Josephine S. 1917. "The Negro Migration." *The Southern Workman* 46:410–411.

Campbell, Angus, and Howard Schuman. 1968. *Racial Attitudes in Fifteen American Cities: Supplement Studies for the National Advisory Commission on Civil Disorders.* Washington, DC: U.S. Government Printing Office.

Cantey, Inez V. 1927. "Jesse Binga Illustrates." *The Crisis: A Record of the Darker Races* 34 (10): 329.

Caroll, Raymond G. 1920. "Negro City in New York." *The Southern Workman* 49:433–435.

Cassell, James. 1973. "Army of Rats Take Over North Philadelphia Apartment Bldg." *Philadelphia Tribune*, September 1.

Cayton, Horace R. 1943. "Migration West." *Pittsburgh Courier*, August 21.

Center on Urban Poverty and Community Development. 2016. "Northeast Ohio Community and Neighborhood Data for Organizing." Case Western Reserve University. http://povertycenter.case.edu/data-systems/neo-cando/.

Chandler, D. L. 2015. "Atlanta, Raleigh, & D.C. Top Cities for Black Economic Success." *NewsOne*, January 20. http://newsone.com/3082983/best-cities-for-blacks-economically/.

Chicago Commission on Race Relations. 1922. *The Negro in Chicago: A Study of Race Relations and a Race Riot.* Chicago: University of Chicago Press.

Child Trends. 2015. *Births to Unmarried Women: Indicators on Children and Youth.* Bethesda, MD: Child Trends. https://www.childtrends.org/?indicators=births-to-unmarried-women.

City of Cleveland. 2011. "Cleveland Neighborhood Fact Sheet." http://planning.city.cleveland.oh.us/census/factsheets/spa34.html.

Clark, Kenneth B. 1965. *Dark Ghetto: Dilemmas of Social Power.* Hanover, NH: Wesleyan University Press.

Claytor, Glenn. 1971. "The Urban Cancer." *Chicago Daily Defender*, April 26.

Cleaver, Eldridge. 1969. "Community Imperialism." *The Black Panther*, April 20.

Cleaver, Jim. 1975. "Compton Officials Blast Grand Jury's Report." *Los Angeles Sentinel*, April 10.

Clegg, Claude Andrew. 1997. *An Original Man: The Life and Times of Elijah Muhammad*. New York: St. Martin's Press.

Clemetson, Lynette. 2002. "Pittsburgh's Hill District Undergoing Gentrification." *Baltimore Sun*, September 8.

Colbert, Robert E. 1946. "The Attitude of Negro Residents Toward Recent Migrants in the Pacific Northwest." *Journal of Negro Education* 15 (4): 695–703.

Collier, Aldore. 2002. "Blacks in Los Angeles." *Ebony*, May.

Collins, W. J. 2004. "The Housing Market Impact of State-Level Anti-discrimination Laws, 1960–1970." *Journal of Urban Economics* 55 (3): 534–564.

Collins, W. J., and Robert A. Margo. 2000. "Residential Segregation and Socioeconomic Outcomes: When Did Ghettos Go Bad?" *Economics Letters* 69:239–243.

Commonwealth of Pennsylvania Department of Public Welfare. 1927. *Negro Survey of Pennsylvania*. Harrisburg: Commonwealth of Pennsylvania.

Coplon, Jeff. 2013. "The Tipping of Jefferson Avenue." *New York Magazine*, March 7.

Crockett, Stephen A., Jr. 2012. "The Brixton: It's New, Happening, and Another Example of African American Historical 'Swagger-Jacking.'" *Washington Post*, August 3.

Crossney, Kristen B., and David W. Bartelt. 2005. "The Legacy of the Home Owners' Loan Corporation." *Housing Policy Debate* 16 (3–4): 547–574.

Crowe, Charles. 1906. "Racial Massacre in Atlanta September 22, 1906." *Journal of Negro History* 54 (2): 150–173.

Cullen, Countee. 1925. "Heritage." *Survey Graphic* 53 (11): 674–675.

Cutler, David M., Edward L. Glaeser, and Jacob L. Vigdor. 1999. "The Rise and Decline of the American Ghetto." *Journal of Political Economy* 107 (3): 455–507.

Dastrup, Samuel, Ingrid Gould Ellen, and Anna Jefferson. 2016. "Staying for Opportunity: Gentrification and Public Housing." *Cityscape* 18 (3): 87–108.

Davis, Hugh. 2011. *We Will Be Satisfied with Nothing Less: The African American Struggle for Equal Rights During Reconstruction*. Ithaca, NY: Cornell University Press.

Dawes, Laina. 2015. "What It Means to Be a Black Gentrifier." *Archipelago*, February 23. https://medium.com/the-archipelago/what-it-means-to-be-a-black-gentrifier -f3ef15b2674c.

Delany, Sarah L., A. Elizabeth Delany, and Amy Hill Hearth. 1993. *Having Our Say: The Delany Sisters' First 100 Years*. New York: Kodansha America.

Dent, David J. 1992. "The New Black Suburbs." *New York Times Magazine*, June 12.

Detroit Bureau of Governmental Research. 1926. *The Negro in Detroit*. Detroit: Mayor's Inter-racial Committee.

Devine, Edward T. 1905. Introduction to *The Negro in the Cities of the North*, edited by Edward T. Devine, 1–6. New York: Charity Organization Society.

Dobbie, Will, and Roland G. Fryer Jr. 2015. "The Medium-Term Impacts of High-Achieving Charter Schools." *Journal of Political Economy* 123 (5): 985–1037.

Donaldson, Jeff. [1969] 1997. "The Role We Want for Black Art." In *Modern Black Nationalism from Marcus Garvey to Louis Farrakahn*, edited by William L. Van Deburg, 217–221. New York: New York University Press.

Dorn, Mel. 2011. "Oral Histories for the Desegregation of Girard College." Recording in *Civil Rights in a Northern City: Philadelphia*, edited by Diane Turner. Philadelphia: Temple University. http://northerncity.library.temple.edu/exhibits/show/civil-rights-in-a-northern-cit/collections/desegregation-of-girard-colleg/who--oral-histories-for-the-de.

Douglas, Davison M. 2005. *Jim Crow Moves North: The Battle Over Northern School Desegregation, 1865–1954*. New York: Cambridge University Press.

Douglass, Frederick. 1880. "Southern Questions: The Negro Exodus from the Gulf States." *Journal of Social Science* 11:1–21.

Drake, St. Clair, and Horace R. Cayton. [1945] 1993. *Black Metropolis: A Study of Negro Life in a Northern City*. Chicago: University of Chicago Press.

Du Bois, W. E. B. 1899. "Results of the Investigation." In *The Negro in Business: Report of a Social Study Made Under the Direction of Atlanta University*, edited by W. E. B. Du Bois, 4–46. Atlanta: Atlanta University.

——. 1901. *The Black North in 1901: A Social Study*. New York: Arno Press.

——, ed. 1909. *Efforts for Social Betterment Among Negro Americans*. Atlanta: Atlanta University.

——. 1914a. "Editorial." *The Crisis: A Record of the Darker Races* 7 (3): 133–134.

——. 1914b. "Editorial." *The Crisis: A Record of the Darker Races* 7 (4): 174.

——. 1933. "Along the Color Line: Housing." *The Crisis: A Record of the Darker Races* 40 (11): 257.

——. 1934a. "The Board of Directors on Segregation." *The Crisis: A Record of the Darker Races* 41 (5): 149.

——. 1934b. "Postscript." *The Crisis: A Record of the Darker Races* 41 (2): 52–53.

——. 1934c. "Postscript." *The Crisis: A Record of the Darker Races* 41 (5): 147–148.

——. [1899] 1996. *The Philadelphia Negro*. Reprint. Philadelphia: University of Pennsylvania Press.

Dunbar, Paul Laurence. 1902. *The Sport of the Gods*. New York: Dodd, Mead.

Duncan, Otis Dudley, and Beverly Duncan. 1957. *The Negro Population of Chicago*. Chicago: University of Chicago Press.

Durham, Richard. 1945. "Millionaire Plots Tighter Noose on 'Black Ghetto.'" *Chicago Defender*, February 24.

Dworkin, Julie, and Casey Wittekind. 2010. *A Drop in the Bucket: An Analysis of Resources to Address Home Foreclosure in Chicago*. Chicago: Sweet Home Chicago Coalition.

Edin, Kathryn, and Maria Kefelas. 2005. *Promises I Can Keep: Why Poor Women Put Motherhood Before Marriage*. Berkeley: University of California Press.

Ellen, Ingrid Gould, Keren Horn, and Katherine O'Regan. 2012. "Pathways to Integration: Examining Changes in the Prevalence of Racially Integrated Neighborhoods." *Cityscape* 14 (3): 33–53.

Ellen, Ingrid Gould, and Katherine O'Regan. 2011. "How Neighborhoods Change: Entry, Exit, and Enhancement." *Regional Science and Urban Economics* 41 (2): 89–97.

Ellis, Eddie. 1965. "A Man Named Jones Builds Theatre School in Harlem." *Chicago Daily Defender*, August 23.

Erskine, Hazel. 1967. "The Polls: Demonstrations and Race Riots." *Public Opinion Quarterly* 41 (4): 655–677.

Escridge, Hattie G. 1899. "The Need of Negro Merchants." In *The Negro in Business: Report of a Social Study Made Under the Direction of Atlanta University*, edited by W. E. B. Dubois, 61. Atlanta: Atlanta University.

Farley, R., and W. H. Frey. 1994. "Changes in the Segregation of Whites from Blacks During the 1980s—Small Steps Toward a More Integrated Society." *American Sociological Review* 59 (1): 23–45.

Farrell, C. R., and B. A. Lee. 2011. "Racial Diversity and Change in Metropolitan Neighborhoods." *Social Science Research* 40 (4): 1108–1123.

Farris, Bessie. 1976. "Saving Ogontz Avenue" (letter to the editor). *Philadelphia Tribune*, August 31.

Fischer, Mary J., and Douglas S. Massey. 2000. "Segregation and Ethnic Enterprise in US Metropolitan Areas." *Social Problems* 47 (3): 408–424.

Fligstein, N. 1983. "The Transformation of Southern Agriculture and the Migration of Blacks and Whites, 1930–1940." *International Migration Review* 17 (2): 268–290.

Forman, James, Jr. 2017. *Locking Up Our Own: Crime and Punishment in Black America*. New York: Farrar, Straus and Giroux.

Fortner, Michael Javen. 2015. *Black Silent Majority: The Rockefeller Drug Laws and the Politics of Punishment*. Cambridge, MA: Harvard University Press.

Frazier, E. Franklin. 1929. "Chicago: A Cross-Section of Negro Life." *Opportunity* 7 (3): 70–73.

Freedman, Samuel G. 1994. *Upon this Rock: The Miracles of a Black Church*. New York: Harper Perennial.

Freeman, Lance. 2005. "Displacement or Succession? Residential Mobility in Gentrifying Neighborhoods." *Urban Affairs Review* 40 (4): 463–491.

——. 2006a. "Comment on Kirk McClure's 'The Low-Income Housing Tax Credit Program Goes Mainstream and Moves to the Suburbs.'" *Housing Policy Debate* 17 (3): 447–459.

——. 2006b. *There Goes the 'Hood: Views of Gentrification from the Ground Up*. Philadelphia: Temple University Press.

——. 2010. "African American Locational Attainment Before the Civil Rights Era." *City & Community* 9 (3): 235–255.

——. 2018. "The Siting Dilemma." In *Facing Segregation: Housing Policy Solutions for a Stronger Society*, edited by Molly Metzger and Henry S. Webber, 35–57. New York: Oxford University Press.

Freeman, Lance, and Frank Braconi. 2004. "Gentrification and Displacement—New York City in the 1990s." *Journal of the American Planning Association* 70 (1): 39–52.

Freeman, Lance, and Tiancheng Cai. 2015. "White Entry Into Black Neighborhoods: Advent of a New Era?" *Annals of the American Academy of Political and Social Science* 660 (1): 302–318.

Freeman, Lance, Adele Cassola, and Tiancheng Cai. 2015. "Displacement and Gentrification in England and Wales: A Quasi-experimental approach." *Urban Studies* 53 (13): 2797–2814.

Frey, William H. 2004. *The New Great Migration: Black Americans Return to the South, 1965–2000*. Living Cities Census series. Washington, DC: Brookings Institution.

Gabreyes, Rachel. 2015. "Grappling with Gentrification as a Middle Class Black American." *Huffpost Black Voices*, May 26. http://www.huffingtonpost.com/2015/01/20/black-gentrification_n_6502104.html.

Galster, G. C., and S. P. Killen. 1995. "The Geography of Metropolitan Opportunity—a Reconnaissance and Conceptual-Framework." *Housing Policy Debate* 6 (1): 7–43.

Gans, Herbert J. 1962. *Urban Villagers: Group and Class in the Life of Italian-Americans.* New York: Free Press.

Gatewood, Willard B., Jr. 1990. *Aristocrats of Color: The Black Elite, 1880–1920.* Bloomington: Indiana University Press.

Gay, Eustace. 1938. "Will Not Use Funds to End City's Slums: Negroes Will Feel Program Least Projects Will Allow Slum Areas to Remain in Present State." *Philadelphia Tribune*, January 13.

Gelman, Erik S. 2016. *Death Blow to Jim Crow: The National Negro Congress and the Rise of Militant Civil Rights.* Chapel Hill: University of North Carolina Press.

General, Lloyd. 1964. "Woman, 72, Slain in Project." *Chicago Defender*, January 6.

Gibson, Bob. 1968. *From Ghetto to Glory: The Story of Bob Gibson.* Englewood Cliffs, NJ: Prentice-Hall.

Gibson, Campbell, and Kay Jung. 2005. *Historical Census Statistics on Population Totals by Race, 1790 to 1990, and by Hispanic Origin, 1970 to 1990, for Large Cities and Other Urban Places in the United States.* Working Paper no. 76. Washington, DC: Population Division, U.S. Census Bureau.

Glaeser, Edward, and Jacob Vigdor. 2012. *The End of the Segregated Century: Racial Separation in America's Neighborhoods, 1890–2010.* New York: Manhattan Institute.

Glass, Ruth. 1964. *London: Aspects of Change.* London: MacGibbon & Kee.

Godsil, Rachel D. 2013. " The Gentrification Trigger: Autonomy, Mobility, and Affirmatively Furthering Fair Housing." *Brooklyn Law Review* 78 (2): 319–338.

Goffman, Alice. 2014. *On the Run: Fugitive Life in an American City.* Chicago: University of Chicago Press.

Goffe, Leslie. 2014. "The Harlem Gentrification: From Black to White." *The New African*, June 25.

Goldstein, Brian D. 2017. *The Roots of Urban Renaissance: Gentrification and the Struggle Over Harlem.* Cambridge, MA: Harvard University Press.

Goodman, Ellen. 1969. "The New Brownstone Breed." *Boston Globe*, April 16.

Gosnell, Harold F. 1925. *Negro Politicians: The Rise of Negro Politics in Chicago.* Chicago: University of Chicago Press.

Graham, Lawrence Otis. 1999. *Our Kind of People: Inside America's Black Upper Class.* New York: Harper Collins.

Grand Master Flash and the Furious Five. 1979. *Superrappin.* Enjoy Records.

Gregory, James N. 2005. *The Southern Diaspora.* Chapel Hill: University of North Carolina Press.

Grier, Eunice, and George Grier. 1958. *In Search of Housing: A Study of Experiences of Negro Professional and Technical Personnel in New York State.* New York: New York State Commission Against Discrimination.

Grigsby, William G., Michael A. Stegman, Louis Rosenburg, and James Taylor. 1973. "Summary of Housing and Poverty." In *Abandoned Housing Research: A Compendium*, 41–46. Washington, DC: U.S. Department of Housing and Urban Development.

Grisom, John H. 1845. *The Sanitary Condition of the Laboring Population.* New York: Harper Brothers.

Gross, Allie. 2015. "Freddie Gray Went to an 'Apartheid School.'" *Mother Jones*, April 29.

Grossman, James R. 1989. *Land of Hope: Chicago, Black Southerners, and the Great Migration*. Chicago: University of Chicago Press.

Guilmant, Pierre. 1970. "Fear Pervades Black Ghettos." *Chicago Daily Defender*, March 3.

Hall, Chatwood. 1943. "Kiev, City of Jim Crow During Nazi Rule." *Atlanta Daily World*, November 14.

Harlem Children's Zone. 2017. "Harem Children's Zone: Our Programs." http://hcz.org /our-programs/.

Harris, Ron. 1979. Death Almost Destroys Family. *Ebony*, August.

Hartt, Rollin Lynde. 1921. "I'd Like to Show You Harlem." *The Independent* 105 (3): 334–338.

Hayes, R. Drummond. 1974. "Many Blacks Returning 'Home' to South in a Reverse Migration." *New York Times*, June 17.

Haynes, George E. 1924. "Negro Migration: Its Effect on Family and Community Life in the North." *Opportunity* 2 (22): 303–305.

Headley, Madge. 1928a. "Equipment and Condition of Houses." In *Negro Problems in Cities*, edited by T. J. Woofter Jr., 115–120. Garden City, NY: Doubleday, Foran.

——. 1928b. "Home Buying." In *Negro Problems in Cities*, edited by T. J. Woofter Jr., 136–151. Garden City, NY: Doubleday, Doran.

Height, Dorothy. 1966. "South Ward Newark Changing; Whites Move Out, Negroes Move In: But the Power Remains the Same." *New York Amsterdam News*, July 2.

Heinicke, Craig W. 2006. "Demographic Patterns of the Great Migration (1940–1970)." In *Encyclopedia of the Great Black Migration*, edited by Steven A. Reich, 239–243. Westport, CT: Greenwood Press.

Helper, Rose. 1969. *Racial Policies and Practices of Real Estate Brokers*. Minneapolis: University of Minnesota Press.

Herbers, John. 1970. "Paradox of Big Cities: Houses Are Abandoned Despite Shortage." *New York Times*, February 9.

Herman, Max Arthur. 2013. *Summer of Rage: An Oral History of the 1967 Newark and Detroit Riots*. New York: Peter Lang.

Hillier, Amy. 2003. "Redlining and the Homeowners' Loan Corporation." *Journal of Urban History* 29 (4): 394–420.

Himes, Chester. 1945. *If He Hollers Let Him Go*. New York: Doubleday.

——. 2000. *The Collected Works of Chester Himes*. Edited by Leslie Himes. New York: Thunder Mouth Press.

Hirsch, Arnold R. 1983. *Making the Second Ghetto: Race and Housing in Chicago, 1940–1960*. London: Cambridge University Press.

Hirsch, James S. 2010. *Willie Mays: The Life, the Legend*. New York: Scribner.

Hoffman, Alexander von. 2003. *House by House, Block by Block: The Rebirth of America's Urban Neighborhoods*. Oxford: Oxford University Press.

Hope, John. 1899. "The Meaning of Business." In *The Negro in Business: Report of a Social Study Made Under the Direction of Atlanta University*, edited by W. E. B. Du Bois, 56–60. Atlanta: Atlanta University.

Hoyt, Homer. 1939. *The Structure and Growth of Residential Neighborhoods in American Cities*. Edited by Federal Housing Administration. Washington, DC: U.S. Government Printing Office.

Hughes, Langston. 2001. "Hope for Harlem." In *The Collected Works of Langston Hughes*, edited by Arnold Rampersad, 207. Columbia: University of Missouri Press.

Humphreys, Keith. 2016. "There's Been a Big Decline in the Black Incarceration Rate, and Almost Nobody's Paying Attention." *Washington Post*, February 10.

Hunter, Kim D. 1997. "Detroiters Remember the 1967 Rebellion." Solidarity, n.d. http://www.solidarity-us.org/node/824.

Hwang, Jackelyn, Michael Hankinson, and Kreg Steven Brown. 2015. "Racial and Spatial Targeting: Segregation and Subprime Lending Within and Across Metropolitan Areas." *Social Forces* 93 (3): 1081–1108.

Hwang, Jackelyn, and Robert J. Sampson. 2014. "Divergent Pathways of Gentrification: Racial Inequality and the Social Order of Renewal in Chicago Neighborhoods." *American Sociological Review* 79 (4): 726–751.

Hyra, Derek. 2017. *Race, Class, and Politics in the Cappuccino City.* Chicago: University of Chicago Press.

Hyra, Derek, and Jacob S. Rugh. 2016. "The US Great Recession: Exploring Its Association with Black Neighborhood Rise, Decline, and Recovery." *Urban Geography* 37 (5): 700–726.

Innis, Roy. [1969] 1997. "Separatist Economics: A New Social Contract." In *Modern Black Nationalism from Marcus Garvey to Louis Farrakahn*, edited by William L. Van Deburg, 176–181. New York: New York University Press.

Innis, Roy, and Victor Solomon. 1967. "Harlem Must Control Its Schools." *New Generation*, Fall.

Inside the Battle for Fair Housing in 1960s Chicago. 2014. Atlantic Documentaries.

Jackson, Kenneth T. 1985. *Crabgrass Frontier: The Suburbanization of the United States.* Oxford: Oxford University Press.

Jackson, Mahalia, and Evan M. Wylie. 1966. *Movin' on Up.* New York: Hawthorn Books.

Jargowsky, P. A. 1994. "Ghetto Poverty Among Blacks in the 1980s." *Journal of Policy Analysis and Management* 13 (2): 288–310.

Jarrett, Vernon. 1952. "Slum Clearance—Is It Negro Clearance." *New York Amsterdam News*, October 4.

Jenkins, Morgan. 2015. "I'm a Black Gentrifier in Harlem—and It's Not a Good Feeling." *Guardian*, August 25.

John F. Kraft, Inc. 1966a. *A Report of Attitudes of Negroes in Various Cities: Prepared for the Senate Subcommittee on Executive Reorganization.* New York: John F. Kraft, Inc.

——. 1966b. *The Report of a Survey of Attitudes of Harlem Residents Toward Housing, Rehabilitation, and Urban Renewal.* New York: John F. Kraft, Inc.

Johnnson, Thomas A. 1967. "Buffalo Negroes Blame the Police." *New York Times*, July 1.

Johnson, Charles S. 1923. "Urbanization and Negro Mortality." *Opportunity* 1 (11): 323.

——. 1924. "Segregation and Votes." *Opportunity* 2 (24): 354.

——. 1928. "A Negro Congressman." *Opportunity* 7 (122): 359.

——. 1930. "A Negro Bank Closes Its Doors." *Opportunity* 8 (9): 264.

Johnson, Charles S., Herman H. Long, and Grace Jones. 1944. *The Negro War Worker in San Francisco.* San Francisco: YWCA.

Johnson, John H. 1979. "Publisher's Statement." *Ebony*, August.

——. 2004. "John H. Johnson Interview." Recorded interview. History Makers, n.d. http://www.thehistorymakers.org/biography/john-h-johnson-40

Johnson, Ronald M. 1984. "From Romantic Suburb to Racial Enclave: LeDroit Park, Washington, D.C., 1880–1920." *Phylon* 45 (4): 264–270.

Johnson, Thomas A. 1967. "Violence Called Only Language." *New York Times*, June 30.

Jones, Paul L. 1950. "Pittsburgh's Housing for Negroes." *Pittsburgh Courier*, April 29.

Joseph, Peniel E. 2006. *Waiting 'til the Midnight Hour: A Narrative History of Black Power in America*. New York: Holt Paperback.

Justice Mapping Center. 2010. "National Justice Atlas of Sentencing and Corrections." https://csgjusticecenter.org/nrrc/publications/national-justice-atlas-of-sentencing-and-corrections-2/.

Kain, J. F. 1968. "Housing Segregation, Negro Employment, and Metropolitan Decentralization." *Quarterly Journal of Economics* 82 (2): 175–197.

Kalt, Brian C. 2003. "The Exclusion of Felons from Jury Service." *American University Law Review* 53 (1): 65–189.

Kan, Kamhon. 1999. "Expected and Unexpected Residential Mobility." *Journal of Urban Economics* 45 (1): 72–96.

Katzman, David M. 1973. *Before the Ghetto: Black Detroit in the Nineteenth Century.* Urbana: University of Illinois Press.

Keber, George T., Jr. 1965. "Cutting a Vital Need." *New York Amsterdam News*, January 23.

Kelly, Kimberly, John Sullivan, and Steven Rich. 2015. "Broken by the Bubble: In the Fairwood Subdivision, Dreams of Black Wealth Were Dashed by the Housing Crisis." *Washington Post*, January 25.

Kim, Sukkoo. 1998. "Economic Integration and Convergence: U.S. Regions, 1840–1987." *Journal of Economic History* 58 (3): 659–683.

Kopf, Dan. 2016. "Quantifying the Changing Face of San Francisco." Priceonomics, May 5. https://priceonomics.com/quantifying-the-changing-face-of-san-francisco/.

Kotlowitz, Alex. 1992. *There Are No Children Here: The Story of Two Boys Growing Up in the Other America*. New York: Doubleday.

Kotlowski, Dean. 1998. "Black Power–Nixon Style: The Nixon Administration and Minority Business Enterprise." *Business History Review* 72 (3): 409–445.

Krysan, M., M. P. Couper, R. Farley, and T. A. Forman. 2009. "Does Race Matter in Neighborhood Preferences? Results from a Video Experiment." *American Journal of Sociology* 115 (2): 527–559.

Kucheva, Yana, and Richard Sander. 2014. "The Misunderstood Consequences of *Shelley v. Kraemer*." *Social Science Research* 48:212–233.

Kusmer, Kenneth L. 1978. *A Ghetto Takes Shape: Black Cleveland, 1870–1930*. Urbana: University of Illinois Press.

Lacoe, Johanna, and Ingrid Gould Ellen. 2015. "Mortgage Foreclosures and the Changing Mix of Crime in Micro-neighborhoods." *Journal of Research in Crime and Delinquency* 52 (5): 717–746.

Lacy, Karyn. 2007. *Blue-Chip Black: Race, Class, and Status in the New Black Middle Class*. Berkeley: University of California Press.

Lane, Roger. 1986. *Roots of Violence in Black Philadelphia: 1860–1900*. Cambridge, MA: Harvard University Press.

Latzer, Barry. 2017. *The Rise and Fall of Violent Crime in America*. New York: Encounter Books.

Lawrence, Michael A. 1985. "Gentrification: Is It a New Form of Oppression or an Opportunity?" *The Crisis: A Record of the Darker Races* 92 (9): 20–45.

Lee, Barrett A., and Peter B. Wood. 1991. "Is Neighborhood Racial Succession Place-Specific?" *Demography* 28 (1): 21–40.

Lee, Felicia. 1994. "On a Harlem Block, Hope Is Swallowed by Decay." *New York Times*, September 8.

Lee, Kwan Ok. 2014. "Why Do Renters Stay in or Leave Certain Neighborhoods? The Role of Neighborhood Characteristics, Housing Tenure Transitions, and Race." *Journal of Regional Science* 54 (5): 755–787.

Lemann, Nicholas. 1994. "The Myth of Community Development." *New York Times Magazine*, January 9.

Lesthaeghe, R. 2010. "The Unfolding Story of the Second Demographic Transition." *Population and Development Review* 36 (2): 211–2551.

Levin, Sam. 2015. "Racial Profiling Via Nextdoor.com." *East Bay Express*, October 7.

Lewis, Cary B. 1914. "Cornerstone Laying of 8th Regiment Armory Event in Race History." *Chicago Defender*, October 17.

Lewis, David Levering. 1979. *When Harlem Was in Vogue*. New York: Oxford University Press.

Lincoln, C. Eric. 1994. *The Black Muslims in America*. Trenton, NJ: Africa World Press.

Lindsay, Arthur G. 1929. "The Negro in Banking." *Journal of Negro History* 14 (2): 156–201.

Liou, Y. T., and R. C. Stroh. 1998. "Community Development Intermediary Systems in the United States: Origins, Evolution, and Functions." *Housing Policy Debate* 9 (3): 575–594.

Logan, John R., Zengwang Xu, and Brian Stults. 2012. "Interpolating U.S. Decennial Census Tract Data from as Early as 1970 to 2010: A Longitudinal Tract Database." *Professional Geographer* 66 (3): 412–20.

——. 2015. *Longitudinal Tract Database*. Providence, RI: Spatial Structures in the Social Sciences, Brown University. https://s4.ad.brown.edu/projects/diversity/researcher/bridging.htm.

Logan, John R., and Charles Zhang. 2010. "Global Neighborhoods: New Pathways to Diversity and Separation." *American Journal of Sociology* 115 (4): 1069–1109.

Logan, John R., Weiwei Zhang, Richard Turner, and Allison Shertzer. 2015. "Creating the Black Ghetto: Black Residential Patterns Before and During the Great Migration." *Annals of the American Academy of Political and Social Science* 660 (July): 18–35.

Long, L. H. 1975. "Untested Hypothesis—Effect of Size of Public Assistance Benefits on Migration—Reply." *American Sociological Review* 40 (6): 847–849.

Long, L. H., and L. R. Heltman. 1975. "Migration and Income Differences Between Black and White Men in North." *American Journal of Sociology* 80 (6): 1391–1409.

Lyons, Ken. 1945. "Workers Quit South for NY Seeking Jobs." *New York Amsterdam News*, September 15.

Madison, Arthur A. 1951. "Says There's Treachery in City Housing Plans" (letter to the editor). *New York Amsterdam News*, May 12.

Malcolm X. 1963a. "Message to the Grassroots." Speech presented at the Northern Negro Grass Roots Leadership Conference, November 10, Detroit. http://teachingamericanhistory.org/library/document/message-to-grassroots/.

——. 1963b. "Racial Separation." Speech presented at the University of California, Berkeley, October 11. http://www.blackpast.org/1963-malcolm-x-racial-separation.

Mallory, Milton J. 1956. "Sidewalk Interviews." *New York Amsterdam News*, March 24.

Manson, Steven, Jonathan Schroeder, David Van Riper, and Steven Ruggles. 2017. *IPUMS National Historical Geographic Information System: Version 12.0*. Database. Minneapolis: University of Minnesota.

Marcuse, Peter. 1997. "The Enclave, the Citadel, and the Ghetto." *Urban Affairs Review* 33 (2): 228–264.

Mark, Mary Louise. 1928. *Negroes in Columbus*. Columbus: Ohio State University Press.

Martin, Isaac William, and Kevin Beck. 2016. "Gentrification, Property Tax Limitation, and Displacement." *Urban Affairs Review* 54 (1): 33–73.

Martin, Louis. 1974. "Claim Blacks Going Back 'Home.'" *Chicago Defender*, June 22.

Marwick, Arthur. 1998. *The Sixties: Cultural Revolution in Britain, France, Italy, and the United States*. Oxford: Oxford University Press.

Massey, Douglas S., Len Albright, Rebecca Casciano, Elizabeth Derickson, and David N. Kinsey. 2013. *Climbing Mount Laurel: The Struggle for Affordable Housing and Social Mobility in an American Suburb*. Princeton, NJ: Princeton University Press.

Massey, Douglas S., and Nancy A. Denton. 1993. *American Apartheid*. Cambridge, MA: Harvard University Press.

Massey, Douglass S., and Garvey Lundy. 2001. "Use of Black English and Racial Discrimination in Urban Housing Markets." *Urban Affairs Review* 36 (4): 452–469.

Mauer, Marc. 2006. *Race to Incarcerate*. New York: New Press.

Maurer, Daniel. 2014. "When Amiri Baraka Was LeRoi Jones, 'King of the Lower East Side.'" Bedford+Bowery, January 10. http://bedfordandbowery.com/2014/01/when-amiri-baraka-was-leroi-jones-king-of-the-lower-east-side/.

McCoy, Terrence. 2015. "Freddie Gray's Life a Study on the Effects of Lead Paint on Poor Blacks." *Washington Post*, April 29.

McKee-Ryan, F. M., Z. L. Song, C. R. Wanberg, and A. J. Kinicki. 2005. "Psychological and Physical Well-Being During Unemployment: A Meta-analytic Study." *Journal of Applied Psychology* 90 (1): 53–76.

McKinnish, T., R. Walsh, and T. K. White. 2010. "Who Gentrifies Low-Income Neighborhoods?" *Journal of Urban Economics* 67 (2): 180–193.

McLanahan, Sara, and Gary Sandefur. 1994. *Growing Up with a Single Parent: What Hurts, What Helps*. Cambridge, MA: Harvard University Press.

Medoff, Peter and Holly Sklar. 1999. *Streets of Hope: The Fall and Rise of an Urban Neighborhood*. Boston: South End Press.

Middlesex Real Estate Association. 1887. "Middlesex Real Estate Association Composed of Colored Men." *New York Freeman*, July 9.

Montgomery, George. 1973. "King Crime." *Chicago Daily Defender*, February 12.

Montgomery, Marvin. 2002. "Invasion of the 'Hood Snatchers': How Black Neighborhoods Are Being Gentrified." *Smooth*, January.

Moore, Joseph Thomas. 2011. *Larry Doby: The Struggle of the American League's First Black Player*. Mineola, NY: Dover.

Moore, Kesha S. 2009. "Gentrification in Black Face? The Return of the Black Middle Class to Urban Neighborhoods." *Urban Geography* 30 (2): 118–142.

Muhammad, Khalil. 2010. *The Condemnation of Blackness: Race, Crime, and the Making of Modern Urban America*. Cambridge, MA: Harvard University Press.

Murchison, John P. 1935. "The Negro and Low-Rent Housing." *The Crisis: A Record of the Darker Races* 42 (7): 199–200, 210.

Myrdal, Gunnar. 1944. *An American Dilemma: The Negro Problem and Modern Democracy*. New York: Harper & Brothers.

National Advisory Commission on Civil Disorders. 1968. *Report of the National Advisory Commission on Civil Disorders*. New York: National Advisory Commission on Civil Disorders.

National Negro Congress. 1936. *The Official Proceedings of the National Negro Congress*. Chicago: National Negro Congress.

National Urban League. 1973. "Summary of the National Survey of Housing Abandonment." In *Abandoned Housing Research: A Compendium*, edited by U.S. Department of Housing and Urban Development, 39–40. Washington DC: U.S. Department of Housing and Urban Development.

National Visionary Leadership Project. 2004. *John H. Johnson: The Importance of Black Media*. Alexandria, VA: National Visionary Leadership Project.

Neal, Larry. 1968a. "The Black Arts Movement." *Drama Review* 12 (4): 1–2.

——. 1968b. "The Black Arts Movement." *Drama Review* 12 (4): 28–39.

Neckerman, K. M., G. S. Lovasi, S. Davies, M. Purciel, J. Quinn, E. Feder, N. Raghunath, B. Wasserman, and A. Rundle. 2009. "Disparities in Urban Neighborhood Conditions: Evidence from GIS Measures and Field Observation in New York City." *Journal of Public Health Policy* 30:S264–S285.

Nesbitt, George B. 1949a. "Break Up the Black Ghetto?" *The Crisis: A Record of the Darker Races* 56 (2): 48–52.

——. 1949b. "Relocating Negroes from Slum Clearance Sites." *Land Economics* 25 (3): 275–288.

Neuman,William and Samantha Schmidt. 2016. "After Congressional Primary, Harlem's Reign as a Power Base May Be Over." *New York Times*, June 29.

New York Association for Improving the Condition of the Poor. 1856. *Thirteenth Annual Report*. New York: New York Association for Improving the Condition of the Poor.

Newton, Huey P., and Bobby Seale. 1966. *Ten Point Program*. Oakland, CA: Black Panther Party for Self-Defense.

Northridge, M. E., and Lance Freeman. 2011. "Urban Planning and Health Equity." *Journal of Urban Health: Bulletin of the New York Academy of Medicine* 88 (3): 582–597.

Ohio History Connection. 2016. "John P. Green." http://www.ohiohistorycentral.org/w /John_P._Green.

OhNeeksTV. 2015. *A Short Documentary on Gentrification*. Online video clip, YouTube, posted December 18. https://www.bing.com/videos/search?q=OhNeeksTV%2c+A+ Short+Documentary+on+Gentrification&view=detail&mid=EB3CEC7B6A4E533 F589FEB3CEC7B6A4E533F589F&FORM=VIRE.

Osofsky, Gilbert. 1971. *Harlem: The Making of a Ghetto*. 2nd ed. New York: Harper Torchbooks.

Osthaus, Carl R. 1973. "The Rise and Fall of Jesse Binga, Black Financier." *Journal of Negro History* 58 (1): 39–60.

Ovington, Mary. 1911. *Half a Man: The Status of the Negro in New York*. New York: Longmans, Green.

Owens, Michael Leo. 2007. *God and Government in the Ghetto: The Politics of Church–State Collaboration in Black America*. Chicago: University of Chicago Press.

Painter, Neil Irvin. 1976. *Exodusters: Black Migration to Kansas After Reconstruction*. New York: Norton.

Parker, Karen F., and Scott R. Maggard. 2009. "Making a Difference: The Impact of Traditional Male Role Models on Drug Sale Activity and Violence Involving Black Urban Youth." *Journal of Drug Issues* 39 (3): 715–739.

Parker, Karen F., and Amy Reckdenwald. 2008. "Concentrated Disadvantage, Traditional Male Role Models, and African-American Juvenile Violence." *Criminology* 46 (3): 711–735.

Pattillo, Mary. 1999. *Black Picket Fences: Privilege and Peril Among the Black Middle Class*. Chicago: University of Chicago Press.

——. 2007. *Black on the Block: The Politics of Race and Class in the City*. Chicago: University of Chicago Press.

Paul, Mark, William Darity Jr., and Darrick Hamilton. 2017. "Why We Need a Federal Job Guarantee." *Jacobin*, February 4.

Payton, Seth B., Thomas D. Stucky, and John R. Ottensmann. 2015. "The Spatial Extent of the Effect of Foreclosures on Crime." *Social Science Research* 49:288–298.

Petry, Ann. 1946. *The Street*. Boston: Mariner Books.

Pew Center on the States. 2009. *One in 31: The Long Reach of American Corrections*. Washington, DC: Pew Center on the States.

Plunz, Richard. 1990. *A History of Housing in New York City*. New York: Columbia University Press.

Poger [*sic*]. 2016. "Moving to Columbus, Tell Me the Differences Between South, East, West, Suburbs?" Westerville, Apartment Complexes, Renting. http://www.city-data .com/forum/columbus/2697064-moving-columbus-tell-me-differences-between .html.

Poindexter, Fred. 1955. "Power in Ghettos" (letter to the editor). *Chicago Defender*, November 26.

Powell, Michael. 2009. "Suit Accuses Wells Fargo of Steering Blacks to Subprime Mortgages in Baltimore." *New York Times*, June 6.

President's Conference on Home Building and Home Ownership. 1931. *Negro Housing: Report of the Committee on Negro Housing*. Washington, DC: President's Conference on Home Building and Home Ownership.

Prince, Sabiyha. 2014. *African Americans and Gentrification in Washington, D.C.* Surrey, UK: Ashgate.

Pritchett, Wendell E. 2002a. *Brownsville Brooklyn: Blacks, Jews, and the Changing Face of the Ghetto*. Chicago: University of Chicago Press.

——. 2002b. *The Romance of Home: The Fair Housing Movement in the 1950s*. Philadelphia: University of Pennsylvania Law School.

Rampersad, Arnold. 1997. *Jackie Robinson: A Biography*. New York: Knopf.

Reed, Christopher Robert. 2005. *Black Chicago's First Century*. Columbia: University of Missouri Press.

——. 2011. *The Rise of Chicago's Black Metropolis, 1920–1929*. Urbana: University of Illinois Press.

Reich, Steven A. 2009. "The Great Migration and the Literary Imagination." *Journal of the Historical Society* 9 (March): 87–128.

Reynolds, Barbara. 2012. "Minorities Fall Victim to Predatory Lenders." *Washington Post*, July 16.

Richardson, William Jamal, Lori Glantz, and Robert M. Adelman. 2014. "'Ain't Nothin' Here in Buffalo': Residents' Perceptions About Living in a Racially Isolated, High-Poverty Neighborhood." *Journal of Children and Poverty* 20 (2): 73–90.

Ricketts, Erol R., and Isabel V. Sawhill. 1988. "Defining and Measuring the Underclass." *Journal of Policy Analysis and Management* 7 (2): 316–325.

Riis, Jacob A. [1890] 1971. *How the Other Half Lives: Studies Among the Tenements of New York*. New York: Dover.

Rinder, Irwin D. 1955. *The Housing of Negroes in Milwaukee: 1955*. Milwaukee: Intercollegiate Council on Intergroup Relations.

Risen, Clay. 2008. "Legacies of the Riot." *Washington Post*, April 4.

Rob Paral and Associates. 2015. *Chicago Community Area Data*. Chicago: Rob Paral and Associates.

Roberts, Sam. 2006. "Black Incomes Surpass Whites in Queens." *New York Times*, October 1.

Robeson, Paul, Jr. 2001. *The Undiscovered Paul Robeson*. New York: Wiley.

Robinson, Bill. 1970. "Black Vote Can End Black Crime." *New Pittsburgh Courier*, April 4.

Rohe, William M. 2009. "From Local to Global: One Hundred Years of Neighborhood Planning." *Journal of the American Planning Association* 75 (2): 209–211.

Roof, W. C., T. L. Vanvaley, and D. Spain. 1976. "Residential Segregation in Southern Cities—1970." *Social Forces* 55 (1): 59–71.

Roosevelt, Franklin D. 1937. Inaugural Address, January 20. American Presidency Project. http://www.presidency.ucsb.edu/ws/index.php?pid=15349.

Rosen, Louis. 1999. *The Southside: The Racial Transformation of an American Neighborhood*. New York: Ivan R. Dee.

Roster, Edgar. 1936. "New Deal Ignored Negro Needs." *Philadelphia Tribune*, October 22.

Roth, Randal. 2009. *American Homicide*. Cambridge, MA: Belknap Press of Harvard University Press.

Rubinowitz, Leonard S., and James E. Rosenbaum. 2002. *Crossing the Class and Color Lines: From Public Housing to White Suburbia*. Chicago: University of Chicago Press.

Ruggles, Steven J., Trent Alexander, Katie Genadek, Ronald Goeken, Matthew B. Schroeder, and Matthew Sobek. 2010. *Integrated Public Use Microdata Series: Version 5.0*. Machine-readable database. Minneapolis: University of Minnesota.

Sacks, Marcy S. 2006. *Before Harlem: The Black Experience in New York City Before World War I*. Philadelphia: University of Pennsylvania Press.

Saegert, Susan. 1989. "Unlikely Leaders, Extreme Circumstances: Older Black Women Building Community Households." *American Journal of Community Psychology* 17 (3): 295–316.

Sampson, Robert J. 2012. *Great American City: Chicago and the Enduring Neighborhood Effect*. Chicago: University of Chicago Press.

Sampson, Robert J., and Dawn Jeglum Bartusch. 1998. "Legal Cynicism and (Subcultural?) Tolerance of Deviance: The Neighborhood Context of Racial Differences." *Law & Society Review* 32 (4): 777–804.

Sampson, Robert J., and Charles Loeffler. 2010. "Punishment's Place: The Local Concentration of Mass Incarceration." *Daedalus* 139 (3): 20–31.

Sampson, Robert J., Jeffrey D. Morenoff, and Thomas Gannon-Rowley. 2002. "Assessing Neighborhood Effects: Social Processes and New Directions in Research." *Annual Review of Sociology* 28:443–78.

Sampson, Robert J., Stephen W. Raudenbush, and Felton Earls. 1997. "Neighborhoods and Violent Crime: A Multilevel Study of Collective Efficacy." *Science* 77 (August): 918–925.

Savage, Charles. 2012. "Wells Fargo Will Settle Mortgage Bias Charges." *New York Times*, July 13.

Schaffer, Richard, and Neil Smith. 1986. "The Gentrification of Harlem?" *Annals of the Association of American Geographers* 76 (3): 347–365.

Schuyler, George S. 1930. "Views and Reviews." *Pittsburgh Courier*, June 28.

Schwartz, Joel. 1986. "The Consolidated Tenants League of Harlem: Black Self Help vs. White, Liberal Intervention in Ghetto Housing, 1934–1944." *Afro-Americans in New York Life and History* 10 (1): 31–52.

Schwulst, Earl B. 1956. "A Banker Relates Experience in Financing Nonwhite Housing." *Journal of Housing* 13 (April): 128–129.

Scott, Emmett J. 1919a. "Letters of Negro Migrants of 1916–1918." *Journal of Negro History* 4 (3): 290–340.

——. 1919b. "More Letters of Negro Migrants of 1916–1918." *Journal of Negro History* 4 (4): 412–465.

——. 1920. *Negro Migration During the War.* New York: Oxford University Press.

Scott, James C. 1977. *The Moral Economy of the Peasant.* New Haven, CT: Yale University Press.

Sears, David O., and T. M. Tomlinson. 1968. "Riot Ideology in Los Angeles: A Study of Negro Attitudes." *Social Science Quarterly* 49 (3): 485–503.

Sentencing Project. 2015. "Trends in U.S. Corrections." December. https://www.sentencingproject.org/publications/trends-in-u-s-corrections/.

Sharkey, Patrick. 2013. *Stuck in Place: Urban Neighborhoods and the End of Progress Toward Racial Equality.* Chicago: University of Chicago Press.

Sides, Josh. 2003. *L.A. City Limits: African American Los Angeles from the Great Depression to the Present.* Berkeley: University of California Press.

Simmons, Clarence L. 1937. "Cleveland Committee Charges Jim-Crow in Government Housing Projects." *Pittsburgh Courier*, October 23.

Sitkoff, Harvard. 1978. *A New Deal for Blacks: The Emergence of Civil Rights as a National Issue.* New York: Oxford University Press.

——. 1993. *The Struggle for Black Equality: 1954–1980.* New York: Hill and Wang.

Small, Mario Luis. 2008. "Four Reasons to Abandon the Idea of 'the Ghetto.'" *City & Community* 7 (4): 389–398.

Smethurst, James Edward. 2005. *The Black Arts Movement: Literary Nationalism in the 1960s and 1970s.* Chapel Hill: University of North Carolina Press.

Smith, James P., and Finis R. Welch. 1986. *Closing the Gap: Forty Years of Economic Progress for Blacks.* Santa Monica, CA: RAND Corporation.

Smith, Pamela J. 1977. "Elderly Live in Constant Fear of Being Attacked." *Philadelphia Tribune*, April 19.

Smith, Preston H. 2012. *Racial Democracy and the Black Metropolis.* Minneapolis: University of Minnesota Press.

Snides, Josh. 2003. *L.A. City Limits: African America Los Angles from the Great Depression to the Present*. Berkeley: University of California Press.

Solomon, Victor. 1968. "An Independent Board of Education for Harlem." *Urban Affairs Quarterly* 4 (1): 39–44.

Sorrells, Carl. 1972. Letter to the editor. *Los Angeles Sentinel*, October 19.

Spear, Allan H. 1967. *Black Chicago: The Making of a Negro Ghetto, 1890–1920*. Chicago: University of Chicago Press.

Spielman, S. E., C. A. Golembeski, M. E. Northridge, R. D. Vaughan, R. Swaner, B. Jean-Louis, K. Shoemaker, S. Klihr-Beall, E. Polley, L. F. Cushman, B. Ortiz, V. E. Hutchinson, S. W. Nicholas, T. Marx, R. Hayes, A. Goodman, and E. D. Sclar. 2006. "Interdisciplinary Planning for Healthier Communities—Findings from the Harlem Children's Zone Asthma Initiative." *Journal of the American Planning Association* 72 (1): 100–108.

Spraggs, Venice. 1949. "U.S. Housing Chief Sets Policy: Race No Factor in Home Loans." *Chicago Defender*, April 16.

Sternlieb, George, Robert W. Burchell, James W. Hughes, and Franklin J. James. 1974. "Housing Abandonment in the Urban Core." *Journal of the American Institute of Planners* 40:321–332.

Stewart, Rhonda. 1999. "Living the Dream." *Emerge*, September.

Stierholz, Katrina. 2014. "Manufacturing Is Growing Even When Manufacturing Jobs Are Not." *FRED Blog*, December 18. https://fredblog.stlouisfed.org/2014/12/manufacturing-is-growing-even-when-manufacturing-jobs-are-not/.

Stoecker, Randy. 1997. "The CDC Model of Urban Redevelopment: A Critique and an Alternative." *Journal of Urban Affairs* 19 (1): 1–22.

Stome, Chuck. 1963. "2 Wks. Old Baby in Apt. with No Windows, Heat." *Chicago Defender*, December 17.

Sugrue, Thomas J. 1996. *The Origins of the Urban Crisis*. Princeton, NJ: Princeton University Press.

——. 2008. *Sweet Land of Liberty: The Forgotten Struggle for Civil Rights in the North*. New York: Random House.

Taeuber, Karl E., and Alma F. Taeuber. 1965. *Negroes in Cities: Residential Segregation and Neighborhood Change*. Chicago: Aldine.

Taitt, John. 1925. "The Binga Block: A Visit of Mrs. Booker T. Washington to the Associated Business Club of Chicago, July 10th, 1924." New York Public Library Digital Collections.

Tavernise, Sabrina. 2011. "A Population Changes, Uneasily." *New York Times*, July 17.

Taylor, Monique M. 2002. *Harlem Between Heaven and Hell*. Minneapolis: University of Minnesota Press.

Taylor, Quintard. 1994. *The Forging of a Black Community: Seattle's Central District from 1870 Through the Civil Rights Era*. Seattle: University of Washington Press.

Tinawina. 2015. "Is a White Person Moving to a Majority Black Neighborhood Automatically Gentrification?" *City-Data Forum*, September 6. http://www.city-data.com/forum/baltimore/2441965-white-person-moving-majority-black-neighborhood-2.html#ixzz4hRJ5zH58.

Tolbert, Richard C. 1968. "Needed: A Compatible Ideology." *Negro Digest* 17 (10): 10–11.

Tsai, Alexander C. 2015. "Home Foreclosure, Health, and Mental Health: A Systematic Review of Individual, Aggregate, and Contextual Associations." *PLOS One* 10 (4): 1–21.

Turner, Margery Austin, Stephen L. Ross, George Galster, and John Yinger. 2002. *Discrimination in Metropolitan Housing Markets: National Results from Phase 1 of HDS 2000.* Washington, DC: Urban Institute.

Unger, Craig. 1984. "Can Harlem Be Born Again?" *New York*, December 17.

United Kingdom Board of Trade. 1911. *Cost of Living in American Towns.* London: His Majesty's Stationery Office.

United States Housing and Home Finance Agency. 1963. *Our Nonwhite Population and Its Housing.* Washington, DC: United States Housing and Home Finance Agency.

Urban America. 1969. *One Year Later: An Assessment of the Nation's Response to the Crisis Described by the National Advisory Commission on Civil Disorders.* New York: Urban America and Urban Coalition.

U.S. Census Bureau. 1935. *Negroes in the United States 1920–1932.* Washington, DC: U.S. Census Bureau.

——. 1977. *Reference Manual on Population and Housing Statistics from the Census Bureau.* Washington, DC: U.S. Census Bureau.

——. 1992. *Tracking the American Dream: Fifty Years of Housing Changes.* Washington, DC: U.S. Census Bureau.

——. 2016. "American Community Survey 2010–2014: 5 Year Data." http://www.census .gov/en.html.

——. 2017. *Quarterly Homeownership Rates by Race and Ethnicity of Householder for the United States: 1994–2016.* Washington, DC: U.S. Census Bureau.

U.S. Department of Housing and Urban Development (HUD). 2008. *A Picture of Subsidized Households.* Washington, DC: U.S. Department of Housing and Urban Development.

——. 2015. *Affirmatively Furthering Fair Housing Data Documentation.* Washington, DC: U.S. Department of Housing and Urban Development.

U.S. House of Representatives, Committee on Internal Security. 1971. *Gun Barrel Politics: The Black Panther Party, 1966–1971.* Washington, DC: U.S. Government Printing Office.

Vacca, Carolyn S. 1991. "Housing Conditions as a Predictor for Riot: Rochester, New York, 1964." *Afro-Americans in New York Life and History* 15 (2): 45–61.

Veiller, Lawrence. 1903. "Tenement House Reform in New York City, 1834–1900." In *The Tenement House Problem,* edited by Robert W. DeForest and Lawrence Veiller, 69–113. London: Macmillan.

Venkatesh, Sudhir. 2002. *American Project: The Rise and Fall of a Modern Ghetto.* Cambridge, MA: Harvard University Press.

Wacquant, Loic. 1993. "Urban Outcasts: Stigma and Division in the Black American Ghetto and the French Urban Periphery." *International Journal of Urban and Regional Research* 17 (3): 366–383.

——. 2008. "Ghettos and Anti-ghettos: An Anatomy of the New Urban Poverty." *Thesis Eleven* 94:113–118.

Waldinger, Roger. 1996. *Still the Promised City? African-Americans and New Immigrants in Postindustrial New York.* Cambridge, MA: Harvard University Press.

Waldman, Amy. 2001. "In Harlem's Ravaged Heart, Revival." *New York Times*, February 18.

Waldron, Edward E. 1978. *Walter White and the Harlem Renaissance*. Port Washington, NY: Kennikat Press.

Wang, Wendy, and Kim Parker. 2014. *Record Share of Americans Have Never Married as Values, Economics, and Gender Patterns Change*. Washington, DC: Pew Social and Demographic Trends Project.

Washington, Booker T. 1905. "Why Should Negro Business Men Go South?" *Charities* 15 (1): 17–21.

——. 1907a. *The Negro in Business*. Boston: Hertel, Jenkins.

——. 1907b. "The Negro in the North: Are His Advantages as Great as in the South?" *Congregationalist and Christian World* 92:403–404.

——. 1912. *Is the Negro Having a Fair Chance?* New York: Century.

——. 1913. "Must Be Less Talk of Racial Friction." Speech to National Negro Business League, Muskogee, OK, August 19.

Washington, Forrester B. 1920. *The Negro in Detroit: A Survey of the Condition of a Negro Group in a Northern Industrial Corridor During the War Prosperity Period*. Detroit: Associated Charities of Detroit.

Washington, Sam. 1966. "EXCLUSIVE: Most Negroes Would Reject Change At Open Housing." *Chicago Defender*, October 29.

Watson, Jamal E. 2003. "The Whitening of Black Neighborhoods." *New York Amsterdam News*, July 10.

Weaver, Audrey. 1943. "Living Wages Lure Migrants out of Dixie." *Baltimore Afro-American*, December 11.

——. 1972. "From the Weaver." *Chicago Defender*, January 15.

Weaver, Robert C. 1948. *The Negro Ghetto*. New York: Harcourt, Brace.

Werner, Lawrence R. 1964. "City Applauds Pittsburgh Slum Kids for Decency." *Chicago Defender*, January 18.

White, Alvin, Warren Gardener, and J. Maceo Young. 1953a. "Philadelphians." *Our World*, September.

——. 1953b. "The Riverton." *Our World*, May.

——. 1954. "Pittsburgh's New Look." *Our World*, August.

White, Frank, III. 1985. "The Yuppies Are Coming." *Ebony*, April.

White, Khadijah. 2015. "Belongingness and the Harlem Drummers." *Urban Geography* 36 (3): 340–358.

White, Walter F. 1920. "The Success of Negro Migration." *The Crisis: A Record of the Darker Races* 19 (3): 112–115.

Widener, Daniel. 2010. *Black Arts West: Culture and Struggle in Postwar Los Angeles*. Durham, NC: Duke University Press.

Wiese, Andrew. 2005. *Places of Their Own: African American Suburbanization in the Twentieth Century*. Chicago: University of Chicago Press.

Wilkerson, Isabel. 2010. *The Warmth of Other Suns: The Epic Story of America's Great Migration*. New York: Random House.

Williams, Monte. 2000. "Harlem Journal; Gay White Pioneers, on New Ground." *New York Times*, November 19.

Williams, Robert. 1968. "U.S. Open to Urban Guerrillas." *The Black Panther*, November 2.

Williams, Timothy. 2008. "An Old Sound in Harlem Draws New Neighbors' Ire." *New York Times*, July 6.

Wilson, William Julius. 1987. *The Truly Disadvantaged: The Inner-City, the Underclass, and Public Policy.* Chicago: University of Chicago Press.

Winston, Smith. 1936. "Better Housing for Negroes Gift of New Deal." *New York Amsterdam News*, September 19.

Wolfers, Justin, David Leonhardt, and Kevin Quealy. 2015. "1.5 Million Missing Black Men." *New York Times*, April 20.

Wolfinger, James. 2009. "The Limits of Black Activism: Philadelphia's Public Housing in the Depression and World War II." *Journal of Urban History* 35 (6): 787–814.

Woods, Louis Lee, II. 2012. "The Federal Home Loan Bank Board, Redlining, and the National Proliferation of Racial Lending Discrimination, 1921–1950." *Journal of Urban History* 38 (6): 1036–1059.

Woodson, Carter G. 1918. *A Century of Negro Migration.* Washington, DC: Association for the Study of Negro Life and History.

——. 1929. "Insurance Business Among Negroes." *Journal of Negro History* 14 (2): 202–226.

Woofter, T. J., Jr., ed. 1928a. *Negro Problems in Cities.* Garden City, NY: Doubleday, Foran.

——. 1928b. "Racial Separation." In *Negro Problems in Cities*, edited by T. J. Woofter Jr., 37–77. Garden City, NY: Doubleday, Foran.

Works Projects Administration. 1942. *Report of the Chicago Land Use Survey.* Chicago: Chicago Plan Commission.

Wright, Richard. 1940. *Native Son.* New York: Harper. Kindle edition.

——. 1951. "The Shame of Chicago." *Ebony*, December.

Wright, Richard R. 1908. "The Economic Condition of Negroes in the North: Recent Improvement in Housing Among Negroes in the North." *The Southern Workman* 37 (November): 601–612.

Wright, Robert E. 1969. "Black Capitalism: Toward Controlled Development of Black America." *Negro Digest* 19 (December): 27–33.

Young, A. S. 1960. "The Big Beat." *Los Angeles Sentinel*, August 25.

Young, Earni. 2014. "The Problems and the Promise: Gentrification in Philadelphia." http://www.philly.com/philly/news/Gentrification_in_Philadelphia.html.

Young, Stacie. 2008. *The Foreclosure Crisis in the Chicago Area: Facts, Trends, and Responses.* Chicago: DePaul University Real Estate Center.

Young, Whitney M., Jr. 1970. "Heroin Killing Boys as 'Mr. Big' Thrives." *Philadelphia Tribune*, March 17.

Zelder, Raymond E. 1972. "Poverty, Housing, and Market Processes." *Urban Affairs Quarterly* 8 (1): 76–95.

Zhang, Haifeng, and Eric S. McCord. 2014. "A Spatial Analysis of the Impact of Housing Foreclosures on Residential Burglary." *Applied Geography* 54:27–34.

Zimmermann, Christian. 2014. "The Decline of Manufacturing." *FRED Blog*, April 21. https://fredblog.stlouisfed.org/2014/04/the-decline-of-manufacturing/.

Zukin, Sharon. 2009. *Naked City: The Death and Life of Authentic Urban Places.* London: Oxford University Press.

INDEX

Note: page numbers followed by *f* and *t* refer to figures and tables respectively. Those followed by n refer to notes, with note number.

employment/income guarantees, 250; gentrification and, 245–47, 251–52; neighborhood-based programs, Harlem Children's Zone (HCZ) initiative as model for, 248–50; neighborhoods unlikely to benefit from, 246; past failures of, 244; pilot programs for, 246; political will to implement, 250; and potential loss of neighborhood's black identity, 251–54; and return of ghetto as haven, 251–54; social justice arguments for, 243–44

political machines, and black patronage jobs: in nineteenth century, 33–34; in twentieth century, 60

political offices held by blacks: benefits to black community, 161; black pride in, 61–62, 108; and community nationalism, 160–62; in nineteenth-century cities, 33–34; in World War II era, 108, 131

political power, black: community nationalism and, 154–55, 160–62; elected officials as source of pride, 61–62, 108; and election to political office, 61–62; federal programs enhancing, 161–62; gentrification of ghettos and, 223, 226–27; ghetto as haven for development of, 6, 42–43, 55, 60–62, 241; in nineteenth-century northern cities, limited development of, 33–34, 61; northward migration in World War II and, 99, 107–8; urban renewal and, 111–12

Portland: development of ghettos in, 103; prewar segregation in, 101; segregation, in pre-World War II era, 102, 102t

Post, Langdon, 91

Powell, Adam Clayton, Jr., 91, 108

press, black: and advertising, ghetto's concentrated population as market for, 65–66; comparison of U.S. racism to Nazi practices, 14, 85, 122; development of, 33; on federal mortgage programs, 76, 84, 85; on

gentrification of ghettos, 218; ghetto as haven for development of, 65–66; on middle-class blacks' accomplishments, 129–30; on public housing program, 88, 89–91, 90f, 93–94; responsibility for racial uplift, 84; on school segregation, 96; in South, and danger of frank reporting, 65; support for black return to South, 169–70; on urban renewal, 109, 111, 114

press, black, before Great Migration: advertisements for black-only housing, 23–24, 23f, 24f; criticisms of black elite in, 37–38; on housing discrimination, 19–21

press, white, portrayal of blacks in, 129

progressive reformers: on housing discrimination, 22–23; views about blacks, 56

Promise Neighborhoods Program, 249

Promise Zone Program, 249

protest movements, black, rise in 1930s–40s, 94–95. *See also* riots

public housing: and high-rise slums, 116; integrated housing in, 116; long-time progressive calls for, 86; as still predominantly black, 71

public housing program, 86–98; black enthusiasm about, 86, 88, 91, 92, 94, 239; black need for decent housing and, 91–92; black press on, 88, 89–91, 90f, 93–94; and construction jobs for black workers, 86, 88; criticisms of segregationist goals of, 89–91; grassroots organizations' support of, 91; high quality of units vs. other ghetto housing, 92–93; as response to Great Depression, 71, 86; and seed of future inequality, 72–73; share of units for black community, positive perceptions of, 87–88, 91, 93; as slum-clearance program, 86, 87, 91

public housing program, segregationist intent of, 86, 87, 243; lack of public objections to, 94–98; as less important than decent housing, 91–92, 97–98; objections to, 93–94